Y0-BXV-475

Politics of the Northwest Passage

Politics of
the Northwest
Passage

Edited by
FRANKLYN GRIFFITHS

McGill-Queen's University Press
Kingston and Montreal

© McGill-Queen's University Press 1987
ISBN 0-7735-0613-6

Legal deposit third quarter 1987
Bibliothèque nationale du Québec
Printed in Canada

Printed on acid-free paper

Canadian Cataloguing in Publication Data

Main entry under title:
Politics of the Northwest Passage
   "A study prepared for the Dalhousie Ocean Studies
   Programme, Dalhousie University, Halifax."
   Includes bibliographical references and index.
   ISBN 0-7735-0613-6
   1. Territorial waters – Northwest Territories –
   Arctic Archipelago. 2. Shipping – Political aspects –
   Northwest Territories – Arctic Archipelago.
   3. Canada – Boundaries – Arctic regions. I. Griffiths,
   Franklyn, 1935–   . II. Dalhousie Ocean Studies
   Programme.
   FC192.P64 1987   971.9'2   C87-093746-4
   F1090.5.P64 1987

54,791

Contents

Preface vii

1 Where Vision and Illusion Meet 3
FRANKLYN GRIFFITHS

PART ONE   SETTING
2 Bringing the Outside Inside: Towards
Development of the Passage 25
GRAHAM ROWLEY
3 Inuit Politics and the Arctic Seas 46
PETER JULL

PART TWO   INTERNATIONAL ARCTIC POLITICS
4 The *Manhattan* Voyages and Their
Aftermath 67
JOHN KIRTON AND DON MUNTON
5 The Negotiation of Article 234 98
D.M. MC RAE
6 Arctic Shipping: An American Perspective 115
ORAN R. YOUNG
7 Greenlandic and Danish Attitudes to Canadian
Arctic Shipping 134
LARS TOFT RASMUSSEN

PART THREE   CANADIAN ARCTIC POLITICS
8 Lessons of the Arctic Pilot Project 163
JENNIFER LEWINGTON
9 Environmental Politics and Inuit
Self-Government 181
PETER BURNET

CAMROSE LUTHERAN COLLEGE
LIBRARY

10 Defence and Policing in Arctic Canada 200
   W. HARRIET CRITCHLEY
11 Polar Icebreakers: The Politics of Inertia 216
   KIM RICHARD NOSSAL

   PART FOUR   CONCLUSIONS
12 Beyond the Arctic Sublime 241
   FRANKLYN GRIFFITHS

   Appendix: Statement on Sovereignty,
      10 September 1985 269
   Notes 275
   Contributors 303
   Index 305

MAPS

The North American Arctic 6–7
Main Surface Routes of the Passage 28–9
Canadian Arctic Marine Jurisdictions 68–9
Greenland and the Eastern Canadian Arctic 136
The Circumpolar North 258

Preface

In August 1985, the United States sailed a Coast Guard icebreaker through Canada's portion of the Northwest Passage. This it did without having sought Canadian permission to proceed. The voyage of the *Polar Sea* was conducted in a manner consistent with the American claim that the many and varied channels of the Canadian Arctic archipelago are, in the ensemble, an international strait through which the surface vessels, submarines, and even aircraft of all states are entitled to move virtually without limitation. The transit of the *Polar Sea* could be construed as a denial of Canada's view that the waters of the archipelago are internal Canadian waters and historically an integral part of the national domain. Not surprisingly, the appearance of the *Polar Sea* provoked an outburst of public indignation and concern over Arctic sovereignty in Canada. What was surprising was the subsequent action of the Canadian government.

Statements of Canada's claim to the Passage as internal waters had previously been limited by Ministers and officials. Either they avoided a precise delineation of the waters considered as Canadian, or they affirmed only a specific authority to act, for example in the prevention of Arctic marine pollution. This self-limitation in public definitions of the scope of Canadian authority was rooted in a belief that an explicit and comprehensive claim to exclusive jurisdiction over the waters of the archipelago would not be able to withstand the combined opposition of the United States and other maritime powers, whereas more selective assertions of the right to act could cumulatively be made to succeed. As well, it was understood that an outright sovereignty claim would be unlikely to prevail if Canada were not "up there" to demonstrate effective control of the waters in question. For this, expensive regulatory and enforcement capabilities would be required, as would good reason to make use of them in practice. Some of these instruments, for example, a polar icebreaker that permitted year-round mobility in the Passage, would however remain underemployed as long as regular commercial shipping failed to materialize. Others, for instance anti-submarine capabilities to deal with foreign nuclear submarines operating in violation of Canada's claim, would risk being ineffectual in the absence of a readiness to accept the consequences of their use. But now, in the aftermath of the *Polar Sea* episode, the government of Canada decided to state its claim to the Passage in no uncertain terms by formally enclosing the channels of the Arctic archipelago as internal waters.

The historic decision to enclose the Passage, effective 1 January 1986, was announced in a statement by Secretary of State for External Affairs Joe Clark in the House of Commons on 10 September 1985 (included as an appendix to this volume). It was accompanied by a series of supporting actions. These included a reaffirmation of Canada's previously declared readiness to welcome commercial shipping in the channels that make up the Passage; a decision to acquire an exceedingly powerful icebreaker, the Polar 8, at an initially estimated cost of some $500 million; an announcement of Canada's willingness to have its claim adjudicated by the International Court of Justice (ICJ) in the event of a challenge; and a statement that bilateral talks would be sought with Washington in an effort to resolve American-Canadian differences over the Passage and its status in international law. Clearly the voyage of the *Polar Sea* had brought the Canadian government to a much more forthright defence of the Passage than had previously been thought appropriate. Some would even say that 10 September 1985 marked the beginning of a new era in Canada's Arctic waters policies.

Although the considerations that made for restraint in the advancement of Canada's claim before 1985 have by no means been banished, a new situation, with new policy requirements, has been created. Canadian Arctic sovereignty could now be vindicated or denied fairly promptly if bilateral talks with the United States yield either international acceptance of enclosure or a trip to the ICJ from which Canada returns empty-handed. Alternatively, as seems more likely for reasons to be made clear in this volume, Canada may be denied early resolution of its dilemmas in the Passage. Given continued disagreement with the United States on the basic legal issue, Canadian policy may very well have to aim simultaneously to secure international acceptance of enclosure and to open the archipelago to commercial navigation as appropriate. These two aims, seemingly contradictory, go hand in hand in ways that will be explained in the chapters that follow. As to the formidable problem posed by the activities of U.S., Soviet, and possibly other foreign nuclear submarines under the ice, this is best handled by explicit or tacit agreement with the United States while Canada proceeds to strengthen its occupancy of the surface waters of the Passage. One thing at a time, provided we are able to gain the time we need.

This book is therefore concerned primarily with the challenge of opening the Passage to commercial navigation. Attention is given as well to international legal aspects of Canadian Arctic waters policy, to environmental and socioeconomic implications of Arctic marine transportation, and of course to the issue of subsurface activities. On all counts, there is much for Canada to accomplish in the years ahead. Ultimately, however, the question for Canada is not so much what to do as how to follow through.

Make no mistake about it, the twin aims of securing acceptance of exclusive Canadian jurisdiction and providing for safe and efficient navigation in the Passage are highly ambitious. Their achievement will test the ingenuity and determination of the small population that is stretched out along the southern reaches of a vast northern domain, a population that has thus far evinced only sporadic interest in its Arctic heritage. If Canadians are to become true keepers of the Passage, they will need to assimilate and act upon new knowledge not only of the situation they face in their Arctic marine spaces but also of the strengths and weaknesses that they themselves bring to the situation.

The chapters you will read here seek to provide baseline information on Canada's Arctic dilemmas and on Canadian propensities in dealing with them during the decade and more before the September 1985 decision to lay the claim to the Passage on the line. To know better where we are coming from is to improve the prospect of getting where we want to go as a country with much to give as well as keep in the Arctic.

F.G.
1 June 1986

This volume is sponsored by the Dalhousie Ocean Studies Programme (DOSP), an interdisciplinary institution concerned with ocean law, policy, and management studies at Dalhousie University in Halifax, Nova Scotia. With the support of the Donner Canadian Foundation, DOSP initiated a research project on Canada's northern waters in October 1982 and subsequently commissioned the present study. Other books produced by the project are *Transit Management in the Northwest Passage* (forthcoming 1987), edited by Cynthia Lamson and David VanderZwaag, and *The Waters of the Canadian Arctic Archipelago in International Law* (forthcoming 1987), by Donat Pharand. The editor of the present volume gratefully acknowledges the encouragement and support he received from Professor Douglas Johnston of DOSP and from the Donner Canadian Foundation. This book has been published with the help of a grant from the Social Science Federation of Canada, using funds provided by the Social Sciences and Humanities Research Council of Canada.

Politics of the Northwest Passage

CHAPTER ONE

Where Vision and Illusion Meet

FRANKLYN GRIFFITHS

The Northwest Passage is as much a cultural artifact as an Arctic navigation route. It is as much a metaphor for human perseverance and ingenuity as a physical reality. The challenge of the Passage is as much one of self-discovery as of the discovery of ways and means to move at will through the Arctic waters of North America. As the twenty-first century draws near, and with it the prospect of year-round surface shipping in the Passage, Canadians in particular may have an opportunity to discover something new about themselves.

For nearly 500 years, men have been drawn by the vision of a commercially viable and strategically advantageous seaway that runs west and north from Europe to the Far East and back. The early and rather practical visionaries of a way through turned out to be victims of illusion when their courage and the technology of the day were tried against the irreducible severities of the Arctic environment. Their ventures and those of subsequent explorers nevertheless acquired symbolic reality as a measure of the best that Western civilization could advance against nature at its most unforgiving.[1] The existence of a passage through the ice-choked labyrinth of what later became Canada's Arctic archipelago was established only in the search for the Franklin expedition of 1845, itself an enterprise animated more by the vision of British greatness than by practical considerations of commercial and strategic gain. As of the end of the last century, failures and partial successes alike had revealed more about the men who made the effort than about the Northwest Passage as a seaway.

The great difficulties experienced in making a way through the Canadian archipelago contributed in turn to today's custom of referring to Canada's portion of the much longer sea route as the Northwest Passage itself. Lest an unhistorical and parochial perspective prevail, we shall refer here to the seaway that links Europe and the Far East through the varied channels of the Canadian archipelago as the Northwest Passage. The several alternative waterways that make up the Canadian portion (see map, pp. 28–9) of the much longer sea route will be referred to simply as the Passage. This book is about the politics of surface shipping through the Passage and its eastern and western approaches.

Since Canada stands astride the central portion of the Arctic waters of North America, Canadian actions will be decisive in determining what ultimately happens in the area. If surface navigation in the Passage should at last become commonplace, Canada will have had to summon the vision and the ingenuity to lead the way in accomplishing a task that has long stood for all that is most difficult to achieve on the face of this planet. Conversely, should Canada fail to meet the challenge and if traffic in the Passage nevertheless becomes increasingly frequent, something important will have happened to Canada and to the Canadian people. The book that follows gives greater attention therefore to Canadian policy concerns than to those of the other two Arctic coastal states of North America, the United States and Denmark/Greenland, or to those of interested parties such as Britain, France, Japan, the Soviet Union, West Germany, and the oil multinationals.

In the course of the twentieth century, the commercial and strategic significance of the Passage has once again appreciated. Visions of greatness, not all of which are hype, continue to surface in the language of private-sector and official promoters of marine development ventures in the North American Arctic. But practical concerns are now uppermost, as they were in the days of the earliest explorers. Let us therefore focus on the practical before returning to the unavoidable realm of metaphor.

TOWARDS YEAR-ROUND SHIPPING

Since the historic first transit of the entire Passage in 1903–6 by the Norwegian explorer Roald Amundsen in the tiny *Gjoa*, the Canadian archipelago has been crossed by surface vessels and nuclear submarines on more than two score known occasions.[2] The most recent were the exceptionally easy crossing of the Swedish cruise ship *Lindblad Explorer* in August–September 1984 and separate transits by the American cruise ship *World Discoverer* and the U.S. Coast Guard icebreaker *Polar Sea* in the summer of 1985.

As well, beginning with the two voyages of the American supertanker *Manhattan* in 1969 and 1970, pilot projects have been mounted and provisional commitments made to employ various portions of the North-west Passage for the transportation of oil and natural gas from the North American Arctic to markets in the southern part of the continent and in Western Europe. The Japanese investment of $400 million in Dome Canada's Arctic operations also suggests that oil might be shipped westward if a major discovery were made in the Beaufort Sea and the price were right. The voyages of the *Manhattan* demonstrated that the technology is indeed available to permit regular surface shipping from as well as through the Passage. Petro-Canada's Arctic Pilot Project, in contrast, revealed the inability of Canadians to steer a high-technology Arctic natural gas transportation megaproject through the shoals of changing international energy prices and domestic regulatory requirements between 1977 and 1983. Similarly, Dome's plans to run icebreaking oil tankers year-round from the Beaufort Sea to east coast ports, still on the books, ran afoul of the company's acquisitions binge in 1978–81, the vast debt burden that ensued, and a continuing inability to locate threshold reserves of Beaufort oil. More recently, in 1985, Panarctic Oils of Calgary succeeded in obtaining official approval for an annual summer-months venture to ship small amounts of oil to Montreal from Cameron Island in the Canadian archipelago. As well, hard minerals have been shipped eastward on a limited-season basis from two locations in the Passage and one in Greenland. Meanwhile, unnumbered subsurface transits of the Passage have been made by the nuclear submarines of the United States and conceivably the Soviet Union and other nuclear-submarine states since the USS *Seadragon* first went through from east to west in 1960. These submarine voyages have almost certainly run along south-north as well as east-west axes through the Canadian archipelago.

Although costs currently outweigh benefits for most commercial uses of the Arctic waters of North America, it is generally agreed that the oil and natural gas of the Beaufort Sea and the Canadian Arctic islands will be exploited and that the marine mode will be one of the transportation options.[3] It is also agreed that nuclear submarine and anti-submarine warfare (ASW) operations will become increasingly frequent in Arctic waters, probably including those of North America.[4] Although the prospect of direct shipping between Europe or Eastern North America and the Far East continues to be distant, a gradual increase in the volume and annual duration of surface and subsurface navigation in and about the Passage does seem likely in the years ahead. Hard fact is hard to come by where Arctic subsurface operations are concerned, but a significant increase in military-strategic uses of the waters of the Canadian archipelago by foreign nuclear attack submarines could already be under way.

Further, there is the perennial possibility of a surge towards year-round commercial shipping as the consequence of an acute crisis in the Middle East, specifically in the Persian Gulf: heightened energy prices and demand for secure supplies could bring on a large volume of traffic, particularly in the transportation of Arctic natural gas which is already known to be available in substantial quantities. Moreover, the ages-old notion of direct navigation between Europe and the Far East could itself move a step nearer

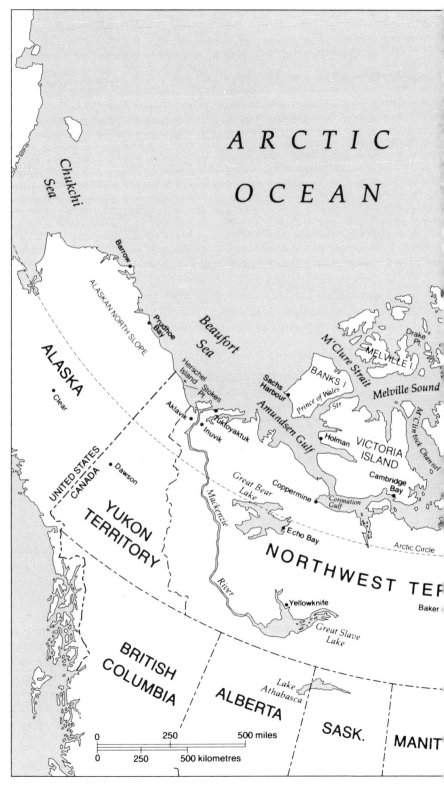

The North American Arctic

- North Pole

Lincoln
Sea

Alert

ELLESMERE ISLAND

Nares Strait

GREENLAND

JAMESON LAND

Harry Inlet

Ittoqqortoormiut
(Scoresbysund)

Grise
Fiord

Qaanaaq
(Thule)

Jones
Sound

solute

DEVON I.

Baffin
Bay

Upernavik

Marmorilik

Strait

Lancaster Sound

Pond Inlet

Disko Bay

Sondre
Stromfjord

Nanisivik

Gulf of Boothia

BAFFIN ISLAND

Davis Strait

Fury and Hecla
Strait

ence
Bay

Igloolik

Nuuk
(Godthåb)

oa Haven

Pelly
Bay

Hall
Beach

Repulse Bay

Foxe
Basin

Pangnirtung

Foxe
Channel

Iqaluit

ITORIES

Hudson Strait

Rankin Inlet

Ungava
Bay

Hudson

Nain

Bay

QUÉBEC

Churchill

Schefferville

LABRADOR

A

to realization once year-round commercial shipping from the North American Arctic had begun. As the twentieth century ends, reality appears to be drawing closer to the vision of the earliest explorers and promoters of a Northwest Passage.

THE NEW LABYRINTH

And yet, even as preconditions for regular surface shipping in the Passage have been accumulating in the form of the requisite knowledge, capabilities, and need, new obstacles have arisen to set us back in terms of the ability to get through. These obstacles, largely unexplored, are essentially political: a political labyrinth has been superimposed on the complex physical geography of the region.

Those who would now engage in regular commercial navigation from the North American Arctic or across it must find their way through a quickly thickening maze of competing and overlapping jurisdictions, regulations, and purposes that would surely amaze and depress John Cabot if he were to be returned to us. Only one country, the United States, has the ability, in principle and in a national emergency, to break a way through the political impediments to regular navigation. In exercising this ability, the American government would incur considerable political and military-strategic costs, the acceptance of which is all the less likely in the absence of urgent necessity. As will be seen, all states are best advised to negotiate a way through, dealing along the way with elaborate domestic as well as international bargaining agendas.

The political labyrinth that overlays and indeed in many ways itself constitutes the modern Northwest Passage may be entered at any number of points. Most noteworthy perhaps is the point that the international legal status of the Canadian portion of the larger waterway is in dispute: the United States regards the many channels of the Canadian Arctic archipelago as a set of international straits, whereas Canada declares these to be historic Canadian waters subject to exclusive Canadian jurisdiction. Indeed, in response to the voyage of the *Polar Sea*, which took place with the U.S. Government having informed and consulted but not sought permission to cross the Passage, Canada strengthened its claim with the announcement on 10 September 1985 that it was enclosing the channels of the archipelago as internal waters within straight baselines and that new measures were to be taken to reinforce Canadian control of these waterways.[5]

To the degree that the Canadian view is accepted, non-Canadian shippers in the Passage will be obliged to take the time and pay the money to meet a series of demanding ship-construction, pollution-prevention, navigational, and other requirements. Similarly, unless transit rights were granted tacitly or formally by Canada, American or Soviet nuclear submarines proceeding through the Passage would be engaged in illicit operations. Conversely, should the waters of the archipelago come to be regarded as an international strait in which rights of transit passage applied, non-Canadian and Canadian shippers alike could proceed under minimal regulations.[6] By the same token, Soviet as well as American nuclear submarines would be unencumbered in their right to move through the area. As matters stand for would-be Canadian shippers, they as a rule must work their way through an arduous and expensive regulatory process that in the ensemble entails the participation of scores of bodies–federal government departments, inter-agency committees, impact assessment boards, implementing agencies, and public interest groups, all of whose activities are suffused in the bureaucratic and constitutional politics of the Canadian north.

If this were not enough, today's potential surface shipper is obliged to chart a course through the politics of the eastern and western approaches to the Passage. To the east, in the Davis Strait and Baffin Bay area, the governments of Canada and Denmark and their respective Inuit populations in Canada's eastern Arctic and Greenland may be expected to seek legitimate powers of determination in responding to and managing shipping ventures likely to produce local environmental and social effects. As matters stood early in 1986, the Canadian and Greenlandic Inuit, joined with their Alaskan counterparts in the Inuit Circumpolar Conference, were opposed to the shipping of hydrocarbons through the Passage and adjacent waters. And to the west, the American and Canadian governments and conceivably that of the Soviet Union, together with the state of Alaska and the Alaskan and Canadian Inuit, may all have proper things to ask of oil and natural gas shippers in the Beaufort, Chukchi, and Bering seas. Add to all of this the contributions of conservation organizations such as the Canadian Arctic Resources Committee and the Audubon Society of America, mix in the media in Canada, Denmark/Greenland, and the United States, and the full magnitude of the political problem in making large-scale use of the Passage and its surrounding waters becomes increasingly evident.

The situation is still further complicated by the subsurface operations of nuclear submarines. These will evolve according to their own dynamic and will affect the realization of international arrangements to facilitate surface shipping through the Passage. Despite the veil of secrecy that shrouds u.s. and Soviet submarine activities in Arctic waters, a few things are reasonably clear. First, the waters of the Canadian archipelago are likely to experience greater use by attack submarines moving to and from the Arctic Ocean and between the Atlantic and Pacific oceans.[7] Second, to the extent that the military-strategic value of the Passage appreciates, the United States is likely to display an underlying preference for obfuscation, as distinct from precision, in the elaboration of international arrangements for surface shipping and in discussions with Canada over the status of the Passage in international law.

Washington may be expected to assert rights of transit passage through the Canadian archipelago with gradually diminishing vigour, since if generally accepted they would allow unimpeded access in peacetime not only to Soviet attack submarines but as well to Soviet surface vessels and airborne ASW.[8] Indeed, Soviet ballistic and cruise missile-firing submarines and strategic bombers carrying air-launched cruise missiles (ALCMS) would be entitled to a free ride through the archipelago, should Moscow wish to exercise rights of transit passage – an outcome that would run counter to the Reagan Administration's "Star Wars" effort to build a strategic nuclear defence of North America and to the joint Canadian-American commitment to modernize the Distant Early Warning (DEW) bomber detection line which runs parallel to the Passage and is right on the Passage at some points. However, the American government will no doubt seek maximal freedom of action for its own vessels by resisting the assertion of exclusive Canadian jurisdiction and by endeavouring to engage Canada and Denmark/Greenland in various northern undertakings that stand to create a political environment favourable to U.S naval mobility in the region. Accordingly, in international discussions to further surface shipping through the Passage, the United States is likely to prefer informal arrangements that maximize, and certainly do not impede, its existing freedom of subsurface access.

Now that Canada has made clear its determination to exercise the full array of jurisdictions that come with sovereignty over the Passage, Washington has additional choices. It could seek to negotiate a treaty with Canada that provided for naval and commercial access to the archipelago under agreed conditions. Alternatively, insofar as a treaty might enable a future Canadian government to deny U.S. national security interests by withdrawing access rights originally granted by agreement, Washington could opt to contest Canada's claim by challenging it before the International Court of Justice (ICJ) or by acting unilaterally to deploy nuclear submarines into the Passage without Canadian consent. Although an American decision that favoured either bilateral agreement or unilateral action cannot be excluded, constructive ambiguity and "agreement to disagree" with Canada may still seem most advantageous to Washington.

As to Canada and Denmark/Greenland, they too have good reason to favour obfuscation in the evolution of Arctic surface shipping arrangements, since they are allies of the United States and themselves lack the ability to prevent the passage of nuclear submarines. If what goes on under the surface of the Passage may be an embarrassment to or even a denial of Canadian claims of exclusive jurisdiction, how can Canada be expected to lead the way in developing international arrangements to govern commercial navigation? Bilateral agreement with the United States on the status of the Passage and on naval operations there would seem to be a precondition for Canadian leadership in the elaboration of a surface shipping regime. As to Denmark, we may anticipate a continuing avoidance of developments that serve to heighten the concern of Greenlanders with international security affairs. As a home rule area of the Danish realm, Greenland is not formally entitled to deal with questions of foreign and defence policy. As will be seen, Greenlanders have nevertheless been moving into these areas as they strain at Danish control. Whether or not Greenland is judged to be moving toward independence, Denmark has a continuing interest in avoiding additions to the Greenlanders' foreign affairs agenda. Copenhagen will therefore do what it can to prevent Greenlandic opinion from becoming alarmed over nuclear submarine activities in Baffin Bay and Davis Strait. To this end, it will seek to avert or delay international discussions that might draw attention to subsurface as well as surface navigation in the eastern approaches to the Passage.

As occurs with the United States, Canada and Denmark have cause not to deal directly with questions of jurisdiction and enforcement that must be resolved or finessed in the elaboration of a regime for surface shipping in and about the Passage. The creation of such a regime, already made exceedingly difficult by the need to reconcile a wide range of political and legal issues, is further complicated by the military-strategic interests of North America's coastal states in leaving well enough alone.

Finally, any attempt not only to engage in large-scale shipping but also to prepare the way for it in North America's Arctic waters will be inhibited by a series of economic uncertainties. Oil and natural gas will presumably be the principal cargoes for extended-season and then year-round navigation. But reserves of oil sufficient to justify a vigorous commitment to Arctic shipping have yet to be discovered in the Beaufort Sea or the Canadian archipelago. Although there is increasing assurance that scattered smaller reserves, as distinct from a major discovery, will suffice for exploitation, the view is gaining ground that these are energy supplies for the twenty-first century. Aside from the availability of Arctic oil now and in future, the international demand for and price of natural gas as well as oil continue to remain well below levels required to warrant the extraction and transportation of costly frontier supplies for markets in North America, Western Europe and Japan. Although hydrocarbon prices are widely predicted to rise in the 1990s, they are currently marked by previously unexpected declines. As well, should all the preconditions be fully met for the exploitation of North American oil and gas, overland pipeline routes to continental consumers could still be preferred instead of marine transportation systems. And where the marine mode itself is concerned, continuing technological innovation might yet produce an option to avoid surface ice

the constricted waters of the Passage altogether by employing
marine tankers on under-ice Arctic Ocean routes to and between ports
in southern North America, Western Europe and Japan. Should such a
transportation option prove cost-effective, the Northwest Passage could
yield to the North Passage, which for centuries has been recognized as the
shortest shipping route between Europe and the Far East.

If we left the argument at this, any major commitment of economic and
political resources in the 1980s to shipping and to opening the way for it in
the Passage could only be termed illusory. The difficulties are so great, the
cost-effectiveness ratios are so adverse, and the perceived need to act is so
slight that those who would now promote the development of an integrated
transit management regime would seem all but certainly destined to join
the host of unrequited Northwest Passage visionaries from Sir Humfrey
Gilbert down to Jack Gallagher of Dome Petroleum. As well, it would have
to be conceded that an attempt in the 1980s to design the technical features
of a Northwest Passage shipping regime risks being proved illusory in view
of likely changes in the relevant political, economic, and technological
contexts between now and the time of need, if indeed there is to be a need.
Overall, we would have to recognize that whereas the historic trend of
marine transportation in the North American Arctic suggests that key
preconditions for commercial navigation are indeed taking shape, the
question of employing the Passage and surrounding waters for extended-
season and year-round bulk cargo transportation is not ripe for policy. But
is it wise to leave the argument this way?

PRECAUTION AND ITS LIMITS

The encounter with high levels of uncertainty and imposing obstacles is
typical of the attempt to make use of the Northwest Passage. The terms of
discussion have changed dramatically, but the essence of the question for
those in Canada and the other North American states who would consider
arrangements for more intensive shipping in their Arctic waters is the same
as was confronted by Cabot's backers in 1497: should we put something
into it, and, if so, for what purpose and how much?

Though a vigorous commitment to build a seaway through the Arctic
waters of North America might well be unjustifiable as of the mid-1980s,
unwarranted risks would be incurred if Canada's response to the growing
likelihood of commercial traffic in the Passage were largely one of inaction.
Risk arises primarily from the long lead times required not only to resolve
national and international political disagreements about the use of the
Passage and its approaches but as well to develop the physical capacity and
procedures that will be needed. The ability to support and regulate
Canadian and foreign shipping on a year-round basis includes require-

ments for icebreaking, local ice-condition and weather forecasting, satellite-based and local communications and aids to navigation, bathymetry or mapping of the depth of channels and wider bodies of water, and operational experience, including knowledge of the effects of vessel traffic on birds, marine mammals, and above all the Inuit way of life. Lead times vary with the requirement, but in 1986 we are contemplating capabilities that by and large could come into being only in the next decade. Should Canada fail now to anticipate and act on the Arctic marine transportation requirements of the 1990s or for that matter of later years, it could find itself caught short. The same applies to the United States and to Denmark/Greenland.

Canada has, however, taken a major step towards preparedness. On 10 September 1985 Canada announced, together with its decision formally to enclose the channels of the archipelago as Canadian internal waters, its intention to build the world's largest icebreaker, the Polar 8. Following the voyage of the *Polar Sea* through the Passage, the commitment to acquire the Polar 8 was made primarily as a means of affirming Canadian sovereignty. This commitment certainly deserves support, and care should be taken to ensure that the impetus to follow through is maintained. But it remains to be seen what will come of the venture. Up to five years will be required for construction of the Polar 8 at an estimated cost of $500 million (or possibly rather less if the vessel is designed as well as built by private industry). In the early 1990s sea trials will begin, as will acquisition of practical experience in year-round navigation in the Passage. Well before then Canada will have had an opportunity to explore the potential for a bilateral settlement with the United States that resolves the two countries' differences over the status of the Passage in international law.

In the event that a deal were made and Canadian sovereignty affirmed, the impetus to follow through with construction of the Polar 8 would surely diminish, as would Canadian interest in gaining the wider array of national capabilities and international arrangements required for safe and efficient commercial navigation in the Arctic waters of North America. The Polar 8 could thus turn out to have been a bargaining chip that was cashed in when a game of sovereignty had ended. Alternatively, should Canada and the United States agree to disagree without actively contesting one another's claims, a less precipitous reduction in Canadian readiness to commit resources to Arctic marine development could still occur as inevitable budgetary constraints had their effect, programs were elongated, and the Canadian sense of urgency diminished. A central problem in Canada's present approach to the Passage is that requirements for preparedness are defined very largely in terms of sovereignty and its defence. Currently it is political control, rather than sound use of the Passage, that matters most.

The government of Canada has nevertheless declared its readiness to assist Arctic shipping in conformance with Canadian regulations.[9] Suppose that aside from acquiring the Polar 8, it broadly preferred inaction or half-hearted action as distinct from an effort to make good on stated policy, and that in 1991 an American, Canadian, or Western European consortium announced a plan to build a fleet of icebreaking tankers for extended-season or year-round hydrocarbon transportation eastward through the Passage. Arctic tankers being relatively quick to construct, Ottawa could find itself in a position neither to support nor effectively to regulate such a venture if it went through. Avoidable risks of accident would arise, as might the danger of pollution and other threats to the Arctic marine environment and to Inuit communities. Insurance rates could become unnecessarily high, thereby affecting the profitability of a shipping project that Ottawa might wish to encourage. In effect, the government of Canada could become a bystander in the presence of Canadian or foreign marine transportation operations. Or it could find itself in the position of having to delay and thus possibly to deny a proposal that was otherwise in the national interest. Or it could be forced to deny outright a foreign shipping venture in circumstances where the validity of its claim to exclusive jurisdiction over the waters of the Passage was still in doubt.

The point here is that the thought of surging forward to meet commercial shipping needs once they are clearly evident is not workable. On simple grounds of prudence, not only Canada but also Denmark/Greenland and the United States are well advised to undertake preparatory measures on a national basis well in advance of the need.

Aside from the acquisition of needed national capabilities, lead times are also substantial in negotiating an optimal way through the political labyrinth of the Passage and its adjacent waters. Two obvious outcomes can be envisaged in the absence of an enabling national and international policy framework. On the one hand and more likely, a proposed shipping project could come to naught in the midst of debilitating national regulatory processes and interstate discord on the merits of the venture, on specifications for ship design and handling, or on procedures for the evaluation of social and physical impact. On the other hand, if the project acquired the momentum required to proceed, it could engender environmental damage and political conflict by overriding national interests or by denying the legitimate demands of domestic actors that shipping not produce adverse social and physical consequences – to say nothing of a sharpened sense of powerlessness on the part of those most immediately affected in the Arctic coastal communities. An attempt to commence shipping in the Passage and its approaches before the elements of an enabling regime were in place would thus be likely to generate an excessively uneven distribution of benefits and deprivations: either there would be no shipping despite the existence of good reason to encourage it; or there would be unwarranted environmental, social, and political damage despite the best effort to avoid it.

Clearly there is a need to further the expectation of more even-handed outcomes in the event that Arctic marine transportation megaprojects are put forward in the next decade. Time requirements being what they are for the creation of an integrated transit management regime for the Arctic waters of North America, an effort should now be made by Canada and its neighbours to encourage the development of background conditions for such a regime. In view of Canada's central role in any future commercial use of the Passage and its approaches, Canadians could well take the initiative in fostering the emergence of a knowledge base for the effective adaptation of large southern-generated marine transportation projects to the Arctic setting. What is required to begin with is consensual knowledge or "technical information … and theories about that information which commands sufficient consensus at a given time among interested actors to serve as a guide to public policy designed to achieve some social goal."[10] Given progress in the elaboration of consensual knowledge about shipping in the Arctic waters of North America, a particular commercial proposal could be processed with greater assurance nationally and with greater likelihood of effective international co-operation.

Consensual knowledge on the wide array of technical issues posed by Arctic commercial shipping will be difficult to obtain on a national basis, where there is as yet little perceived need to address questions of Arctic marine transportation in earnest. Discussions among experts from the three coastal states could nevertheless yield a measure of politically significant agreement on technical matters such as ship design and navigation requirements, pollution prevention, conservation of the marine environment, avoidance of damage to the renewable-resources way of life of the Inuit, and legal issues of jurisdiction, enforcement, and liability. International expert consultations could in turn energize national efforts to deal with similar agendas. The development of consensual knowledge about Arctic marine transportation would seem to offer part of the solution to finding a way through the political labyrinth of the Passage and its adjacent waters. Prudence suggests that the effort should be made.

In Canada's case, the varied disabilities that could be encountered if a major marine transportation project caught the North American countries unprepared are compounded by uncertainties that may continue to surround its claim to the waters of the Passage. Were the project an undertaking of an American consortium that enjoyed the backing of the U.S. government, and were the latter still committed to the view that the Passage was an international strait, Canada would be obliged to seek adjudication by the ICJ. To build a successful case in court and with international opinion, Canada could very well have to demonstrate that it had enclosed the Passage not to deny foreign shipping but to facilitate it in accordance with stated Canadian policy. To make this a credible purpose, Canada would in turn need to adduce evidence that it had undertaken a variety of measures to support commercial navigation.[11] Again, to lurch into action only once the requirement had been fully identified would not do.

This much said, it still has to be recognized that governments, the Canadian government included, do not as a rule invest substantial economic and political resources in undertakings with long lead times when the need to act is by no means clearly established. Prudence suggests good reasons to put something into the creation of technical capabilities and arrangements for the support and regulation of commercial shipping in the Passage well before a pressing need arises. But uncertainty returns to undermine precaution in a situation where significant risks are offset by apparent low probabilities that they will materialize and high costs of action to anticipate them.

The need to prepare for commercial navigation in the Northwest Passage epitomizes Canada's larger dilemma as a northern country: not only to do things in the Arctic but to do them right when there is no common perception of a compelling need to do anything much at all, when there is time to learn to do things right but little sense of urgency in doing so. Canada's response to its northern dilemma has on the whole been to minimize commitments, to prefer ad hoc activity to an overriding sense of purpose, to react rather than to initiate. In these circumstances, the appeal to prudence and a major concern with technical solutions are unlikely to move Canada very far towards recognizing, much less dealing with, the potential for commercial navigation in the Passage. The terms of the discussion will have to change if justification is to be found for a vigorous commitment to the management of Canada's Arctic waters.

MAKING IT HAPPEN

Everything we know about the Passage tells us that for regular commercial use to occur, it must be wanted very strongly. Faint-heartedness has no place here. Nor does a self-image in which Canadian actions are effectively governed by large and uncontrollable forces such as the international price of oil. The question of whether or not Canada should make a substantial commitment to commercial development of the Passage ought to be reframed. Rather than asking whether large-scale transportation will occur and then what, the basic question is whether there is reason for Canada to want to make it happen in the first place.

Since the transfer of the high Arctic from Britain over a century ago, Canada has declined to do much more than defend the waters of the Arctic archipelago against foreign encroachment and pollution. The outpouring of public concern over the *Manhattan* voyages of 1969–70, and over the transit of the *Polar Sea* in 1985, nevertheless suggests that latent attachments to the Passage and to the Arctic spaces it represents are lodged deep in Canadians' conceptions of themselves as a people.

Others should be aware that Canadians have long believed that their writ extends to the whole of the archipelago and indeed northward across the waters beyond in a wedge-shaped sector that comes to a fine point at the North Pole. Although the evolution of international law makes it clear that Canada's northernmost reach is to the outer edge of the 200-mile exclusive economic zone and possibly beyond for its portion of the continental margin, Canadians – decision-makers included – do not believe that they are changing anything in declaring that the country is entitled to the exclusive political control that comes with sovereignty over the waters of the archipelago. Quite simply, this is the way it always was and should be.[12] But there is more to it than this.

As others have noted, the Victorian imagination viewed the Arctic and with it the Passage as sublime.[13] To this I would add that the Arctic is still sublime for southern Canadians, who remain in the thrall of a nineteenth-century vision of the region.

In presenting the southern mind with the image of unspoiled and truly awesome natural greatness, the thought of the Arctic at once lifts up the human spirit and appals with its harsh and overpowering immensity. To the extent that it is perceived as sublime, the Arctic evokes a dual political response in Canadians: it both attracts and repels. It brings forth deep-seated attitudes of possessiveness on the one hand and fear and passivity on the other. As well, Canadians seem to be aware that the people who stand as guardians over such natural greatness are themselves in a way greatened. These are not things that Canadians ordinarily speak or even think about. They are quite unexamined. Nevertheless, to the Arctic sublime Canadians do have a subliminal commitment that may on occasion be made manifest. Hence the surfacing of powerful hidden attachments in 1969–70 and 1985, when challenges to their legal position in the Passage threatened to diminish Canadians' self-regard and distinctiveness as a people, when pollution threatened to mar the splendour of their Arctic spaces.

To persist in a Victorian vision of the Arctic sublime would seem to suit southern Canadians who have yet to reflect seriously on their Arctic heritage and its place in the nation's future. Certainly there was little reason to question the cultural and political implications of accepting such an orientation to the Arctic in 1886, or even 50 years ago. But in 1986, some vigorous questioning is long overdue. As we have seen, the Arctic is changing. Technological innovation, military-strategic rivalry, new re-source requirements, and the lengthening reach of governments and peoples all demand of Canada a continuing and not an episodic occupation with Arctic affairs and the Passage in the first instance. No longer can

Canada afford to rise to meet imminent threats and then subside into inaction born of unstated fear. No longer can southern Canadians afford to appreciate the Arctic from a safe distance. As the twenty-first century draws near, an alternative vision of the Arctic is required, one that evokes the expectation of future achievement, overcomes passivity, and brings forth a united effort on behalf of a distant goal. What such a vision might consist of is an additional concern of this book.

In considering whether to make active use of the Passage, Canada is presented with an opportunity to become an increasingly assured Arctic country with a destiny of its own on the North American continent. Canadians could make use of the opportunity to affirm their distinctiveness, and to make good on their northernness, by rendering a distinguished performance in the management of their Arctic and their portion of the Northwest Passage to begin with. Without ill will to the United States and the pervasive influence of its ways, and indeed preferably in active co-operation with it, an increasingly effective Canadian occupancy of the Passage could affirm Canada's separate identity and provide proof of its capacity to offer an alternative way. As previously occurred with the construction of a transcontinental railway across the southern reaches of the country, the building of an Arctic seaway could demonstrate anew the ability of Canadians to summon the inner resources to achieve great things in difficult circumstances.

Viewed this way, the challenge presented to Canada by the prospect of shipping in and about the Passage is not so much to devise technical means of moving through the physical and political labyrinth, as to make manifest the attachments of Canadians to the Arctic, to make the transition from a passive to an active demonstration of Canada's northernness where its Arctic waters are concerned. The prospect of commercial shipping in the Arctic waters of North America becomes not so much an awkward problem as an opportunity for nation-building into the next century.

Arctic marine transportation will strike some as a prosaic theme far removed from the visionary business of national self-discovery. Nevertheless, it may be evident by now that the task of opening the way for and then managing commercial navigation in the Passage presents a fundamental challenge to Canada. It brings together in a single requirement most of the concerns that should occupy a live northern country. To the degree that Canadians succeed in meeting these concerns, they will have realized their northernness without detriment to other attributes of their identity.

To do what it takes to become authentic keepers of the Passage, Canadians would need to be persuaded that the attempt to lead in the development of Arctic marine transportation was feasible as well as desirable. Uncertainty intrudes here once again. In particular, if there are no ships yet in sight and none likely for some time to come, why begin to consider an ambitious northern venture of self-discovery that centres on Canada's portion of the Northwest Passage? But now we are looking at the problem through a different optic. Rather than waiting for shippers to appear and then reacting, Canada could attempt to induce potential shippers to make use of the Passage. As of the mid-1980s, Japan may provide a promising prospect.

Japan clearly has an interest in reducing its dependence on Middle East oil and in gaining a leading position in the construction of tankers for the transportation of Arctic and Antarctic hydrocarbons.[14] Many of the major Japanese integrated firms are moving to acquire not only information on ice conditions in Canadian waters but also ice simulation tanks to test vessel design concepts. IHI (Ishikawajima-Harima Heavy Industries) in particular has entered into an arrangement with the world's leading builder of icebreakers and ice tankers, Wartsila of Finland. This agreement is evidently aimed at capturing a good part of the world market for polar tankers, a market that is expected to be large, diversified, and long-lasting once polar hydrocarbons come on stream. IHI is also active in conducting ice studies for Mobil Oil in the Hibernia field off Newfoundland.

Hibernia oil is both more secure and closer to Japan than that of the Persian Gulf. Might the governments of Canada and Newfoundland be able to interest the Japanese in purchasing Hibernia oil and making use of the Passage to ship it westward once the field begins to produce in the 1990s? Economics of transportation argue for extended-season rather than all-year shipping of oil through the Passage, the Panama Canal being preferred for the winter and spring months. Nevertheless, the proposal would entail preliminary but regular shipping in the Passage and, perhaps most important for Japanese industry, an early opportunity to gain experience in the design of icebreaking tankers by co-operating with Canada in a trial project to test polar hydrocarbon transportation technology. Much in the Japanese decision would presumably depend on oil price considerations and the distribution of industrial benefits between Canada and Japan. Canada has an industrial co-operation agreement with Japan, and Hibernia oil is said to be producible despite reductions in world oil prices as of late 1985. It should also be noted that from a Japanese perspective, the Northwest Passage, as distinct from the North Passage, could offer relatively secure waters and thus a strategic advantage in view of the impressive surface and subsurface mobility of the Soviet Union in the Arctic Ocean.

If Japan were to participate in a pilot project that could lead to the purchase of Hibernia oil and its movement westward through the Passage, an essential precondition for Canada's realization of a new northern vision would have been met. This could also be the case if the Federal Republic of Germany were to be interested in an analogous technological development and shipping project from the Beaufort Sea. With substantial tanker traffic in the offing and in keeping with Canadian and international law, the scene would be set for a multifaceted effort to affirm Canada's northernness in the building of a transcontinental Arctic seaway. But now the leisurely pace of Canada's marine development programs in the Arctic would be replaced by the need to act with a clear sense of purpose. Arctic shipping would become a priority of a country firmly committed to the assertion of its northern identity in domestic and foreign affairs. Commercial use of the Passage, and all that it entails, would indeed have become a ripe subject for national policy.

WHERE VISION AND ILLUSION MEET

Where then does Canada stand? As of January 1986, the question of preparing actively for year-round navigation in the Passage is not ready for official action. The need to commit the required economic and political assets is by no means recognized. The inhibitions and difficulties are far too imposing. Awareness of and interest in Arctic shipping are deficient at the public and decision-making levels alike. Current Canadian interest in the waters of the Arctic archipelago is centred not so much on commercial shipping as on the defence of sovereignty. The focus here is more on legal and political means of affirming control over the Passage than on furtherance of sound uses of Canada's Arctic waters. This is part of the reason why the Polar 8 icebreaker started to run into trouble after the decision to acquire was announced.[15] In such an internal political context, those who would recommend an integrated and costly Canadian effort to lead the way in resolving the many issues associated with commercial navigation in the Passage and surrounding waters are indeed likely to be dismissed as advocates of a quixotic venture or at best one that is ahead of its time.

Equally illusory are the views and unstated assumptions that justify Canadian inaction or low-level precautionary measures against the eventuality of commercial shipping in the Passage. Despite inevitable short-term fluctuations, the second half of the twentieth century is marked by a continuing evolution of technological and economic preconditions for navigation in the Arctic waters of North America. Sooner or later a viable shipping venture will emerge. When it does, the long lead times required to cope effectively will almost certainly give rise to excessive and avoidable deprivations to the Arctic social and physical setting, to shipping and associated interests, and to one or more of the Arctic states of North America. Canada and Canadians have nevertheless been acting as though their secret hope is not to be tested on their declared readiness to welcome shipping in the Passage. To base policy, or more precisely the lack of it, on hope of this kind is not only foolish but unworthy.

Rather than continue to live with a conundrum in which action and inaction alike seem ill-founded, and in which half-way measures today will not serve to meet the potential for shipping in the 1990s, Canadians surely ought to develop a new approach to the Passage. As I see it, the problem is ultimately quite elemental. Stated colloquially, it is one of "put up or shut up": either Canada does more to honour its undertaking to support commercial navigation, or it effectively leaves it to others to look after their own interests. Should Canada continue to leave it to chance, it may well leave the Passage to others. Were this to be the case, the underlying dilemma of "use it or lose it" might also have been resolved: effective control over the waters of the archipelago could well be surrendered even if it received formal recognition in a bilateral agreement with the United States or a decision of the World Court. If it is assumed that Canadians would prefer not to leave the Passage to others, then they have no option but to bestir themselves and attend more vigorously to the evolving requirements of Arctic marine transportation and *all* that goes with it – from excellence in Arctic science and icebreaking through co-operation with the circumpolar Inuit to a gradual resolution of the national defence issues associated with foreign nuclear submarine operations in Canada's Arctic waters.

For Canada to move forward not only to effective control over the waters of the archipelago but also to a safe and open Northwest Passage, a mobilizing vision or guiding sense of national purpose will be needed. If the effort were confined to technical measures devised and implemented in government and corporate offices, it would almost certainly grind to a halt. The magnitude of the challenge to do things right in the Passage and its surrounding waters is such that an authentic national commitment is required. And yet there is no assurance that a new national vision can be created and communicated with success. Were it improperly constructed, as occurred with the "Northern Vision" of the Diefenbaker years, it would lead the country back into passivity. The effect of another disillusionment with the Arctic could be to demobilize Canadian interest for an extended period during which the scope and pace of international and national operations in the region will continue to grow. A workable vision, in contrast, will be based on a realistic assessment of Canadian abilities and of what the domestic and international context will allow. It will also be founded on realistic assumptions about the northernness of southern Canadians. These are the ultimate concerns of the chapters that follow.

PART ONE

Setting

CHAPTER TWO

Bringing the Outside Inside: Towards Development of the Passage

GRAHAM ROWLEY

The possibility of a quick and easy route to the silk and spice markets of the Orient was the lure that attracted the European search for a Northwest Passage, but man must already have discovered a way north of the North American continent some thousands of years earlier while extending his dominion over the world. Before 2,000 BC people of the Arctic Small Tool Tradition had entered northern Canada from Alaska, continued east, and passed through the islands of the Canadian Arctic archipelago to reach Greenland. We do not know how they travelled. The journey would be possible today by land and over sea ice, but they probably had boats of some kind. The Passage was, therefore, known to man long before its geographical significance was recognized – indeed before it had any significance except as a place to hunt and a way that led to other hunting grounds. Archaeologists called the route these hunters followed the "Musk-ox Way" because they had lived to a large extent on the musk-oxen they had found there.[1]

A second discovery of the Passage must have been made about three thousand years later when Inuit of the Thule Culture invaded the Canadian Arctic from Alaska. They spread rapidly along the Arctic coasts of Canada and crossed into Greenland. These people had kayaks and umiaks and were able to hunt the larger whales. The framework of an umiak constructed in the Alaskan tradition, if not actually built there, was found by the Danish archaeologist Count Eigil Knuth on the coast of the most northern part of Greenland and has been dated by radiocarbon analysis to be about 500 years old.

The sea mammals on which the life of the Inuit was so firmly based appear to have had little interest in the Passage. The whales that were hunted in the Eastern Canadian Arctic were a different population from that hunted off the Alaskan coasts. The Pacific walrus in the west is a different subspecies from the Atlantic walrus in the east, and many other species of sea mammals are different. No animals are known to migrate regularly through the Passage. Narwhal and harp seal, both of which must have come from the east, have however been reported occasionally west of Bellot Strait.

EUROPEAN EXPLORATIONS

European activity in the area began with the Vikings. The Norse settlers in Greenland made voyages to Vinland in the west and to Baffin Bay in the north.[2] Accounts that have survived in Icelandic sagas and a runic inscription found in 1824 at Kingigtorsuak on the west coast of Greenland in latitude 72°55'N provide convincing evidence of these journeys. Material of Norse origin has been discovered at a few archaeological sites in the Eastern Canadian Arctic, as well as at L'anse aux Meadows in northern Newfoundland. In particular many Norse artifacts were recently excavated at a site on Skraeling Island, a small island off the east coast of Ellesmere Island. This shows that there was some contact between the Norse and the Inuit in the Eastern Canadian Arctic and may indicate actual Norse presence there.[3] The approaches to the Passage from the Atlantic were, therefore, becoming known by the thirteenth century, but this knowledge was lost with the disappearance of the Norse settlements in Greenland, if it had not already been forgotten.

Commercial interests in Europe were attracted by the possibility of a Northwest Passage soon after the rediscovery of America by Christopher Columbus. The new continent was seen as a barrier to a direct route to the markets of the Orient. In 1497 John Cabot became the first to seek a way around it to the north, a route that would avoid the Spanish sphere of influence to the south. Other attempts during the next eighty years added little to the geographical knowledge of the north before Martin Frobisher reached Baffin Island in 1576. He was diverted from his quest for the Northwest Passage by the belief that he had found gold ore in Frobisher Bay, but the search was continued in the next half-century by Davis, Hudson, Button, Baffin, Bylot, and others who probed the continent for a passage to the west that would take them to the East. When these attempts failed to find an easy route, the merchant companies that had supported them lost interest. For nearly two hundred years there were no significant discoveries in the eastern approaches to the Passage.

Frobisher's Arctic voyages took place at the time when Mercator's projection was coming into general use for maps and charts. The projection did not of course make navigation through the Passage any easier or more difficult, but, owing to the exaggeration of both north-south and east-west distances at high latitudes, the route appeared much longer and less direct than it is. This may have had, and possibly still continues to have, an unconscious psychological effect even on those well aware of the limitations of the projection.

For the remainder of the seventeenth and all the eighteenth centuries the exploration of northern Canada sprang from the fur trade. Agents of the fur-trading companies travelled overland and by canoe along the rivers and across the lakes, guided by Indians and making great use of Indian knowledge, techniques, and support. Both Hearne and Mackenzie reached the northern coast of the continent, at the mouths of the Coppermine and Mackenzie rivers respectively. Toward the end of this period naval and scientific interest in the north took root and led to Cook's expedition to the north Pacific. Cook in 1778 and, after Cook's death in Hawaii, Clerke in 1779 entered Bering Strait and followed the northern coast of Alaska as far as Icy Cape, where they met impenetrable ice. This expedition established the western approach to the Passage.

The fifty years following the end of the Napoleonic Wars saw a great revival of British interest in the north. National prestige, fear that the Russians, already firmly established in southern Alaska, might sail north of America to reach the Atlantic from the west before Britain had reached the Pacific from the east, apprehension about the increasing maritime strength of the United States, the growing thirst for scientific knowledge, and especially the availability of naval ships and crews after the Napoleonic Wars were among the factors that persuaded the British Admiralty to mount Arctic expeditions and to renew an earlier offer of a reward for the accomplishment of a Northwest Passage.[4] The success of Parry in reaching as far west as Melville Island in 1819, the discoveries of other expeditions, and the explorations of the Hudson's Bay Company indicated that a passage existed, and it was in a wave of optimism that Sir John Franklin with HMS *Erebus* and *Terror* sailed in 1845 on what was confidently expected to be the final attempt to accomplish the Northwest Passage. When this large and well-equipped expedition vanished after entering Lancaster Sound, the search for the missing ships led to many more expeditions, which explored the majority of the islands of the Canadian Arctic archipelago and the channels betwen them. The Franklin expedition was lost in the search for a Northwest Passage, but the Northwest Passage was found in the search for the lost expedition.[5] It had also become evident that the Passage was not a practicable route for the shipping of the time and that it therefore had neither commercial nor military importance. Not until 1906 did a ship complete the Northwest Passage, when Amundsen reached the Pacific in the *Gjoa* after a voyage that had begun in the Atlantic in 1903.

THE SEVERAL PASSAGES

Historical accounts and common usage have always referred to "the

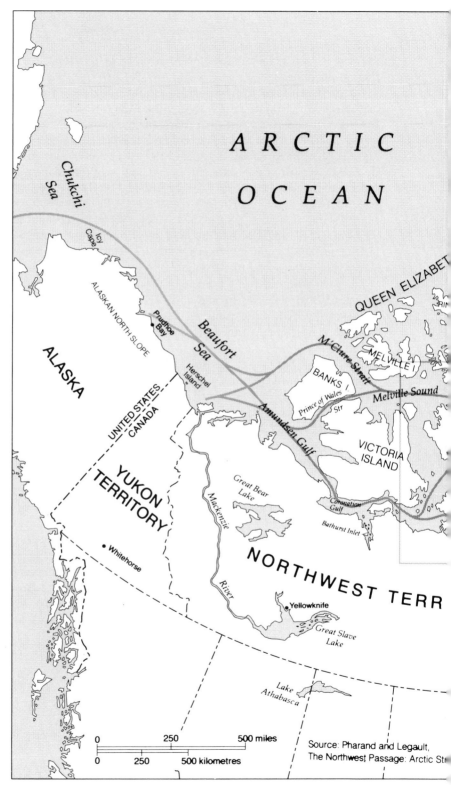

Main Surface Routes of the Passage

Northwest Passage." It would probably be more accurate to say that Amundsen had completed "a Northwest Passage" because there are many ways between the Atlantic and the Pacific through the Canadian Arctic archipelago. A navigator has the choice of several different routes, at least in theory, depending on which way he decides to go around each island and on the size and type of his ship. Since the transit of the *Gjoa* much has been learned of the waters of the Passage and about navigating them. The best route for any particular voyage and ship will depend on several factors, some of which had not been thought of in Amundsen's day.

The dominating factor that makes navigation of the Passage difficult and sometimes dangerous and often dictates the route that must be followed is of course the presence of sea ice. During the fall practically all the channels between the islands of the archipelago freeze over, the only exceptions being a few narrow straits where the current is strong enough to preserve patches of open water. The sea ice grows in depth throughout the winter and into June, reaching a thickness of up to about eight feet. By this time, however, the surface of the ice is beginning to rot in the long days of the Arctic summer, and the sea ice breaks up in July or August to form fields of pack ice. Some of this melts in the north during the summer, some is carried south by the wind and currents to melt in the North Atlantic, and some of the pack remains in the north where it may be compressed, especially during the storms of the fall and early winter. Pieces of ice are pushed against one another and can be raised into ridges or slide one above another to form what is known as rafted ice. This rough old ice is much harder and often thicker than new ice, and pack ice that contains old ice floes is much more difficult for a ship to penetrate and can cause more severe damage. Icebergs, formed by the calving of the tongues of glaciers that reach the sea, are common in Baffin Bay because of the many active glaciers flowing from the Greenland ice cap. In the Canadian Arctic archipelago, however, few glaciers reach the sea, and they are not very active, and so icebergs are not a serious problem for shipping. The prevailing winds in the Canadian Arctic are from the northwest and north-northwest and drive the pack ice against those shores that face north and into bays and channels that are open to these winds. A ship caught in the pack can be crushed by the pressure of the ice or driven ashore.

There are essentially two practical routes for east-west shipping through the Passage, though there are variations of each. One is suitable for ships of any size and submerged nuclear submarines, and the other is possible only for ships of limited draught. The deep-draught route runs directly from east to west through Lancaster Sound, Barrow Strait, Viscount Melville Sound, and M'Clure Strait, which are collectively known as Parry Channel. The most difficult part is M'Clure Strait, as it is usually choked with heavy pack ice driven in from the Beaufort Sea. Prince of Wales Strait and

Amundsen Gulf offer surface ships a way of avoiding the worst of this, and in any event the ice will usually allow no choice. In the east an alternative to entering Parry Channel through Lancaster Sound appears to lie in the route Hudson Strait, Foxe Basin, Fury and Hecla Strait, and Prince Regent Inlet, but it would not be feasible in most years. The ice in Foxe Basin breaks up very late, and the ice that packs into the southern part of the Gulf of Boothia often extends north of the entrance to Fury and Hecla Strait.

The second route, for vessels of limited draught, also enters the archipelago through Lancaster Sound, but follows the northern coast of the mainland from Queen Maud Gulf to Bering Strait. The greatest difficulties along this route in normal years are to be expected in the channels between Lancaster Sound and Queen Maud Gulf. Three channels lead south from Lancaster Sound or Barrow Strait: Prince Regent Inlet, Peel Sound, and M'Clintock Channel. They are all open to the north, and ice is likely therefore to move into them. M'Clintock Channel in particular acts as a funnel for heavy ice and in most years is filled with pack throughout the summer. It is the longest route and would also be the most difficult except in a very unusual year. The ice in Prince Regent Inlet and the northern part of Peel Sound melts by late summer in a normal year. The route through Prince Regent Inlet, however, continues through Bellot Strait to join Peel Sound where it leads into Franklin Strait. Bellot Strait is very narrow and has strong currents, and there would be little advantage in attempting this route unless ice conditions happened to be appreciably easier in Prince Regent Inlet than in the northern part of Peel Sound. The most severe ice conditions are likely to be found in Franklin Strait and Larsen Sound, which receive ice from M'Clintock Channel. There is then the choice of taking the direct route through Victoria Strait to Queen Maud Gulf or of following the northeast coast of King William Island through James Ross Strait and then through Rae Strait and Simpson Strait.

Ships drawing up to 30 feet have sailed through Victoria Strait, but ice conditions there are almost always very difficult, as it receives heavy ice direct from M'Clintock Channel. It was near the entrance to Victoria Strait that Franklin's *Erebus* and *Terror* were beset. The longer route around King William Island is usually easier despite its shallower water, irregular bottom with many drumlin shoals, and incomplete hydrographic charting. James Ross Strait was believed to be the shallowest section, but in 1984 the *Lindblad Explorer* established a line of track soundings through it with a minimum depth of nearly 30 feet, which is more than the 26-foot minimum in the deepest known channel through Simpson Strait. From Lancaster Sound to Queen Maud Gulf, where ice conditions differ greatly from year to year and even from day to day, ice reconnaissance information is invaluable.

Greenland lies east of the archipelago, and the sea currents flow clockwise round most of the great island. The cold East Greenland Current mixes with warm, Gulf Stream water before turning north up the coast of west Greenland to the head of Baffin Bay. The West Greenland Current is therefore comparatively warm, resulting in open water for much of the year along the west Greenland coast. For this reason the easiest approach to the Passage is along the Greenland coast to Melville Bay and then across the North Water to enter Lancaster Sound. The North Water is the name given by the whalers during the last century to an area in Smith Sound that remains open in winter. This leads to early warming of the sea and hence to an early break-up in northern Baffin Bay.

West of the archipelago navigation depends on the position of the Beaufort Sea pack. In some years this moves in the summer far to the north of the north coast of Alaska. It is normally between 50 and 100 miles offshore, but strong winds from the north or west can drive it against the coast of the continent with little warning. This shallow coast has no harbours, but offshore islands and grounded heavy ice can provide some protection to small ships. In the nineteenth century many whalers were trapped between Herschel Island and Icy Cape and crushed by the ice. Ice reconnaisance now gives much greater warning of this danger. In exceptional years this coast may become impassable by early September.[6]

ENVIRONMENTAL AND SOCIAL IMPLICATIONS OF SHIPPING

Until recently little consideration had been given to the implications that shipping through the Passage might have for both the environment and the native people. If it were to become an important commercial route, used by large ships possibly on a year-round basis, the environment would certainly be affected to some extent. Animals and birds in the north often congregate in large numbers, especially when migrating, as for instance at polynias in the winter or where nutrients are brought to the surface by ocean currents. Ships are potential sources of pollution, and a major oil spill could become an ecological disaster of the first magnitude. Large ice-breaking tankers break up significant areas of sea ice and might disturb the sea mammals, possibly to the extent of changing their migration patterns. The noise of the propellers of these very powerful ships could also affect the sea mammals. Whales in particular are believed to rely on sound waves through water for communication between individuals, often over large distances as well as for locating their food. Some parts of the northern seas are biologically more productive than others, and the dangers are correspondingly greater there. The entrances to Lancaster Sound and to Fury and Hecla Strait are two areas of relative richness; any practical route through the Passage would have to pass through one or the other. These are examples of ways in which shipping might interfere with the environment, and little is known of how severe the interference might be or how far it would extend. The north is one of the few areas left in the world that have been almost untouched by the industrial or agricultural practices of man, and conservationists will rally to defend it. Any proposal for development that ignored the interests of the environment and the native people would be sure to arouse widespread opposition, possibly to the extent that development would become politically unacceptable.

The Inuit are a maritime people and have relied on the sea for most of their food and until recently for virtually all their fuel. The sea has been the source of their energy, and a threat to the sea mammals, the fish, and the sea birds is seen by them as a threat to their existence as individuals and as a people, despite increased reliance on modern energy sources and food-stuffs. They hunt on, from, and through the sea ice, and it is also the highway on which they travel by dog team or over-snow toboggans to visit their neighbours. There is therefore a strong political reaction to any development that could disturb maritime resources or the environment that nurtures them. This is particularly the case in Greenland, where commercial fishing is by far the most significant industry and the largest employer, where many people still depend on hunting sea mammals for most of their food, and where more than 95 per cent of the population of some 50,000 live along the west coast of the island, the preferred route for shipping through Davis Strait. Greenland, formerly a colony of Denmark and completely sheltered from the rest of the world, has recently achieved home rule and is increasingly active politically. The perceived threat that shipping presents led the Greenland government to oppose strongly a plan to use very large ships to carry Canadian liquefied natural gas from the Queen Elizabeth Islands to the south along the west coast of Greenland. The credibility of their case has, however, been called into question by their recent approval of petroleum development in Greenland that would be open to much the same ecological objections as the Canadian plan – the Arctic Pilot Project which is discussed in detail in chapters 7 and 8.

In Canada, Pond Inlet, a settlement of nearly 1,000 inhabitants, lies about 100 miles south of the entrance to Lancaster Sound. Igloolik, much the same size, is at the eastern entrance to Fury and Hecla Strait. Its hunting economy would be directly affected if the possible, but unlikely, alternative route through Hudson Strait and Foxe Basin were used. The only inhabited place within 50 miles of the deep-draught route is Resolute Bay, with rather more than 100 Inuit residents and a largely transient white population, which reaches about the same number at the busiest times of the year. The Inuit hunt on the ice in Barrow Strait and occasionally cross it to visit Prince of Wales Island. The shallow-draught route passes close to the Inuit settlements of Spence Bay, Gjoa Haven, Cambridge Bay, Holman

Island, and Tuktoyaktuk, but ships of much the size that could use this route have been supplying these places for years and do not cause the same problems as very large ships.

Point Barrow is by far the largest Inuit settlement on the north coast of Alaska. This coast is already the scene of major oil exploration and production, and the Inuit, through native development corporations, are themselves involved in industrial activities. Any conflict between conservation and exploitation there is likely to be internalized and resolved within the Inuit community.

GREATER EASE OF SHIPPING

The stories of the Franklin search expeditions and the hardships and dangers they endured have entered so deeply into the Canadian consciousness and image of the north that they are likely to hide the changes that have taken place since that time. These changes have made transit of the Northwest Passage by no means simple but much easier than it was. Even the climate of the Canadian Arctic has improved. Temperatures are appreciably higher than they were, though there are indications that this ameliorating trend may now have been reversed. Ships are stronger, with engines that are much more powerful, reliable, and efficient. There is now much greater knowledge of the geography of the north and of Arctic conditions. Hydrographic charting, though far from complete, is steadily improving in quality. There may yet be well-hidden surprises, such as the unsuspected pingos on the seabed of the Beaufort Sea that were not discovered before the voyage of the supertanker s/t *Manhattan*, but more detailed hydrography is more likely to reveal deeper channels than to add restrictions. A navigator prefers known hazards to uncertainty.

As the north magnetic pole lies practically on the route of the Northwest Passage, the horizontal component of the earth's magnetic field is very weak in this area, and the magnetic compass, so important for navigation in Franklin's day, is of little use. The introduction of the gyroscopic compass, and later of electronic positioning, was a great improvement, and satellite navigation now provides latitude and longitude to within a few metres instantaneously.

Major improvements have been made in other technological fields. Radio, though subject to blackouts during magnetic storms, allows ships to keep in touch with the world, and satellite communications now provide complete reliability in most but not yet all areas. It is a far cry from the hot air balloons, homing pigeons, and collars for messages on captured foxes that were supplied to the Franklin search expeditions. Two other inventions have added greatly to the safety of navigation in the north. One is the echo-sounder, particularly valuable owing to the incomplete hydrography.

The other is radar, which detects ice fields and icebergs, but not always growlers, in waters where sea fog often accompanies ice.

Weather reporting and forecasting are as useful to ships in the north as they are elsewhere, but knowledge of the presence and movements of sea ice is of vital importance. Special ice reconnaissance flights and satellite imagery now provide detailed information on ice distribution to Arctic shipping, together with short-term and long-term ice forecasts. Large ships can carry helicopters to guide them along the easiest paths through the pack ice, a great improvement over the crow's nest.

It is difficult to compare the task that faced Franklin and Amundsen with modern voyages in the north. Today's navigator is not sailing into the unknown, he has far superior equipment, he has navigation aids that Franklin would have considered miraculous, and he has the means to call on various supporting services and to summon icebreaker assistance if needed.

CANADIAN CONTRIBUTIONS
UP TO 1945

Many nations, beginning with the people of the Arctic Small Tool Tradition and including the Vikings, the British, the Americans, and the Norwegians have taken part in the discovery and exploration of the Passage and in the development of the technology needed to navigate in these waters. They are, however, essentially Canadian waters, since any passage must pass within twelve miles of Canadian territory and since these waters have now been enclosed by the government of Canada. It is of interest, therefore, particularly to Canadians, to review the role that Canada itself has played and the contribution it has made.

By the time of Confederation in Canada in 1867 a northern way around the continent had been found. Even after the transfer to Canada of Rupert's Land and the Northwest Territory from the Hudson's Bay Company in 1870, it remained questionable whether the Canadian Arctic archipelago, through which the route lay, was included in the new dominion. The situation was made somewhat clearer by an Imperial Order in Council in 1880 placing all remaining British possessions in what is now the Northwest Territories under Canadian jurisdiction. These possessions were not defined, but Britain had played by far the greatest part in the exploration of the land area surrounding the Passage, and Canadian title to that part of the archipelago has never been seriously challenged.

Canada could claim little credit for the exploration of this extension to its empire. Even the expeditions dispatched by the fur trade, which had done so much to determine the northern limits of the continent, had been carried out by men who looked to Great Britain as their home. An important and frequently unrecognized part had been played by the native people, who must themselves have found the Passage long before anybody was looking for it. They had also taught the explorers how to survive and travel in the north and had always acted as their guides through the continent; but Indians and Inuit had no thoughts of shipping routes around the continent or of a northern dominion. There was, however, one exception, in which a Canadian had played a leading role in northern exploration and must have had some concept of a Canada that would stretch far into the north. William Kennedy was a Metis whose mother was a Cree and whose father was a chief trader in the Hudson's Bay Company. In 1850 he was selected by Lady Franklin to become captain of the *Prince Albert* and to lead one of the most competent Franklin search expeditions. Many of his crew were chosen for their knowledge of Canadian conditions, and the sledge parties from his expedition used Canadian native travelling techniques; they were able to set out much earlier in the year and to cover greater distances than those of the preceding search expeditions. Kennedy had also been a long-time exponent of absorbing the Hudson's Bay Company territories within the colony and was an early advocate of building a railway to Churchill. A small but increasing number of Canadians must have shared his concept of a northern destiny.

The Canadian government, however, and most of the Canadian population could spare little time for the north. There were so many pressing things to do closer to home, and the east-west dimension of the country was of much more concern to the politicians and was better able to seize the public imagination. When the north was considered at all, it was as a potential corridor across the country, and there were proposals for railways to the Pacific from Churchill and even from Chesterfield Inlet. This was the Northwest Passage by land, rather than by sea. The Canadian attitude towards the north was well illustrated at the time of the First International Polar Year, when a co-ordinated program of scientific observations was carried out from August 1882 to August 1883 at a number of stations established in the polar regions. Three of these stations were in Arctic Canada; one was established by the United Kingdom at Fort Rae, one by the United States at Fort Conger in Ellesmere Island, and one by Germany in Cumberland Sound in Baffin Island. Canada took no part. The only significant Canadian activity in the Arctic seas during the nineteenth century was in the Hudson Strait area, where a series of three expeditions under Gordon established and supplied a number of stations to report on ice conditions and a later expedition under Wakeham investigated navigation conditions. Development of a shipping route into Hudson Bay was of much higher priority than investigating the waters of a passage that seemed to have no value.

The new century brought a great change in the attitude of the Canadian government towards the north. The stations established by the United

States and Germany for the First International Polar Year, Peary's attempts to reach the North Pole from Ellesmere Island, Sverdrup's expedition to the northern islands of the archipelago, Amundsen's interest in the Northwest Passage, and the activities of American whaling vessels in the Beaufort Sea, at Herschel Island, and in Hudson Bay must have made it evident that continued Canadian inactivity, while foreign expeditions were doing so much, would result in parts of the Canadian north passing into other hands.

Among the first Canadians to express concern was J.E. Bernier, a sea captain from L'Islet, Quebec, with a long-standing interest in Arctic exploration. As early as 1898 he proposed to lead an expedition to the North Pole, but he failed to gain sufficient public support. Partly no doubt because of his appeals, the government became aware of the developing threat to Canadian sovereignty and in 1903 dispatched an expedition under A.P. Low in CGS *Neptune* to Hudson Bay to license any foreign whalers there as a demonstration of Canadian authority. The same year the decision of the Alaska Boundary Commission caused widespread indignation in Canada, where many considered it to be unfair and to indicate that the United States would not hesitate to extend its boundaries at Canadian expense. The next year the government bought the *Gauss*, a vessel that had wintered in the Antarctic, renamed it the *Arctic*, and had it prepared under Bernier's direction for a polar expedition. In August, however, it was decided that instead the *Arctic*, with Bernier in command, would relieve the *Neptune* in Hudson Bay.

In 1904–5, "The Title of Canada to the Islands North of the Mainland of Canada," a confidential report to the Minister of the Interior by W.F. King, the Chief Astronomer, concluded that Canada's title to some at least of the northern islands was imperfect. While this report was being drafted, Sverdrup announced the discovery of Axel Heiberg Island and the Ringnes Islands and claimed to have taken possession of approximately 100,000 square miles of the archipelago in the name of the King of Norway. Shortly after this, Amundsen's ship, *Gjoa*, after a voyage that had lasted four seasons, became the first ship to complete the Northwest Passage. The government decided to act on King's report, and Bernier, after completing his voyage back from Hudson Bay in 1905, received instructions to return to winter in the north in 1906–7 and to demonstrate Canadian sovereignty throughout the archipelago by serving notices on any whalers he found there and by formally proclaiming sovereignty and leaving records on the islands he visited. Two similar voyages followed, and these provided a continuing if sporadic Canadian presence in the area. Concern over sovereignty also prompted the government to accept Stefansson's proposal for a major expedition in the western Arctic. The result was the Canadian Arctic Expedition of 1913–18, which made important geographical discoveries in the Arctic archipelago and also carried out scientific studies in a number of disciplines along the northern coast of the continent as far east as Bathurst Inlet.

In the years following the First World War, a regular annual seaborne Canadian Eastern Arctic patrol was initiated, at first with CGS *Arctic* under Captain Bernier, and Royal Canadian Mounted Police (RCMP) detachments were established on Baffin Island and Ellesmere Island. The northern fur trade was expanding, and trading posts were built wherever there was a significant local Inuit population. The number of Anglican and Roman Catholic missions increased. Such measures made Canadian sovereignty more secure, but there was little to encourage seaborne traffic across the top of the continent. For carrying freight to posts in the western Arctic the use of the route around Alaska, which had been pioneered by the whalers, was discontinued in favour of the Mackenzie River route, with transshipment from river barges to small coastal vessels at Tuktoyaktuk. It was a very costly route, especially to the more eastern posts it served. The first alternative that the Hudson's Bay Company tried was by land. In the winters of 1926–7 and 1928–9, experiments were made with tractors hauling freight by sled from Wager Bay in Hudson Bay to Cockburn Bay on the Arctic coast, but the company did not persevere with this concept. By sea the expansion of the fur trade to the west through Lancaster Sound had been brought to a halt by creation of the Arctic Islands Preserve and a government decision to discourage trading in that area. It was not until 1937 that the Hudson's Bay Company was able to establish a trading post at Fort Ross at the eastern entrance to Bellot Strait. There the first commercial use of the Passage was achieved, when token packets of freight, brought from the west by the Hudson's Bay Company schooner *Aklavik*, and from the east by the RMS *Nascopie*, were exchanged between the two ships. Like the token barrel of oil shipped from Prudhoe Bay to the east in the *Manhattan* more than 30 years later, it betokened a promise that has yet to be fulfilled.

During the 1920s the north had not obtruded far into the national consciousness, and one year there passed into another with little change. As a peripheral area it was very vulnerable to the financial crisis of 1929. The gradual expansion of the fur trade came to a halt, and the deepening depression brought retrenchment and stifled initiative. To the Hudson's Bay Company it restored the virtual monopoly the company had enjoyed in the nineteenth century, but now in a shrinking economy. For the Inuit it meant that they had to rely more on their traditional skills and practices. They could afford to buy very little from the south, but, because they had never become accustomed to much, there was no dramatic change. In an Ottawa struggling to restore financial stability, even the small northern expenditures could not be allowed to escape the drastic cuts throughout the government. The few civil servants involved were reduced in number and influence. The annual Eastern Arctic Patrol, which had been the means of demonstrating Canadian sovereignty and concern in the eastern Canadian Arctic, lost its ship; the patrol became a government party carried in the Hudson's Bay Company's RMS *Nascopie*. There were nevertheless some encouraging signs in the north, though not in the far north. The Second Polar Year of 1932–3 saw special Canadian stations at Chesterfield Inlet and Coppermine. The railway to Churchill and the port of Churchill were completed, bringing grain carriers into Hudson Bay. In the west, bush flying opened new fields for prospecting, and mining for gold, silver, and radium began in the Mackenzie District.

The Passage lay far from the main scenes of action during the Second World War, but Canadian public interest was stirred by the voyages of the RCMP schooner *St. Roch*. In the years 1940–2 it completed the passage from west to east, and in 1944 it returned from Halifax to Vancouver, making the voyage in a single season. This demonstrated the use of the Passage for a practical purpose, and completion of the whole voyage in under three months made commercial use appear feasible. It was also an achievement of which Canada could well be proud. The *St. Roch* had been built in Canada. Its captain, Staff Sergeant (later Superintendent) Henry Larsen, had been born in the same part of Norway as Amundsen, at that time the only other man to have navigated the Passage, but Larsen had become a Canadian many years before the voyages that made him so well-known. He and all his crew were members of the RCMP, the most Canadian of institutions in the eyes of the world.

NORTHERN DEVELOPMENT AND SOUTHERN AWARENESS

The end of the Second World War saw the beginning of rapid changes in the Canadian north. There were several reasons for this: political considerations, increased strategic significance with the consequent defence measures, growing public awareness of the north, an expanding economic frontier in a time of relative prosperity, and new technology that brought new possibilities. They were interrelated in many ways, and together they gave northern development a momentum much greater than any single factor could have produced.

Politically there was renewed concern on the part of the Canadian government. Large wartime defence projects in the north such as the air staging routes, the Canol pipeline, and the Alaska Highway had been carried out almost exclusively by the armed services of the United States, and American citizens outnumbered Canadians in many parts of the north. There was no threat to Canadian de jure sovereignty, but Canadian de facto sovereignty was much less secure. Canadian government activities in the north therefore began to be given a higher priority, and northern development was recognized as something that should be encouraged rather than as an expense that could be put off indefinitely.

Though the wartime defence projects were soon terminated, with Canada purchasing from the United States any useful parts of their infrastructure, defence interest in the north increased. The Cold War took shape and brought recognition of the new vulnerability of the North American continent to long-range aircraft equipped with nuclear weapons. Arctic weather stations to provide meteorological information, low frequency Loran stations for navigation, air refuelling bases, and radar warning lines, together with their airfields and communications, were some of the new defence measures. Canada participated in these projects, though the United States often played the leading role. The Canadian armed services themselves began to look on northern operations as an essential part of military training.

Largely as a result of defence activities the Canadian public as a whole became aware of the north for the first time. It learned that over a large part of its country there were neither schools nor health services, and that people could, and sometimes did, die of starvation. It was a shocking and embarrassing discovery for a people that had considered itself beyond reproach and whose representatives at international meetings had deplored such conditions in other countries. Politicians could be confident that they would have wide public support for any program designed to improve living standards and social services in the north.

Interest in the north was not entirely altruistic. Memories of the Yukon Gold Rush were still fresh and nourished a belief that the north held almost unlimited mineral wealth waiting for discovery. Times were prosperous, and the economy was expanding. The industrial frontier was being pushed north with large-scale developments like Kitimat, the Yellowknife gold mines, Port Radium, Lynn Lake, and Schefferville. Mining was seen by both the government and the public as the engine that would drive the economy of the north and pay rich dividends to the nation.

Little of this activity could have been contemplated without the wartime advances in technology. In no field was this more marked than in transportation. Improvements in equipment and techniques allowed development to proceed at a much more rapid pace and at the same time were major influences in determining the pattern of events in the north. The extent of technological change brought about by the war was well illustrated in the Canadian army's "Exercise Muskox." This operation involved nearly 50 men using army equipment, carried in ten Canadian military oversnow vehicles and supplied by air. They travelled in the winter and early spring of 1946 from Churchill to Cambridge Bay in Victoria Island and then to Dawson Creek on the Alaska Highway. They covered more than 2,500 miles with no roads – part of the way along Amundsen's route through the Passage – in less than two and a half months. This journey would have been inconceivable a few years earlier.

With the development of long-range aircraft, the whole north became more accessible: journeys that had lasted months and might be possible at only one season of the year could now be carried out in a matter of hours and at any time. Mail could arrive every week or even more frequently, instead of once a year. Women, as wives or nurses, went north to join what had been for the small white population of the north an almost entirely male preserve, and a white society, separate and different from the Inuit society, evolved. Movements of personnel and of light, valuable, or urgent freight were soon made almost invariably by air, and ships' cargoes were progressively restricted to heavy or bulky items and especially to fuel.

This new freedom of transportation changed the white man's concept of the north. To the Inuit the north had always been a geographical continuity, with change occurring gradually from west to east, and with frequent contact between adjacent Inuit groups. To the white man there had been two Arctics, the eastern Arctic and the western Arctic, defined by the routes used to supply them, and with little contact between the two. In every organization they were included in different administrative regions. Men were divided, consciously or unconsciously, into eastern Arctic men and western Arctic men. Rasmussen's unprecedented journey in 1923–4 by dog-sledge from Hudson Bay to Alaska along the northern coast of the continent had already emphasized how far they were apart. What contact there was between these two Arctics remained through Ottawa in the case of the government, through Winnipeg and Montreal in the case of the Hudson's Bay Company, and through Toronto and Montreal for the churches. This distinction between east and west began to blur as air travel across the north increased, and it became possible to think of one Arctic and gradually to administer the north as a whole.[7]

Those who lived in the north began to feel less isolated from the rest of the country and from the world. Until comparatively recently "outside" was a geographical description used in the north to denote anywhere that was not in or of the north. "When were you last outside?" meant "When were you last in the south, or anywhere else that is not the north." "They do it differently outside" meant that some practice was unique to the north. This word, which used to occur in almost every conversation, is now less often used. The outside has come inside. In the same way the expression "down north," common some years ago in the Mackenzie District, began to slip out of usage by the late 1950s. The north was no longer thought of as being isolated at the end of a single and slow transportation system.

The Inuit had considered themselves not as being isolated but rather as being alone. They had known little of the outside world, but this too began to change after the Second World War. New schools brought knowledge of the wider world to the children, while the large number of Inuit taken to hospitals in the south for treatment of tuberculosis – which soon reached over 10 per cent of the population – received a rapid and sometimes traumatic introduction to how people lived in the rest of Canada. In the north the receipt of family allowances and other social benefits showed them that they were part of a larger, though incomprehensible community.

One of the first northern projects in the post-war period was the development of Resolute Bay. This was not a planned move. An advance base was required from which to service the joint Canadian-U.S. weather stations being built in the Queen Elizabeth Islands to meet both military and civilian needs. It was to be at Winter Harbour on Melville Island, but the convoy was held up by ice in Barrow Strait and suffered some damage. A decision was made against attempting to penetrate farther west, and the base was established instead at Resolute Bay on Cornwallis Island, not far from the most western point the convoy had reached. The site had several disadvantages, but the bay provided some shelter and the terrain was level enough for construction of an airstrip. The position of Resolute Bay in the centre of the Canadian Arctic archipelago and nearly half-way through Parry Channel made it a very suitable base for resource exploration in the Queen Elizabeth Islands, as well as an important factor in any activities centred on the Passage.

The most widely known of the northern defence projects, the Distant Early Warning Line (DEW Line) had stations spaced out along most of the northern coast of the mainland of North America. Sea freight was sent to the western stations from the Pacific or the Mackenzie Delta and to the eastern stations from the Atlantic. A few stations in the centre were inaccessible by sea owing to ice conditions and depended solely on air transport. No attempt was made to follow up the Hudson's Bay Company's experiments with tractors from Hudson Bay to supply these stations. The federal government, faced with a substantial construction program at Pelly Bay, also chose air transport rather than exploiting the opportunity to use tractors from Repulse Bay, an operation in which the Inuit could have become involved. The Passage was not used at all by the DEW Line, the government, or commercial interests for through freight. Between the voyages of the *St. Roch* and the *Manhattan* the only vessels to complete the passage were Canadian icebreakers, U.S. Coast Guard ships, and U.S. Navy nuclear submarines.

Post-war development of the Arctic was begun under Liberal federal governments, which made political capital out of their discovery of the north. Federal government departments realized that they had responsibilities in the north of the country as well as in the south, and the Advisory Committee on Northern Development, composed mainly of their deputy ministers, was established to formulate coherent policies, to co-ordinate military and civil activities there, and to advise Cabinet on northern matters. The Department of Resources and Development was renamed the Department of Northern Affairs and National Resources, social services were expanded and often had to be initiated, and publicity was given to any northern event to ensure continuing public support. When the Hudson's Bay Company's RMS *Nascopie* sank, it was replaced by a government ship, the *C.D. Howe*, giving the Canadian Eastern Arctic patrol its own ship again.

Ironically it was the Conservatives, with John Diefenbaker's "Northern Vision," who made full use of the political potential of the north in the federal election of 1958 and harvested the crop sown by the Liberals. The program of "Roads to Resources" captured the public imagination, and the media, well aware of the value of telling the public what it wanted to hear, supported the concept. Lester Pearson's criticism of the program as one of building highways from igloo to igloo was ineffective, though it proved more realistic. Irrespective of which party was in power, wishful thinking and official optimism continued unabated. The warning of the Royal Commission on Canada's Economic Prospects – that northern development would not be easy – fell on deaf ears. Despite government support in such forms as geological and other surveys, very generous conditions governing prospecting for minerals and petroleum, tax incentives, and even equity participation in companies involved in the north, extensive exploration failed to yield the resources that had been so confidently expected.

In the process of encouraging commercial development of the north, many activities that had been carried out by the Department of National Defence were transferred to civilian departments of government or to private enterprise. They included air photography, operation of many airfields, maintenance of the Alaska Highway, provision of telecommunications, and the supply of several northern stations. As a result the armed forces, which had in the first instance been responsible for introducing change into the north, had raised much of the infrastructure to higher standards than could have been justified for civilian purposes and had continued to keep the north in touch with technological advances, lost much of the impact they had had there.

The need for transportation in the north had expanded in pace with the exploration of non-renewable resources and with the growth of government involvement in response to the assumption of responsibilities to a rapidly increasing native population. Much of this need was met by air. Air transport had had a renowned history in the Canadian north. The exploits of the early bush pilots in the Mackenzie Valley in the 1920s had become legendary, and the ambition of every northern boy was to follow in their footsteps. During the 1930s more freight was carried by air in the

Mackenzie District and in the northern parts of the provinces than anywhere else in the world. After the Second World War the extension of commercial flying north from the bush to the barrens seemed a natural move. The wartime airfields served as stepping stones, and there was no shortage of pilots. The icebreakers of the Department of Transport, later of the Canadian Coast Guard, did not enjoy the same prestige. They provided what was essentially a supporting service to northern shipping in the summer months only. Their capacity was fully occupied in escorting merchant ships through ice and maintenance of navigation aids in waters that were comparatively well-known, with little time for pioneering. The Canadian Hydrographic Service was also expanded but was faced with the formidable task of improving the accuracy of charts covering routes that were already in use. The Royal Canadian Navy's icebreaker HMCS *Labrador* was able to do more to explore Arctic waters and to test the possibilities of developing new routes, but this initiative was lost when it was transferred to the Department of Transport for routine duties in 1958.

Freight rates to the north were much lower by sea than by air – often only about a tenth – but the speed, convenience, and year-round service by air, combined with high interest rates, reduced this advantage. The annual sea lift to practically any settlement in the Arctic continued with increasing tonnage, largely owing to a greater need for fuel and the heavy and bulky nature and low value of construction materials. Freight movements of this comparatively small size could be met by using normal coasters and small tankers; they were much too small to justify the expense and risk of designing and building special ships for the short Arctic shipping season. The continued failure to find northern non-renewable resources meant that there were no substantial cargoes to move and brought a state of virtual stagnation to Canadian commercial shipping in the north. In 1968 the discovery of the largest oil field in North America at Prudhoe Bay on the Arctic coast of Alaska meant sudden and dramatic change. It provided a possible large-scale use of the Northwest Passage and gave reasonable grounds to expect that large reserves of petroleum would be discovered in the Beaufort Sea. Attention was again drawn to the Northwest Passage, not as a route to the East, but as a route from the north.

When viewed from Canada and Alaska, the Passage appears in a different light from how it is seen from elsewhere. For the rest of the world it is essentially part of a longer route between the Atlantic and the Pacific – a way to avoid the North American continent. In this context its importance will therefore rise and fall with changes in marine technology and techniques. For example, development of massive ice-breaking freighters able to sail through the polar pack of the Arctic Ocean or of commercial submarines that could operate under it could serve to maintain the Passage as a back water. For the United States the Passage will nevertheless remain a possible short cut from Alaska and the Pacific to the Atlantic. For Canada it is a way between the eastern Arctic and the Pacific or between the western Arctic and the Atlantic. It is potentially far the cheapest way to carry freight into and out of the Canadian north, and its importance will increase with the growth of the nation and as development extends into the north.

CHAPTER THREE

Inuit Politics and the Arctic Seas

PETER JULL

Along the western end of the Northwest Passage stretches the low-lying Beaufort coast of Alaska, the North Slope. At the eastern end are the great fiords and ice cliffs of Greenland. Between the two are the islands of the Canadian Arctic archipelago and the mainland north coast. This is the homeland of Inuit, a people of Siberian origin who from the shores and islands of the Bering Sea came in successive migrations across the top of North America after the conclusion of the last Ice Age.

Inuit or Eskimo society has undergone greater transformations in recent years than perhaps any on earth. Left for so long to pursue their characteristic life-style of hunting sea mammal, polar bear, and caribou, moving in winter from place to place and quickly building the famous domed snow-house, clad in clothes of furs and skins, they established a remarkable rapport with the natural environment, symbolized perhaps by the image of the smiling Inuit as known to us all. There was some truth in the image. But in a few short decades, most notably since the end of the Second World War, everything has changed.

Now the Arctic seems to be a land of airplanes and empty oil drums, the litter of industrial projects, jerry-built homes, and disoriented individuals. But if that is what the visitor may see from a window in a creaking or modern Arctic hotel, he is missing the continuity. Every community except transient bases or camps for outside labour is still pervaded by extended family kinships, ancient sharing patterns of food gathering and consumption, the presence of children – an apparently endless stream of children, with all the wants and demands and whimsy of children anywhere – and by expressions and habits of mind and language that are the keys to a rich and ancient world-view.

THE CURRENT SITUATION

Alaska

Some of the most dramatic contrasts may be seen on the North Slope of

Alaska. In Barrow, new bungalows with clean lines, complete with garages, have driveways often shared by a station wagon and umiak whale-boat with a creamy walrus-hide stretched tight over its wooden frame. The hide has certain valuable qualities, including silence, in closing on the whale. Whaling is a near obsession on the North Slope and the object of the year's great festival. But the whalers may have university degrees and may have worked in southern nuclear industries, as well as holding major public offices in the North Slope Borough. Homes blend many traditions – evidence of the whaling culture of the New Englanders who exploited the area in times past – while whale ribs and other bones litter a site that has recently been dug up for archaeological surveys and reveals an endless cycle of lives reaching into the distant past. At this point of land, which separates what maps call the Chukchi Sea from the Beaufort Sea, all the jarring elements of the Inuit present and future are available.

On this cold and windswept shore which marks the northernmost point of the United States, community living conditions were dismal a few years ago. But the strength and determination of young leaders, and some older ones of whom the late Eben Hopson is always most honoured, have changed everything. A land claims settlement, improved at the last minute by a brilliant North Slope political effort, benefited all Alaskan natives. It also saw the creation of the North Slope Borough, which proceeded to lay its hands on all available revenue, to apply it to social, housing, and community services of every description, and thus to turn the local life-style upside down. Job creation and training have been a main Borough concern, and a success. But not all of native Alaska has been successful under the claims settlement of 1971.

The North Slope Inuit took the lead in setting up the Alaska Native Review Commission in 1983, to study the operation of the claims settlement. The sponsoring agency for the review was the Inuit Circumpolar Conference, which is discussed at length below. Canadian judge Thomas Berger, renowned for his Mackenzie Valley study of development effects on northern peoples, accepted the job of Commissioner. He travelled throughout Alaska's Inuit and Indian villages and held week-long expert panels in Anchorage. His conclusions, published as a best-selling book, *Village Journey*, contain a powerful indictment of the business corporation model for native development and argue for a more collective and community-based form of self-government.[1] A debate on his findings is now going on throughout Alaska.

Inupiat (as the North Slope Inuit are known) leaders approach issues with great vigour as they seize every legal tool to advance the people's case for more control of the seas offshore and of the resources, living and fossil, that they may yield. As the non-Inuit population grows in certain areas of the Borough – a vast territory that is essentially all of Alaska north of the

Brooks Range – discussion mounts on the risks of the future. The advantages of more traditional structures of Inuit government, allowed for under existing u.s. federal legislation, are being debated, as are other forms of managing and controlling resources and public services.

The traditional and modern synthesis on the North Slope is nowhere better evident than in sea management. While the whale hunt is the main Inupiat cultural, food, and social focus, it has been conducted in the midst of vigorous national and international politics. Protecting the rights of Inupiat to their bowhead whale quotas has challenged many assumptions in international gatherings. At the same time, various agencies in the Borough have used their funds to invest in advanced technology to study, monitor, and develop the economic potential and to protect the environment of the Arctic coastal zone. Given the present level of attention to cultural and heritage values, and to renewable resource harvesting, non-renewable potential, and the entire interaction of natural systems, the Inupiat coastal zone management and its place in the life of the community are probably unique in the world. Bringing in scholars and consultants, the local people also gain access to the best outside knowledge and bolster their own capabilities.

What is most notable about Barrow is the self-confidence and enthusiasm of the people, mingled with their strong sense of tradition. Visitors are shown permafrost cellars full of whale meat and *maktaaq* and entertained in old ways. But one can never fail to note that this is a dynamic society. The Inupiat are experienced and successful combatants in all levels of politics and may be counted on to be in the forefront of Arctic change.

Greenland

Greenland was an isolated preserve when Americans arrived during the Second World War. Demand then grew for a major change of direction, a rethinking of the long isolation of Greenland from the industrial revolution in the world around it. A number of ambitious post-war Danish development plans succeeded one another. They served to concentrate the population in larger centres built around an industrialized fishery. They also provided social and community services and infrastructure in the Scandinavian social-democratic style. The traditional hunting culture continued, however, to thrive in numerous small outports along the rugged western coast.

From the end of the 1960s, young Greenlanders being educated in Denmark led the way for a movement of national renewal. Then through the campaign for home rule and subsequently the creation of new political parties, they took over direction of the country. In May 1979, home rule came into effect, with Greenlandic Inuit politicians acquiring control from Denmark of virtually all fields of policy except foreign affairs, defence, and currency. As for on- and offshore resources, Denmark and Greenland each have a veto on policies and projects. In practice, plans are worked out by compromise through a joint administration and a high-level joint Greenlandic-Danish committee.[2]

Now the hosts of transient outsiders have largely gone. Those who remain often bear a strong commitment to Greenland and its future. The Greenland that remains is also in many ways a European country that requires European techniques and technologies to run. Nevertheless, a resurgence of Inuit culture, and a flowering of new forms of art and music, theatre and poetry, provide compelling examples for Inuit in Canada and Alaska. Co-operation among all the Inuit regions of North American through computer and telecommunication lines also promises to have a profound impact.

Ocean issues are the most active topics in Greenlandic politics, along with the national question itself. When Canadian tankers seemed set to sail through west Greenland's iceberg-laden waters in what appeared as the beginning of a new era of Arctic hydrocarbon transport, Greenland rose to the challenge together with the Canadian Inuit, and the Arctic Pilot Project was eventually halted. More on this and related marine political issues appears in chapter 7.

Greenland's population of 50,000 has challenging years ahead as it seeks national consensus on the issues of development for the sake of revenue versus environmental protection, relations with Denmark and other countries, and a form of economic management to succeed the largely Danish-run, centralized state enterprise that has long controlled most of Greenland's economy. Meanwhile, Greenland plays an active role in international affairs, notably in ocean-related forums[3] and through the Inuit Circumpolar Conference, whose Greenlandic president and staff were for some years headquartered in Nuuk. An Inuit country proud of being the first aboriginal society in recent times to acquire self-rule, Greenland is also capable of being flexible when seeking, as a government among governments, the full perquisites and dignities of statehood.

Labrador

Labrador Inuit and their forerunners once lived along the north shore of the St Lawrence, as well as on the northern portions of the island of Newfoundland. They also moved north and around the coasts of Ungava Bay, Hudson Strait, and Hudson Bay. They populate the latter areas to this day, which accounts for the strong linguistic and cultural affinities between Quebec and Labrador Inuit. The present-day Inuit population of Labrador is centred on the north Labrador coast, Nain being the main community.

As one of the most isolated areas of Canada, coastal Labrador is further distinguished by being a poor region in Canada's poorest province. Without benefit of federal public services received by Inuit elsewhere in Canada, Labrador Inuit now are preparing to negotiate their claims with Ottawa and Newfoundland as a first step in establishing collective status. Marine issues will be an important subject in these talks.

With characteristics common to many maritime areas around the North Atlantic, as well as the Inuit tradition, and with a larger supply of skilled and educated individuals than other Inuit regions, Labrador could in principle provide leadership within the larger Canadian Inuit movement. However, local problems and preparation for claims negotiations have to date preoccupied the Labrador leadership. Organizationally the Labrador Inuit have largely kept to themselves. However, in one area, protection and management of Arctic seas, the Labrador Inuit Association and its ocean science consultants have played a major role. They have been leaders in Inuit work before regulatory and environmental impact bodies, notably the Arctic Pilot Project hearings and the Beaufort Sea assessment panel, as well as in Inuit constitutional staff work relating to ocean matters.

Quebec

Quebec Inuit, partly because of their negotiating experience with the James Bay and Northern Quebec Agreement (Canada's first land claims settlement), and partly because of their insecurity in a province that had a separatist government, have consistently displayed leadership on national constitutional issues among Canadian Inuit. A major element of their proposals has been the readiness to link the basic definition of Inuit interests to questions of marine management of and Inuit benefit from the sea. This theme has been raised repeatedly in briefs and letters relating to Inuit national constitutional work (conducted formally by the Inuit Committee on National Issues in Ottawa). The interest of Quebec Inuit is not abstract. Like all Canadian Inuit, they live largely from the sea. But their rights to the islands and waters offshore – which formally lie within the Northwest Territories – have yet to be negotiated with Ottawa. Federal officials have privately encouraged the Inuit to expect a major settlement,[4] but other priorities and disagreement on the funding of the negotiation process have impeded progress. All Inuit, but especially Quebec Inuit, became alarmed in 1979 when the federal government was preparing to transfer offshore jurisdiction to the provinces, at a time when Inuit and other aboriginal peoples had unsettled coastal claims. Prime Minister Joe Clark responded that aboriginal interests would be taken into account in any such transfer.[5]

Quebec Inuit were an administrative responsibility of Ottawa until increasingly nationalistic Quebec governments began to replace federal services. The long presence of Anglican missionaries and Hudson's Bay traders, plus an essentially anglophone federal administration in the region, left Inuit a Quebec minority by virtue of their second language, English, as much as by their first, Inuktitut. This has had unfortunate consequences for the Inuit, who have found themselves pawns in struggles between Ottawa and Quebec. In the last several years, however, Inuit initiatives, coupled with more responsiveness, first by the Quebec Liberals and then by the Parti québécois government, have improved communications and relations greatly.

When Quebec Inuit, acting with Quebec's Cree Indians, made use of court action to halt the initial phase of the province's James Bay hydroelectric power development, they precipitated Canada's first serious land claims negotiation. The resulting package, agreed to in 1975, provided an Inuit school system, an Inuit-run regional government (albeit open to non-Inuit, of whom very few live in the region), and considerable financial compensation. The latter is administered by a corporation, Makivik, which is collectively owned by Quebec Inuit and works for economic development and the representation of Inuit interests. As well, various categories of reserved lands were set aside, and commitments were made to processes and structures in handling development, development effects, and public services. Regional government has been slow to develop, owing to limited funds and delays on the part of the Quebec government and an initial lack of attention from Ottawa, which is now partly corrected as the result of an all-party parliamentary demand in 1981. Nevertheless, the visible services and infrastructure that Inuit had expected to result from the agreement have been slow to appear, while Makivik has devoted itself to fighting for further benefits and for the letter and spirit of the agreement to be implemented.

The federal intention to decentralize administration to aboriginal peoples collided, in Quebec, with a relatively *dirigiste* provincial government trying to establish a presence strongly throughout its territory. This resulted in a basic division between the province and Inuit. Although the climate has improved, it remains to be seen if provincial and Inuit interests travel much further together under the current Liberal government in Quebec. The various Inuit organizations have established a task force that is touring the communities and developing plans for a new and stronger regional government serving Inuit interests. Community services in Quebec have lagged far behind those of Inuit communities in the neighbouring Northwest Territories, since Ottawa and Quebec began to bargain over their respective roles in the early 1960s. This has necessarily fuelled frustration among Quebec Inuit.

Controversial as the first Quebec-Inuit land claims agreement was, the boost to Inuit morale and self-confidence, so evident in a community like Kuujjuaq (formerly Fort Chimo) where outsiders used to dominate and treat the local Inuit with condescension, is indisputable. The imagination with which Quebec's Inuit leaders are approaching their people's problems and developing new approaches to collective and individual well-being represents a significant new contribution to Canadian society and political life. Even though some three-quarters of Canada's land area will eventually be dominated by majority Inuit, Indian, and Metis political authorities at local and regional levels, with communal ideals of economic and social life and dramatically atypical interpretations of the fairness and course of Canadian law and history, this revolution in Canada's northern identity and make-up is barely perceived in the urban culture to the south.

Northwest Territories (Nunavut)

It is the central area of the Canadian Inuit that embraces the most constricted portion of the Northwest Passage. In this large area the culture and life-style of the Inuit have been less affected by change. The Inuit of the eastern parts of the Northwest Territories have, however, seen a major upheaval.

Nunavut means "our land" and is an unexceptional term used by Inuit of many regions. But in the eastern regions of the Northwest Territories (NWT) – Keewatin, Baffin, and Kitikmeot (or central Arctic, including the communities from Pelly Bay in the east to Holman Island in the west) – Nunavut is a special term for an Inuit-dominated government now being developed actively by the federal and NWT governments along with Inuit associations in the area.[6] Plans for this new government and its boundaries are the subject of much discussion and delay. As well, fluctuating reactions by people in the southwestern NWT who have never had much enthusiasm for the scheme – after all, it would divide an NWT that they now quite dominate – create uncertainty and delay. Nevertheless, the concept of Nunavut is so strongly rooted among the Inuit of the eastern Arctic that delays and obfuscation only hamper a project that will succeed sooner or later, but succeed surely.[7] A 1982 plebiscite throughout the NWT found that 80 per cent of voters in Keewatin, Baffin, and the eastern half of Kitikmeot, in a very high voter turnout, favoured creation of Nunavut.

From a life of scattered hunting camps, where individuals had only their own resources and a material culture of their family's manufacture, Inuit since the 1950s have been concentrated by government in villages with modern prefabricated bungalows complete with furniture and federal advice on homemaking. In these villages the full range of Canadian public services and facilities have been provided – schools, nursing stations, social assistance offices, recreational and social centres, and locally run co-operatives to compete with Hudson's Bay Company trading and retail shops. This form of social organization has not been optimal for the traditional economy of the Inuit – hunting on land and sea, trapping, fishing. Nor have technical, organizational, or productivity changes been such as to improve the renewable resource harvest. Material change has been followed by a welter of local advisory and decision-making bodies. By their very limitations, these have served to remind Inuit forcibly that they have little political control over what matters most to them: the offshore, wildlife generally, protection of their land and sea environment from use and degradation by outsiders, development and use of their Inuktitut language, the content of schooling, economic development, or important decisions about their future and the future development of their homeland, now marginalized as a minority region in the vast context of Canada and its Northwest Territories.

In terms of material commitment, Canada's investment in improvements for people in the NWT can hardly be faulted. Many painful, even tragic mistakes have been made, but the aims and the persistence of government have been clear and well-intended. Nevertheless, in the vital matter of enabling men and women to take charge of their lives – a prerequisite for mental and social well-being – delay has been recognized as the most effective form of denial. Village powers of little interest to a hardy outdoors population – for example, street-lighting where there are no streets – were extended for Inuit to practise on. The idea here, urged in the Carrothers Report of 1966,[8] was that by first developing local political skills and experience, Inuit would progress up a hierarchy to full political citizenship as Canadians. Whether the powers extended were or are relevant, and whether the theory has worked, are open to doubt.[9] But Inuit in the scattered villages of Nunavut – every one of them on tide water – have become frustrated.

A major theme in this search for renewed control has been the ocean and its management. At the first meeting of the Nunavut Constitutional Forum with leaders of the regional councils to discuss powers for a Nunavut government, in Cambridge Bay on 9 September 1984, only one specific jurisdictional subject was raised, the meeting otherwise devoting itself to principle. On several occasions the participants voiced the complaint that Inuit needed powers relating to vessel operations and offshore resource development, that the NWT government had no powers in that regard, and that a Nunavut government must be able to represent Inuit interests strongly on marine matters.[10] During earlier rounds of community hearings on the Nunavut proposals, many individuals spoke of the importance of marine management, powers, and benefits for Inuit. The Nunavut Constitutional Forum has committed itself to seeking an arrangement whereby a Nunavut government can participate effectively in

marine matters, while not demanding a transfer of federal jurisdiction that
has been denied even Canada's provinces to date.[11]

In the NWT Legislative Assembly, Inuit control the largest block of votes.
The Nunavut caucus (which now includes three white politicians elected by
Inuit) has worked effectively and consistently to promote Inuit interests.
The assembly has powers similar to those of a provincial legislature in
Canada, and in practice a large say in the administration of the NWT. But
Inuit remain alienated culturally and politically from the NWT government,
and seek the greater responsiveness to their interests that a Nunavut
government is expected to bring. The only doubt in the eastern Arctic is the
frequently noted lack of education and training of Inuit on a scale adequate
to the staffing needs of a new Nunavut government, a problem to be solved
rather than taken as an excuse for postponement. While Inuit reiterate that
they do not wish to drive out all the whites, they see Inuit staff as a
necessary part of Nunavut both for reasons of administrative responsiveness to local culture and for providing meaningful work to the large
population of un- and under-employed Inuit youth.

Canada has no positive reason to maintain outside control in Nunavut,
only a series of negative ones: the local people must not get control of too
much wealth, they might not be favourably disposed to resource development, the Inuit may not be ready for their own government, the population
is not very large, a new territory must not become ethnocentric, etc.
Despite all the fuss over them, the Inuit of Nunavut are mostly unaware of
these concerns. They take it for granted that they are ready to run their
lives – which they did successfully for many thousands of years without
federal administrators and social scientists. They believe they cannot
reconstruct their families and their personal lives until they are in charge of
their own communities. While every other part of Canada developed
politically for what were ultimately self-centred local reasons of convenience and commerce, the native north has apparently to meet purer
standards of political virtue for Ottawa to give the go-ahead for Nunavut.

Western Arctic

Within the NWT also, but constituting a dramatically unique region, is the
western Arctic, with its handful of Inuit communities in the Mackenzie
River delta and around the Beaufort Sea. Represented by the oldest Inuit
organization, COPE (Committee of Original Peoples Entitlement), the
people of this region – the Inuvialuit – have suffered the most tremendous
jolts of Canadian Inuit in recent years. First the site of the model town of
Inuvik, a model to be avoided from the viewpoint of Inuit, the region then
became the focus of large-scale oil and gas exploration and now is the centre
of the efforts of Dome, Gulf, and Esso Resources to develop production

from drill-ships, rigs, and artificial islands offshore. Using pipelines, and/or tankers sailing westward through the Beaufort and Chukchi seas and Bering Strait, or eastward through the Passage and Davis Strait, oil and natural gas would be shipped to continental or world markets. COPE concluded a land claims settlement with the federal government early in 1984 but still faces considerable uncertainty in relation to the region's political destiny.

The proposal of COPE for a Western Arctic Regional Municipality (WARM) raises various complications for political development in the NWT. Although COPE states that it hopes to include its area within a new Nunavut territory, the powers it would give WARM are rather more than those envisaged for regions by the Nunavut Constitutional Forum (NCF). Indeed, in some of its particulars it would allow for an overriding of territorial government powers, which is foreign to local government practice in Canada. However, using a model based on federal proposals for Indian self-government in southern Canada, acceptable arrangements might yet be worked out.[12] Until the future place of WARM is settled, i.e. whether it is to be included in the eastern territory (Nunavut) or to form a separate western territory, the Nunavut boundary cannot be drawn. This uncertainty has inhibited progress to date on creation of Nunavut. The issue has yet to be faced squarely: NCF and COPE continue to talk at cross purposes; neither side apparently chooses to notice.[13]

Although COPE did not specifically claim the offshore in its negotiations with Ottawa, many of its proposals were contingent on marine issues. The final settlement provides for preferential harvesting of sea mammals by Inuit.[14]

Overview

A number of points may be made about the overall situation of Inuit today. Subjected to rapid and crushing changes in their homelands, Inuit in all areas except perhaps Labrador have had their lives, individually and collectively, turned upside down in the period since the Second World War. They have experienced extremes of dislocation and hardship while the most modern of technology has reshaped their lives. They have been humiliated and have responded aggressively by using the political weapons of the white man to fight back. Now they are seeking to regain control of their lives and to restabilize their society. In reaffirming their traditional culture and mastering the latest methods of development, they are striving to create a balanced and agreeable future.

Like any society, any civilization, created in a hurry, the Inuit north is bound to have some rough edges. What seems miraculous is that the Inuit regions have reconstituted themselves so well after such great upheaval. Greenland seems to have taken the lead in artistic and intellectual life,

Alaska in the spirit of enterprise, and Canada in the maintenance of inherited cultural values. Such generalizations are not absolute or altogether accurate, but they are roughly correct. All Inuit regions use modern technology comfortably; all have a strong corps of young nationalist politicians and, behind them, a less visionary and better educated managerial and professional corps. The greatest threat to evolutionary progress may not be radical young leaders but young leaders hanging on to positions and remuneration that they could not expect to obtain outside the established structures of regional and ethnic politics.

Marine policy and politics are critical elements in the volatile mix of Inuit life. The sea is, after all, the centre of Inuit livelihood. In attempting to sum up the basic Inuit concern here, we may cite the proposals of the Canadian Inuit to the Macdonald Royal Commission on Canada's economic and political future: "Recognise the importance of the Arctic seas to the economy of Inuit, and to the potential economy of Canada and the world; highlight the importance of Canada first securing its own sovereignty and then developing its policies and programs for the intelligent and productive management of Arctic waters; and recommend that governments move to provide for formal Inuit participation in marine decision-making through public bodies (e.g. a Nunavut government), special purpose authorities set up under land claims settlements, or other regional or functional mechanisms as may be appropriate."[15] In this context we should also be aware of the role that Inuit use of the sea and of the sea ice could play in establishing Canada's claim to full sovereignty over its Arctic waters by virtue of historic occupancy.[16]

THE INUIT CIRCUMPOLAR CONFERENCE (ICC)

Thanks to the drive and vision of Eben Hopson of the Alaska North Slope, the man who more than any other built the North Slope Borough, a gathering together of Inuit from the circumpolar north took place in Barrow, Alaska, in 1977. This meeting left an indelible impression on all who attended. Feeling was high as a long-scattered civilization regrouped amid celebration of traditional songs and dances, urgent discussion of political and legal struggles of all the member groups, and an exchange of ideas on the rebuilding of an ancient culture. But environmental worries, notably those centred on offshore development in the Beaufort Sea and other Arctic waters, had perhaps been the main motive for gathering at that particular time. As Mayor Hopson said in his welcome, "The defense of the world's Arctic environmental security must rest upon the strength of local home-rule government. The motivation behind the North Slope Borough's work in the planning and conduct of this conference should be clear to all.

The environmental security of our long municipal coastline depends upon the strength of home-rule government in Canada and Greenland."[17] This was the beginning of the Inuit Circumpolar Conference (ICC).[18]

The Inuit of Canada, Greenland, and Alaska share many concerns, not least their interest in the situation of the Inuit in a fourth state, the Soviet Union. Repeated attempts to make contact with Soviet Inuit have been rebuffed by Moscow. As Soviet Ambassador A.N. Yakovlev told Canada's Inuit leaders in Ottawa before the third ICC general assembly in July 1983, the Soviet Union views internationalization of the Arctic as undesirable. Since 1985, some progress has been made on bilateral cultural contacts between Soviet Inuit and Inuit elsewhere. For now the ICC keeps an empty chair in its executive council as a symbol of the Soviet absence.

The first ICC assembly, in Barrow, was followed by a difficult period during which there was confusion about the nature, structure, and operations of the body. At this stage the ICC was still more an ideal than a going concern. Financed by North Slope interests and driven by Alaskan enthusiasm, it still required organizational and policy development. The difficult work began in earnest in the six months leading up to the second ICC assembly in Nuuk, in the summer of 1980. Welcomed by Greenland's new Home Rule government leaders, notably Premier Jonathan Motzfeldt and his Cabinet, the setting was auspicious for the future of Inuit and their political objectives.

A charter was adopted, with a preamble stating what Inuit collectively hope for and can agree upon across great distances, national boundaries, and long separation from one another. To quote in full:

Recognizing
That we, the Inuit, are an indigenous people, with a unique ancestry, culture and homeland;
that the world's Arctic and sub-Arctic areas which we use and occupy transcend political boundaries;
That due to our historical inheritance and use and occupancy of our homeland we enjoy cultural rights unique to indigenous peoples and share common traditions, values and concerns;
That the Inuit homeland and its resources are of critical importance to the international community;
That renewable and non-renewable resources of the Inuit homeland are essential to the present state and future development of Inuit economies and cultural identity;
That international and national policies and practices should give due consideration to protection of the Arctic and sub-Arctic environment and to the preservation and evolution of Inuit culture and societies;
That our right to self-determination must be confirmed and Inuit participation in policies and activities affecting our homeland assured;

That in furtherance of our spirit of co-operation with the international community, we seek to promote world peace and the objectives of this Charter;

That an international organization of Inuit, known as the Inuit Circumpolar Conference dedicated to protect and advance Inuit rights and interests on the international level, has been created by a resolution unanimously adopted on June 15, 1977 in Barrow, Alaska;

Therefore:

A formal charter for the Inuit Circumpolar Conference is necessary in order to continue the endeavours initiated by the conference and to implement its resolutions and we, the Inuit of the circumpolar region, in accordance with the principles of equality, friendship and respect, hereby accept and agree to this charter, the provisions of which are set forth below.

The charter had great appeal from the moment of its adoption. It also lent strength to the organization that now proceeded to take shape.

The Canadian delegation at Nuuk was particularly anxious that the ICC not be empowered to take positions on or enter into national controversies too readily, certainly not without the agreement of executive members from the country involved, and the charter reflects this concern.[19] On balance, however, Canadian Inuit have been able to influence ICC activities in only a limited way because of their inability to make financial contributions. While supporting certain ICC activities in Canada, and now a Canadian ICC office in Ottawa,[20] Canadian Inuit, apart from Quebec's Makivik Corporation, have not had the funds to do more. Makivik has, however, contributed financially through the years and has provided both staff and executive time for ICC work. In 1985, the Canadian government provided initial funding for the ICC's Canadian operations. At present, about three-quarters of the international budget is provided by the North Slope Borough, and the other quarter by the Greenland Home Rule government. From the beginning, the North Slope has carried the ICC. Contributing much energy and inspiration, the Alaskans have been discreet to a fault about the fact they are ICC's paymaster.

Apart from the limited Canadian financial contribution to the ICC, another problem that has faced the organization is the diffuse nature of its concerns and administration. Cultural and social issues, environmental and economic development problems, political hopes and the special interests of women, youth, and the aged – all these and more are on the ICC's agenda for action. Specific resolutions have been passed at each of the three assemblies, but implementation has been spotty. Particular concern has been voiced on the subject of nuclear power in the Arctic and, of course, nuclear weaponry. In practice the issues most effectively dealt with have been those already the province of existing bodies, which can therefore be pursued outside the small ICC administrative structure – for example, Inuit broadcasting and language development.

With its executive members scattered across the Arctic and more than fully committed to pre-existing leadership roles, with its administrative and financial and co-ordinating centres widely separated, and with no clear division of administrative responsibilites, the ICC functions thanks to the closeness of the handful of executive and staff members who make up its permanent core. Experienced and sympathetic observers have recommended that the priorities of the organization be narrowed,[21] but other voices would like to maintain the full eight or nine working commissions.[22]

The ICC is very different from other international organizations of minorities, for example the World Council of Indigenous Peoples. The work is close to home, involves familiar issues, and can in large part be carried forward by the lobbying, political, legal, and communications techniques that are employed by its members on a daily basis in the liberal democracies where they live. Indeed, this consideration was cited by former Canadian ICC executive member Mary Simon, now President, on behalf of the Canadian delegation at Nuuk in 1980, as favouring the restriction of ICC interests to the Arctic world instead of venturing prematurely into international human rights politics.[23]

The members of the ICC begin with the assumption of a unity of purpose whose celebration in cultural and social events is an important part of all ICC get-togethers. But time and space, history and different economic cultures have provided Inuit with a variety of outlooks. Inuit unity underlies many of the hopes and sentiments of the ICC's work, but the reality of unity is elusive. The relative lack of experience in international relations of many ICC personnel and delegates, and the insistent "family feeling" that is the hope of Inuit groups long subjected to condescending alien majorities in their own homelands, place great demands for high achievement on the ICC. A shrewd observer has suggested that the ICC be more relaxed about the differences that have grown up across the Inuit north.[24]

Having noted some of the difficulties that accompany creation of an effective international vehicle for Inuit co-operation, we should make clear the basic political thrust of the ICC. The stated priority of the organization during the period leading up to the fourth assembly in Kotzebue, Alaska, in the summer of 1986, was the elaboration of an Arctic policy. Through Inuit groups and their academic friends in the three member countries, ideas on public policies that should be pursued across the Arctic by individual states and states collectively are being brought together. Many of the background data needed for this basic policy project already exist. Once they have been assembled in the form of a policy manual, they should facilitate Inuit co-operation with governments in translating principles into practice.

CAMROSE LUTHERAN COLLEGE
LIBRARY

Clearly the first principle is that Inuit themselves should have the greatest possible control over Arctic policy through public institutions in their homelands. As Mayor Hopson stated in his opening address to the first ICC meeeting, the development of self-governing or home rule authorities across the Arctic was a fundamental goal of Inuit.

The ICC has proved most comfortable, directed, and passionate when involved in questions of the Arctic seas. The great early project of ICC was its opposition to Petro-Canada's Arctic Pilot Project, which would have used the Northwest Passage to transport liquefied natural gas as a test scenario for later transport in greater volumes of all forms of hydrocarbons. Greenland and Canadian Inuit worked together through a joint secretariat in Ottawa, supported by the Alaskans. The dramatic intervention by non-Canadian Arctic peoples in a Canadian regulatory board setting in 1983 made a significant impression in official Ottawa, and Inuit leaders may be forgiven for taking much credit for the ultimate defeat of this project, which is discussed at length in chapters 7 and 8.

INUIT POLITICAL OBJECTIVES

Political, social, economic, and cultural upheaval and reconstruction are the characteristics of the international Inuit world today.[25] Regardless of nuances, the common features are the most striking. These include: the rapid development of new forms of self-governing structures with increasingly wide powers; the establishment of clear rights vis-à-vis lands, waters, and resources traditionally used and occupied; and active interest and demands for participation in marine management and development.

Inuit are pushing energetically for changes that their national governments have not been ready to make. Institutional forms that give Inuit control, now and in future, are preferred to ad hoc one-time solutions (although in Canada Inuit are lucky enough to get even these in relation to major developments). The reasons are obvious. If one reads the Beaufort Sea environmental assessment panel report, the product of one of the biggest and most costly exercises in "government responsiveness," one finds that the summaries of Inuit community hearings give a very simple and clear picture of Inuit concerns, but that the report itself simply does not reflect them adequately.[26] Another reflection on the ad hoc approach is given in the fine and perhaps final Lancaster Sound report, which saw studies of the studies, and hearings on the hearings, to make up for the inability of officialdom to come to grips with Inuit interests in that region.[27]

Even when Canadian Inuit are invited to participate or comment on processes under way, the amount of paper, the number and location of meetings, and the limited staff available mean that only the topmost priorities can be dealt with by Inuit organizations at any one time. The invitations to participate get governments off the hook – they have, after all, offered Inuit a chance to be involved. Freedom-of-information procedures, streamlined government administrations, and predictable regulatory and decision processes are of assistance in that they could give small Inuit organizations a fighting chance to track the issues if not to respond to all of them. But it is hard to see how major issues can be adequately dealt with until a Nunavut government can do the staff work and representation on behalf of the people in its area, or until some similar structure is created, for example a body like Quebec's Makivik, set up under a land claims settlement.

While ultra-sensitive to the natural environment, especially the Arctic seas, Inuit are also painfully aware of the disparities in living standards that their people have suffered in comparison with the white majorities of the United States, Denmark, and Canada. Inuit leaders, mostly in their thirties, were often brought to political action in the first place by their awareness of social ills, including ills wrought by change managed by whites. In schools and training centres they experienced humiliation or condescension by whites who felt they had a superior culture to bestow. That culture, as experienced on the "frontier," was typically the gadgetry and accumulation of material items. Material equality is a matter, therefore, of sensitivity.

The seas, long the source of most Inuit well-being, now appear to be the source of new riches. Inuit see themselves threatened in their basic livelihoods by others coming to scoop up the living species or to take away the undersea hydrocarbons with the attendant dangers of pollution. They have felt first helpless, and then robbed. Inuit, new to legal theories about the open seas, simply regard their ocean environment as theirs as much as the familiar hunting lands.[28] They have also seen that governments – and the industrial interests governments seem so assiduously to support and protect in the Arctic – take too little into account, do not understand the consequences of their proposals, and return little to the local people. Quite understandably, Inuit believe that they themselves would be wiser and would not only better protect their locales and ocean economy but would also know how to balance such interests with new wealth-generating activities at sea.

Whether this hope is sanguine or not, Inuit clearly cannot look on idly while the seas of their homeland are used for the benefit of others. Nor can they be expected to let others take risks with their livelihood and source of food. Many regimes for Inuit participation in ocean matters may be contemplated. Ownership or exploitation rights, guaranteed revenue shares, the jurisdiction of Inuit-run governments (e.g. Nunavut) or land claims bodies, guaranteed representation in decision-making bodies, joint management and revenue agreements with higher levels of government – the possibilities and combinations are almost endless.

As well, Inuit have new problems to contend with. The possibility of oil exploration in the Jameson Land area of east Greenland has become what former ICC president Hans-Pavia Rosing termed a "hot issue."[29] There is vigorous debate over hydrocarbon exploitation and environmental conservation within Greenland itself. And in Canada, oil company personnel who suffered at the hands of the ICC's campaign against the Arctic Pilot Project have pointed out that the same people in Greenland who defended the environment now seem ready to risk it for new wealth.[30] Rosing replied that the "economic benefit" of development to Greenland could not be ignored.[31] While such developments will make for major difficulties in Inuit public relations, and obscure the image of stalwart Inuit environmentalists, they are consistent with the desire of Inuit no longer to accept a sideline status in their homelands. Given the political ambitions of Greenland's government and its current severe deficit position vis-à-vis Denmark, the attractions of a major new revenue source and the freedom it could confer are obvious.

In Canada, Inuit have shown a sophisticated regard for the institutions and traditions of the state. They have made proposals that would fit with prevailing political practice while giving Inuit greater powers and benefits in relation to the offshore. If Canadians consider these proposals carefully, they may well conclude that having vigorous indigenous northern partners in development, who know the Arctic environment and what protections are needed, is a happy prospect. They would also find that predictability and equity would satisfy all those involved in northern development and would offer an end to the repeated conflicts that are the main outcome of the current emphasis on ad hoc economic and political development.

A recent publication, capping many years of research and discussion on the eastern Arctic, would seem to discount the possibility that Ottawa can continue to deny institutional change. The cost of denial in dollars, federal credibility, and obstacles to resource development, as well as the problems created for Inuit and other northerners, will be truly exceptional. Regardless of what Ottawa policy-makers may say, the study concludes, resource development, progress on self-government, and settlement of claims are inextricably intertwined in the Inuit north.[32]

There is at present no prospect of a political realignment of the Inuit areas of the Arctic into a pan-Inuit state, or of any degree of Inuit political integration. Of course, major revisions of the map do occur, so one should "never say never." Alaska and its native peoples were bought and sold a century ago, from Russian to American sovereignty. And during the Second World War Greenland saw its Danish kingdom disappear into

Nazi occupation while it remained free. The twentieth century could yet surprise cartographers.

PART TWO

International Arctic Politics

CHAPTER FOUR

The Manhattan *Voyages and Their Aftermath*

JOHN KIRTON AND DON MUNTON

On 8 April 1970 the government of Canada introduced into the House of Commons the Arctic Waters Pollution Prevention bill. Designed to prevent the pollution of waters adjacent to the mainland and islands of the Canadian Arctic, it asserted offshore jurisdiction within a 100-mile pollution prevention zone. An accompanying bill amended the Territorial Sea and Fishing Zones Act to authorize the establishment of new fishing zones in areas of the sea adjacent to the coast of Canada. The Canadian government was thereby empowered to establish control zones behind fisheries closing lines across the entrances to bodies of water requiring fisheries conservation and to which Canada had geographic, economic, and historic claims. In this bill, the government also replaced its existing three-mile territorial sea and nine-mile exclusive fishing zone with a twelve-mile territorial sea.

Together these measures represented a carefully constructed, three-tiered approach to protecting the sovereignty and marine environment of the Canadian Arctic. At the outer 100-mile perimeter the government asserted jurisdiction for the specific purpose of pollution control. Within the archipelago formed by the Arctic islands it strengthened its ability to secure jurisdiction for further purposes in the future. And in the vital core of the Northwest Passage, it enlarged Canadian control over the critical eastern and western gateways at Barrow and Prince of Wales straits, where the channels were less than 24 miles wide. With these moves the Canadian government effectively protected its fragile Arctic maritime environment from the ecological threats presented by the u.s. supertanker s/t *Manhattan* in its summer 1969 transit of the Passage and prospective voyage in the spring of 1970.

These bills also constituted one of the largest geographic extensions of the Canadian state's jurisdiction in the country's history. Moreover, by acting unilaterally, by exempting its pollution and fisheries measures from the compulsory jurisdiction of the International Court of Justice (ICJ), and

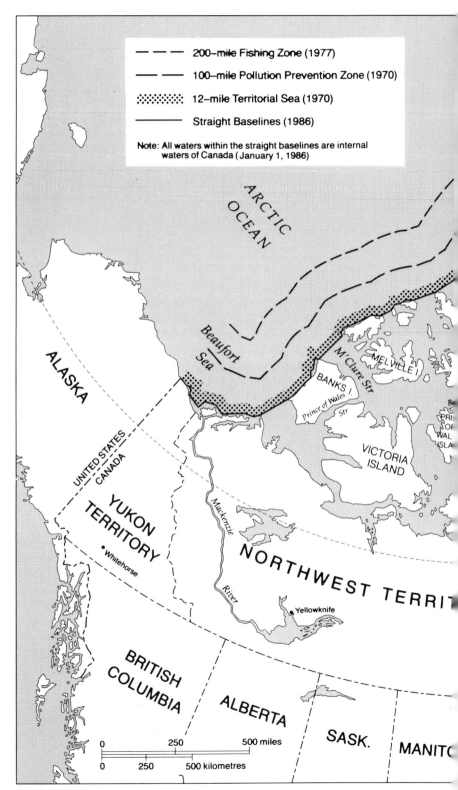

- — — — 200–mile Fishing Zone (1977)
- —— — — 100–mile Pollution Prevention Zone (1970)
- ∷∷∷∷∷∷ 12–mile Territorial Sea (1970)
- ———— Straight Baselines (1986)

Note: All waters within the straight baselines are internal waters of Canada (January 1, 1986)

ARCTIC OCEAN

Beaufort Sea

ALASKA

UNITED STATES
CANADA

MELVILLE I.

M'Clure Str.

BANKS I.

Prince of Wales Str.

VICTORIA ISLAND

YUKON TERRITORY

• Whitehorse

Mackenzie

River

NORTHWEST TERRIT

• Yellowknife

BRITISH COLUMBIA

ALBERTA

SASK.

MANITO

| 0 | | 250 | | 500 miles |
| 0 | | 250 | | 500 kilometres |

Canadian Arctic Marine Jurisdictions

by avoiding an American alternative plan for a multilateral conference on the Arctic environment, the Canadian government broke decisively with the liberal-internationalist traditions that had dominated Canadian foreign policy since the Second World War. Finally, by basing Canadian claims on the concept of custodianship, under which Canada was taking initiatives on behalf of a lagging international community, Canada assumed a leadership role in the development of international law that was normally the special function of the great powers.

However far-reaching these changes were, the Canadian initiatives were also significant for the domestic process that gave rise to them. Externally, the events of April 1970 showed the capacity of a Canadian government armed with few physical resources to act unilaterally in ways that potentially threatened important security interests of the United States. Domestically, they displayed the government's ability to withstand the sustained pressure of an assertive Canadian public demanding considerably more ambitious actions. And above all they revealed the capacity of the government of Canada to act with creativity and confidence in advance of what national capabilities and international realities were thought to allow.

In its performance the Canadian government was far from the sluggish, passive, and timid entity portrayed in much of the existing literature on this case.[1] Rendering this portrait inaccurate, and the government's international success all the more remarkable, were the novelty, complexity, and fundamental character of the issues and the profound divisions existing within Ottawa over their resolution. These divisions reflected a basic ideological cleavage over principles central to Canada's national beliefs and its role in world affairs. This cleavage emerged and was resolved over a period of a year and a half, as a new dominant tendency in Canadian foreign policy evolved to replace the traditional liberal internationalism that had prevailed, largely without challenge, for decades.[2] Ultimately, the Arctic Waters Pollution Prevention Act and its supplementary legal reinforcements were the product of a strong Canadian state redefining its foreign policy to complement its emerging new position in the world.[3]

THE OPENING GAMBIT: NOVEMBER–DECEMBER 1968

The 1968 discovery of commercially significant quantities of oil at Prudhoe Bay on the Alaskan North Slope led to intense study of the most cost-effective means of getting it to the lower 48 states. Various tanker and pipeline schemes were mooted, and in October 1968, Humble Oil, a private U.S. company acting on behalf of the giant multinational EXXON, announced that it would send a refitted tanker, the *Manhattan*, through Canada's portion of the Northwest Passage in the summer of 1969 to test its feasibility as a delivery route. The *Manhattan* left an eastern seaboard port on 25 August 1969, to begin its Arctic journey, and broke through to ice-free waters off northern Alaska on 14 September. It returned for a second voyage, confined to the area north of Baffin Island, in April–May 1970.

From the start, it was clear that Humble's project presented Canada with both threats and opportunities. The *Manhattan*'s voyage might lead to regular commercial transits of the Passage, thereby enhancing its status in law as an international strait (as the u.s. government argued it was), and increasing the chance of oil spills in the vulnerable Arctic environment. Yet it was more likely that the *Manhattan* experiment would show the Northwest Passage to be a poor transportation route, thereby sustaining Canada's case that the special ice-related qualities of the Passage gave it a different international legal status.[4] Moreover, by being prepared to notify Ottawa of the transit (even though this was not an established legal necessity), and by asking Ottawa for information on ice conditions, Humble seemed willing to recognize Canada's jurisdictional rights and operational position in the Passage. And because it was the beneficiary of a very small amount of u.s. government money for research to be conducted as part of the experiment, Humble's co-operation with Canada could be taken indirectly as recognition by the u.s. government of Canada's claims.

Moreover, the u.s. government seemed co-operative, even if it carefully avoided offering de facto support for Canada's jurisdictional claims. The u.s. Coast Guard volunteered to let Canada help in the experiment, and, in keeping with past practice, informed its Canadian counterpart that it would send a ship to escort the *Manhattan*. Even though u.s. Coast Guard vessels were considered military vessels by Canada, they were under no obligation to request permission from Canada, and to do so would be an admission by Washington of Canada's sovereignty. It is thus hardly surprising that Washington refused to respond to a suggestion from Ottawa that the u.s. Coast Guard request permission to accompany the *Manhattan*.

Why did Ottawa make such a suggestion? There was little public concern within Canada at the time. But there were established views and forward thinking on the topic within Ottawa. Even before the first Prudhoe Bay discovery, the government's leading bureaucratic body for Arctic affairs, the Advisory Committee on Northern Development (ACND), was aware that intense oil exploration could be anticipated in northern waters, that Canadian control over foreign shipping was inadequate, that the u.s. Coast Guard had an interest in research on northern transportation, and that there were potential benefits for Canada of northern oil discoveries. By late November 1968 Department of Transportation (DOT) officials anticipated a possible u.s. request for a joint Canadian-u.s. development agency in the Arctic and searched for navigational safeguards to protect Canada's position. The recently created Department of Energy, Mines and Resources (EMR), under prime ministerial urging, began a comprehensive survey of Canada's energy resources. External Affairs (DEA) observed the U.S. probing of other countries' maritime jurisdictional claims and monitored the internal U.S. debate about the desirability of transporting Prudhoe Bay oil by overland pipelines through Alaska or Canada, rather than by a Northwest Passage route.

Because pipelines, which had few implications for Canada's sovereignty, were the early favourites as the means of transportation, many in Ottawa shared the hope of the Department of Indian Affairs and Northern Development (DIAND) and EMR that the Prudhoe Bay discoveries would enhance Canada's northern economic development and balance-of-payments situation through increased Canadian oil exports to the United States by joint pipeline systems. No discrepant signals came from a new Prime Minister and Cabinet preoccupied with the far more direct and acute threat to Canadian sovereignty arising from Quebec's separatist efforts. Thus DEA's informal suggestion to Washington that the U.S. Coast Guard ask for permission to accompany the *Manhattan* was at most an attempt to further Canada's Arctic sovereignty claims without much ado, and at least a signal from the start that these claims would be firmly asserted in a new era of Arctic marine transportation.

Ottawa quickly followed with practical moves to facilitate the *Manhattan* experiment, ensure de facto Canadian sovereignty, and enlist co-operation from the United States. Ottawa decided to have DOT co-operate fully with the *Manhattan's* voyage, to send the icebreaker *John A. Macdonald* to accompany it, and to suggest that icebreakers of both countries travel with the *Manhattan* in both Canadian and American waters. Simultaneously the government created a new internal body, the Task Force on Northern Development (TFNOD), to provide advice on the issues in a co-ordinated and comprehensive manner.

These decisions were catalysed by the U.S. failure to respond to Canada's informal suggestion of an official request for U.S. icebreaker transit. Yet with the Canadian public still unaroused, Ottawa's decisions were largely defined by the perceptions of Canadian officials. These officials recognized that the United States was sensitive to restrictions on the mobility of its naval and commercial vessels and that Canada's international legal position on the Arctic was not widely supported. They further identified a possible danger to Canada's oil exports to the United States from the actual delivery of Alaskan supplies to the lower 48 states and from possible U.S. oil import restrictions in retaliation for a lack of Canadian co-operation in delivering U.S. supplies. Finally, they saw that U.S. interest in a special continental energy relationship with Canada might be used to maximize both Canada's oil export objectives and its sovereignty claims.

The policy of practical co-operation with the *Manhattan* voyage was thus designed to avoid or delay a major confrontation or even bilateral diplomatic talks with the United States over sovereignty, to reinforce Canadian claims to effective occupation of the Passage, and to solidify the support of the u.s. companies for Canada's regime. It also gave TFNOD time to define Canada's energy objectives and to construct an internationally defensible legal position. A desire to enhance Canadian economic development through practical co-operation with the United States, and to respect existing international law, dominated the government's thinking and appeared able to support Canada's particular sovereignty concerns.

DECLARING DETERMINATION: JANUARY–MAY 1969

By the spring of 1969, however, Ottawa began publicly to signal its determination and to set out its position on the sovereignty issue. Prime Minister Trudeau and Secretary of State for External Affairs Mitchell Sharp noted that Canada was discussing with other countries Canadian continental shelf rights and the possibility of straight baseline legislation, which would extend Canada's territorial waters outward from lines that ran from headland to headland, rather than following the sinuosities of the coastline. They also disclaimed the relevance to the problem of the sector principle, under which Canada had a claim to the entire area enclosed by lines projected northward from Canada's eastern and western continental boundaries, up to the North Pole. In early March the Prime Minister indicated that he had asked concerned departments to review Canada's international legal position on the Arctic waters, noting that the key issue was the distinction between a territorial and inland sea.[5] In March, he informed u.s. President Nixon of Canada's concern over territorial sea and fishing rights issues and his hope that Canada would take a position that would be respected by the entire international community. Further, he described Canadian oil as secure, continental oil and agreed to further discussions on a continental oil policy.

A much stronger emphasis on sovereignty appeared soon after. On 27 March the government announced a tour of the Arctic by Governor-General Roland Michener, to take place 22 April to 4 May. On 3 April, the Prime Minister presented Canada's new defence priorities, which emphasized surveillance of Canadian territory and coast lines and protection of its sovereignty.[6] On 22 April, the government introduced a bill to amend the Territorial Sea and Fishing Zones Act to allow all waters above the continental shelf to be declared fishing zones exclusively for Canadian fishermen (while respecting traditional rights). DIAND Minister Jean Chrétien further noted that drilling on Melville Island by government-controlled Panarctic Oil was being undertaken to show Canadian sovereignty in the Arctic.

Then, in a major speech on 15 May, the contents of which were delivered to the United States in a diplomatic note, the Prime Minister declared Canada's sovereignty over the Arctic lands, its exclusive rights to the Arctic continental shelf, and its view that Arctic waters were national terrain. He added, however, that differences over the waters' status "should not be settled in an arbitrary way but in scrupulous respect of the established principles of international law."[7]

It was events abroad that had prompted Ottawa to begin devising a long-term Arctic policy. The frenzied pace of oil exploration in Alaska and the Canadian Arctic suggested that the *Manhattan*'s voyage could represent a real threat. Yet the creation by the U.S. government in February 1969 of a Task Force on Oil Policy to review the American oil import program indicated that Washington had still to determine how large a role expensive Arctic supplies would play in meeting U.S. energy needs. Moreover, discussions with Canada about a continental oil policy, continued at the official level on 12 April, held forth the promise of a non-confrontational solution. Washington's position on the sovereignty issue was also muted. In February, U.S. officials stated in Calgary that extension of Canadian territorial waters beyond the three-mile limit then accepted by Washington was not likely to be challenged. Moreover, both the United States and the Soviet Union appeared willing to engage in a broader effort to define further the law of the sea on a multilateral basis.

Domestically, however, significant pressures for an outright Canadian declaration of sovereignty were beginning to develop. Late February witnessed an article in the Toronto *Globe and Mail* that evoked public concern over northern sovereignty, worrying testimony before the House of Commons Standing Committee on External Affairs and National Defence (SCEAND), and complaints in the Commons. In the ensuing months, with press and parliamentary probing fuelling each other, Liberals were joined by Conservative and New Democrat MPs in the demand for a forthright declaration of sovereignty. Fuelling these pleas were visions of an imminent rush into Canada's unprotected north. In early March 1969, a conference held by the Arctic Institute of North America considered the prospects for sea passage by tankers in the Arctic and the interest of Canadian developers in the region. However, in mid-March the government of Alberta and the Independent Petroleum Association demanded that Ottawa maintain U.S. market access for Albertan rather than Alaskan Arctic oil. At the 20–24 March meeting of the Canadian-U.S. Interparliamentary Group, Canadian MPs chose to press the Albertan case. Yet, by May, Arctic sovereignty had become the parliamentary cause célèbre. On 1 May, SCEAND announced that it was considering a review of the issue.

Despite rising public concern and the Cabinet's focus on the issue, the government remained largely free to shape the contents of the Prime Minister's 15 May statement. The statement was based on reviews, carried out primarily by TFNOD, of the legal status of the sea areas, of Canada's military presence in the north, and of the oil and gas situation. In March 1969, TFNOD's first memorandum to Cabinet "stressed the urgency of increased activities of the relevant departments to ensure 'effective occupation' of the high Arctic," rather than recommending a proclamation of sovereignty.[8] By late April recommendations had been made to Cabinet to upgrade the Canadian Rangers, while an interdepartmental study group of National Defence and other departments reviewed Canada's military presence in the north. At this point, consensus prevailed among the relevant departments. DIAND favoured the rapid economic development in the north which the Arctic discoveries promised but also supported the governor-general's Arctic tour. EMR was concerned about Canada's oil exports to the United States, but felt the prospects for substantial Arctic oil production within the next decade to be small. DEA was inclined to prevent a confrontation until Canada's legal position was more firmly established and its northern presence increased.

NARROWING ALTERNATIVES:
JUNE–OCTOBER 1969

By early autumn the emphasis on sovereignty had intensified. In a June 1969 note to the United States, DEA highlighted the Prime Minister's views that Canadian jurisdiction was not affected by the *Manhattan* voyage, even as it warned that Canada "had inevitably the greatest interest in Arctic waters in the Northwest Passage given historic, geographic, climatic and economic factors."[9] At a joint Canadian-U.S. ministerial meeting in June, Canada agreed to hold discussions with the United States before it made a definitive claim to sovereignty over Arctic waters. As September opened Trudeau was still stating that the *Manhattan*'s voyage was a positive development. On 11 September he promised a sovereignty statement and more precise acts during the current parliamentary session. He added that the impending statement would avoid a court challenge, undue offence to the United States, and a prolonged international legal battle. Given the evolution of international law, he argued, time was on Canada's side.

Yet a week later, a sharp shift in tone took place. On 18 September, four days after the *Manhattan* had made its way through the Passage, a *Globe and Mail* article by Mitchell Sharp declared: "Canada's sovereignty over Arctic waters is being steadily strengthened by developing concepts of international law and by our own activities."[10] Sharp argued that the extensive icebreaker support required for the *Manhattan* voyage demonstrated that the Passage was not an international strait. He concluded that "general principles of international law may have to be applied in a special way in the case of frozen waters" and that Canada had the best claim to contribute to the development of international law in this regard. Canada's Arctic waters were, however, open as a transportation route to all nations, for peaceful purposes, by suitable vessels "operating in accordance with minimum standards of safety."[11] On 6 October, Northern Development Minister Jean Chrétien indicated that the government was planning anti-pollution legislation for the Arctic. Minister of Transport Don Jamieson revealed that a federal task force was exploring the unification of civilian and military naval and air operations in the Arctic. Minister of Defence Léo Cadieux announced a distinctive defence role of surveillance of Canada's territory and coast lines, the creation of a task force to consider a headquarters for Mobile Command in the far north, and an increase in Arctic sovereignty patrols by long-range aircraft.

These developments were provoked in part by external pressures. In early June, a u.s. State Department official had described Canadian extension of its territorial sea and fishing rights as contrary to international law and a bad model for others. At bilateral talks later in the month between Alexis Johnson, the third-ranking official in the State Department, and Mitchell Sharp, there was wide disagreement over Canada's claims. The two sides agreed to meet in the autumn to consider Arctic waters issues and related matters before a definitive Canadian statement on sovereignty was made. The message was clear – Washington would resist Canada's sovereignty claims but was as anxious as Ottawa to avoid, or at least delay, a confrontation. This duality was still evident in late September. u.s. officials told visiting Canadian mps that the United States held North America's Arctic waterways, including Prince of Wales Strait and Lancaster Sound, to be an international strait connecting high seas, that a Canadian claim would lead to a reference to the icj, and that the entire issue might best be resolved in a new international convention to extend coastal state authority for certain narrowly defined purposes. Such a convention might specify three maritime bands, with the third extending 50 miles from shore to meet coastal state responsibilities for navigational assistance and pollution control, but with the right of innocent passage preserved. By October it was clear that the u.s. Department of Defense would strenuously resist unilateral declarations that would establish precedents harmful to its strategic interests in Southeast Asian waters (Indonesia and the Philippines) and in the Mediterranean and Middle East (the straits of Gibraltar and Hormuz). Canada's legitimate but subordinate pollution concerns in the Arctic could be taken care of by concerted international action, probably through the Intergovernmental Maritime Consultative Organization (imco).

If the u.s. government's statements provided no immediate need for bold Canadian action, the progress of American industry's most famous tanker did. In August and September the *Manhattan*, accompanied by the powerful Canadian icebreaker *John A. Macdonald* and the lighter u.s. Coast Guard icebreaker *Northwind*, steamed to and through the Northwest Passage, breaking into clear water on the western end on 14 September. There was much in the voyage that sustained Canada's jurisdictional case. The tendency of the two u.s. ships to get stopped in ice and to rely on Canadian support showed that the Passage was not like the high seas and that Canada's presence was essential to successful transit. Moreover, a weather-induced shift in the *Manhattan's* route from the broad but ice-infested M'Clure Strait to the more hospitable but much narrower Prince of Wales Strait indicated that a commercial waterway would probably have to include sea lanes less than 24 miles across, which Canada could claim as territorial waters. Finally, the damage done to the u.s. ships and their reluctance to test the polar ice pack on the return voyage demonstrated just how difficult routine commercial transportation would be.

These same facts also showed how severe might be the threat of oil pollution, in the highly vulnerable Arctic environment, should tanker traffic become frequent. And Humble spokesmen were suggesting it would. By early September, it was rumoured that Humble, Arco, and British Petroleum were each preparing tankers for Arctic oil transportation and that the *Manhattan* would probably return to the Arctic between March and May 1970. Canada, it was suggested, should provide Herschel Island off the Beaufort Sea coast as an international tanker terminal. On 13 September, Humble declared its $39 million *Manhattan* experiment a success in proving the feasibility of commercial shipping through the Northwest Passage and announced its calculation that tanker transport would be 60 cents per barrel less expensive than pipeline alternatives. At the same time, Humble officials continued to participate in the Mackenzie Valley Pipeline study, explore tanker submarine designs, and look at the Trans-Alaskan Pipeline System (TAPS), which would start snaking across Alaska that winter if u.s. government permission were given. Moreover, in early September Humble indicated that it would accept Canadian standards for vessel construction and manoeuvrability.

Other international developments were also encouraging to Canada. The Soviet Union tacitly signalled its support for Canada's efforts to enhance coastal state control of Arctic waters. Other states and Canada discussed convening another law of the sea conference to deal with fishing zones and territorial waters. And by September Canada was also securing signs of interest in a United Nations system of marine pollution control.

Within Canada, however, pressures to act unilaterally were becoming sharper. During the summer, opposition leaders continued to demand an immediate, forthright declaration of Arctic waters as internal waters subject to Canadian sovereignty. By September Toronto's *Globe and Mail*, *Telegram*, and *Star* all editorially demanded a declaration of sovereignty. Former Prime Minister Lester Pearson suggested an assertion of Canadian sovereignty to keep the north nuclear-free. Public apprehension had been fuelled in August, when two supply barges were sunk in the Arctic, raising the spectre of a pollution disaster. And in early September, after an "inspection tour" of the *Manhattan* by 11 of its members, the chairman of the House of Commons Standing Committee on Indian Affairs and Northern Development (SCIAND), Ian Watson, demanded measures "to assert sovereignty over these waters for pollution control and navigation control," given the imminent use of the Passage for shipping.[12]

Within the government, there was much less certainty and more priorities in play. Officials in DOT and in DIAND saw the *Manhattan*'s voyage as a stimulus to economic development. EMR was concerned about Albertan oil exports to the United States. Transport estimated that regular tanker transit would require, at a time of government austerity, two to four new icebreakers and associated navigational aids, for a total cost of over $200 million. Defence Minister Cadieux saw expanded roles for the forces in Arctic national development as a promising opportunity in an era of defence spending cutbacks.

The concerns of External Affairs lay elsewhere. Its legal officers had, by September, concluded that the *Manhattan*'s voyages, while not directly challenging Canada's sovereignty, showed the need for a definitive legal statement. As transit through the Passage would require Canadian aid and pollution and navigational controls, the department wanted to consider the waters internal, but with a potential for innocent passage as long as Canadian pollution and navigation regulations were followed. Following the 1958 UN Convention on the Law of the Sea, these regulations would apply to all waters within the Canadian Arctic archipelago and would offer other states open, maintained, assisted, and regulated passage. Canada should probably assert its claim by unilateral declaration accompanied by domestic legislation for anti-pollution and other regulations. However, DEA officials were worried about the overall friction level in bilateral Canadian-U.S. relations and about the consequences if Canada had to start seizing vessels that deliberately ignored the declared rules. They were also fearful that Canada might not win a court case.

These judgments were debated in a three-hour Cabinet meeting on 11 September 1969, the results of which were unveiled in the Prime Minister's and Mitchell Sharp's September statements. It was clear that Ottawa had gone far in developing its position and that its approach differed from the dominant positions abroad and at home. Yet within Ottawa, two competing tendencies were emerging. The first, reflecting the traditional approach and led by Sharp, assigned high priority to economic development objectives, to applying existing general international law to ice-covered waters, and to doing so in a way that corresponded to the slowly evolving international consensus on this subject. Critically, this tendency saw domestic law as having to meet the test of international acquiescence. In Sharp's words, "Action taken internally must therefore be either compatible with the current state of international law or at least be defensible in a court of law."[13] This position was modest in its geographic extent, its functional comprehensiveness, and its limitations on the traditional doctrine of innocent passage.

The second and competing tendency was centred on the Prime Minister and those close to him. It gave priority to pollution control over economic development, to creating new international law in areas such as ice-covered waters where little or none existed, and in leading rather than remaining abreast of or following the international consensus. This tendency was far less concerned about international legal acquiescence and, given the imperatives of the anti-pollution task, ready to contemplate a geographically and functionally ambitious regime. The emerging conflict thus focused on how far, how fast, and for what ultimate purpose Canada should proceed.

Despite this divergence, Ottawa had moved a considerable way from the traditional ideological foundations of liberal internationalism and the demands of those at home and abroad. It had affirmed its sovereignty over the waters of the archipelago, its need to assert jurisdiction for the functions of navigation, safety, and pollution control, and the priority of these tasks over the traditional doctrine of innocent passage. It further accepted the need for occupancy initiatives, a major reorientation of traditional defence priorities, rapid legislative action, and a more definitive statement of Canadian claims. But how much of a departure these new beliefs represented depended importantly on which competing tendency would define the answer to several questions: just how much effective control was needed over how much of the Arctic waters; for how many functions beyond fisheries the assertion of jurisdiction was needed; how numerous, comprehensive, and expensive initiatives to enhance Canada's presence should be; and how far from the prevailing international legal consensus Canadian actions should go.

DEFINING THE POLICY:
OCTOBER—DECEMBER 1969

The last three months of 1969 saw the Canadian government move tentatively towards answering these questions. Its basic approach –

national jurisdiction reinforced by international co-operation – was unveiled on 23 October 1969 in the Speech from the Throne, which announced legislation for measures to prevent pollution in Arctic waters. Speaking in the debate the next day, the Prime Minister elaborated a policy of strictly regulated use of Arctic waters to prevent pollution through Canada's exercise of authority over the use of the waters and through the setting of standards for ships and cargoes therein. He also promised that Canada would seek international agreement on Arctic pollution prevention measures, beginning with a prime ministerial visit to UN Secretary General U Thant. The Prime Minister declared, "We invite the international community to join with us and support our initiative for a new concept, an international legal regime designed to ensure to human beings the right to live in a wholesome natural environment."[14] The government thus switched the focus of debate from sovereignty to pollution and the form of its claim from possession to custodianship. Yet it also suggested that national legislation would proceed regardless of international co-operation. The Prime Minister warned that Canada "would not bow to the pressure of any state."[15]

Trudeau met with U Thant on 11 November 1969 to discuss his idea for an "international regime" to protect the Arctic's natural environment and to call for a co-ordinated, urgent effort to develop international control for the non-Canadian portion of the Arctic. Simultaneously, Minister of Transport Don Jamieson delivered a strong speech to the Brussels IMCO conference on pollution of the sea by oil. Backing these diplomatic efforts were announcements of plans for a highly mobile Arctic strike force with airlift and naval support in an ice-free port; new military detachments in Yellowknife and Whitehorse; a $2 million program to construct six new airfields on the fringes of the Arctic Circle; and plans for the first-ever military exercises in the Arctic islands.

The Canadian government now set out to determine if the potential sovereignty threat posed by the United States was an isolated or widely shared challenge. On his visit to Ottawa, Soviet Foreign Minister Gromyko spoke with Mitchell Sharp about the possibility of Canadian-Soviet co-operation in the Arctic. At IMCO's International Legal Conference on Maritime Pollution Damage, held in Brussels 10–28 November 1969, Canada sought without much success support for rules that would protect against pollution of maritime waters, beyond the voluntary regime recently created by some major tanker owners to establish shipowners' responsibility to national governments that incurred expenditures in avoiding or alleviating damage from pollution.[16] Prime Minister Trudeau, meeting with U Thant, was assured that no UN member then had an objection to Canada's plan to set anti-pollution and environmental control standards for the waters of the Arctic archipelago. Thant added that the UN system was unlikely to devise an appropriate international regime in the near future.

All the while Canada was carefully monitoring u.s. actions. u.s. officials were cautious in assessing the economic feasibility of moving Alaskan oil to the u.s. east coast by tanker through the Passage. Discussion of the new Canadian position with the United States had still not taken place, although the Prime Minister again acknowledged this as a necessity and stated that on security grounds not all countries would be given equal access to the Arctic waterways. However, as the United States was currently considering abandoning the Distant Early Warning radar line, it apparently was not vitally interested in the effects of Canadian actions on Arctic security as such. One contrary sign came in late December, when President Nixon ordered that priority be given to u.s. Arctic environmental and resource research, more than doubled the u.s. Navy's funds to develop a military vessel to skim across the Arctic ice, and allocated an additional $22 million to 11 federal agencies.

At home the pressures were intensifying. In November Panarctic Oils, in its first wildcat well, hit gas at Drake Point on Melville Island in what seemed to be a commercially viable find if economic transportation were available. In mid-December, 44 oil companies, including the Canadian subsidiaries of the u.s. Alaskan permit holders, formed Operation Polarquest, a four-year exploration and data-gathering venture in over 100 million acres of Canada's Arctic Islands. Industry interest bred parliamentary vigilance. On 16 December, the Liberal-dominated SCIAND urged the government to declare sovereignty immediately over the waters of the archipelago in order to protect Canada's Arctic environment. The committee demanded "that the Government of Canada take whatever steps are necessary, consistent with international law, to assume recognition of Canadian Sovereignty by all vessels, surface and submarine, passing through the Arctic Archipelago."[17]

"Consistent with international law" was, however, beginning to become less of a sacred principle within some parts of the executive branch. The Prime Minister himself had already asserted Canada's responsibility to itself and the world to impose some controls on the use of this uniquely vulnerable environment, the world's last large natural reserve. As only Canada could take the lead in protecting its portion of this reserve, it would have to do so as an ecological or conservation trustee on behalf of the world community, until the latter was able to assume the responsibility. As the trusteeship role explicitly took precedence over "freedom of the seas" and economic development, the conflict with established international law, and traditional domestic priorities, was clear.

While the Prime Minister's instincts were certain, their dominance in the internal government debate was not. By late October the government had not yet decided how expansive Canadian authority would be. Three primary options had emerged. The most geographically ambitious was enclosure of the entire archipelago as internal waters by drawing straight baselines around the perimeter, with or without a right of innocent passage within. The least geographically assertive option was, in accordance with the 1958 Convention, to extend the Canadian territorial sea from three to twelve nautical miles, with a right of innocent passage, and thereby place key chokepoints in Barrow Strait and Prince of Wales Strait explicitly within Canadian sovereignty without prejudice to the wider claim to all the waters of the Canadian archipelago. The third option was to convene an international conference to seek multilateral agreement on more innovative concepts of international law, perhaps by proceeding with general national legislation and seeking international agreement on a special pollution zone of up to 50 miles.

During October and November, the major departments gravitated toward one or other of these options. The department least involved in the specific debate, but most in line with the logic of the ambitious first option, was National Defence (DND). DND supported an expanded presence in the north out of simple loyalty to the Prime Minister, as a way of developing an attractive new mission at a time when forces were being reduced in Europe and subjected to a government-wide budgetary freeze, and because it liked the Prime Minister's declaration that Canada might well discriminate among foreign nations in granting access to the Arctic on national security grounds. DOT shared this sense of departmental opportunity; it argued that the opening of the north was welcome and that this required greater pollution and navigation controls. However, it also believed that the principal multilateral organization in which it participated, IMCO, could respond to the challenge. DIAND suffered from acute internal tension. While it contained a constituency in favour of rapid northern development, its experts opposed repeating the sins of the Soviet Union in its northern development, notably widespread despoliation of the environment. On the jurisdictional issue, DIAND's position was to await agreement on international guidelines covering pollution in Arctic waters outside the coastal zones clearly under Canadian jurisdiction, while actively promoting a bill to regulate shipping within the Canadian zone.

Elsewhere, positions were more predictable. Fisheries and Forestry, with the Wildlife Service, was strongly conservationist, fearing a tanker or drilling accident that could destroy the surrounding environment for decades. Energy, Mines and Resources, still concerned about the implications for Albertan oil exports of Alaskan oil, and increasingly worried about the U.S. Oil Import Task Force and Continental Energy Policy proposals, was inclined to oppose both overly rapid development and the imposition of strong environmental regulations. It was also comforted by a belief, shared by many in Ottawa, that in the end most Alaskan and Arctic oil would travel not by ship but by pipe along the Mackenzie River Valley. External Affairs, led by its international lawyers, saw the 12-mile territorial sea extension as adequate for the pollution control task and as resting on the firmest international legal foundation then available, i.e. "its" multilateral agreement, the 1958 UN Law of the Sea Convention. And the Treasury Board Secretariat, managing the Prime Minister's austerity program, cast a suspicious eye over anything likely to cost money.

Given this diversity of perspectives, the Prime Minister was relatively free to provide direction. He pressed both for an increase in Canada's military and scientific presence in the north for sovereignty reasons and for recognition of Canada's moral responsibility as an Arctic environmental trustee. And at the United Nations he and Ivan Head (his special assistant and an expert on the international law of the Arctic) concluded that a more co-ordinated, rapid, and effective approach than the UN currently provided was both politically acceptable abroad and functionally necessary.

The task of meshing these various perspectives into a single strategy began late in the autumn of 1969 in the deliberations of a very senior group of officials.[18] At its first meeting this group tentatively decided to limit the "target" by excluding from the proposed legislation measures to control pollution of Canada's coastal seas as a result of atmospheric factors such as nuclear fallout. By early November it decided upon a new law based on Canada's concern over the pollution of its coastal seas, from such vantage points as the protection of fisheries and other resources of the sea, and safeguarding the welfare of Canada's aboriginal peoples and those living by, or depending for their livelihood on, the sea. It also agreed to proceed without prejudicing the government's decision on the Territorial Sea and Fishing Zones Act or the Fisheries Act and to frame the new law so that some of its protective provisions could apply to Pacific and Atlantic coastal areas as well as to the high Arctic. The group thus agreed upon an act focused on the pollution threat posed by new resource exploitation and transportation technology to the Arctic waters and on the consequent need for determined Canadian government action as part of a larger problem of growing global concern. The act envisaged government-designated special "pollution control zones," which might be announced in advance of formal legislative action (so other countries and parties might object) but that would not be subject to parliamentary review. To these zones would be applied prohibitions, preventative requirements, and financial responsibility and liability provisions.

At the group's 20 November meeting, the chairman noted the Prime Minister's view that Canada had a clearly identifiable interest in preventing pollution in the Arctic seas. He stressed that while international acquiescence was important, it could take years to reach agreement on an international regime for the control of pollution of the seas and that Canada must effectively protect its Arctic waters while continuing to seek ways of acting on an international scale. After a lengthy discussion, the group decided to proceed unilaterally with legislation limited to Canada's Arctic waters. It concluded its deliberations by giving follow-up mandates to three bodies: DIAND for defining the area of application and detailed drafting, the Privy Council Office (PCO) for preparing a memorandum to Cabinet proposing legislation for pollution prevention in the Arctic seas, and External Affairs for preparing a memorandum recommending the position that Canada should adopt internationally with respect to the proposed legislation.

By early December the PCO had prepared its memorandum. From Transport it got a request for another interdepartmental meeting before the PCO memo went to the Prime Minister. Transport argued that the new legislation's rules should have national coverage. As Transport was revising its own Canada Shipping Act in accordance with the results of the Brussels Conference, its central objection was clear. There were positive results at Brussels, and Canada should defer to this hopeful multilateral movement. Diverging tendencies had now grown into active resistance to Ottawa's potentially far-reaching new Arctic waters regime. The foundation of this resistance was an instinctive reluctance to abandon Canada's traditional adherence to international rules, as defined by multilateral institutions linked to the UN system.

THE HARD CHOICES:
JANUARY–FEBRUARY 1970

In January and February 1970 this fundamental issue was confronted and resolved, as Cabinet approved its strategy and successfully tested it during the second voyage of the *Manhattan*. The new strategy was unveiled on 22 January by Mitchell Sharp. Avoiding a direct claim or declaration of sovereignty, Canada would give priority to the prevention of pollution damage from oil tankers by imposing regulations on Arctic shipping in the form of a bill to establish pollution controls for the entire archipelago. In February Sharp, accordingly, welcomed a return of the *Manhattan* to the Arctic, as Canada needed to know more about the conditions under which "Canadian waters" could be used. Sharp later announced that Canada would provide icebreaking assistance to the *Manhattan* if asked but would enact laws against oil pollution in the Arctic before approving voyages through the Passage of any tankers actually carrying oil.

On 19 and 20 February, the Canadian position strengthened considerably. Sharp declared of the Arctic archipelago: "These are our waters."[19] Trudeau added that the *Manhattan* could not proceed until Canada was satisfied that there was no risk of oil pollution. Transport Minister Jamieson noted that Canada could bar tankers from journeying through the Passage by simply refusing to provide icebreaker assistance. Canada informed Humble and Washington of its position. Meanwhile it continued negotiating with other governments to establish territorial limitations on coastal waters, drawing up a headland-to-headland straight baseline system, and preparing to introduce a bill in the next few weeks.

A week later Canadian demands increased. Mitchell Sharp ruled out the use of non-Canadian icebreakers for the *Manhattan* voyage. Don Jamieson added that Humble's *Manhattan* would have to comply with the anti-pollution regulations of the legislation not yet passed or even introduced into the House, or else no Canadian icebreaker assistance would be provided. Ottawa was using the one physical resource on which it had a temporary monopoly – a heavily powered icebreaker – to force an impatient multinational company to accede to a set of anti-pollution standards and procedures that would provide the basis for later Canadian law.

Canada's escalation was certainly not the result of any relaxation in the U.S. government's position. In mid-January, a press leak from Washington and a statement by former U.S. Secretary of State George Ball had suggested that the United States, as part of its revised oil import program, would press for a continental energy policy with Canada that would include unimpeded transit rights through the Passage. On a diplomatic level, Washington pressed its aide-mémoire, delivered on 6 November 1969, that welcomed Prime Minister Trudeau's invitation to the international community to support Canada's initiative for an international regime regarding the Arctic and the protection of its environment. Washington pressed for bilateral talks on the subject focused initially on the Arctic environment but then broadening to include the future development of Arctic resources and the operational aspects of transportation. It specifically suggested a discussion of the requirements for keeping the sea lanes open all year through "the North American Arctic."[20] The United States asked Canada's views on the desirability of extending the proposed bilateral talks to include other circumpolar states and interested countries. It requested an early Canadian response.

The sense of urgency rose in February. Humble formally notified DOT of the second *Manhattan* voyage, which was planned to test the ship, without cargo, against the much stronger spring icepack in April. A Liberian oil tanker, the *Arrow*, ran aground off Nova Scotia, placing one million gallons of oil on the shoreline and causing widespread coastal damage. On 18 February, President Nixon, in his State of the World address, referred to the need to "head off the threat of escalating national claims over the oceans."[21] Shortly thereafter he announced that he was authorizing the

State Department to pursue with Canada a continental energy policy that included access to the Passage for u.s. tankers. He did so on the basis of a report that recommended also that until negotiations were completed, oil imports from Canada should be cut back to 615,000 barrels a day, beginning 1 July. As Canadian oil exports to the United States were already running at levels one-third higher than permitted under previously negotiated arrangements, the report offered an exceedingly attractive carrot and highlighted an easily available American stick.

As external pressures intensified, so too did domestic ones. For months Progressive Conservative and NDP MPs had maintained a daily ritual of criticizing the government on the Arctic sovereignty issue and expressing fears that government negligence over the second Manhattan voyage would sell Canadian sovereignty short. The opposition parties did succeed in forcing a Commons debate on 21 January over the report of the Northern Development Committee and may have helped inspire Mitchell Sharp's sovereignty statement. Moreover, the Cabinet came under heavy pressure from the Liberal caucus and party to force Humble to ask for permission for a second voyage. Yet the parliamentary debate seemed primarily to strengthen the government's hand, providing a forum in which Canadian and u.s. military officials could be cited to support demands for an augmented Canadian military presence in the north, Liberal backbenchers could vent their own and their constituents' frustrations, and the anti-pollution passions of the Canadian people could be demonstrated to audiences abroad.

Outside Parliament, positions were even more strident. Led by the Toronto *Star*, with the *Globe and Mail*, the *Telegram*, and the Ottawa *Journal* following, editorialists constantly applauded the expansion of Canada's Arctic presence, while demanding further action and a straight-forward sovereignty declaration. The anti-pollution concerns of the press were shared by groups such as the Canadian Wildlife Federation, which declared its 175,000 members to be in favour of a moratorium on Arctic energy development. And 51 per cent of the Canadian public in a January poll thought that Canada owned the North Pole. While these demands may have tempered business influence in favour of rapid economic develop-ment, neither the moratorium nor the declaration acquired any major advocates within the government.

In large measure this was because the government began the new year with a firmly established policy of passing legislation to control shipping and pollution in the Arctic, exercising Canadian sovereignty through these actions, and avoiding any prior or subsequent sovereignty declarations. By 23 January, the government had almost finished drafting its bill. Yet while its position was thus firmly established before the external and domestic eruptions of February, it was subject to varying emphases. Those emphasizing development, most notably Energy Minister Joe Greene, were anxious to "open up" the north by improving tanker access, albeit under Canadian law. Those favouring technical co-operation, represented publicly by Capt. Thomas Pullen (perhaps with sympathy from Transport), argued that Canada and the United States should co-operate in instituting a vessel management system in the Arctic and welcomed the second *Manhattan* voyage, viewing the existing public sensitivities over sovereignty and pollution as secondary. A related emphasis on "presence" in the Arctic was best expressed by Public Works Minister (and former Minister of Northern Affairs and Natural Resources) Arthur Laing. Sustained by his status as a minister from British Columbia (whose coasts would be endangered by the tanker component of the TAPS system), Laing opposed TAPS as well and strongly promoted a Mackenzie Valley pipeline. The emphasis on sovereignty-by-declaration, so popular outside the Cabinet, had no major proponents inside.

Translating the government's position into legislation provided the occasion for these differing approaches to become serious disagreements. As January opened, the Cabinet was considering five interrelated pieces of water and water-pollution legislation, including two versions of draft amendments to the Territorial Sea and Fishing Zones Act and a proposed new Arctic Waters Pollution Prevention Act. The first version of the revised Territorial Sea and Fishing Zones Act authorized the creation of wider coastal fishing zones and extended the zones to Arctic waters. The second and stronger version, based on a proposal approved by Cabinet prior to the 1969 Speech from the Throne, extended the width of Canada's territorial sea from three to twelve miles. This version, which would geographically extend the application of several other acts, was advanced primarily for its impact on the Arctic seas. The package of a special Arctic pollution prevention zone with a 12-mile territorial limit had thus to contend with the far more limited option of a mere extension of fishing zones legislation into the Arctic. This latter option, its advocates argued, markedly lessened the chances of evoking U.S. retaliation or running afoul of international law.

Cautious voices arose over other issues as well. Transport proved reluctant to press ahead with an interim National Contingency Plan for the Arctic. Its minister, Don Jamieson, envisaged an approach based on accepting the Brussels coastal state jurisdiction convention, extending the Canada Shipping Act to the high seas, and introducing new legislation on liability in the case of major incidents. EMR argued, in opposition to a 12-mile territorial limit, that Canada should merely assert jurisdiction over activities connected with the exploration and exploitation of the continental shelf outside territorial limits. EMR urged Cabinet to re-examine its approach to the Arctic in the light of the effects on Canada's oil exports to the United States.

Against this caution was arrayed the activism of the two other departments. DIAND pushed vigorously for an interim National Contingency Plan for the Arctic region. Public Works, led by Arthur Laing, pressed for a 12-mile coastal limit for all purposes save those that would prohibit innocent passage of ships. Most important, support for a highly active approach came from Ivan Head at the Prime Minister's Office. His early studies and subsequent research on the Arctic provided much of the conceptual and analytical foundation for the Arctic Waters Pollution Prevention bill.

The real battle came over the issue of whether the Arctic Waters Pollution Prevention bill, now entailing a 100-mile zone, would be sacrificed to maintain Canada's traditional support for international law and its central institutional embodiment, the ICJ. On 19 January 1970, Prime Minister Trudeau himself recommended Cabinet approval for preparation of Arctic pollution prevention legislation to be introduced as soon as possible in the current session of Parliament. Yet the deep divisions on this issue were revealed by a simultaneous direction for the Secretary of State for External Affairs, Mitchell Sharp, to prepare a memorandum to Cabinet recommending action to deal with possible international reaction to the proposed legislation. Sharp was also to consider, in consultation with the Prime Minister, the extent, nature, and timing of discussions with other countries that would be interested in and might react to the legislation. Moreover, the Prime Minister also forwarded an alternative course of action that would confine the application of the legislation establishing pollution control over ships to an outer limit of twelve miles, thereby establishing a nine-mile contiguous pollution control zone beyond the three-mile territorial sea.

The next day, 20 January, Sharp concluded before Cabinet that Canada need not protect itself over ICJ action regarding a 12-mile contiguous zone or a 12-mile territorial sea but would need a reservation for an assertion of pollution control jurisdiction over the waters of the Arctic archipelago. He also recommended that Canada should inform the United States before announcing legislative action on any of the alternatives.

Thus when the Cabinet Committee on House Planning and Legislation met to consider the Arctic-related bills, the basic alternatives were clear: a wide Arctic waters pollution control zone with a reservation on the jurisdiction of the ICJ, as forwarded by the Prime Minister; and a narrow 12-mile pollution control zone without an ICJ reservation, sponsored by Sharp.[22] In reference to the Prime Minister's recommendation, the Committee felt that it went beyond international law and would require at least a temporary ICJ reservation. In reference to Sharp's position, it accepted his recommendation for Cabinet to consider, simultaneously with the Prime Minister's proposal, a 12-mile territorial sea without a reservation.

Although Sharp's position had shifted to the 12-mile territorial control zone proposal, overall legislative policy was still very much in doubt when Cabinet met on 4 February to consider the matter. It was still in doubt afterward. Cabinet did decide to introduce during the current session Arctic pollution prevention legislation, to apply to a 100-mile zone, and to make no claim at that time to a 12-mile territorial sea. But this clear victory was accompanied by a decision that the Cabinet Committee on External Policy and Defence consider and report back to Cabinet on the issue of a reservation to Canada's acceptance of compulsory ICJ jurisdiction, the timing of such a measure, and, in the same context, changes in Canada's exclusive fishing zones.

When the External Policy and Defence Committee met on 10 February, Sharp took full advantage of the opportunities that his chairmanship allowed. Although supposed to focus on the narrow issue of whether Canada should make its ICJ reservation at or just before enactment of the Arctic waters bill and the Territorial Sea and Fishing Zones Act, the Ministers returned to the broader issue of what method would best assert Canadian jurisdiction over Arctic waters. It was a prolonged, wide-ranging, and heated discussion. Led by Paul Martin and Sharp, there was a trend back toward the 12-mile territorial sea proposal on the grounds that it required no ICJ reservation. Sharp concluded that as the ICJ reservation was an important question which the Committee could not decide, Cabinet might well reopen the whole subject. The one individual firmly opposed to proceeding without an ICJ reservation covering all elements of the Canadian approach was Allan Gotlieb. He argued that given the uncertain state of international law on the territorial sea, following the failure of the 1960 Law of the Sea Conference, the United States might be under no obligation to recognize a decision on Canada's part to enact a 12-mile territorial sea limit and could, therefore, possibly be in a position to take Canada to court over any enforcement action against its vessels.[23] While his opposition prevented a clear-cut decision being made, the majority present, led by Sharp, Martin, and Jean-Luc Pepin, were loath to recommend any ICJ reservation. They argued that such an action would be seen domestically and internationally as inconsistent with Canada's professed respect for the rule of law in international affairs.

So the big issue went back to full Cabinet. With it went a report that *if* Cabinet decided to proceed with the Arctic waters bill, it would be necessary to submit an ICJ reservation before or on the day the legislation was introduced. Here again discussion was both passionate and prolonged, extending through a Priorities and Planning Committee meeting and the Cabinet session of 19 February.

The dispute centred on the fundamental principle involved in Canada exempting its Act from the compulsory jurisdiction of the ICJ, thereby avoiding the risk of the United States opposing it in the Court. The individual most strongly in favour of Canada reserving its position before the Court was Donald Macdonald, a Toronto lawyer and government House Leader. While Macdonald understood the importance of building the international legal system through the use of the Court, he argued that Canada's interests were more important than the system in the particular case at hand. In addition, he had consulted a number of academic international lawyers and found agreement with his views.

Macdonald's major antagonist was Paul Martin, who was very strongly opposed to an ICJ reservation.[24] Martin argued that it was inconceivable that Canada would break away from its belief in the international system, of which the Court was a vital part. As an international lawyer himself, Martin felt that the weight of academic international legal opinion would be behind him. And he argued that Canada could persuade the Japanese, who might be asked by Washington to act as a surrogate in taking Canada to the ICJ, not to challenge the Canadian act.

The Prime Minister's position appeared to be more neutral.[25] Trudeau recognized that it was dangerous to weaken the Court with a reservation. Indeed, he spoke on several occasions to indicate the importance of Martin's argument and the significance of Canada's membership in the United Nations. Yet as the debate continued he did not oppose Macdonald's view and gradually accepted it. In this he followed most of his Cabinet, who had easily accepted Macdonald's view.[26] Finally, the Prime Minister went around the cabinet table and asked his ministers where they stood. Only Sharp and Martin voted against, standing alone with the internationalist principles they had done so much to promote and defend over the preceding decades. It was left only for Cabinet at its 26 February meeting to mandate External Affairs to consult rapidly with the United States over the Arctic and fisheries zones legislation in order to respond to U.S. requests for such consultations and to secure information as to possible U.S. reactions.

FINALE: MARCH—APRIL 1970

The succeeding two months provided the dénouement. Here again Humble's compliance provided a needed opening. During the first week of March, Sharp informed the House that Canada had agreed to a second *Manhattan* voyage, to begin 1 April, but had established anti-pollution rules that the ship must obey. DOT would inspect the ship's hull, navigation aids, and other equipment. The Canadian government would again have an agent aboard, but this time with additional duties. Most important, by early April a letter from DOT to Humble established that the captain of the Canadian icebreaker accompanying the *Manhattan* would have the ultimate responsibility, in liaison with Canadian authorities, for ending the voyage if necessary. Thus before the legislative initiatives of early April were introduced into the House of Commons, their anti-pollution provisions and the underlying principle of Canadian jurisdiction had been given a successful field test.

Reinforcing these highly practical acts was a variety of public relations initiatives. On 9 March, Don Jamieson, on CBC-TV's *Encounter*, mused about the international conflict of interest on pollution he had discovered in Brussels. Pierre Trudeau, from an Arctic location on the same date, told the audience of NBC's *Today Show* that Canada claimed its Arctic waters on the basis of the sector principle and continental shelf. On 30 March, Public Works Minister Arthur Laing publicly described ships like the *Manhattan* as fragile "apple boxes" in the harsh Arctic environment. Finally, in early April, Defence Minister Léo Cadieux and the Chief of Defence Staff began a five-day tour of the Arctic while stating that they would soon receive a plan for Arctic defence.

Such brave words seemed appropriate, given the rising tension between Ottawa and Washington and Canada's blunt refusal to accede to American requests in early March when Trudeau sent Ivan Head and Alan Beesley (head of the External Affairs legal division) to brief U.S. officials. On 20 March, Johnson and a U.S. negotiating team journeyed to Ottawa for talks with Sharp, Chrétien, and senior officials. They got nowhere, even though the week before Sharp had stated that Canada's Arctic sovereignty claims would be challenged by the United States and that Canada would "go along with what turns out to be international law."[27]

This pledge was, of course, absent on 8 April, when the government introduced into the House of Commons a bill to establish the Arctic Waters Pollution Prevention Act and a bill to amend the Territorial Seas and Fishing Zones Act. These bills established a 100-mile control zone in the waters around the Canadian Arctic archipelago, within which Canada would exercise jurisdiction in specified ways to prevent pollution. The 100-mile limit followed the prevailing international legal standard applying to oil pollution from tankers. The size of the zone had only an indirect functional rationale. It was, however, "legal" enough to appeal to the international community, large enough to satisfy the appetite of the Canadian public, and limited enough to sustain the distinction between full zonal sovereignty and purpose-specific jurisdiction – and hence to complicate the diplomatic response of the U.S. government.

The government's bills also extended the territorial limit of Canada's coastal waters from three miles (with an additional nine-mile fishing zone) to twelve miles. This action increased the size of Canadian territory by one-eighth and brought Canada into line with the 56 other countries claiming a 12-mile territorial limit. Most important, the extension created territorial waters "gates" of less than 24 miles in Prince of Wales Strait and in Barrow Strait, thus asserting additional control over the Passage even if M'Clure Strait at the western end would one day prove to be regularly navigable.

Finally, immediately prior to introduction of the legislation, the government informed the United Nations that Canada was reserving from the compulsory jurisdiction of the ICJ "disputes arising out of or concerning jurisdiction or rights claimed or exercised by Canada in respect of the conservation, management or exploitation of the living resources of the sea, or in respect of the prevention or control of pollution or contamination of the marine environment in marine areas adjacent to the coast of Canada."[28] Although this was Canada's fourth reservation to the jurisdiction of the Court, it was the first dealing with a subject area category. It could thus be viewed as a repudiation of support for international law which Canada had provided since the establishment of the Court.[29]

Equally innovative were the concepts the government stressed in its ensuing public diplomacy campaign.[30] Canada argued that the threat posed by oil-laden tankers in the fragile Arctic environment made their passage inherently non-innocent and thus required an assertion of coastal state jurisdiction. It asserted that there was no international law covering the pollution threat from advanced technology in ice-infested areas and that a Court dominated by maritime powers ought not to foreclose international legal development of this kind by asserting jurisdiction based on technologically outmoded concepts of the law of the sea. Canada claimed that it was engaged in an act not of asserting or extending sovereignty but of exercising purpose-specific jurisdiction, as with fishing or aircraft identification zones, in its role as a custodian of a global resource for the world community. It declared that it would not be swayed by the opposition of the United States, which was said to have been the largest obstacle to the creation of an international law of the sea effective in preventing marine pollution. And finally, the government stressed that it believed fully in international law, was searching for an international, multilateral, or bilateral agreement on the pollution prevention issue, supported the American call for an international conference on territorial sea limits, and would accept ICJ jurisdiction over Canada's extension to 12 miles (an area where international law did exist). Armed with these arguments, Canada held firm in the face of the predictable U.S. response.

In early March, Humble acquiesced by requesting the assistance of a Canadian icebreaker for the *Manhattan's* second voyage, inviting a Canadian government representative to be on board, and fulfilling the

Canadian pollution prevention standards. It also identified the ship's route as being merely an excursion into the waters of Baffin Bay. On 18 March, Humble agreed to post a bond and accept responsibility for the voyage. And on 26 March, Humble agreed to give Canada ultimate control over the *Manhattan*'s voyage.

The reaction of the U.S. government was strikingly different. It bombarded Ottawa with notes asking for more talks. And on 10 March President Nixon declared that "as a means of interim control during the period of transition to an alternative United States-Canada energy policy," oil imports from Canada for 1 March to 31 December east of the Rockies would be reduced by 20 per cent.[31] Although this measure was produced by the U.S. Assistant Secretary of State for Economic Affairs to secure Canadian agreement to the prized Continental Energy Plan (CEP), the Arctic access dimensions of the latter gave it a direct relevance to the issue at hand. The CEP and Arctic issues were also joined on 11 March, at the 13th meeting of the Interparliamentary Group, when the U.S. delegation insisted that the Northwest Passage was an international strait. This refrain was repeated at a meeting of Canadian and U.S. officials on 20 March. With Canada holding firm, the mood did not improve. On 1 April, the *Manhattan* began its voyage, just as a U.S. Federal District Court judge granted a temporary restraining order preventing the issuance of permits for the construction of TAPS. Simultaneously the U.S. Congress approved the construction of the most powerful non-nuclear icebreaker in the world, one that promised to be far superior to anything Canada possessed. Its sister ship, the *Polar Sea*, was to appear in Canadian Arctic waters amid renewed controversy 15 years later.

THE AFTERMATH

After the introduction of the Arctic legislation on 8 April 1970, the government was free to concentrate on the task of convincing audiences at home and abroad and of coping with persistent U.S. efforts to lure Canada into a less unilateral and ambitious approach. The frustrations faced by domestic and external actors throughout the *Manhattan* episode were underlined by the ease with which the government accomplished these tasks. The domestic demand for a straightforward declaration of sovereignty died almost instantly, as the public responded enthusiastically to Ottawa's creativity and cleverness. Within Parliament, the Conservatives unleashed a barrage of condemnation, but its effectiveness was greatly reduced by its striking inconsistency.

Dealing with the Americans and the rest of the international community proved only somewhat more difficult. The appeal of the anti-pollution principle, the creative approach to international law, and a carefully orchestrated campaign of public diplomacy did much to dampen the opposition of attentive Americans.[32] U.S. government protests, in diplomatic notes and a presidential phone call, produced little, despite press reports from Washington indicating that the United States was considering economic sanctions or a navy submarine transit of the Passage to show Canada's lack of effective control.

While the Canadian government was well prepared to withstand these moves, Washington's suddenly sophisticated multilateral diplomacy proved to be a more formidable challenge. In a 14 April note and in a 15 April aide-mémoire, the United States proposed to convene in Washington during the fourth week of June 1970 a multilateral conference to establish an international regime for Arctic areas beyond national jurisdiction. It invited the Canadian government to join in the call for a conference. The multilateral alternative, American sponsorship, and the implied willingness to proceed without Canadian co-sponsorship each constituted a major problem, particularly as the Canadian government's bills had not yet been enacted into law.

In a 16 April note and a subsequent aide-mémoire of 28 April, Canada indicated that it had no intention of submitting issues of territorial limits and national jurisdiction to the conference but welcomed multilateral discussions on agreed rules of environmental protection and the safety of navigation in the Arctic waters. On 6 May, the United States accepted Canada's willingness to participate in the multilateral discussions Canada specified and suggested immediate bilateral consultations to prepare for and determine the participants of the conference. The United States stressed its desire for a consensus approach at the conference, its lack of interest in provoking a jurisdictional dispute, and its agreement with Canada that the question of rules for the Arctic environment and Arctic navigation transcended traditional concepts of sovereignty. Despite these alluring signals, Canada remained concerned about U.S. unwillingness to rule out other agenda items at the proposed conference. Canada thus sought to delay the conference, restrict its agenda, and shape its membership by lining up supporters for its April measures, even as the United States enlisted adherents to its multilateral conference approach.

In the end Canada proved able to secure the support of enough of the key states to block the U.S. approach. Canadian victory was in sight. While most diplomats judged the United States to have a strong legal case against Canada and recognized the self-interest in Canada's measures, most also felt that Canada would win the battle for world public opinion. Their judgment rested on the appeal of environmental protection, the acknowledged cloudiness and bias of the international law of the sea with regard to pollution, and Canada's effective use of the precedent of U.S. President Truman's unilateral 1948 extension of jurisdiction over the continental shelf. Perhaps more important was the desire of other countries, particularly coastal states, to break the three-mile territorial sea regime.

In its competition with the United States over the April measures themselves, Canada did lose, in varying degrees, all of the large Western countries – such traditional Canadian associates as the Netherlands and Belgium and the old dominions (notably Australia). Yet it secured the support of the critical circumpolar Scandinavian states of Sweden, Norway (an important shipping power), and Iceland. More important, it obtained the support of the other Arctic superpower, the Soviet Union, with a visit by Ivan Head to Moscow in June 1970. Moscow treated the u.s. conference proposal with suspicion and reserve and evinced no desire to see international discussions develop that might disturb the existing situation in the Soviet Arctic.

Thus, with the possible exception of Denmark and Finland, which remained noncommittal, all Arctic powers apart from the United States had gravitated to the Canadian side. The intellectual leader of the un-sponsored Law of the Sea Conference, Malta, was sympathetic as well. Led by Brazil, all the Latin American coastal states had come to the Canadian side. Moreover, the two major flag-of-convenience shipping states that the United States invited to its proposed conference (Panama, which claimed a 200-mile limit, and Liberia, the only African country invited) both had expressed sympathy for the Canadian legislation.

Most important, of the 14 states (apart from Canada) that the United States was known to have approached with invitations to its proposed conference as of early May, only the Dutch seemed in favour, with the Spaniards and Finns noncommittal. Japan, Britain, Belgium, and Denmark refused to accept until the terms of reference were clarified by the United States and/or the conference was limited to technically based aspects of pollution and navigation. Italy went further, saying that any conference without Canadian participation would be worthless and Italian involvement in it a hostile act toward Canada. The Soviet Union, Iceland, Norway, and Sweden were opposed to the u.s. conference proposal. Indeed, Sweden considered the proposal a ganging-up operation and suggested that Canada call a counter-conference to develop an international regime based on the Canadian legislation.

Thus by the summer of 1970 it became clear that the United States no longer had an international constituency for its efforts to shape the development of international law in this area. And despite the formidable array of unilateral economic, military, and political instruments at Washington's disposal, it chose not to deploy them alone on behalf of the old regime. By 1970, the United States was unable to define the new and unwilling by itself to defend the old international order in the field.

CONCLUSION

The voyages of the *Manhattan* through the Passage were the occasion of significant change in the Canadian government's foreign policy behaviour. They evoked competing tendencies that defined anew the alternative courses of action available to the state. Canada's response to the *Manhattan* transits illuminates the process of change in Canadian foreign policy itself. The episode reveals a government whose physical assets, creative professionalism, and internal debates were ultimately more important in determining Canadian behaviour and international outcomes than the strong, competing pressures exerted by actors at home and abroad. It points to an intragovernmental policy-making process that was centred on deeply held convictions backed by pervasive belief systems, with none more powerful than the classic liberal internationalist ideology that was created and applied during the Pearson-Martin era in Canadian foreign relations. And it suggests that Trudeau's revolution in Canadian foreign policy was neither the passing concern of an international neophyte nor an easy, unthinking repudiation of a gracious internationalism in favour of national greed. What we see in the *Manhattan* episode is instead an effort to build an international order more in keeping with the values and responsibilities of a Canada that had become more powerful than in the initial phases of the post-war era.

The new Trudeau decision-making system did allow the voice of classic liberal internationalism forceful expression. In doing so it revealed the deeply ideological character of the traditional Canadian approach to foreign policy and the fundamental values of the emerging alternative. It is wrong to see this latter alternative as a choice between sovereignty and pollution prevention goals, with the latter serving only as a convenient cover for the former. Canada's pollution concerns were real and in some respects determining. They arose as a major element in the government's thinking as early as October 1969. They provided the general legislative context in which the Arctic measures took shape. And when reinforced by the damage done to the *Manhattan* on its first voyage and the accidents to barges and tankers elsewhere, they led to measures far more forceful, and far more focused on pollution, than those originally contemplated. Moreover, the concern with pollution was not a transitory, fashionable theme, nor a simple response to environmentalist pressure. Rather it was a direct emanation of the commitment of the Prime Minister and his closest associates to the integrity and legitimate interests of dispossessed communities.[33] For Pierre Trudeau, pollution *prevention* was essential to protect the distinctive way of life of Canada's northern native communities. It was a fellow French Canadian and Minister of Indian Affairs, Jean Chrétien, who first signalled the pollution-prevention approach. And the Prime Minister himself went to considerable personal effort to ensure that the Third World states within the global community would not see Canada's pollution prevention initiatives as merely a rich man's luxury, let alone a convenient cover for national greed.

Nor was this a simple choice between "internationalism" and "nationalism." Rather the interests of the international community were compelling throughout the period. The Prime Minister's earliest statements – in the spring of 1969 – reveal an explicit and instinctive desire to abide by international law and a distaste for the expansive claims of the sector principle or the sovereignty-by-declaration approach. It was the Prime Minister who travelled to the United Nations to see if a workable international regime were possible and who moved unilaterally only after the UN generally and the Brussels process specifically had proved inadequate. And it was Pierre Trudeau who, in the final Cabinet debate, acted more as an international lawyer who understood the requisites of the international system than as the protagonist of a new nationalism or a secure Prime Minister humouring a former leadership rival, Paul Martin, now devoid of even a seat in the House of Commons, who was voicing the verities of another age.

Uniting the concern with pollution and the interests of the global community was the concept of custodianship – a doctrine that appears to have had a real moral force in the minds of its progenitors. This doctrine conceived of Canada's Arctic waters as an essential component of the global ecological system and as part of the common heritage of mankind. It saw Canada, by virtue of geographic location and functional expertise, with the responsibility to serve as the custodian of the resource until the global community generated the institutional mechanisms for coping. And in the face of an urgent pollution threat, it saw Canada compelled to act and to lead, legally and institutionally, in the evolution of a new international regime. The concept of Canada as an agent, par excellence, of the international system linked the Arctic initiatives to the finest traditions of the liberal-internationalist era in its most creative phase. Indeed, the belief that Canada must exercise leadership, unilaterally and multilaterally, on behalf of a global community incompletely knit together by the existing array of regimes, institutions, and great power managers suggested that the immediate legacy of the Arctic initiatives of April 1970 would lie in an effort to shape a new UN convention on the law of the sea.

CHAPTER FIVE

The Negotiation of Article 234

D. M. MC RAE

Canada's Arctic aspirations, expressed in Senator Poirier's famous motion in the Canadian Senate in 1907 as the "possession of the lands and islands situated in the north of the Dominion, and extending to the north pole,"[1] have always posed fundamental questions of jurisdiction and title. These have found expression, in terms of both legal and political philosophy, as a problem of sovereignty. Initially attention was focused on the islands themselves, which were the specific concern of Senator Poirier. But as confidence over the strength of Canada's title to the land areas grew, attention was directed to the waters of the Arctic archipelago.[2]

The waters, however, have posed more troublesome problems than the land. The question of title to land territory touches on fundamental rules of international law of long standing. Discovery, effective occupation, and contiguity, concepts that over the centuries have had a greater or lesser weight in determining who has acquired title to territory, can readily be called in aid.[3] The problem of title or sovereignty to water areas is much less clear in international jurisprudence, both generally and specifically in relation to Arctic waters. There are a number of reasons for this.

First, the concept of historic title to waters was not, nor is it perhaps even today, fully developed. The prevailing philosophy since the seventeenth century had been one of freedom of the seas, with only narrow belts of sea falling within the jurisdiction of coastal states.[4] Claims to historic waters had been made, and their legitimacy rested largely on the acquiescence or acceptance by other states to the assertion of jurisdiction over waters enclosed or substantially surrounded by a state.[5] But no precise rules were developed in relation to claims to historic title to areas of water, and not even the 1982 Convention on the Law of the Sea, the most comprehensive attempt yet made to codify the law of the sea, contains such rules.

Second, the remoteness of the Arctic marine area militated against substantial attention being devoted to the question of sovereignty over the waters.[6] Apart from the indigenous inhabitants, no one traversed the waters, and early European explorers seeking the Northwest Passage found the waters decidedly inhospitable. Since no one was claiming to use the waters, and therefore there was no challenge to a Canadian claim to title over them, there was little reason for the question of Canadian sovereignty to become a major issue.

Third, the area has never been perceived simply as water. The existence of permanent ice raised the question whether for legal purposes the "waters" of the Arctic archipelago should be treated as "water," or whether the correct analogy is with land. The problem of characterization had a major impact upon early thinking about the legal status of the waters of the Canadian Arctic.[7] It raised, for example, the question whether Arctic waters were sui generis or whether they should be treated no differently from other large enclosed or semi-enclosed waters around the Canadian coast – the Gulf of St Lawrence, the Bay of Fundy, Hecate Strait, Dixon Entrance, and Queen Charlotte Sound.

It was not until 1951 that there was an important clarification in the law regarding the jurisdiction of states over waters adjacent to their coasts, one that put into perspective some of the questions relating to both Arctic and other bodies of Canadian coastal waters. This occurred in the decision of the International Court of Justice (ICJ) in the *Fisheries Case (United Kingdom v. Norway)*.[8] The Court recognized the concept of historic title to coastal waters and accepted that where a coastline is broken up with indentations and off-lying islands then its territorial sea could be measured from straight lines drawn from points on the coast to islands, or from island to island. Behind those baselines, the waters would be subject to the full sovereignty of the coastal state.

Seven years later the first United Nations Conference on the Law of the Sea, held at Geneva, reinforced the position taken in the *Fisheries Case*. The Convention on the Territorial Sea and Contiguous Zone[9] included an express reference to the concept of historic waters, thereby endorsing it as an accepted concept of the modern law of the sea. The "straight baselines" technique for the measurement of the territorial sea[10] in respect of particular coastal configurations was also adopted.

Thus, by the late 1950s Canada had two clear options on which to base a legal claim to the waters of the Arctic archipelago – a claim to historic title to the waters, and the enclosure of the waters by straight baselines around the perimeter of the archipelago. The waters inside those baselines would therefore be internal waters of Canada and thus subject to Canadian sovereignty.

To have claimed formally at that time that the waters of the Arctic archipelago were internal waters either by virtue of historic title or by the drawing of straight baselines would, however, have been an extremely radical gesture. Canada had no general legislation establishing a territorial sea,[11] and a more pressing need was the extension of fisheries jurisdiction in response to demands for measures to protect the Canadian fishing industry against foreign vessels.[12] At both the 1958 and 1960 conferences on the law of the sea the question of a contiguous fishing zone beyond the territorial sea was one of major concern to Canada.[13] The particular question of jurisdiction over Arctic waters was not an issue at either of these conferences.

Moreover, the anticipated reaction from the United States to any formalizing of a Canadian position that the waters of the Arctic archipelago were internal waters of Canada discouraged precipitate action. Traditionally the United States opposed claims by states to exclusive control over the waters of adjacent straits,[14] and the United States quickly manifested its opposition to the inclusion of the straight baseline concept in Canada's 1964 Territorial Sea and Fishing Zone Act. Such lines were not drawn on the east coast of Canada until 1967,[15] and on the west coast until 1969.[16]

There was, therefore, no clear policy during the 1950s and early 1960s on the status of Arctic waters. Public statements by ministers appeared to suggest that the waters were Canadian internal waters, but these statements were not free from ambiguity.[17] Although co-ordinates for the territorial sea were designated for the east and west coasts of Canada, under the Territorial Sea and Fishing Zones Act, no such co-ordinates were ever promulgated for Canadian Arctic waters. In other words, Canada had not committed itself by legislation on the juridical status of Arctic waters. However, the events of 1969 were to put a new perspective on the matter.

ARCTIC WATERS POLICY: THE FUNCTIONAL APPROACH

The voyage of the supertanker s/т *Manhattan*, in 1969, forced the issue for Canada.[18] If transit through the Passage was commercially feasible, then Canada had to assert a position on the legal status of the waters or run the risk of having a practice develop among states of using the Canadian archipelago for international navigation. In such circumstances the Passage could become in law an international strait through which there would be a right of innocent passage that could not be suspended. Canada would, therefore, have lost the opportunity to ensure that the waters were the internal waters of Canada through which no right of passage exists.

In response to this challenge Canadian officials developed a novel approach to the exercise of Canadian regulatory authority over Arctic waters, one that would enable Canada to exercise jurisdiction over shipping in order to protect the Arctic marine environment and at the same time put to one side, without giving up, a Canadian position on full sovereignty over the waters of the Arctic archipelago. This was the functional approach, under which Canada was to "exercise only the jurisdiction required to achieve the specific and vital purpose of environmental protection."[19]

The functional approach was, in legal terms, as radical as it was novel. It was novel because it put environmental considerations to the forefront as a justification for the exercise by the coastal state of jurisdiction over adjacent maritime areas. It was radical because it rested on a philosophy that called for a rethinking of the traditional doctrine of the law of the sea. One of the leading exponents and authors of the Canadian position put it this way: "The traditional law of the sea in general is oriented towards the concept of unfettered freedom of navigation on the high seas and thus favours flag-state jurisdiction while seeking to limit the jurisdiction of coastal states. As a result this essentially *laissez-faire* system is inadequate in its provisions for the prevention and control of marine pollution."[20] The legal justification for action by Canada therefore lay not on a traditional basis of sovereignty but rather in the concepts of "self-defence" and "self-preservation." A state is entitled to defend its environmental integrity, the argument went, just as traditional doctrine allows it to defend its territorial and political integrity.

The result of this new orientation in Canada's approach to the legal justification for exercising jurisdiction over Arctic waters was the Arctic Waters Pollution Prevention Act, enacted with the unanimous consent of the House of Commons in 1970. The Act, as is well known, extended Canadian jurisdiction for the prevention of pollution in waters north of 60°N to a zone 100 miles from the baseline from which the territorial sea is measured. Within this zone Canada would have the authority to regulate all shipping, including the authority to prohibit shipping from the whole or part of the area, and to prescribe standards on such matters as design, construction, and manning for ships entering the zone. In order to enforce these provisions, powers of arrest and prosecution were included.

The Act came into direct conflict with traditional doctrine on freedom of the seas, for it applied Canadian jurisdiction to foreign-flag vessels – and it extended that jurisdiction to an area apparently broader than the three miles still regarded by many states at that time as the appropriate limit for the territorial sea. It was inevitable, therefore, that there would be reaction from other states, particularly from the United States.

That the Arctic waters legislation represented something novel in international law was acknowledged implicitly by Canada, for when the legislation was enacted Canada's acceptance of the jurisdiction of the ICJ was altered in order to avoid the question of the legality of Canada's pollution prevention legislation under international law from being challenged in the Court. The Prime Minister openly conceded that "it was important to make the reservation the moment we introduced the law for fear that at any moment there may be some litigation begun which we would be too late to withdraw from.[21] This new approach also served to manifest a new political style in Canada's external relations. It came just after the 1968 review of Canadian foreign policy and signalled a change of direction towards the vigorous pursuit internationally of national interests, if necessary by unilateral action.[22]

But it was not sufficient just to claim the jurisdiction asserted over Arctic waters and to circumvent any challenge to that jurisdiction in the ICJ. Ultimately, the viability of the legislation depended upon international acceptance. The real question was how to achieve such acceptance.

SEEKING INTERNATIONAL ACCEPTANCE

There were three principal options in securing international acceptance of the Arctic waters legislation. The first option was to treat the matter simply as a Canadian-U.S. bilateral issue on the assumption that if the approbation of the United States was secured then the acceptance of other states would follow. One kind of bilateral approach, that is by having the question of the international legal validity of the legislation tested before the ICJ had been ruled out by Canada from the outset. The alternative of entering into direct negotiations with the United States held little promise. The position taken by the United States had appeared quite uncompromising.

The second option was to treat the matter as a regional issue, affecting the Arctic littoral states alone and therefore to be resolved among them. In fact, the United States in its response to the Canadian legislation had proposed the convening of a conference of Arctic user and coastal states. But such an approach could have placed Canada in a minority in alliance with the Soviet Union against the United States and other states whose primary interest was in navigation in the Arctic and not in environmental controls. In any event the Soviet Union was not interested in such a conference, and although Canada engaged in consultations with other Arctic states, no such conference was held.[23]

The third option was to try to secure general international acceptance of the Arctic waters legislation through a wider multilateral forum. Several opportunities presented themselves. The Stockholm Conference on the Human Environment, to be held in 1972, would provide an opportunity to influence the development of general principles on the protection of the marine environment favourable to the Canadian approach; at a more technical level the Intergovernmental Maritime Consultative Organization (IMCO) was preparing a comprehensive convention on the control of marine pollution.[24] And plans were under way for a Third United Nations Conference on the Law of the Sea (UNCLOS). The UN conference would provide a forum for the negotiation of special measures for shipping in the Arctic within the context of a reconsideration of traditional doctrines on the law of the sea. Each of these forums had its own advantages for Canada, and they all provided an opportunity for obtaining the support of other, non-Arctic states for the Canadian position – support that would not have been available if the issue had been dealt with only as a bilateral or regional matter.

Canada chose the multilateral option. The Canadian delegation participated actively in the preparations for Stockholm and in the 1972 conference itself,[25] in particular in the formulation of the "23 principles on marine pollution" prepared by the Intergovernmental Working Group on Marine Pollution for the conference. Canada had proposed, in addition to those principles, a further three, one of which was as follows: A state may exercise special authority in areas of the sea adjacent to its territorial waters where functional controls of a continuing nature are necessary for the effective prevention of pollution which could cause damage or injury to the land or marine environment under its exclusive or sovereign authority.[26] Although not adopted by the Intergovernmental Working Group, the three Canadian principles were submitted by Canada to the Stockholm conference, which took note of them without accepting or rejecting them and referred them to both the 1973 IMCO Conference on Maritime Pollution and the UN General Assembly's Seabed Committee.[27] The foundation for the Arctic exception was being laid.

In the February 1973 preparatory meeting for the IMCO conference on the prevention of marine pollution from ships, Canada proposed articles that would provide international recognition of the right of a coastal state to take "special measures" in respect of shipping off its coasts. These measures were to apply within the limits of the coastal state's national jurisdiction, "including environmental protection zones," pending or following the establishment of international measures, if, inter alia, they were "necessary in the light of local geographical and ecological characteristics." Not surprisingly, this approach ran into considerable opposition in an organization for which the concept of flag-state jurisdiction was an unquestioned assumption, and the "special measures" approach was defeated. It was reintroduced, with some modifications, at the conference itself in October 1973, but it was again defeated.[28]

The IMCO exercise was far from futile. Although the idea that coastal states should be free to enact measures relating to design, construction, and manning standards within the economic zone in the light of local geographical and ecological characteristics was not acceptable to the major shipping states, the initial Canadian proposal brought forth a set of counter-articles that recognized that certain "special measures" might be taken by coastal states in waters "the particular characteristics of which render the environment exceptionally vulnerable."[29] However, the counter-articles did not go as far as the Canadian approach in allowing the coastal state to adopt its own design, construction, and manning standards applicable to non-flag vessels. Although no "special measures" provisions were ultimately adopted by the IMCO conference, the shipping states were now clearly on notice. Moreover, the draft articles sponsored by the group of shipping states provided an indication that the need was being understood. The idea of "exceptionally vulnerable areas" had developed, and this was to become an essential element of the Canadian "special measures" approach at the Law of the Sea Conference. The 1973 IMCO conference had provided a useful "dry run" for the Canadian position.

CANADIAN POLICY AT UNCLOS

Although UNCLOS offered an opportunity for Canada to promote international acceptance of the Arctic waters legislation, it also presented a number of dangers. The very multiplicity of issues to be resolved meant that it might be difficult to get enough states to focus on the specific problems of Arctic waters. In part this turned out to be true. Many states took the view that like the problems of anadromous species (principally salmon) the question of ice-covered waters concerned only a small number of states and was to be resolved by them. Additionally, one of the major issues on the agenda at UNCLOS was a regime for passage through international straits, an issue that had a far higher profile than that of Arctic marine pollution. But the inclusion of the Passage within an international straits regime would, as far as Canada was concerned, nullify any concessions made for Arctic waters.

Moreover, Canada had a variety of other interests to pursue at UNCLOS. These included securing an acceptable regime for coastal state jurisdiction over fisheries (particularly over anadromous species), confirming the sovereign rights of states out to the continental margin, and protecting Canada's land-based producers in any regime for the exploitation of the minerals of the deep seabed. Determining priorities among these issues would be difficult, and although no attempt was made to set specific priorities, observers concluded that acceptance of the Arctic waters regime was a dominant objective in Canada's UNCLOS policies.

Canada was therefore faced with a number of choices in the UNCLOS negotiations. Some were plain from the outset; others emerged as the negotiations progressed. Two were of particular and continuing significance and were ultimately critical in achieving a successful outcome. These were the severing of specific needs for Arctic waters from other "exceptionally vulnerable areas" in the global marine environment and the formulation of a Canadian position on a regime for international straits.

Although Canada's attempt to secure international acceptance for the Arctic waters legislation had been framed as part of a general rule applicable to specially vulnerable areas, not as a specific rule for ice-covered areas, there was no doubt from the outset that it was the Arctic waters legislation that was really at stake. Yet the argument for the protection of Arctic waters paralleled the argument for other "exceptionally vulnerable areas." And a broader approach had its advantages in the context of UNCLOS negotiations, for it struck a chord with non-Arctic states, such as Australia, which also had coastal areas that they regarded as "exceptionally vulnerable" and for which a special regime would be appropriate. However, the Soviet Union, whose support for the Canadian position was essential, had only Arctic concerns. A broad-ranging provision for "exceptionally vulnerable areas" would therefore be contrary to the general position of the Soviet Union on freedom of the seas and could conflict with the Soviet interest in a regime for international straits. As the negotiations progressed it became clear that Canada had to make a choice between a general provision for "exceptionally vulnerable areas" and a specific regime for Arctic waters, even at the risk of losing the potential support of some non-Arctic states.

The question of the regime for international straits posed a particular problem for Canada. Both the United States and the Soviet Union were concerned that the trend towards broader coastal state jurisdiction over the oceans would restrict freedom of movement for their naval vessels, in particular for their submarines. This concern led them to favour a regime that would grant even less rights to a coastal state bordering an international strait. They wanted a right of unimpeded transit through international straits and not merely a regime of "innocent" passage, even though such passage could not be suspended.[30] Prior to the convening of the conference, the two states had contemplated calling an international conference to deal specifically with this question. The "straits" issue was therefore of fundamental importance to both of them. Although Canada had no reason, as a matter of general principle, to oppose a new regime for straits, it would certainly be opposed to the application of such a regime to the Passage (or in fact to other waters off the Canadian coast). Canada had to ensure that the Northwest Passage was not to be treated as an international strait.

One alternative, therefore, was simply to oppose this new straits regime. Canada would then have been in the company of the many coastal states that were reluctant to recognize any right of passage through international straits beyond that embodied in Article 16(4) of the 1958 Convention on the Territorial Sea and Contiguous Zone, that is, a right of "non-suspendable" innocent passage. This would have been a natural move for Canada, which in many respects was a leading member of the coastal states group. Another alternative was not to oppose a straits regime, but rather to ensure that the

Northwest Passage would be treated as an exception to any regime for international straits. Such an approach might, however, weaken Canada's coastal state affiliations which were important for other issues being negotiated at UNCLOS. A further alternative, the one ultimately adopted, was to refrain from making a commitment on the straits issue until the question of special provisions for Arctic waters was resolved. In this way Canada could hope to obtain the best of both worlds.

A particular question concerning the appropriate group of states with which to ally was posed by the archipelagic group. The Canadian Arctic geographically constitutes an archipelago, and archipelagic states were asking for special recognition at UNCLOS. States like Indonesia and Fiji wanted recognition of the unity of their territory, even though it was constituted not by a single substantial land mass but rather by many islands of varying size and often a considerable distance apart. Their particular claim was to use straight baselines around the outer edges of the islands to enclose them within a single group and to treat the waters so enclosed as internal waters. Such a claim paralleled the Canadian claim, and thus there was a temptation to throw Canada's lot in with the archipelagic states. But there was a fundamental difference between Canada and those states. The latter were "mid-oceanic archipelagos" – the Canadian Arctic was a coastal archipelago, contiguous to a coastal mainland. The mid-oceanic archipelagos have no mainland as such, and this very reason strengthened their claim to preferential treatment. Moreover, many of these archipelagic states straddle some of the world's major shipping lanes, and the proposals for "transit" passage through international straits concerned some of these states directly. Canada did not let its position stand or fall with the archipelagic states. Although these states were successful in achieving recognition of the special status of archipelagic waters, they were unable ultimately to avoid the application of the unimpeded or "transit passage" regime to those waters. Moreover, provisions for archipelagic states finally included in the convention were not applicable to "coastal archipelagos."[31]

As the negotiations developed, other questions arose. Should Canada negotiate solely within the framework of UNCLOS or should it seek to use other forums? The exclusion of the Northwest Passage from the regime for international straits might be achieved in NATO, where consultations were occurring on law of the sea issues, in particular on the straits regime. But this approach had its dangers. If the United States were to take the position that free transit through the Passage was vital to alliance security, this could do irreparable harm to Canada's position on Arctic waters. Further, would it improve Canada's negotiating position if the Arctic waters legislation were modified to remove some of its more objectionable provisions? In particular, should the claim to set hull design and construction standards for vessels using Arctic waters be forgone? Such an approach had its attractions in the context of multilateral negotiations. In the end the Arctic waters legislation remained intact, and the issue was not taken to forums outside UNCLOS – it was resolved through negotiations among a small group of states within the UNCLOS framework.

THE PROGRESS OF NEGOTIATIONS

Many of the above issues were the subject of debate within the Department of External Affairs and in the Interdepartmental Committee on the Law of the Sea in the early months of 1974, while preparations were under way for the first substantive session of UNCLOS in Caracas. The formulation of a policy for Arctic waters did not go unchallenged. There were some, particularly in the Department of Transport, who favoured a free transit regime through straits, including the Passage. However, it was unlikely that any modification of the Canadian position – for example, by limiting the "specially vulnerable areas" proposals to ice-covered areas (in other words by making a special exception for Arctic waters) – would lead automatically to U.S. acceptance of the Canadian position, although it was likely that such an approach would be more favourably received by the Soviet Union.[32] There was concern, however, that any proposals to allow states to stop and inspect foreign vessels in particular areas of an "economic zone" would be met with united opposition from the major maritime states, including the United States, the United Kingdom and other western European countries, and Japan.

At Caracas the Canadian delegation took steps to mark out its position at an early stage. The defects of a regime that relied solely on international standards were outlined in committee III by the Canadian representative in July 1974. The Canadian position on "exceptionally vulnerable areas" was set out: "ice-covered areas" were presented as an obvious example of the type of area to which such measures would apply; enclosed or semi-enclosed seas, congested traffic situations, and narrow channels were also cited as examples that might require "special measures." No significant progress was, however, made in committee III.

A concern that did emerge at Caracas, both for the issue of Arctic waters and more generally in respect of the issues before the conference, was the possible attitude of the Group of 77, which generally represented the views of the developing world. If the Group of 77 were to take up a position on the question of special measures that was different from the Canadian stance, it might then be difficult to dislodge. Consequently, Canada's consultations with other governments between the Caracas session and the Geneva session the following year were designed partly to enlist the aid of some of the members of the Group of 77 in order to ensure that the group as a whole would not take a position prematurely or do anything incompatible with the Canadian approach.

Throughout this inter-session period Canadian-u.s. consultations also took place. Each side explored the extent to which the other might move. Would the United States contemplate the setting of national standards by coastal states that might differ from generally accepted international standards? Would Canada be prepared to contemplate the restriction of such standards to what was "necessary" or "essential" in any particular area? It was in these consultations that the germ of compromise began to develop. The United States was interested in Canadian support for its views on international straits. By accepting the application of "special measures" in part of the economic zone, particularly with regard to ice-covered areas, the United States might be able to gain support for its preferred international straits regime from an influential member of the coastal states group. Such an approach was certainly of interest to Canada, but the United States was still in favour of an international review process, through the mechanism of imco, for any special coastal state shipping regulations.

Notwithstanding these attempts to reach an accommodation in bilateral discussions, and in the multilateral consultations organized under the aegis of Ambassador Evensen of Norway, the United States and the other maritime powers maintained their formal opposition to the Canadian approach. The maritime powers appeared implacably opposed to "special measures" for vulnerable areas. But it also became clear in bilateral consultations and as a result of inquiries among a number of governments that many states had little knowledge or appreciation of the problem of ice-covered areas. Most states were, by and large, neutral on the question of special provisions for such areas. They were prepared to support whatever could be worked out by the states most directly affected. If there was to be a "deal" on Arctic waters it would have to be arranged between Canada, the United States, and the Soviet Union.

By the spring of 1975 the idea of two streams of "special measures" provisions began to emerge. This would involve on the one hand a regime for ice-covered areas, where the standards enacted by coastal states would not be subject to review, and on the other hand a regime for other vulnerable areas, where the approval of an international organization (imco) would be required before special coastal state standards could become effective. But Canada could not endorse any formal position along these lines until the details of a regime for ice-covered areas were worked out. Moreover, a separation of "Arctic" from other areas at this stage might have appeared to be an abandonment of the non-Arctic supporters of the "special measures" approach. Also, the position of Canada at the Geneva session was being made difficult by the characterization of the Canadian approach in the press as expansionist and greedy. Canada was seen to be in the forefront of "creeping jurisdiction."

In most respects the Geneva session in the summer of 1975 did little to advance the Canadian position on special measures generally or on ice-covered areas in particular. As a result of general frustration over lack of progress in all areas, the conference chairman took the initiative in having each committee chairman draw up a set of draft articles representing the "trend" in negotiations, hence giving rise to the "single negotiating text" (SNT). This text went through several revisions, both in name and in substance, and ultimately emerged as the 1982 Convention on the Law of the Sea. There was no provision in the SNT applicable to Arctic waters as such. The chairman of committee III had instead included – in Article 20(c) – the more general "special measures" provision, under which the coastal state had authority to enact such measures in "areas of the economic zone where particularly severe climatic conditions create obstructions or exceptional hazards to navigation."

Following the Geneva session the same pattern continued – bilateral consultations between Canada and the other two major Arctic states, and multilateral consultations in the "Evensen Group." The problem was to find a formulation that would not go beyond what would be acceptable to the United States but at the same time would go far enough to satisfy the Soviet Union that its own, more extensive claim to full sovereignty over its Arctic waters was not compromised. Of course, any form of international review of nationally established standards through IMCO, as advocated by the United States, was not acceptable to the Soviet Union.

The question of specially vulnerable areas had still not been resolved by the time the spring 1976 session of UNCLOS began in New York. But the nature of the compromise seemed increasingly clear. The area in which national standards would be applied would be restricted to "ice-covered areas," and Canada would acquiesce in U.S. proposals on the transit passage regime for international straits. Intensive trilateral negotiations continued, and by April 1976 the compromise had been obtained. There was to be a special provision for ice-covered areas, the langauge for which had been carefully negotiated, under which coastal states would have the right to "adopt and enforce non-discriminatory laws and regulations for the prevention, reduction and control of marine pollution from vessels in ice-covered areas within the limits of the exclusive economic zone," subject to certain specified conditions.[33] A new article was to be included as a separate section of the revised single negotiating text (RSNT) (section IX), under the heading "Ice-Covered Areas." The earlier "special measures" provision, which applied more broadly to special areas of the economic zone, was restricted in scope, and the measures so adopted were to be subject to review by IMCO.[34] Thus a price for the "Arctic exception" was the depreciation of the wider claim to a right of the coastal state to enact its own standards in non-Arctic exceptionally vulnerable areas of the economic zone.

The ice-covered areas provision also effected a careful compromise on the question of the relationship of the Northwest Passage to the "international straits" regime under the Convention. No express provision was made to exclude the Northwest Passage from that regime, and thus neither the United States nor Canada was required to take a position on the matter. However, the intention of the compromise is readily apparent. The ice-covered areas provision is not included in the sections of part XII of the Convention that are subject to the international straits regime. Since the ice-covered areas provision clearly applies to the Northwest Passage, and since the ice-covered areas provision is not subject to the international straits regime, *ergo* the international straits regime is not applicable to the Northwest Passage.[35] Canada was not required to seek a special dispensation for the Northwest Passage, nor was the United States required to make a formal exception to the international straits regime. The result was satisfactory for the Soviet Union as well. The issue of Arctic waters was essentially removed from the UNCLOS agenda without any attack on the Soviet position of full sovereignty over its Arctic waters.[36]

Thus the "Arctic exception" was established as of 1976. Although the conference continued for another six years, this provision was not in dispute and it emerged as Article 234 in the final Convention adopted on 12 December 1982.

THE SUCCESS OF A STRATEGY

The negotiation of Article 234 is a major achievement of Canadian foreign policy. In the space of six years, Canada went from the assertion of a claim to jurisdiction in domestic legislation that was protested by other states, and the international validity of which was sufficiently in doubt for Canada to withdraw its acceptance of the jurisdiction of the ICJ, to international recognition of the acceptability of that legislation. How was this achieved? Several factors – timing, forum, personnel, tactics – contributed to the result.

The matter arose at a propitious time. There was world-wide awareness of the need for the protection of the marine environment, coupled with a general movement away from the old laissez-faire concept of freedom of the seas. The question of jurisdiction over Arctic waters, which in isolation might as a matter of principle have engaged the interest of other states, was simply one of many issues to be negotiated as part of a much larger law of the sea package. States not directly concerned with Arctic waters were content therefore to leave the matter to those states with a direct interest. If, for example, non-Arctic states had shown the interest in Arctic areas that is now being shown in the Antarctic by states with no traditional interest in the area, then the prospects for the negotiation of Article 234 might well have been diminished.

The Law of the Sea Conference provided an opportune forum for the negotiation of an Arctic waters provision. Notwithstanding the fact that actual negotiations ultimately involved only three countries (the United States, the Soviet Union, and Canada), the broader framework provided an opportunity to gain support from other countries which was essential in the early stages of the "special measures" provisions. It also provided a context in which there could be a trade-off between Canadian support for u.s. international straits provision and u.s. support for an "Arctic exception." The pressure for a "package deal" within the conference framework provided an incentive for some accommodation on all issues. In this regard, the position of the Soviet Union was key, in its explicit support for the Canadian position, and in the fact that by comparison with the more extreme Soviet position on full sovereignty over its adjacent Arctic waters the Canadian functional approach appeared much more reasonable. Moreover, the techniques of negotiation that were developed at UNCLOS, which involved informal consultations and negotiations outside the formal conference framework, and consensus decision-making,[37] enhanced the opportunity for the three states to work out their own deal and then incorporate it within the conference package.

There is no doubt that a major factor in the achievement of Article 234 was the skill and tenacity of an able team of officials, spearheaded by the deputy representative of Canada to the Law of the Sea Conference, J. Alan Beesley. Its approach to the issue was co-ordinated within the Legal Bureau of the Department of External Affairs, which controlled the Interdepartmental Committee on the Law of the Sea. It thus was able to ensure that a consistent position was maintained, notwithstanding the lack of unqualified support in some departments. Backed by a clear political mandate, enunciated in the 1970 Arctic waters legislation and affirmed in statements of the Prime Minister and the Secretary of State for External Affairs, these officials were able to use their negotiating skills to ensure that the Canadian position was understood, to ensure that incompatible "special measures" positions were not put forward by other states, and to forge alliances. At the same time they were able to maintain bilateral dialogues with the United States and with the Soviet Union.

The Canadian position on the other items on the agenda of the conference was also maintained, and the "Arctic exception" was achieved without the sacrifice of major Canadian interests. Canada, it is true, came to lend its support to the new international straits regime, but Canada had no particular interest in opposing the straits regime once the question of Arctic waters was resolved.[38] Thus the critical issue in the negotiation of the "Arctic exception" was how and when Canadian support for the straits provision was to be offered. The Canadian negotiators did not lend that support too early; rather they waited until the opportune moment presented itself. In sum, the Canadian negotiating stance was characterized by cohesion, perseverance, and pragmatism.

THE NEGOTIATION OF

ARTICLE 234: AN ASSESSMENT

There is no doubt that the Canadian international legal strategy in respect of Arctic waters, from the first voyage of the *Manhattan* through to the conclusion of UNCLOS at the end of 1982, was enlightened. The functional approach, it became clear, was precisely the strategy that would secure Canadian objectives. The pursuit of a claim to treat the waters of the Arctic archipelago as the internal waters of Canada at that time might well have resulted in insuperable opposition from the United States and other maritime states to *any* claim by Canada to exercise jurisdiction over those waters. In the context of a multilateral negotiation regarding the oceans, in which different positions were to be traded off or compromised, an explicit internal waters claim might well have been too extreme. Yet, as Canada took care to point out upon the enactment of the Arctic waters legislation of 1970, a functional claim to jurisdiction was not a renunciation of any claim on historic or other grounds to treat the waters of the Arctic archipelago as the internal waters of Canada. It was nevertheless implicit that if the jurisdiction claimed by Canada under the 1970 legislation were to receive international acceptance, there would be less need to pursue an internal waters claim in order to protect Arctic waters from the consequences of navigation.

Although securing Article 234 was a major policy success, the failure of the United States and some other maritime states[39] to sign the Convention leaves a question about the future of the Convention and of certain provisions within it. Unless a future U.S. administration decides to become a party to the Convention, Article 234 cannot be binding as between Canada and the United States as a matter of treaty law, although it has been argued that the provision is accepted in customary international law.[40] Thus the future attitude of the United States towards rights over Arctic waters independently of the Convention becomes of particular importance. There are two questions to be considered. Will the United States recognize that the right embodied in Article 234 is, for all practical purposes, part of customary international law and applicable in its relations with Canada apart from the 1982 Law of the Sea Convention? Will the United States accept that Canada's Arctic waters legislation is a valid exercise of the jurisdiction permitted under Article 234?

In this regard there are indications that the U.S. position on Article 234 is ambiguous. There have been suggestions that the Canadian claim to jurisdiction over Arctic waters under the Arctic Waters Pollution Prevention Act goes beyond the extent of acceptable coastal state jurisdiction over such waters,[41] but it has also been said that Article 234 lends legitimacy to the Canadian legislation.[42] The opportunity to make the position clear was not taken in the U.S. proclamation of a 200-mile exclusive zone in March 1983.[43] There is, therefore, a need for clarification of the U.S. position.

It might nevertheless be asked whether it was really necessary to obtain a provision such as Article 234. If the protection of the Arctic marine environment is the desired end, what is the most effective method of achieving that end – a claim to sovereignty, a claim to functional jurisdiction (Article 234), or co-operative arrangements with potential users of Arctic waters, in particular, with the United States? The question is important. Given the current state of uncertainty over U.S. attitudes towards Article 234 and towards Canada's Arctic waters legislation, there will be pressure for Canada either to hold to its claim to the waters of the Canadian Arctic as the internal waters of Canada, or to put aside the question of sovereignty and establish a "management regime" over the waters of the Arctic archipelago in co-operation with the United States and other states.

There are a number of arguments in support of a co-operative regime for the management of the waters of the Arctic archipelago,[44] and there are examples of Canadian-U.S. bilateral arrangements – the International Joint Commission is the pre-eminent instance – that give a practical illustration of how such a regime might be carried out. Moreover, proposals for co-operative management regimes tend to focus on the administrative and technical advantages of the arrangement and play down jurisdictional or sovereignty questions. This gives the impression that the latter are issues that complicate the "real" issues of management. Yet, as the Canadian negotiators of Article 234 recognized, it is impossible to sever the question of jurisdiction from the technical and administrative side of "management" of the waters. Ultimately, in any management arrangement between two states there has to be an answer to the question: who has jurisdiction over a particular area or over a particular activity? In the absence of a clear delineation of jurisdiction, a co-operative management regime amounts to recognition that the states concerned share jurisdiction over the area. In other words, a co-operative management regime over Arctic waters between Canada and the United States would be tantamount to recognizing that jurisdiction over Arctic waters was *shared* between Canada and the United States.

Questions of jurisdiction inevitably come down to pragmatic considerations of the exercise of criminal and civil authority and the enforcement of standards. Any regime designed to manage the transit of shipping through Arctic waters and to establish a regime of environmental standards will find that such questions are central rather than secondary. The application of civil and criminal authority presupposes the existence of jurisdiction in one state or another. The question of jurisdiction simply cannot be avoided.

The Canadian negotiators of Article 234 correctly perceived that there were only two options to pursue in achieving Canadian objectives for environmental management in Arctic waters – a claim to sovereignty over the waters or a claim to functional jurisdiction. They also saw that in the circumstances of that time only a more restrictive claim was likely to meet with success. Events proved them correct. The Canadian "special measures" provision had as its objective international recognition of the jurisdiction asserted by Canada under its Arctic waters legislation. The wording of Article 234 specifically embodied that recognition.[45] There was no doubt in the minds of the UNCLOS negotiators, Canadian or otherwise, that the Canadian legislation was the reason for the Arctic exception, and there was no doubt that Article 234 was designed to give it specific approval. What the Canadian negotiators were not able to foresee was that events unrelated to the Arctic would leave some doubt about U.S. acceptance of the package deal embodied in the Convention, and therefore of the "Arctic exception." The efficacy of Article 234 as a generally accepted basis of authority for the exercise of environmental jurisdiction in Arctic waters has yet to be proved beyond doubt.

CHAPTER SIX

Arctic Shipping:
An American Perspective

ORAN R. YOUNG

Since the s/т *Manhattan*, an ice-strengthened American supertanker, steamed through the Northwest Passage in 1969, informed observers on both sides of the border have anticipated an increasingly severe conflict between Canada and the United States over Arctic shipping. Canada reacted to the voyage of the *Manhattan* swiftly and unilaterally, asserting authority to control pollution in Arctic waters by means of the Arctic Waters Pollution Prevention Act of 1970. The United States has consistently refused to accept the validity of this legislation as far as non-Canadians are concerned. Canadian representatives lobbied hard at sessions of the Third United Nations Conference on the Law of the Sea (UNCLOS) through the 1970s for the inclusion of Article 234, a special provision extending the regulatory authority of coastal states in ice-covered areas. American representatives pressed equally hard for provisions guaranteeing "non-suspendable" transit rights in the articles pertaining to international straits (Articles 34-45). What is more, the United States has refused to sign the completed Law of the Sea Convention, raising doubts about the future status of this convention with regard to Canadian-American relations.

The thesis of this chapter, nonetheless, is that Canadian-American conflict over Arctic shipping is more apparent than real. This putative conflict is largely an artifact of the propensity of the parties to formulate issues relating to Arctic shipping in jurisdictional terms, thereby forcing themselves to address the problem in the mode of distributive bargaining. Yet Canada and the United States need not adopt this approach. There is nothing to prevent them from setting jurisdictional questions aside without prejudice and proceeding to develop an international regime for Arctic shipping. Approaching the matter in this way would open up numerous opportunities to explore mutual interests through a process of integrative bargaining, in contrast to distributive bargaining.[1]

PROSPECTS FOR ARCTIC SHIPPING

Swept along by evidence suggesting the technical feasibility of Arctic shipping and by the expansive spirit underlying the idea of a "great Arctic energy rush," most observers simply assume that the next two or three decades will witness a rapid growth in Arctic shipping.[2] But this is hardly a foregone conclusion. Even among those who confidently expect marked growth in Arctic shipping, moreover, the relative merits of ice-breaking supertankers and submarine tankers of varying proportions are far from settled.

The future of Arctic shipping rests on a series of factors that will determine the course of non-renewable resource development (and especially oil and natural gas development) in the region. These include: the magnitude of recoverable reserves of hydrocarbons located in the Arctic, the attractiveness of Arctic oil and gas in economic or commercial terms, the political attractions of the non-renewable resources of the Arctic, and the relative merits of alternative methods of transporting Arctic resources to southern markets. Significant uncertainties regarding each of these factors make it difficult to predict the future of Arctic shipping with any confidence.

Many commentators believe that up to 50 per cent of the earth's remaining undiscovered reserves of hydrocarbons are located north of 60°N latitude. Since the massive strike at Prudhoe Bay in 1968, however, discoveries of proved reserves of oil and gas in the North American Arctic have been few and far between. Several significant (though much smaller) fields have turned up in areas adjacent to Prudhoe Bay, and scattered deposits of gas and oil have been located in the Canadian high Arctic islands and the Beaufort Sea.[3] But there have also been major disappointments in areas widely expected to contain sizeable deposits of oil and gas (for example, the u.s. lease sale no. 71 area). At the same time, exploratory efforts in several areas outside the Arctic (for example, eastern Canada, the Gulf of Mexico, the South and East China seas) have produced promising evidence of large recoverable reserves of hydrocarbons. None of this demonstrates that there will be no Arctic "energy rush" during the foreseeable future. But it does remind us of the profound uncertainties surrounding the search for hydrocarbons in areas like the Arctic.

No matter how large the recoverable reserves of the far north, Arctic oil and gas will always be expensive to produce.[4] This is a function of the severity of operating conditions in the Arctic coupled with the problems of transporting Arctic hydrocarbons to distant markets, and it is not subject to change. As a result, the commercial attractiveness of Arctic oil and gas will be particularly sensitive to fluctuations in supply and demand in world markets. If demand fails to rise steadily (due to such things as energy conservation), or if supplies prove plentiful (due to the development of alternative energy sources or discoveries of oil and gas elsewhere), the marginal hydrocarbons of the Arctic will be among the first to become unattractive in purely commercial terms. What is more, the fact that Arctic oil and gas are expensive to produce and ship makes Arctic development economically vulnerable to the activities of organizations like OPEC which influence world market prices for oil and gas over and above the normal interaction of supply and demand. Because most OPEC oil is relatively cheap to produce and deliver, OPEC could destroy the commercial attractiveness of Arctic oil and gas should it choose to do so. It is therefore hard to escape the conclusion that the development of Arctic oil and gas reserves will always be risky in purely commercial terms.

What ultimately drives the search for Arctic oil and gas is the attractiveness of this energy source in political terms. Because the North American Arctic is controlled by the United States and Canada, many Americans regard the development of Arctic hydrocarbons as a promising route to energy independence.[5] But even this impetus does not ensure that we will witness an Arctic "energy rush" during the foreseeable future. Many thoughtful Americans are more interested in the pursuit of conservation, enhanced efficiency, and energy alternatives than in deploying ever more advanced technology to conquer the Arctic. The development of the Strategic Petroleum Reserve has ameliorated the fears of many concerning new oil embargoes.[6] Both environmentalists and native peoples are presenting powerful arguments in important political arenas concerning the disruptive potential of oil and gas development under Arctic conditions. For its part, Canada has ample energy reserves outside the Arctic to ensure energy self-sufficiency for itself for years to come.[7] Given the influence of nationalist sentiment in Canada in recent years, moreover, we cannot simply assume that Canadian governments will be moved to join an Arctic "energy rush" in order to promote energy independence for the United States. While the political attractions of Arctic oil and gas are real, therefore, they are not so overwhelming that we can confidently predict that recoverable reserves of oil and gas in the Arctic will be developed at a rapid pace.

Beyond this, the relative merits of alternative methods of transporting Arctic oil and gas are anything but settled.[8] Many analysts suggest that marine transport, whether by ice-breaking supertanker or by submarine tanker, has great attractions in terms of flexibility. It is possible for ships to roam widely, loading oil or gas even from relatively small fields. At the same time, it appears that pipelines are more reliable than marine transport and that this may continue to be the case for years to come. Perhaps because pipelines have become a fact of life in the north, opposition to proposals for new pipelines is now somewhat less vociferous than opposition to plans for marine transport on the part of environmentalists and native peoples.[9] What is more, there are many cases in which it is possible to configure pipelines in such a way that they fall wholly within the jurisdiction of a single state, thereby avoiding the inevitable complications of international co-ordination regarding the transport of oil and gas.

Within the framework of this broad picture, there are significant national variations regarding the prospects for Arctic shipping. The political attractions of Arctic oil and gas are undoubtedly greater for the United States than for Canada. The United States is a large energy importer possessing few new sources of recoverable reserves of hydrocarbons outside the Arctic. Canada, by contrast, is largely energy self-sufficient, and it has excellent prospects for developing new reserves of hydrocarbons outside the Arctic (for example, the Hibernia area off Newfoundland, if not the Sable Island area off Nova Scotia).[10] However, marine transport is apt to hold much greater attractions for the movement of oil and gas from the Canadian Arctic than from the American Arctic. Reserves in the Canadian Beaufort Sea and the high Arctic islands are likely to take the form of relatively small deposits scattered over an enormous area. American Arctic reserves are more likely to consist of a few large deposits located in the Beaufort fringe or the coastal segment of the Arctic National Wildlife Refuge, where they can be tied into existing or proposed pipeline systems focused on Prudhoe Bay. None of this proves that those who foresee substantial growth of Arctic shipping in the next two or three decades will turn out to be wrong. But it certainly does warrant the observation that developments along these lines hardly constitute a foregone conclusion.

SOURCES OF CONFLICT

Nonetheless, both Canada and the United States have vital interests that could be affected by any significant development of Arctic shipping.[11] Several of these interests will be operative under virtually any foreseeable circumstances. Others will vary in their import as a function of such things as the course of East-West relations, the tone of north-south interaction, and the tides of nationalism or protectionist sentiments in Canada and the United States. It is the configuration of these interests that has led many observers to anticipate an increasingly severe conflict between Canada and the United States regarding Arctic shipping.

Political interests

For shorthand purposes, we can use the term *sovereignty* to characterize Canada's political interests in the high Arctic.[12] Partly, this is a matter of natural sensibilities regarding the physical integrity of the nation.[13] Under the most optimistic of assumptions, Canada's presence in the high Arctic will remain thin for the indefinite future. It is therefore not totally unrealistic to imagine threats to Canada's "effective occupation" of the region. In part, the concern for Arctic sovereignty is a deep-seated symbolic one. Because many Canadians think of Canada as a northern country, it is important to their sense of national identity to exert the widest possible control over the high Arctic. For this reason, commentators frequently treat northern sovereignty as a core objective of Canadian foreign policy.

In fact, no one questions Canadian sovereignty over the islands located in the Canadian sector of the Arctic.[14] The critical issue, therefore, concerns control over the waters of the Canadian Arctic archipelago (some would extend this to the waters of the Arctic sector stretching northward to the Pole). Many Canadians have favoured assertion of total control over these waters, claiming them as internal waters of Canada or at least as parts of the Canadian territorial sea. Indeed, the Canadian government has now moved formally to enclose the waters of the archipelago as internal waters. Yet Canada has other political interests that cut against such an expansive assertion of control. Should Canada persist in this course, others (such as the United States, Greenland/Denmark, and the Soviet Union) could be encouraged to follow suit in their sectors of the Arctic. Developments along these lines might well yield greater losses than gains for Canada in the long run.[15] What is more, taking the lead in the enclosure movement for marine areas runs counter to Canada's long-standing policy of promoting international co-operation in many realms. While adopting a relatively extreme position on Arctic sovereignty may satisfy the nationalistic aspirations of certain Canadians at the present time, such a posture could prove costly in terms of Canada's larger role and reputation in the international community.

The political interests of the United States in the high Arctic, by contrast, can be captured in the terms *security* and *energy independence.*[16] Until recently, it was widely held that the strategic significance of the Arctic had waned as a consequence of the decline of the manned bomber as a delivery vehicle for strategic weapons. But several recent developments have radically altered this situation, focusing renewed interest on the Arctic in terms of security.[17] These developments include the deployment of cruise missiles, the increased vulnerability of land-based missile systems, and the growing importance of the Arctic ice pack as a hiding place for submarine-based missile systems. As a result, the United States has moved vigorously to initiate such projects as the construction of a North Warning System (an upgraded version of the DEW Line of the 1950s) and the development of more sophisticated anti-submarine warfare (ASW) devices for use in the Arctic. What all this means is that it is exceedingly unlikely that the United States will acquiesce during the foreseeable future in any form of Canadian control over the waters of the Arctic archipelago that substantially reduces the transit rights of American vessels in these waters, allows Canada to require submarines to pass through Arctic waters on the surface (which would mean no passage unless a comic new type of ship were to be built – the icebreaking submarine), or limits the use of the superjacent airspace.

No doubt, the Arctic is less vital to the United States in terms of energy independence than in terms of security. Conservation and alternative energy sources are proving to be live options. Substantial new oil and gas reserves are being located in other parts of the world. The Strategic Petroleum Reserve is becoming a reality. Yet the goal of energy independence is a powerful political force in the United States, and the idea of the Arctic as a store-house of hydrocarbons is firmly implanted in the public mind. It is therefore unrealistic to expect the United States to accept jurisdictional arrangements for the Arctic that could curtail the ability of American companies to move Arctic oil and gas to southern markets. Any such move would appear to undermine the very features of the Arctic that make its oil and gas politically attractive.

Economic interests

Both Canada and the United States have general economic interests as well as specialized economic interests in the Arctic. The United States may come to regard Arctic oil and gas as a secure source of energy, providing protection against energy shocks like those of the 1970s and contributing to continued growth of productivity in the American economy. Canada may exploit Arctic hydrocarbons to develop an export market in the hopes that this will help to restore a sagging Canadian economy. In more specific terms, the Canadian government may experience irresistible pressure to promote Arctic oil and gas development to prevent a total collapse of Dome Petroleum or to shore up Panarctic Oils Ltd (in which the government of Canada has a large stake).[18] For its part, the government of the United States may experience powerful pressures to bail out companies whose Arctic ventures have run into serious trouble. The efforts of the Reagan administration to facilitate the financing of the Alaska Natural Gas Transport System (ANGTS) illustrate this prospect.

Is there any reason to expect these economic interests to lead to Canadian-U.S. conflict over Arctic shipping? Restrictive Canadian regulations for marine transport in the Arctic could certainly become an irritant. Unwillingness on the part of American financiers to provide funds for future Canadian projects involving Arctic shipping (such as the now defunct Arctic Pilot Project) could cause friction. The Canadian government could even seek to restrict American shipping in the Arctic for the express purpose of forcing the United States to import Canadian oil or gas on Canadian terms. Yet all these possibilities are a little remote and unpersuasive. In reality, the strictly economic interests of the two countries in Arctic shipping do not appear incompatible. In contrast to the case of political interests, there is nothing in these economic interests that cannot be worked out handily through the efforts of technical experts.

Environmental interests

The fact that large-scale shipping has never occurred in the North American Arctic makes it impossible to evaluate the probable environmental impact of such shipping on the basis of experience. Nonetheless, there are good reasons to be highly sensitive to the potential environmental disruptions of Arctic shipping.[19] The Arctic exercises a powerful influence on global climate patterns; the characterization of the Arctic as the world's "weather kitchen" is apt. Arctic ecosystems are undoubtedly fragile in some important respects. It takes extraordinary lengths of time for Arctic ecosystems to recover from serious disruptions. Above all, many Arctic systems are poorly understood, so that it is impossible to make confident predictions regarding the environmental impact of Arctic shipping.

Without doubt, concern about Arctic environmental matters has risen rapidly in recent years in both Canada and the United States, and it seems fair to say that this concern is now becoming institutionalized in both political systems. It is possible to argue over the relative impact of environmental considerations in the policy-making processes of the two countries (for example, is the American environmental impact assessment process more or less effective than the Canadian?). But environmental interests have become important factors in both Canadian and American policy-making. Even more important for this discussion, however, there is no reason to anticipate any serious conflict between Canadian and American environmental interests regarding Arctic shipping. Canada has exhibited great concern about the environmental integrity of the Lancaster Sound area.[20] The United States has displayed similar sensitivity to the welfare of the Bowhead whale stocks of the western Arctic.[21] However, environmental concerns may not have been accorded sufficient weight in the Canadian controversy over port facilities at Stokes Point.[22] Much the same can be said regarding the American controversy over seasonal drilling restrictions in the Beaufort Sea.[23] In short, both countries are clearly concerned about the potential environmental consequences of Arctic shipping, but there is no guarantee than environmental interests will dominate policy-making in either country.

Social interests

During the 1970s and 1980s, the Eskimo or Inuit residents of the high

Arctic have acquired an increasingly effective voice regarding plans for Arctic development. Partly, this is a result of growing receptivity in American, Canadian, and Danish societies to the claims of minorities couched in terms of rights. It is no longer politically acceptable in any of these societies simply to ignore the rights of minority groups in the interests of serving the needs of dominant groups. In part, it stems from the growing financial and political capabilities of the indigenous peoples of the North American Arctic. Both the financial resources of the North Slope Borough in Alaska and the significance of the Inuit Circumpolar Conference as a political forum for the articulation of native interests are beyond doubt. [24]

What this means in the present context is that the potential impact of Arctic shipping on the remote communities of the Arctic cannot be ignored. If anything, the Inuit from Alaska to Greenland are more vocal and united in their opposition to Arctic shipping than they are to Arctic pipelines. A single shipping route could produce significant effects on communities from Greenland to Alaska; pipelines seldom affect such a broad array of peoples. What is more, it is reasonable to expect that Arctic shipping will have more severe effects on the subsistence practices of indigenous peoples than pipelines. Most of these peoples have developed maritime adaptations; they are "hunters of the northern ice." [25] Additionally, existing pipelines have compiled a relatively good record in these terms; Arctic shipping may well generate currently unpredictable but potentially frightening consequences. What this means is that both the Canadian and U.S. governments will experience strong pressure to weigh social interests heavily in their decisions regarding Arctic shipping. But it does not suggest the emergence of serious conflict between the two countries regarding Arctic shipping. On the contrary, the United States and Canada will experience significant incentives to co-operate in an effort to minimize social effects in the event that large-scale Arctic shipping eventually occurs.

Research interests

It is probably fair to conclude that research in the North American Arctic has been less extensive over the last several decades than research in Antarctica. [26] But this may soon begin to change. The Arctic Research and Policy Act of 1984 (Public Law 98-373) should give a boost to Arctic research in the United States. Similar pressures to increase support for Arctic research in Canada may produce results in the near future. Of course, the expansion of research may contribute to an intensification of conflict if research programs are harnessed to nationalistic goals. It is a cause for some concern that recent Canadian work in the field of marine geology (for example, the exploration of the Alpha Ridge) is so closely linked to Canadian interests in expansive assertions of northern sovereign-ty.[27] Similarly, the fact that American Arctic research has often been tied closely to the security interests of the United States is hardly a source of comfort.

Yet the rise of serious interest in Arctic shipping could both provide a great boost for Arctic research in a number of fields and serve as a basis for fruitful Canadian-u.s. collaboration in the Arctic. Whatever our preferences may be, most research is stimulated by practical concerns. Undoubtedly, the growth of shipping over the Northern Sea Route has been a major factor underlying the importance attached to Arctic research in the Soviet Union.[28] Regular shipping in the North American Arctic would produce a pressing need for better information concerning such matters as hydrolo-gy, ice dynamics, weather patterns, and Arctic ecosystems. Far from being a source of conflict, the resultant research programs could serve to promote Canadian-u.s. co-operation with respect to Arctic shipping. The research needs of authorities in both countries would be much the same. It would make sense to avoid unnecessary duplication in the area of expensive Arctic research. Scientists also have an outstanding record of being able to collaborate productively, even in cases where their national governments are at odds.

This brief account of the prospects for Arctic shipping over the next several decades as well as the character of Canadian and American interests in Arctic shipping does *not* warrant the conclusion that this issue-area is likely to precipitate a crisis in Canadian-u.s. relations during the foreseeable future. Even so, there is a persuasive case for coming to terms with issues pertaining to Arctic shipping now. Though Arctic shipping has the poten-tial to generate relatively severe frictions between the two countries, no genuinely intractable conflicts have arisen in this area to date. The fact that large-scale Arctic shipping is not an immediate prospect makes it possible to consider issues relating to this subject with a certain calmness and objectivity. As I shall demonstrate in the remaining sections of this chapter, there are solutions to the outstanding issues relating to Arctic shipping that would secure the vital interests of both countries and provide for management strategies that meet the needs of those actually engaged in or affected by Arctic shipping. No doubt, the occasionally abrasive character of Canadian-u.s. relations in recent years could constitute a barrier to the successful resolution of outstanding issues relating to Arctic shipping. Approached from another angle, however, success in resolving Canadian-u.s. differences regarding Arctic shipping could contribute significantly to the initiation of a constructive dialogue between the two countries on a number of other issues (for example, acid rain, fisheries management, defence installations, and economic imperialism v. economic nationalism).[29]

THE POLITICS OF JURISDICTION

Much of the air of conflict surrounding Arctic shipping stems from the propensity of the parties to formulate issues relating to this matter in jurisdictional terms. Broadly, jurisdiction involves the demarcation of boundaries within which authority may be exercised.[30] Many jurisdictional boundaries are geographical in nature. Debates concerning the breadth of the territorial sea or the locus of baselines demarcating the inner boundary of the territorial sea exemplify this class of boundaries. Alternatively, jurisdictional boundaries may be demarcated in functional terms. States may assert jurisdiction over specific functions, such as outer continental shelf oil and gas development or pollution control, without claiming jurisdiction over other activities occurring in the same area. It is conventional to speak of sovereignty or sovereign authority when a state exercises authority over the full range of functional activities taking place within a well-defined geographical area.

These observations make it clear that bundles of jurisdictional claims are not indivisible. There is nothing to prevent one state from exercising authority over certain activities (for example, commercial fishing) in a given area while other states exercise authority over other activities (for example, maritime transport) in the same area. By way of illustration, this is precisely the situation that has arisen in recent years with regard to fishery conservation zones. When the relevant activities affect or even interfere with one another, of course, it is necessary for the states involved to work out some system of rights and rules to resolve the resultant conflicts. Whether they take the form of informal conventions or explicit agreements articulated in formal treaties, the operation of these systems of rights and rules gives rise to international regimes.

There are several reasons why the formulation of issues relating to Arctic shipping in jurisdictional terms has the effect of heightening Canadian-u.s. conflict and promoting undesirable outcomes. At best, the resolution of jurisdictional disputes is apt to become a matter of distributive bargaining. Worse yet, jurisdictional differences may well give rise to disputes in which there is no contract zone or zone of agreement in the positions of the parties.[31] Consider the Canadian-u.s. dispute over Arctic shipping in this light. Canada insists that the waters of the Northwest Passage and the Arctic archipelago should be treated as internal waters of Canada. But "non-suspendable" transit rights and rights to use the superjacent airspace are not guaranteed in internal waters or even in territorial seas. Given the interests of the United States in the high Arctic, it follows that the United States cannot accede to Canada's claims regarding internal waters or territorial seas. Any disposition of the problem formulated in this fashion would therefore require one party to become a clear-cut loser. Not only is it unlikely that either party will accept such an outcome voluntarily, it is also likely to prove costly in terms of the future of Canadian-u.s. relations more generally.

Even where there is a zone of agreement regarding jurisdictional issues, the resultant bargaining will generally take the form of distributive politics. In its essentials, that is, the situation will resemble a negotiation between a buyer and a seller over the purchase price of a house or between labour and management over wage rates. There may be certain outcomes that both sides prefer to an outcome of no agreement, but each party will concentrate on devising tactics designed to procure the best possible outcome for itself in distributive terms rather than developing new opportunities for mutually beneficial relationships. Any jurisdictional claims that the United States concedes to Canada would constitute a deterioration in the "terms of trade" from an American point of view and vice versa. As is well known, distributive bargaining of this type routinely produces a preoccupation with bargaining tactics and often leads to protracted stalemates which are costly to all parties concerned.[32] Because such interactions are frequently seen as tests of bargaining strength, moreover, participants regularly choose to sacrifice the prospects of gains in specific situations in order to avoid any appearance of weakness that might prompt others to press harder for concessions in concurrent or subsequent negotiations.

Even if the United States and Canada were to reach some agreement regarding the jurisdictional status of the waters of the Northwest Passage and the Arctic archipelago, this would do nothing to resolve many of the major management problems that would arise in connection with regular Arctic shipping. Here there are two distinct cases to consider: the case of icebreaking supertankers and the case of submarine tankers. Most plausible routings would take icebreaking supertankers (carrying either oil or liquid natural gas) through the jurisdictional zones of two or more of the following states: Greenland/Denmark, Canada, and the United States. It follows that none of the North American Arctic states can promote this mode of transport without explicitly co-ordinating its management practices with one or both of the others. What this suggests is the importance of joint problem-solving with regard to Arctic shipping, in contrast to the strategic manoeuvring characteristic of distributive bargaining. This point has particular significance for Canadian policy-makers because the most probable impetus to the introduction of icebreaking supertankers in the Arctic during the foreseeable future will be efforts to move Canadian hydrocarbons to the east coast through the jurisdictional zone of Greenland/Canada or to Japan through the jurisdictional zone of the United States.

The case of submarine tankers raises different management problems, because these tankers would not be confined to the waterways of the Northwest Passage, restricted areas of Baffin Bay, and the Beaufort Sea fringe.[33] Submarine tankers taking on oil and gas at terminals in Alaska, Canada, or Greenland would be able to deliver their cargoes to southern markets without entering the jurisdictional zones of other countries. A partial exception to this might occur if every Arctic state were to advance and enforce the most extreme sort of sector claim.[34] Even this might complicate the situation more for submarine tanker routes originating in Canada than for routes originating in Alaska or Greenland. What is important to notice about this case, however, is the fact that the dangers of marine pollution would not decline despite the ability of shippers to escape the regulatory requirements of one or more of the North American Arctic states. This is so because of the natural conditions prevailing in the Arctic. Oil takes years or even decades to degrade under Arctic conditions, and spilled oil (especially spilled oil trapped in ice) would tend to circulate around the Arctic Basin just as ice islands do today.[35] What all this means is that a Canadian-u.s. agreement regarding the jurisdictional status of the waters of the Northwest Passage and the Arctic archipelago would do little to solve the real management problems associated with submarine tanker traffic in the Arctic. If the effort to reach such an agreement produced an atmosphere of strategic manoeuvring and abrasive conflict, moreover, the prospects for dealing with the problems of submarine tanker traffic in a co-operative mode would decline.

Beyond this, the resolution of outstanding issues relating to Arctic shipping through the specification of some system of jurisdictional zones would constitute a bad precedent, or even a step in the wrong direction, when it comes to handling other important Arctic issues. The dangers to Arctic ecosystems associated with maritime transport are real. But several other environmental concerns are equally important, if not more impor-tant, in the Arctic today. Arctic haze has become a severe problem that could generate massive effects on global weather patterns. Oil spills and chronic discharges from offshore platforms are at least as worrisome as the potential disruptive effects of Arctic shipping. The industrialization of the Arctic poses numerous threats to the welfare of marine mammal stocks. A common feature of all these problems is that they cannot be controlled by states acting unilaterally within arbitrarily demarcated jurisdictional zones.[36] Arctic haze pervades the Arctic Basin; the currents of the Beaufort Sea flow back and forth across the Canadian-u.s. boundary, and so forth. Efforts to cope with these problems will require co-operative and co-ordinated actions on the part of all the Arctic states. Under the circum-stances, the precedent that would be set by the resolution of issues relating to Arctic shipping through the demarcation of national jurisdictional zones would inevitably make it more difficult to solve many of the environmental concerns of the future in the Arctic.

Finally, the propensity to formulate issues relating to Arctic shipping in jurisdictional terms promotes inappropriate forms of reasoning in this realm. Jurisdictional issues can be resolved only through consistent application of the principles of either the public order of terrestrial spaces or the public order of non-terrestrial spaces. Faced with this choice, most analysts have endeavoured to subsume Arctic issues under the principles of the evolving law of the sea.[37]But this practice regularly yields disturbing anomalies. The Arctic Basin is an ocean, but most of it has a permanent cover of pack or sea ice and the remainder is ice-covered for much of the year. The coastal littorals of the Arctic Basin, by contrast, are underlain with permafrost, so that a great portion of this "land" actually consists of ice. As the Inuit residents of the Arctic have long known, these conditions make the ice of the Arctic Basin a suitable platform on which to carry out many activities that are ordinarily thought of as land-based activities, whereas the coastal littorals do not constitute a suitable platform for many traditional land-based activities.[38] It follows that efforts to force the Arctic into one or another of the major systems of public order must ultimately fail. They cannot resolve issues relating to Arctic shipping in an unambiguous fashion, and they will undoubtedly serve to hinder initiatives aimed at handling other Arctic issues in a constructive manner.

Even among those who agree that Arctic issues should be approached in terms of the principles of the evolving law of the sea, the propensity to formulate these issues in jurisdictional terms leads to profound problems. Assume for a moment (though even this is subject to dispute) that the new Law of the Sea Convention is the appropriate place to look for authoritative statements regarding the principles of the law of the sea.[39] With respect to the issues raised by Arctic shipping, the most striking feature of the Convention is the loosely textured language of the relevant provisions.[40] How exactly should we evaluate claims regarding internal waters (Article 8)? Is Canada justified in drawing straight baselines around the entire Arctic archipelago (Article 7)? Is the Northwest Passage an international strait, or could it become one in the future (Article 34)? Would the regulatory authority accorded to coastal states in ice-covered areas (Article 234) supersede the transit rights of other states in international straits (Article 38)?[41] These and other similar questions cannot be resolved in a clear-cut fashion from a reading of the Convention and associated documents. Plausible cases for any of a number of interpretations can be constructed in these terms.

Such ambiguities also occur regularly in municipal systems, but they are handled through a series of authoritative rulings handed down by appropriate courts. In the case of the outstanding issues relating to Arctic shipping, this approach to clarification is not likely to work. At the time of the enactment of the Arctic Waters Pollution Prevention Act of 1970, Canada declared that it would not accept the authority of the International

Court of Justice over matters pertaining to jurisdiction in the waters of the Northwest Passage and the Arctic archipelago.[42] Though this reservation was revoked in September 1985, the prospect of a decision by the International Court of Justice cannot be reassuring to Canada. Nor is there any reason to expect the United States to be enthusiastic about this approach to resolving jurisdictional issues in the Arctic. All this means that formulating issues relating to Arctic shipping in jurisdictional terms leads to a legal dead end. It can only complicate distributive bargaining between Canada and the United States with inconclusive legal rhetoric in contrast to facilitating the adoption of a problem-solving approach to common concerns.

What makes the argument of this section concerning the problems of jurisdictional politics particularly apposite is the fact that there is an attractive method of setting aside jurisdictional issues relating to Arctic shipping without prejudice to the claims of either Canada or the United States. The simplest way to achieve this result would be to adapt the formula articulated in Article IV of the Antarctic Treaty of 1959 to apply to all areas that may be affected by Arctic shipping. This formula contains two distinct elements, both of which are important with regard to the case of Arctic shipping. Article IV (1) states that agreement to set aside jurisdictional claims does not constitute a renunciation or diminution of any previously asserted rights or claims on the part of any of the contracting parties. Article IV (2) then enunciates a complementary commitment to the effect that no activities taking place under the Antarctic Treaty regime can form a basis for asserting, supporting, or denying the jurisdictional claims of the contracting parties. The effect of this formula is to leave all pre-existing claims intact while allowing co-operative activities to take place in such a way that they will not have any impact on the future status of jurisdictional claims.[43] This formula says nothing about the framework for organizing co-operative activities in Antarctica. But it does serve to clear away an otherwise intractable complex of conflicting jurisdictional claims so that opportunities for co-operative ventures can be addressed in a spirit of integrative bargaining and joint problem-solving.

AN ARCTIC SHIPPING REGIME

Should Canada and the United States agree to set aside jurisdictional claims relating to Arctic shipping without prejudice, what alternative approach should they adopt? The answer advanced in this chapter is that Arctic shipping constitutes an appropriate area for regime formation at the present time. Regimes, like all other social institutions, are interlocking sets of roles, rights, and rules, which give rise to identifiable practices.[44] They generate recognized patterns of behaviour around which the expectations of participating actors converge. International regimes are institutional arrangements governing practices of interest to members of the international community.[45] These practices encompass activities taking place outside the jurisdictional boundaries of sovereign states (for example, high seas fishing or explorations in space), or cutting across the jurisdictional boundaries of states (for example, international commerce and diplomacy).[46]

Efforts to form mutually beneficial regimes sometimes provide an effective method of resolving otherwise intractable disputes. Disputes relating to regional seas (a category to which the Arctic Ocean belongs) appear particularly susceptible to this approach to resolution.[47] The Convention on the Protection of the Marine Environment of the Baltic Sea, signed in Helsinki in 1974, promotes co-operative activities among a group of central and eastern European states that includes both East and West Germany as well as the Soviet Union. The 1976 Convention for the Protection of the Mediterranean Sea against Pollution (the Barcelona Convention) calls for co-ordinated action to control pollution among 18 states that are divided by the East-West conflict, the Arab-Israeli conflict, and the Greek-Turkish conflict. Comparable efforts are now under way to enhance co-operation among the states bordering on the Caribbean Sea. The United Nations Environment Programme (UNEP) has backstopped several of these developments in capable fashion through the articulation of its regional seas program. While no two cases are identical or even strictly comparable, it seems reasonable to infer from these experiences that the idea of forming an Arctic shipping regime is by no means far-fetched.

Formulating issues relating to Arctic shipping as problems of regime formation would yield substantial advantages in contrast to formulating these issues in jurisdictional terms. Working on the terms of a coherent regime fosters a search for new options likely to yield mutual benefits[48] rather than a preoccupation with dividing a predetermined payoff space (that is, a fixed pie). It leads to the ascendance of integrative bargaining – in which the parties work together to enlarge the payoff possibility set – over distributive bargaining. Likewise, the search for new options promotes attitudes of problem-solving in contrast to an emphasis on devising winning tactics.[49] It becomes more important to think about the relative merits of various joint pollution control programs, for example, than to back the other side into a tight spot in order to wring concessions regarding demarcation of jurisdictional boundaries. Equally important, the integrative processes involved in hammering out a mutually beneficial regime will ordinarily leave the parties with a sense of ownership of the product. Parties are likely to become committed much more to an arrangement that they have worked out together in a spirit of co-operation than to some division of a fixed pie that they feel pressured into accepting in nominal terms. This sense of ownership is likely to play a crucial role in facilitating implementation of resulting agreements and in promoting compliance among those subject to the rights and rules of regimes.

What can we say about the substantive content of a regime for Arctic shipping? It is pointless to attempt to lay out a detailed blueprint for such a regime in this essay. There is a large family of possible regimes for Arctic shipping. The process of negotiating the terms of such a regime should lead to the identification of new options that none of us can foresee at this time. It is important for the negotiating teams to formulate many of the provisions of an Arctic shipping regime on their own so that they will develop strong feelings of ownership regarding the outcome. Nonetheless, it is possible to identify what the principal components of an Arctic shipping regime should be and to spell out some of the basic options with regard to each of these components.[50]

Should an Arctic shipping regime be laid out in a formal treaty or convention, or would it suffice to let this regime take the form of a series of informal understandings among the participants? Those who adopt the perspective of rational planning and social engineering will no doubt prefer to see the terms of such a regime spelled out formally. But it is worth noting that many social institutions operate effectively in the absence of formalization. Similarly, should an Arctic shipping regime involve some centralized institutional arrangements, or would it be sufficient to settle for an agreement on the part of the members to co-ordinate their national policies and regulations on a decentralized basis? Again, centralization seems to offer a more rational approach to management in an area like Arctic shipping. Given the character of the international community, however, decentralized co-ordination may produce more effective results than some form of centralization.

What should be the coverage of an Arctic shipping regime in terms of geographical domain, functional scope, and membership?[51] There are compelling political and managerial reasons to extend the geographical domain of such a regime beyond the waters of the Canadian portion of the Northwest Passage and the adjacent Arctic archipelago. Politically, it is desirable to develop a regime with rights and rules that apply uniformly to all the North American Arctic states. This would foster a sense of equality and equity among the participants. In managerial terms, only a broader domain would be sufficient to handle the problems posed by Arctic shipping. The regime should cover at least the Beaufort Sea, Baffin Bay, and Davis Strait, in addition to the Canadian portion of the Northwest Passage; it should probably encompass segments of the Arctic Basin proper as well.

There is an equally strong case for endowing an Arctic shipping regime with a relatively broad functional scope. Arctic shipping obviously raises fundamental issues relating to pollution control. Such activities also raise unavoidable questions regarding the maintenance of Arctic ecosystems and the viability of the socioeconomic and cultural systems of the human communities of the high Arctic. Efforts to answer all these questions will require substantially expanded programs of research. While there may well be political reasons to restrict the functional scope of an Arctic shipping regime (for example, to relatively technical concerns pertaining to shipping per se), it would be unfortunate if these considerations were allowed to dictate the terms of a final agreement.

The issue of membership in an Arctic shipping regime is apt to be controversial. Should membership be limited to the littoral states (that is, the United States, Canada, and Greenland/Denmark)? Should other states wishing to engage in Arctic shipping (for example, Japan) be included? What about various groups with legitimate interests in Arctic shipping (for example, the Inuit residents of the high Arctic, shipping companies, consumers' and environmental groups)? Is there a danger that the regime will look like an exclusive club to the remainder of the international community? These are all delicate questions that do not have any clearly correct answers.

Underlying every regime or institutional arrangement are some basic principles that serve to set the tone of the resultant practice. A few examples pertinent to the case of Arctic shipping will serve to clarify this observation. The principle of setting aside jurisdictional claims without prejudice is obviously central to the argument for an Arctic shipping regime as set forth in this essay. The essential idea motivating this plan is to transcend the politics of jurisdiction in the case of Arctic shipping. But there is a strong case to be made for the inclusion of several other principles as well. All legitimate interests (including those of the Inuit residents of the high Arctic) should be fairly represented in the decision-making processes of the regime. Not only is this important from the point of view of justice, it is also central to the achievement of compliance with the resultant practice. Participants should accord equal status to the informal, experiential knowledge of the long-term residents of the high Arctic and to the scientific knowledge of Western researchers. It is essential to forge a working partnership between ethnoscience and Western science in managing Arctic systems.[52] Those involved in the regime should make every effort to arrive at major decisions through some consensual process rather than through exercises in coalition-building or coercive diplomacy. This is just as important when it comes to reconciling the divergent interests of indigenous peoples and shipping companies as it is to satisfying the sensitivities of sovereign states like Canada and the United States.

The core of any coherent regime must be a system of rights and rules governing the specific actions of the participants.[53] In the case of Arctic shipping, these substantive arrangements would involve things like construction standards for tankers, rules pertaining to safe operation in Arctic waters, traffic control, aids to navigation (for example, search and rescue, ice-breaking, and ice-forecasting services), user fees, environmental protection, the socioeconomic integrity of nearby communities, liability rules for oil spills or other damages, and clean-up procedures. Though some of these matters are relatively technical, they form the substantive core of any management system for Arctic shipping, and they deserve to be examined with great care. What is more, many of these matters offer considerable scope for the development of co-operative arrangements and the deployment of problem-solving techniques. It is worth nothing the rather remarkable level of co-operation already existing between Canada and the United States with respect to a number of these matters.[54] This suggests that efforts to hammer out the substantive arrangements of an Arctic shipping regime could become an important focus for integrative bargaining and the cultivation of problem-solving attitudes among those likely to become members of the regime.

The distinction between institutional arrangements and explicit organizations is worth emphasizing. Institutions are interlocking sets of roles, rights, and rules; organizations are material entities possessing offices, personnel, equipment, budgets, and so forth. Whereas the Bretton Woods system is an international monetary regime, the International Monetary Fund and the World Bank are organizations. In the present context, the key questions concern the design of suitable organizations (if any) to administer an Arctic shipping regime. The need for organizations is a function of the character of the regime itself. If the chosen regime is highly decentralized, there may be no need for organizations specific to the regime. Should the chosen regime involve a more centralized process of decision-making or administration, designing appropriate organizations would become an important task. To lend substance to these observations, consider the following relevant models: the simple consultative arrangement of the Antarctic regime, the commission established under the provisions of the international whaling regime, and the more elaborate International Seabed Authority envisioned for the seabed regime.[55] While it would be inappropriate to prescribe organizational arrangements for an Arctic shipping regime at this stage, it seems likely that such a regime would require something more than the consultative arrangement of the Antarctic regime but less than the proposed International Seabed Authority. Some sort of Arctic shipping commission coupled with a staff of specialists possessing expertise in such matters as traffic control, ice forecasting, Arctic ecosystems, and socioeconomic effects would probably suffice.

CONCLUSION

The thesis of this essay is that the Canadian-u.s. conflict over Arctic shipping is more apparent than real. It is largely an artifact of the way in which issues relating to Arctic shipping are typically formulated. So long as these issues take the form of jurisdictional problems, the two countries will be unlikely to arrive at any mutually satisfactory agreement regarding Arctic shipping. If the jurisdictional problems are set aside without prejudice and issues relating to Arctic shipping are approached as problems of regime formation, numerous opportunities to pursue mutually beneficial processes of integrative bargaining will arise. In effect, this case illustrates clearly the significance of alternative formulations of the central issues with regard to social conflict more generally.

Despite the existence of opportunities to resolve issues relating to Arctic shipping through processes of integrative bargaining, the occasionally abrasive character of Canadian-u.s. relations in recent years may constitute an effective barrier to seizing these opportunities. Both sides have contributed to this state of affairs. Canada's economic nationalism, expansive attitudes toward marine jurisdiction, and declining interest in defence have undoubtedly irritated American policy-makers. By the same token, the unwillingness of the United States to pay serious attention to Canada's concerns regarding acid rain, fisheries management, and economic autonomy has provoked negative feelings toward the United States among Canadian policy-makers. Approached from a different angle, however, a constructive resolution of Canadian-u.s. differences over Arctic shipping could become a catalyst for an era of more harmonious relations between the two countries in other areas. The governments of Canada and the United States might therefore do well to seize on Arctic shipping as a policy area in which constructive steps of considerable symbolic as well as practical significance could be taken with relative ease.

CHAPTER SEVEN

Greenlandic and Danish Attitudes to Canadian Arctic Shipping

LARS TOFT RASMUSSEN

On a sunny spring day in 1975, Lukas Kruse watched in amazement and anger as the icebreaker *Sigyn* slowly made its way through the frozen waters of the Uummannaq Fiord. Standing on a hill above his home village of Niaqornat, a hunting community of 80 Inuit in northwest Greenland, the old man saw through his binoculars how the small but powerful ship, bound for a lead and zinc mine, was creating a dark track of open water in the ice, which serves as an open road for the indispensable dog sled. The incident was symbolic of things to come: a conflict of interest between the Inuit hunters of the remote and undisturbed north and the industrialized communities to the south. The Inuit won the first round of this north-south dialogue in reverse. As Lukas Kruse puts it, "Soon I saw about twenty hunters racing toward the icebreaker, placing themselves and their dog sleds in front of it." With local politicians as intermediaries, a settlement was negotiated right there on the ice. Since then, no ships have been allowed to call on the mine between December and June.

The *Sigyn* incident illustrates the deeply felt opposition by Greenlanders to all-year icebreaking activity in the Arctic. Normally peaceful to the point of being shy, the Greenlandic hunters of Niaqornat must have been extremely agitated to act with such determination.

The Arctic Pilot Project (APP) – a venture sponsored by Petro-Canada in 1977–82, which promised year-round icebreaking tanker traffic in Baffin Bay and Davis Strait – and similar Canadian proposals have been perceived in Greenland as offering extreme harm to the subsistence culture and fishing on which the people attempt to base their way of life. The Greenland home rule government has gone to great lengths to protect the renewable resources of the island. Its conservation-minded policies have twice taken Denmark/Greenland to the brink of a "cod war" with West Germany and have caused numerous confrontations with European Community (EC) authorities over the size of fishing quotas. The desire to gain control over their resources of fish and to avoid over-exploitation was, in fact, one of the major reasons for the Greenlanders' decision to leave the EC as of 1 January 1985. The APP, with its anticipated pollution, mainly in the form of underwater noise and disruption of marine mammal life, did not sit well with Greenlanders and their policy of protecting renewable resources. Viewed from the eastern side of Davis Strait, the APP offered only problems and no compelling reason to endorse the venture.

The Home Rule Act does not grant the Greenlanders any special jurisdiction in international relations, which continue to be handled by Copenhagen. Nevertheless, the ice-covered island has been able to conduct a foreign policy of sorts, based on the Danish government's loyalty and responsiveness to the wishes of its former colony. Denmark seems determined to go far in keeping the Greenlanders content, evidently because of the strategic importance of their huge land mass. Helping Greenland to get out of the EC and supporting Greenland in its opposition to the APP have been small prices to pay for political and strategic stability.

Although it is recognized by Greenland/Denmark that there is little in the way of international law to prevent Canada from launching projects such as the APP, Canadian insensitivity towards its nearest eastern neighbour could lead to a serious political confrontation. Greenlandic opposition to tanker traffic in Baffin Bay and Davis Strait may, however, lose some of its intensity in the 1980s because of what one Greenlandic newspaper has referred to as "Greenland's Own APP." Hydrocarbon exploration has been taking place in Jameson Land on the east coast of the island. If oil or gas is found, it could be transported only in icebreaking tankers. It seems likely that the home rule government would accept year-round icebreaking activity on the East Coast if the economic benefits were sufficient. In such an event, it would be difficult for Greenland not to scale down its opposition to Canadian tanker traffic along the west coast.

And yet a softening of the home rule government's position would undoubtedly be difficult for the Greenlandic public to accept. Greenlanders have been well educated in the potential hazards of icebreaking supertankers – by the home rule government itself. Lukas Kruse, who has been a hunter all his life, certainly would not be easily converted. "What are we going to do if the seals and whales disappear?" he asks. "Move to the stars, I guess."

FROM PATERNALISM
TO HOME RULE

The first Inuit arrived in Greenland from North America about 4,000 years ago. Known as the Independence I culture to archaeologists, they were followed by three more waves of Inuit immigrants of which the latest, the

Greenland and the Eastern Canadian Arctic

Thule people, arrived around AD 900. They are the ancestors of today's population in Greenland.

Colonization began in 1721 when the Danish-Norwegian missionary Hans Egede went to Greenland to bring the Lutheran faith to the Norsemen who had settled there around AD 1000. He found no Vikings, however. Instead, he began missionary work among the Inuit. Danish colonies were established in several locations on the west coast.

Danish rule during the following 200 years was extremely paternalistic. Greenland was treated more or less as a reservation that could be visited only by special permission. The Royal Greenland Trade Department, established by royal resolution of 18 March 1776, became solely responsible for trade and shipping between Denmark and Greenland, for the sale and marketing of products originating from Greenland, and for the operation of stores in Greenland. These stores carried only essential goods such as flour, salt, ammunition, and rope. Goods that were thought to be incompatible with the Inuit way of life were not made available.

The Second World War and the arrival of American forces in Greenland marked the beginning of the end of this paternalistic policy. Greenland was cut off from Denmark, and the United States took over responsibility for its protection and supply. The massive U.S. presence and Sears & Roebuck mail-order catalogues made the Greenlanders increasingly aware of the world outside.

When the war was over there was no turning back to the old paternalism. Tuberculosis also became a serious problem, and in 1948 Danish Prime Minister Hans Hedtoft visited Greenland to survey conditions there. During a meeting with the Greenlandic provincial council he asked directly if the Greenlanders wanted their country to be opened up to the rest of the world and a modern industrial society to be established. After considering the question for about 48 hours, the council gave an affirmative answer, stating in effect that the desire of the population to reach the same level as other nations in terms of culture and economic development had become so strong that it could not be ignored.

In 1953, Greenland's status as a colony was formally abolished when the Danish constitution was changed to include Greenland as an integral part of the realm. The new constitution also gave the people on the island two seats in the 179-member Danish Parliament. During the following years rapid development took place, including the construction of modern housing, fish processing plants, harbour facilities, and other elements of infrastructure. At the same time attempts were made to concentrate the population in four major towns on the west coast for reasons of efficiency.

There was very little participation by the Greenlanders in the development process. Almost everything from planning to actual construction was carried out by Danes. Not surprisingly, the native population felt increasingly alienated. Social problems, particularly alcohol abuse, followed. Greenland also experienced a baby boom as a result of improved health care and living conditions. A contributing factor to the sense of frustration was the fact that Greenlanders were paid less than Danes. The reason given was that the Greenlanders had to have wages based on the country's own economic capacity or they would be forever dependent on subsidies from Denmark. Danes also had privileges in terms of housing and other matters. On a personal level, this discrimination was perceived as being extremely unfair.

National and political awareness began to develop among the Greenlanders and was strengthened by the 1972 plebiscite on Danish membership in the EC. As a constituent part of the realm, Greenland had to submit to the Danish decision to join the EC, in spite of a negative island vote of 70.2 per cent. Only three years later a Home Rule Commission was established by the Danish Parliament with a mandate to draft its recommendations – including a new Home Rule Bill – for home rule in Greenland within the framework of national unity. Comprising seven Greenlandic members and seven Danish members, the commission finished its work in 1978. On being accepted by the Danish Parliament, the Home Rule Act was made the subject of a plebiscite in Greenland. It was accepted by a 70 per cent majority. Elections followed in April 1979, and the Greenland home rule Parliament began its work on 1 May 1979, in the presence of Queen Margrethe II.

INTERNAL POLITICAL RELATIONS

In spite of occasional anti-Danish rhetoric, the Greenlanders have strong ties to their former colonial rulers. Says Jonathan Motzfeldt, Premier of Greenland, "We have a cultural, biological, and historical fellowship with Denmark dating back 250 years. These are ties that are not easily broken." The relationship between Greenland and Denmark has sometimes been likened to a marriage. The wedding took place in 1953, when Greenland's status was changed from that of a colony to part of Denmark. The bride, resplendent in a wedding gown of ice and snow, was given everything that Denmark thought she needed – better houses, hospitals, schools, and modern factories. But the new wife was left without much responsibility. All major decisions were made in Copenhagen, thousands of miles away on the other side of the Atlantic. And Greenlanders did not have a chance to contribute to the creation of their new society. Unqualified to do construction or technical work, they could only watch and marvel as Danish labourers moved in with heavy equipment to implement programs formulated by Danish politicians and administrators. After a while, the Greenlanders felt like tenants in their own country. And then, at the time of the silver anniversary, after 25 years of marriage, the wife was finally given some spending money and the right to make decisions affecting her own life.

Some may argue that the relationship is based on common sense rather than on love. It was explicitly stated, however, in the terms of reference of the Home Rule Commission that divorce was not the goal, that national unity was to be preserved. According to Isi Foighel, the chairman of the commission, the basic philosophy "may be expressed in terms *that the population of Greenland does not wish national independence but improved possibilities of strengthening and expanding the identity of Greenland through an increased independent responsibility."*[1] The fact that home rule was to be developed "within the unity of the realm," i.e. without violating the Danish constitution, meant that certain fields could not be transferred to the home rule authorities. This applies particularly to external affairs, defence policy, administration of justice, and monetary and currency policy.

The Faroe Islands, another former Danish colony, have had home rule since 1948. A fundamental principle in the islands' agreement is that legislative power and the power of the purse cannot be divided. This principle could not be adhered to in Greenland's home rule agreement because of different geographic and historic realities: it is expensive to provide services to a population that would fit into a football stadium (51,000) but lives on an island that is larger than the rest of the EC combined. Further, Greenland was developed only recently and, unlike the Faroe Islands, is still in the midst of building an economic foundation.

So if Greenland was to take over only those fields that the home rule administration would be able to finance independently, home rule would have had very little real content or meaning. It was decided that subsidized fields could also be transferred to home rule by means of special authorizing acts in which the Danish Parliament expressed a few main principles for the administration of the field in question but otherwise left detailed regulations to the home rule authorities. The Greenlandic administration receives the same amount of money that the Danish administration had previously spent plus compensation for inflation – no more, no less. The total subsidy to non-self-financed fields is transferred to the home rule administration in the form of a block grant in order to give Greenland the opportunity to establish its own economic priorities. The block grant today pays for roughly half of the home rule administration's activities.

Among the most important areas of responsibility under home rule at this time are education and culture; social welfare; taxation; fishing, hunting, and sheep-breeding; organization of local government; environmental preservation; district planning; labour market affairs; and legislation governing trade and competition. The home rule administration is soon to take over the Royal Greenland Trade Department's production and export division and, at a later date, the health service sector, the supply of goods and internal transport of passengers, environmental protection, and others.

The home rule government (Landsstyre) consists of six Ministers. The leader of the government, the Premier, is also Chairman of the home rule Parliament (Landsting). The Premier/Chairman and the five other Ministers are elected by the Landsting, which currently consists of 26 members elected in general, direct, and secret election. Greenland's so-called outlying districts, i.e. Thule, Itteqqortoormiit (Scoresbysund), Ammasalik, Upernavik, and Uummannaq, each elect one member of the Landsting. The Disko Bay area elects five members; the more populous mid-district, comprising Nuuk and several other major towns, elects eight members; and the southern districts elect five members. Up to three additional seats are divided among the parties on the basis of the overall vote to make the composition of the Parliament reflect each party's actual support among the voters more accurately.

All Danish citizens, regardless of origin or ethnicity, who have lived in Greenland for at least six months prior to an election, and who are at least 18 years of age, may vote. The eligibility requirements to sit in Parliament are identical. About one-fourth of the electorate are of non-Greenlandic origin. In the first five years of home rule only one Dane was a member, and only for one year. Apparently Danes living in Greenland either prefer Greenlandic candidates or do not vote.

Greenland's three political parties were established in the 1970s. *Siumut* – "forward" in Greenlandic – started as a movement in 1971 and had as its main goal the creation of home rule. Siumut had an absolute majority in Parliament from 1979 to 1983. In 1984 the party became a member of the Socialist International, of which Canada's New Democratic Party is also a member. In the Danish Parliament, Siumut's member co-operates with the Social Democrats. *Atassut* – "link" in Greenlandic – was founded in 1978 on a platform of preserving strong ties with Denmark and the EC. Although conventional political labels are difficult to apply in Greenland, Atassut may be described as a liberal party. In the Danish Parliament, Atassut's representative has co-operated with the conservative-liberal coalition government. *Inuit Ataqatigiit* – "human (or 'Inuit') fellowship" – started as a movement in 1976. Its goal was to establish a revolutionary party in pursuit of Greenlandic independence and common ownership. A major element in the party platform is to advance the position of Greenland's indigenous population, including Greenlandic ownership of natural resources. In recent years Inuit Ataqatigiit appears to have abandoned some of its socialistic ideals and is rarely heard mentioning independence for

Greenland as a political goal. All three parties seem to be committed to making the current political system work.

Municipal self-government is guaranteed by the Danish constitution. Greenland has 16 municipalities which have the responsibility locally for areas such as social welfare, education, and city planning. Their activities are financed partly through income tax and partly through block grants from the home rule administration and the Danish government. The municipalities are united in the Association of Greenlandic Municipalities, KANUKOKA.

THE ECONOMIC SITUATION: GREENLAND'S STRAIT-JACKET

It may have been the first recorded case of consumer fraud when Eric the Red, the Norwegian-Icelandic Viking, dreamed up the name Greenland so long ago. Eighty-five per cent of this giant treeless island, the largest in the world, is permanently covered by ice up to more than three kilometres deep. Only around the edges, between the glaciers and the sea, is there a narrow strip of habitable land – a fringe of mainly brown and grey on a great white shield. Eric's descendants survived in Greenland for 500 years, at which point they vanished and left the land to a people much better adapted to the inhospitable conditions of the Arctic: the Inuit.

The Scandinavians returned to Greenland 250 years later and settled once more. The Danes are now in control, but in a way history is in the process of repeating itself. For the second time the Inuit are reclaiming their land. The native inhabitants are gradually taking over more and more political responsibility and are making Greenland more Greenlandic again. But this time the Scandinavians are leaving more behind than a few ruins of Viking dwellings and some rusty nails: they are leaving a deep Western imprint on the culture of the Inuit. Where the harsh environment used to supply them with food, clothing, and everything else they needed, the Greenlanders are now dependent on Middle East oil, Canadian-made aircraft, Japanese transistor radios, and Danish beer. Any dump in Greenland is speckled with green bottles and cans from Carlsberg and Tuborg, finally giving some accuracy to Eric's colourful name for the country. Western add-water-and-stir culture is here to stay. In the words of a Danish author and former reporter for Radio Greenland, "They the (Inuit) have become too big around the middle to ever again be able to squeeze into a kayak."

Nowhere in Greenland is the impact of Western culture more visible than in the capital, Nuuk (previously Godthåb). About half of its 10,000 inhabitants live in large multi-storey housing projects. A fleet of shiny Mercedes taxicabs cruises the streets, and the stores carry anything from fishing hooks to stereo equipment. Sealskin, stretched out to dry on wooden frames on the balconies of the apartment buildings, serve as a reminder that this is not some place in Western Europe.

The population of Nuuk has quadrupled in just 25 years, and bulldozers, cranes, and concrete mixers have been familiar sights since the early 1950s. Nuuk is a boomtown, but the boom is not caused by the presence of rich oil deposits or coal mines. Instead, Nuuk's expansion is to a large extent fuelled by Danish kroner flowing from the mother country at a rate of 2,183 million (Can. $250 million) a year (overall Danish government net expenditure in Greenland in 1983).

Lars Emil Johansen, Greenland's Minister for Resources and Industries, has said that in order to make Greenland politically stronger he would like to reduce the need for Danish subsidies by closing the gap between Greenland's exports and imports. "The deficit on our balance of payments serves as a strait-jacket," he says. "One way to loosen it would be to import less." Another way to cut the dependence on Danish subsidies, and to avoid the somewhat humiliating negotiations every year in Copenhagen over the size of the block grant for the home rule government, is, of course, to produce more by expanding the trawler fleet and the fishing industry and possibly by exploiting the oil and the minerals under Greenland's rocky surface.

It is the policy of the home rule administration to maintain harvesting of renewable resources as the backbone of the island's economy. Historically, cod fishing has played a most significant role, although it is now matched in economic importance by shrimp fishing. One of every four Greenlanders is dependent on fishing. An estimated 2,500 are employed in the fishing fleet, which in 1981 consisted of 383 vessels of more than 5 GRT (eight exceeded 500 GRT). Another 2,000 people are employed in the eight government-owned processing plants or in the 15 privately owned plants, of which four are co-operatives.[2]

In the 1950s and early 1960s yearly catches in what is now Greenland's economic zone ranged between 400,000 and 500,000 tons. The figure dropped dramatically at the end of the 1960s because of a combination of climatic changes and over-fishing. On the advice of biologists, a strict conservation policy was implemented and now seems to be paying off. The yearly total allowable catch (TAC), the maximum that may be caught of each species annually, is now 62,000 tons for cod. In order to allow the spawning stock to regenerate, the home rule administration has consistently favored a low TAC reserved for Greenlandic fishermen exclusively. This led to numerous conflicts in Brussels, the seat of the EC, in the negotiation of fishing quotas. West Germany has been particularly aggressive in its demand for a higher TAC and fishing rights for its ocean-going fleet of very large trawlers.

In January 1981, the West German Minister for Agriculture and Fisheries, Joseph Ertl, lost his temper during negotiations on new fishing quotas, saying that it was time for Greenland to contribute to the EC in exchange for all the investments that had been made there. Ertl proceeded to issue fishing quotas for cod off Greenland's east coast without seeking the consent of the Danish/Greenlandic authorities. Denmark, seeing Ertl's move as illegal, sent naval vessels to the area. Ertl replied by threatening to close off the border between Denmark and West Germany, thereby raising the prospect of a halt to vital Danish exports of cheese and other agricultural products. The dispute ended peacefully, but only after Denmark relented, allowing the West German trawlers a small quota of Greenland cod.

In August 1982, West Germany again unilaterally handed out a fishing quota for its trawlers off Greenland. The situation was resolved only after Denmark had sent Bonn a strongly worded diplomatic note, and the home rule government had demanded that Denmark use naval fisheries inspection vessels to stop the West German fishermen. The issue was discussed at the highest level between Danish Prime Minister Anker Jorgensen and West German Chancellor Helmut Schmidt.

These two confrontations drew Greenland closer to Denmark, strained the island's relations with the wicked stepfather in Europe, and strengthened the Greenlanders' desire to get out of the EC. On 13 March 1984, an agreement was finally signed that would end Greenland's involuntary membership in the EC as of 1 January 1985. From that date Greenlandic jurisdiction over the 200-mile fishing zone would be restored. Greenlandic politicians would no longer have to go to Brussels to bargain with the EC about the right of local fishermen to catch cod and shrimp off their own coastline. The authority to decide the TAC was to be transferred from the EC Commission to Greenlandic authorities.

As part of the agreement, Greenland also obtained duty-free access to the European market for the island's vital export of fish. This provision is linked to the right of EC fishermen to catch up to 125,000 tons of fish in Greenlandic waters annually for the next five years in exchange for an amount of 216 million kroner (Can. $30 million) per year, regardless of whether the fish are actually caught. This amount is about equal to the EC subsidy to Greenland in recent years. Termination of EC membership also means that Greenland/Denmark negotiates Greenland's salmon quota in Davis Strait. Until now the EC has negotiated on behalf of Greenland.

About 2,500 Greenlanders, hunters and their dependants, rely on hunting for their livelihood. To an unknown but significant number of people hunting is an important supplement to their income.[3] Hunting is practised all over Greenland but is of particular importance in the outlying districts, i.e. in North and East Greenland and in the municipalities of Upernavik and Uummannaq. In 1981, 77 per cent of the value of sealskin, caribou meat, and other products originating from hunting came from these areas, where there is little else on which to base a living.

The seal is still the animal of greatest economic importance to the hunters, in spite of declining prices of sealskin on the international market as a result of the campaign against the killing of baby seals off the Canadian coast. Other animals of significance are whales, polar bears, foxes, caribou, and birds. Hunting is to a large extent regulated by the local authorities. In most regions the kayak has been replaced by small boats with outboard motors. The traditional dog sledge has not, however, been abandoned. Ski-doos are not allowed for hunting purposes anywhere in Greenland because they are too noisy and scare away the animals.

About 350 persons in southern Greenland depend on sheep-breeding for their livelihood. It is not an easy existence because of the harsh climate. Greenlandic lamb cannot compete with the New Zealand product in terms of price, not even on the domestic market. The number of sheep-breeders has been reduced by about 50 per cent since 1970.

It seems unlikely that Greenland will significantly reduce its dependence on Danish subsidies through the exploitation of renewable resources alone. This goal can be achieved only through mining and oil development. Jurisdiction over non-renewable resources is divided between Denmark and Greenland. All decisions in this regard are made by a Joint Council on Mineral Resources, which consists of five Greenlandic members (appointed by the Landsting), five Danes (appointed by the Danish Parliament), and a chairman (appointed by the Minister for Greenland). The latter position is currently held by Premier Motzfeldt. Each side in the Joint Council has veto power, so that no resource project can be initiated without the consent of both the home rule government and the Danish administration for Greenland. Any income earned from the exploitation of oil and minerals is to replace the Danish subsidies. In other words, the home rule government will not obtain an increase in disposable funds until the income generated by such development exceeds the more than 2 billion kroner that currently come from Denmark every year. Such income would, however, give Greenland more political freedom. The only mine in operation in Greenland today is the Black Angel Mine at Maarmorilik, near Uummannaq in northwest Greenland. It was long owned by Greenex, which was owned entirely by Vestgron Mines Ltd, of which 62.5 per cent was in turn owned by Cominco, a large Canadian company. In 1983 Greenex paid 56 million kroner (Can. $7 million) in royalties to Greenland. The Danish subsidy to the island was reduced by an equal amount. Producing lead, zinc, and silver, Black Angel employs over 300, of whom almost half are Greenlanders. Recently, however, it was sold to non-Canadians.

Significant deposits of uranium, coal, and molybdenum are known to exist elsewhere in Greenland. But the coal is of poor quality, the molybdenum is located in an extremely remote and inaccessible mountain in East Greenland, and the uranium ore is not very pure. As well, all three political parties in Greenland are against uranium mining for environmental reasons. In 1977–8, five dry holes were drilled by Arco, Chevron, Mobil, and TGA-Grepco (a French-Danish consortium) off West Greenland. An internal document from Mobil indicates that expectations had been high. The company expected to find 1.2 billion barrels and would have spent billions on production facilities. The home rule government has since taken the firm position that it will allow no more offshore oil exploration, as is allowed in neighbouring Canada. "We must protect our hunters and fishermen," says Lars Emil Johansen. "We cannot risk an oil spill."

Land-based exploration is taking place in Jameson Land on the east coast. The Joint Council and Atlantic Richfield Company (ARCO) negotiated a concession that was approved in the autumn 1984 session of the home rule Parliament by an overwhelming majority. Only those members elected from the Jameson Land area, which is where the consequences of oil development will most directly be felt, failed to approve. The ARCO concession was thus supported by the Inuit Ataqatigiit Party which, in the six months following the spring of 1984, totally altered its position from opposition to endorsement of oil exploration. Arqaluk Lynge, the party's chairman and now Minister of Social Affairs in the home rule government, explained to a Danish interviewer: "We could not have stopped the project. Instead we chose to seek influence and to limit the damage."[4] His views were not, however, supported by some of the younger and more ideologically motivated members of the party, whose disaffection may be expected to continue. However, if oil were to be found in quantity, it could start flowing in the 1990s, thereby reducing Greenland's economic dependence and altering its overall relationship with the mother country.

FOREIGN RELATIONS

According to the Home Rule Act, the home rule authorities have no jurisdiction over Greenland's relations with other countries and will never be able to obtain it: external affairs must be handled by the national authorities in Copenhagen. Chapter 3, section 11, of the Act states: "The Central authorities of the Realm shall have jurisdiction in questions affecting the foreign relations of the Realm." In order to allow the home rule government some input into the decision-making process, the Act does, however, obligate the Danish Parliament (Folketing) to consult with the Greenlanders: "Treaties which require the assent of the Folketing and which particularly affect Greenlandic interests shall be referred to the Home Rule authorities for their comments before they are concluded" (chapter 3, section 13). In spite of Greenland's limited influence over its own international relations, the home rule government has been able to carry out a foreign policy of its own. This is mainly because the Danish government, no matter what its political coloration, has been extremely responsive to the wishes of the Greenlanders.

Danish responsiveness was clearly expressed when Greenland's new status with the EC was negotiated by Copenhagen on behalf of the home rule administration. After Greenland became an involuntary member of the EC in 1972, the 10 EC nations invested $10–25 million a year in infrastructure and education in Greenland. But the positive image thus purchased was undermined by West German trawlers fishing illegally off Greenland and by disagreements over fishing quotas between the EC Commission and the conservation-minded home rule government. Equally important, EC membership was seen as being incompatible with the cultural and political aspirations of Greenland. "The idea behind home rule was to shed the yoke of Copenhagen. Why replace it with a new one?," asked Finn Lynge, the Greenlandic member of the European Parliament. "The EC is working towards a reduction of the members' sovereignty while home rule was a step towards greater self-determination. These are goals that are not compatible."

During a visit to Greenland in the summer of 1977, two years before the introduction of home rule, Danish Prime Minister Anker Jorgensen declared that his social-democratic government did not intend to force upon Greenland a particular association with the EC. But he also made it clear that he would prefer Greenland to maintain its membership. Greenland didn't agree. On 23 February 1982, voters in towns and tiny villages along the vast and frigid coast said "naagga" ("no" in Greenlandic) to continuing the affiliation with the EC. Rockets and fireworks flared over snow-bound Nuuk, and young EC opponents staged a torchlight parade as the returns came in. They showed 53 per cent against continued membership.

Before the plebiscite, Prime Minister Jorgensen had promised that if a majority, no matter how slim the margin, voted to get out of the EC, his government would assist in the negotiations. Although regretting the outcome of the plebiscite, he kept his promise. His government pressured reluctant EC Commissioners and diplomats who hoped that by dragging their feet, and by adding to the EC's financial support to Greenland, they might persuade the Greenlanders to change their minds.

Part of the reason for the EC's reluctance was a fear that Greenland might set a precedent. This was clear from a letter dated 10 January 1983, from the Political Affairs Committee of the European Parliament to its Legal Affairs Committee: "Were Greenland to secede, it would be the first time in the Community's history that a constituent element of the Community had withdrawn from it. The Political Affairs Committee wishes to express its profound anxiety at this possible diminution of the Community, which would set a dangerous precedent and reflects a politically questionable view of the Community founded by the Treaty of Rome. It would therefore strongly urge the Commission and the Council to think profoundly about the consequences of any course of action tending to undermine the Community as at present constituted."

Greenland's home rule government became more and more impatient with the lack of progress in the Brussels talks. The Danish government, now headed by conservative Prime Minister Poul Schluter, finally announced to the nine other member countries of the EC that Greenland would leave the EC, with or without their consent, on 1 January 1985. The threat of unilateral withdrawal, made with unqualified support in Copenhagen, brought the EC to understand that Greenland meant business. An agreement, generally viewed as being quite generous to Greenland, was finally signed on 13 March 1984. When the agreement was endorsed by the home rule Parliament in March 1984, Premier Motzfeldt praised the governments of Jorgensen and Schluter for their support.

The most important lesson to be learned from the EC example about Greenland's "foreign policy" is that the Danish government, be it social-democratic or conservative-liberal, will go to great lengths in accommodating Greenland's wishes, even if they are not fully shared in Copenhagen. A Danish diplomat who was involved in the EC negotiations reports that it was the Danish attitude all along to negotiate completely on Greenland's premisses: "In the European Communities there was great suspicion about the loyal Danish attitude. Some members thought that Denmark, Greenland and the Faroe Islands were planning a plot that would give them more extensive fishing rights in the North Atlantic." This is confirmed by the head of the Home Rule Office in Copenhagen, Lars Vesterbirk. A former personal aide to the Minister for Greenland, he was present at the negotiations. Aside from the approval of the Greenlanders, "the Danish government clearly gained nothing from its loyal attitude. On occasion there was even suspicion in the EC that Denmark was up to something," he says.

Why this loyalty? And why is Denmark supporting Greenland with more than $200 million a year when there is no indication that this money will ever be returned? "Good question. Why is the sky blue?" says Finn Lynge. "I guess we have almost come to take Danish loyalty for granted. The key words in understanding it, I think, are 'The Emperor of China' and 'security junkies'":

Let me explain. When the first Danish diplomat visited China some time in the 19th century, the Emperor wanted to know where this man came from. A globe was brought out, but the Emperor could hardly see that little country in Europe. Then the diplomat pointed at Greenland and said, "Your Imperial Majesty, this is the least part of our Kingdom." This, of course, impressed the Emperor, and I think that in the Danish public today there is still a feeling that Greenland makes Denmark great. Another reason for Danish loyalty is that an important element in the Danish national character – and Greenland's too, for that matter – is the desire to avoid conflicts and seek security. Danes are sometimes referred to as "security junkies." Denmark has NATO obligations which most definitely also pertain to Greenland. There has never been any unrest in that northern province, and there is certainly no desire to get it. It is my feeling that the Danes try extra hard to understand the Greenlandic point of view in order to avoid alienating the population here. Nobody knows what the result will be if political stability is not maintained. That would probably have some security implications.

"The security aspect was never openly mentioned at the negotiating table," reports one EC diplomat. "But it certainly was informally discussed in the coffee breaks and during the cocktail hour. Although no one would doubt Greenland's commitment to NATO, even in the event of unilateral withdrawal from the EC, it is in the long-term interest to maintain friendly relations. It is a small price to pay, security being infinitely more important than fish."

Although they seldom talk about it, prominent Greenlandic politicians are aware of their giant island's strategic importance. This awareness gives them the sense of possessing an ultimate secret weapon in the conduct of external relations. Positioned midway on the shortest route between the two major superpowers, Greenland politicians see the Western Alliance as willing to pay a price for stable political relations with the island.

If Greenland had not been able to obtain a satisfying agreement with the EC, an obvious alternative would have been unilateral withdrawal and an invitation to non-EC nations to buy fishing rights. East German, Soviet, and other nations of the eastern bloc would have been likely to make high bids, possibly also claiming "historic rights" because of their presence off Greenland before the declaration of a 200-mile fishing zone on 1 January 1977. The Soviet Union has shown interest in the ice-covered island in various ways. Moscow once offered to develop Greenland's fishing industry on favourable conditions in an apparent attempt to gain a foothold, and in the summer of 1983 a submarine, evidently of Soviet origin, was spotted near the village of Akunnaaq when it surfaced next to a native Greenlander who was hunting seals from his little boat.

Operating several large military installations in Greenland, the United States also took an interest in the EC agreement. According to an American diplomatic source, there were consultations between the EC and the United States during the negotiations, the United States recommending that a deal be reached.[5]

The home rule administration has also had at its disposal a few tools for carrying out a foreign policy without direct participation by the Danish government. First, there was the Greenlandic seat in the European Parliament, which was filled by direct election. Finn Lynge from the Siumut party held this office since it was first established in 1979, but had to find another job as of 1 January 1985, when Greenland quit the EC. Greenland will still have a voice in the Parliament, however. Lynge had started a club called "Friends of Greenland" for MPs who have been to Greenland. As of early 1985, 17 individuals had qualified. It is Lynge's hope that the club will take an interest in and to some degree represent to the European Parliament the point of view of Greenland as well as the rest of the Arctic region. Lynge skilfully used his office to advance Greenland's position on such issues as the ban on trade in sealskins and the Arctic Pilot Project (APP).

Second, another foreign policy tool for Greenland is the newly obtained observer status with the Nordic Council. Created in 1952 by Denmark, Iceland, Norway, and Sweden (Finland joined in 1955), the council may take up any area of joint interest except in matters of defence. Third, the home rule government is a member of the Inuit Circumpolar Conference (ICC), an international organization of Inuit in Canada, Alaska, and Greenland. On 3 March 1983, the home rule government ratified the ICC's charter. In the ratification document it is noted: "The Greenlandic Home Rule Government accedes to the Charter with the limitations which at any time emanate from legislation of the Kingdom of Denmark and the Greenlandic Parliament." The ICC has been used to voice the home rule government's opposition to the APP and similar proposals. On most other issues the Greenlandic authorities have chosen to be very careful about not overstepping their limited mandate in foreign relations.

PUBLIC OPINION AND ICEBREAKING TANKERS

In Greenland one needs only the confidence of the staff of the two large weekly newspapers and the staff at Radio Greenland in order to be in close touch with public opinion. Three editors, "gate-keepers" they are, regulate access to the media and shape the public's political concerns. In a larger society such as that of Denmark, public opinion is more "inert" due to the fact that there are almost 50 newspapers and it is much more difficult to gain access to the electronic media. To bring all the gate-keepers to support a particular point of view would be next to impossible because of the political diversity of the media.

In 1980, all three Greenlandic media discovered the APP and quickly made it one of the most important issues on the island's political agenda. The ball started rolling when the little local newspaper in Thule, *Hainang*, published a critical lead article about the supertanker proposal. Most of the story was based on a glossy brochure published by Petro-Canada, "Arctic Pilot Project: What We Are Saying in Our Application." The brochure explained that the supertankers would not get any closer than 150 kilometres to Arctic Bay, 272 to Grise Fiord, 576 to Frobisher Bay, etc. "But nowhere is mentioned that [the tankers] in some places will be as close as 25 kilometres to Greenland's coast," the newspaper declared with indignation. The APP was off to a bad start.

The article also expressed concern about what the APP might lead to. Referring to information from the Canadian Arctic Resources Committee (CARC), *Hainang* calculated that if all proposed American and Canadian tanker schemes at the time were to become reality, there would be, at any given time, 15 or 16 supertankers off the west coast of Greenland. "Greenlandic society cannot tolerate," the article concluded, "that its two most important productive trades are threatened by reckless shipping by foreign wealthy nations who need to satisfy their extravagant consumption of energy." *Hainang's* article was reprinted by Greenland's largest newspaper, *Atuagagdliutit/Grønlandsposten*, in a special edition on the APP. Soon the project made headlines in all Greenlandic media and in the Danish press as well.

For the APP, it was no doubt frustrating to encounter a total lack of support everywhere – in the press, from the public, and among the politicians. APP representatives requested permission from Copenhagen to visit potentially affected communities in Greenland in order to explain the point of view of the oil companies. But they were told, according to Vice-President Douglas Bowie of Petro-Canada, "informally, but very pointedly" to stay away, or "the relations we had built up with Denmark would be ruined."

It was primarily the home rule government that did not want to see the APP's spokesmen. On 15 July 1980, prior to a visit to Nuuk by Minister for Indian and Northern Affairs John Munro, Lars Emil Johansen wrote a letter to the Ministry for Greenland. In it he stated: "The Home Rule Government does not wish to receive representatives of Petro-Canada, neither at the same time nor in connection with the meeting with Canadian Minister for Indian and Northern Affairs, Munro, and further ... Petro-Canada's desire to send representatives to the affected parts of northern Greenland should not be met at this time." "We don't need their propaganda," Finn Lynge said at one point.

The APP, in turn, attempted to keep Greenlandic witnesses away from Canada's National Energy Board (NEB) hearings on the project in Ottawa in March 1982, but unsuccessfully. "What [the Greenlanders] can say about these matters is no less relevant than what those on the Canadian side of these waters can say," the NEB ruled.

Lynge correctly stated at the NEB hearings that the APP had become second to only the EC question in terms of importance among issues in Greenland. Part of the reason why opposition to the APP caught on so well with the press and the public was probably that it was less abstract than most other items on the political agenda. It is easy to envisage a supertanker smashing its way through frozen Arctic waters while seals and whales flee in all directions. It is also important to understand that the sea mammals play a very important role in Greenlandic culture. Anything that might cause these animals to disappear, making the thrill of hunting a thing of the past and their meat unavailable, is bound to touch powerful emotions deep inside almost every Greenlander. Indeed, opposition to the APP became so intense that no one wanted to be associated with it in any way.

On 17 March 1982, *Atuagagdliutit/Grønlandsposten* revealed that APP representatives had met twice with the Danish National Oil and Gas Company (DONG), including its president. DONG immediately issued a statement to the effect that the meetings had taken place on the initiative of APP and that DONG had shown no interest in buying natural gas from the disputed project. This was contrary to what APP's chairman, Donald Wolcott, had told the newspaper's reporter: "The Arctic Pilot Project toured potential customers in Europe, and the Danish National Oil Company asked if we could meet and discuss with them the possibility of future purchases ... and other things."

On 18 February 1982, the Danish daily *Information* created a link between the two most important issues in Greenland. Referring to an EC document titled "Communication from the Commission to the Council Concerning Natural Gas," the newspaper created a sense among Greenlanders of all evil powers ganging up on their island. The document stated: "Canada is of particular interest as a possible supplier to Europe with its significant reserves and promising potential for further discoveries. These 'Arctic' resources would have to be recovered by LNG [liquefied natural gas] tanker and would then be about as close to European as to American markets. Considerable effort is being made to overcome the formidable technical problems presented by very hostile conditions, although it remains for the Canadian Government to give a clear indication of natural gas export policy."

When this story was picked up by the Greenland press, Danish Minister of Energy Poul Nilsson immediately made sure, just as DONG had done, that he would not be associated with the disputed project. He offered assurances that the Danish government had had no part in indirect EC support of the APP as implied by the press reports, saying that the Danish government would oppose the APP everywhere – in Greenland, Denmark, and in the EC.

In the summer of 1983, when it was learned in Greenland that the APP had quietly passed away, Premier Motzfeldt said to Radio Greenland that this was "one of the best messages I have received in years." "This proves," he went on, "that when we stand together here in Greenland we are able to have some influence, in spite of our small population and the giant interests we are up against." Although the failure of the APP was in fact due primarily to falling oil prices, Greenland had the political resources required to mount an increasingly effective opposition to the project if it had gone ahead.

STRATEGIES AND POLITICAL RESOURCES

The Danish authorities were first notified about the APP at a meeting in Copenhagen, in August 1977. Present were representatives of Petro-Canada, the Ministry for Greenland (MFG), and the Danish Ministry of Foreign Affairs. The chairman of Greenland's provincial council was informed by the MFG as to what had been learned about the project (Greenland had not yet obtained home rule). Even at that time Danish authorities pointed to the APP's possible harmful effects on the environment and Greenland's subsistence culture. Petro-Canada's representatives were told that their project looked like "exporting problems from Canada to Greenland." This expression provides a good statement of the Danish/Greenlandic attitude to the project and similar ventures right up to the present day. "There was nothing in it for us," says one Danish diplomat. "Even if there was only a one per cent risk of adverse effects from the project and a 99 per cent chance that it would be safe we would of course oppose it."

So in a way it was a useless exercise when the Danish authorities and Petro-Canada decided to set up a special APP working group, which was to attempt to resolve the scientific and technical objections raised. Several scientific studies, particularly in relation to the noise problem, were undertaken. But when Premier Motzfeldt visited Ottawa in 1982, he noted in a statement to representatives of the Canadian Government: "No further progress or consensus seems to be obtainable due to obvious fundamental differences of opinion that prevail on the technical-scientific level as well." The basic problem was that no scientific study could ever entirely exclude the possibility of adverse impact on the environment. There would always be the 1 per cent risk. The APP representatives stressed the "pilot" nature of their project and said that the best way to assess the environmental impact would be to build the tankers and measure the effects of noise generated by them. This was unacceptable to the Danes and Greenlanders, who were concerned that a $2 billion project would not be easily abandoned even if it had detrimental effects on the environment. In spite of the hopelessness of its task, the APP working group kept meeting up to April 1984. As of 1980, the home rule government was itself directly represented in the working group.

At the political level, the Danish authorities suggested in 1979 a change in the proposed tanker route to go "behind" Baffin Island, through Fury and Hecla Strait. This solution proving unacceptable to Canada, the home rule government expressed the opinion that the "APP and similar projects" should be withdrawn or that the Canadians should consider transporting their Arctic hydrocarbons by pipeline across their own country.

In September 1980 Minister for Northern and Indian Affairs John Munro visited Nuuk, where he had direct consultations with the Home Rule Government. Representatives of the MFG and the Ministry of Foreign Affairs were present. In December 1980 the Danish government sent a diplomatic note through its embassy in Ottawa to Canada's Department of External Affairs, expressing deep concern over the project as it affected Greenlandic interests.

At first it seemed to be the strategy of Denmark/Greenland to rely exclusively on political and technical-scientific contacts with Canada. Later, when no real progress was being made and the pressure from public opinion in Greenland continued to mount, the home rule government began to look for other means to oppose the APP. At the 1981 fall session of the home rule Parliament, the members present (19 of 21) voted unanimously against the project, and a member of the Atassut party raised the idea of bringing the APP before the United Nations.

At a meeting in January 1982 between Motzfeldt, the Minister for Greenland, and representatives of the Ministry of Foreign Affairs, it was decided to take the problems associated with all-year Arctic shipping to the Third United Nations Conference on the Law of the Sea (UNCLOS). This was done in March of that year in the form of a statement about the draft convention's Article 234, which grants coastal states some power to regulate shipping in ice-covered areas:

As regards Article 234, the Danish delegation greatly appreciates the progress which this article reflects as to the possibilities of protecting the highly vulnerable Arctic Sea areas from pollution by oil and other harmful substances ... Another factor to be taken into consideration is the new plans for year-round navigation in areas which are ice-covered for the greater part of the year and where navigation can therefore only be carried out by aid of huge icebreaking vessels which have to use considerable amounts of energy to break the ice. This poses a serious risk that noise, not only from the icebreaking itself, but especially from the propellers of the vessels, will disturb the ecological balance in areas where until now the impact of modern civilization has been on a modest scale. In view of the increasing exploitation of non-renewable resources in Arctic areas, it is therefore of paramount importance to Denmark that a foundation be laid for up-to-date regulation of navigational activities in the waters surrounding Greenland. This should be viewed against the background that the Greenlandic people to a decisive degree are dependent for their subsistence on the living resources of the surrounding seas. Not least the marine mammals, which are the basis for the existence of the local hunters in the northern and eastern parts of Greenland, are extremely sensitive to impacts on their natural habitats. Consequently, year-round navigation with huge vessels such as icebreaking tankers along the coasts of Greenland would be anticipated to cause major harm to, or irreversible disturbances of, the ecological balance. We hope that adoption of Article 234 will strengthen the basis for intervening, in a non-discriminatory manner, against the threats to the Arctic environment which I have just described.

Canada had been extremely active on behalf of Article 234, seeing it as a means of strengthening Canadian jurisdiction over its portion of the Northwest Passage. Accordingly, there was more than a bit of irony to be detected in Premier Motzfeldt's statement to representatives of the Canadian government in March 1982: "Thanks to Canadian efforts, the Conference [UNCLOS] is fully aware of the particular importance of maintaining the ecological balance of the Arctic waters. We find it most useful that such an international instrument will be established through the Law of the Sea Convention. In particular, we draw attention to the provisions of the present draft Convention in Article 234 on ice-covered areas, which we believe will provide a satisfactory basis for negotiations on and regulation of activities like the proposed Arctic Pilot Project."

The Inuit Circumpolar Conference (ICC) co-ordinated Greenlandic participation at the NEB hearings on the APP in Ottawa in March 1982 and supported this intervention financially. The Greenlandic witnesses were not heard in any representative capacity, but merely as individual hunters and other experts from Greenland. The only exception was Mads Christensen, a civil servant from the home rule administration and a member of the APP working group, who spoke in his capacity as a civil servant by permission of the Danish government. Otherwise Denmark made a point of not lending official status to the Greenlandic witnesses. No one from the Danish embassy in Ottawa was anywhere close to the hearing room on Albert Street during the Greenlandic visit. Among the ICC's other initiatives was the establishment of a special APP working group centring its activities around total opposition to the project. In November 1982 the organization arranged an APP seminar in Copenhagen with international participation.

Finn Lynge, the Greenlandic member of the European Parliament, raised the APP issue in the Environmental Affairs Committee, which passed a statement opposing the project.

The APP was brought to the attention of the Nordic Council in the spring of 1982 by Otto Steenholdt of the Atassut Party. He participated in the Council's session as a member of the Danish Social Democratic Party's delegation (until the election in January 1984, Atassut co-operated with the Social Democrats in the Danish Parliament). Steenholdt asked the Nordic countries to support Greenland in its opposition to the APP, pointing to the possible effects that the project might have on the environment, sea mammals, and Greenland's economy.

In a statement distributed to the International Whaling Commission (IWC) at the annual meeting in July 1982, the Danish government spoke in favour of a moratorium on projects such as the APP until solutions had been found that took into account the special environmental and socioeconomic conditions of the area. Denmark, in co-operation with Sweden and the Netherlands, also presented a draft resolution that encouraged the Canadian government to postpone the APP until the environmental problems had been solved in a way that assured that whales would not be endangered by the project. The text was withdrawn before it was voted on, since it had become clear to the three sponsoring countries that sufficient support was lacking.

Tusarliivik, the home rule administration's information service, also published a number of information sheets and brochures explaining Greenland's attitude to the APP. This material was passed out to interested citizens as well as to visiting foreign journalists. Tusarliivik had considerable success in alerting the international press.

GREENLAND'S OWN APP

After the home rule Parliament had discussed the APP at the fall session in 1981 and unanimously voted against it, the Greenlandic newspaper *Sermitsiaq* published an editorial titled "Greenland's Own APP." The newspaper was referring to the oil project in Jameson Land. There, deep under the windswept surface of East Greenland, there may be hydrocarbons in quantities to make Greenland economically and therefore politically more independent.

The prospect of obtaining new revenues of its own and reducing its dependence on Danish subsidies seems so attractive to the home rule government that it is willing to sacrifice some of the principles that were advocated so vigorously against the APP. If oil is found in sufficient quantities in Jameson Land, it will have to be shipped out by "icebreaking tankers, ice-strengthened tankers aided by icebreakers, or submarine tankers," according to an internal report from the Greenland Technical Organization (a Danish government agency under the Ministry for

Greenland) to the Secretariat of the Joint Council on Mineral Resources. Dated 17 January 1983, the report also notes: "The transportation modes that have been mentioned may, under unfortunate circumstances, result in a considerable oil spill. There is also an as yet undetermined risk that icebreaking in the pack ice will cause noise that may scare away whales and seals within a great distance of the shipping lanes." In spite of this report, Premier Motzfeldt is very much in favour of developing Jameson Land.

The evident ambivalence in the home rule government's attitude towards Canadian tanker projects, on the one hand, and its own planned activities off Greenland's east coast, on the other, was underlined by a reporter from Radio Greenland who asked the Premier on Radio Greenland (21 June 1983) if Greenlandic ships were less harmful than Canadian ones. "We [the Joint Council] have not discussed the mode of transportation, although we probably will use ships – we have not considered transporting the oil by airplane," he answered. "But what type of ship is used is something we'll discuss when the time comes. No oil has been found as yet."

The most likely location for the tanker terminal would be at Hurry Inlet, which has the advantage of being sufficiently deep and ice-free. If a harbour is built there – and there does not seem to be a realistic alternative – the tankers will be passing within sight of the hunting community of Itteqqortoormiit (Scoresbysund). The ships would also have to navigate Scoresby Sound, which, in terms of biological importance to the region and in its productivity, is an East Greenlandic equivalent of Lancaster Sound. If predictions by the home rule government's own experts on the effects of the APP on marine life are any measure, there will be nothing for the local hunters to hunt any more. The 500 inhabitants of the Itteqqortoormiit area will be deprived of the basis for their subsistence.

The initial response of the community's municipal council was to voice total opposition to the Jameson Land project. Mayor Jonas Nielsen stated: "We know that even small freight vessels scare away the animals. I don't even want to think about how they'd react if icebreaking tankers are to navigate our fiord."[6] The home rule administration is, in fact, confronted with its own campaign against the APP. The inhabitants of the Itteqqortoormiit area are, like hunters elsewhere in Greenland, well informed about the harmful effects of year-round icebreaking activity. They have been told all about it by their own government. Nevertheless, the home rule administration seems to have managed to soften the position of the municipal council.

The Jameson Land project may even be able to benefit from its disputed Canadian counterpart. Stressing the importance of further research into the noise issue, the GTO report of 17 January 1983 states: "Such scientific investigations as are currently being carried out in connection with the Arctic Pilot Project and the results of this work will be valuable in making an assessment for Jameson Land."

Premier Motzfeldt seems willing to sacrifice Itteqqortoormiit, if necessary, to gain greater self-determination for Greenland. But not all Greenlandic members of the Joint Council are willing to go that far. Lars Emil Johansen, the Minister of Resources and Industries, has said to the council that it is not acceptable for the Jameson Land project's environmental effects to be treated more gently than those of the APP, because that might reduce the credibility of the Greenlandic authorities.[7]

Arqaluk Lynge, the Chairman of Inuit Ataqatigiit, who became a member of the Joint Council in April 1983, had put in a good deal of effort in opposing oil development in Jameson Land. Prior to the election of 6 June 1984, he made his party's support of a coalition government conditional on a five-year moratorium on exploration. But following the election, when a coalition government had been formed by the Siumut and Inuit Ataqatigiit parties, Inuit Ataqatigiit ceased its call for an exploration moratorium. Political concessions being required to obtain two of the seven Cabinet seats, the party appeared to have abandoned major elements of its earlier position on the Jameson Land issue.

Following a meeting of the Joint Council on Mineral Resources at the end of June 1984, Premier Motzfeldt said: "As of the present, there has been no change in the Government's position on oil development." Motzfeldt also made it clear that there would be no objection from his government to ARCO's plan to build a supply base at Hurry Inlet – this in spite of previous assertions by both governing parties that ships would not be allowed entry into Scoresby Sound in connection with oil exploration. Evidently other considerations had entered the picture in addition to the area's environmental sensitivity and importance as a hunting ground for the population of Itteqqortoormiit.

IMPLICATIONS FOR CANADA

The home rule authorities have clearly demonstrated that they will not readily accept all-year navigation in Baffin Bay and Davis Strait. If Denmark's loyalty to Greenland in the EC negotiations is any measure, the Danish government is likely to go far in supporting the preferences of its former colony. Only by applying considerable political pressure, or by going ahead without the consent of Denmark/Greenland, would such tanker traffic be possible as the issue stood late in 1985.

The impact of tanker traffic on Canada's relations with Denmark and Greenland would obviously be very negative. Further, Danish-Greenlandic relations might suffer in the process. Canadian pressure on Denmark to accept the tankers would put the Danish commitment to Greenland to the test. If Denmark were to fail the test – either by giving in to Canadian pressure or by being perceived by the Greenlanders as not doing enough to stop the tankers – feelings of abandonment and alienation in Greenland might well be very strong.

This is precisely the outcome that Denmark has been trying to avoid in fear of Greenland's secret weapon: the island's strategic importance. Just as involuntary membership in the EC became an important motivation for the Greenlanders in striving for home rule, so unwanted icebreaking tankers off Greenland's west coast could inspire them to sever relations with their "disloyal" national government in Copenhagen and take yet another step towards independence. The political instability that would ensue on the strategically important land mass at the northeastern corner of the North American continent would hardly be in the interest of Canada and would seem to outweigh the advantages that Canada might gain from the tanker projects.

Another option would be to keep the tankers on the Canadian side of Davis Strait, which is more heavily ice-infested. Although this might not evoke quite as strong a reaction, the Greenlanders might still not acquiesce: noise and other forms of tanker pollution would not respect such a dividing line. The only way for Canada to assure avoidance of a confrontation with its eastern neighbour would be to build pipelines to move Arctic hydrocarbons to market. In the distant future submarine tankers may also become more than a possibility. The home rule government has not, however, stated its position on this technology, which is still in the early planning stage.

The future may nevertheless bring not only new technology for the transportation of hydrocarbons, but also a more co-operative Greenlandic attitude. If oil is discovered in Jameson Land, the home rule government will have to use icebreaking tankers to get it out. Although Canada has somehow managed to live with its opposition to the *Manhattan* while supporting its own Arctic tanker proposals, Greenland's international credibility would seem to be on the line if the home rule authorities opposed tankers on the west coast while accepting them on the east coast. In Greenland an ambivalent policy like Canada's would not be easily accepted, if only because of the stronger emphasis on "ideology" in Greenland's political life. Indeed, the word "pragmatism" has a negative connotation in Greenland as well as Denmark.

Canada's best options seem to be to choose pipelines or to adopt a wait-and-see attitude. The same undoubtedly applies to others who would use tankers to bring hydrocarbons eastward through the Northwest

Passage. Meanwhile, as of early 1986, drilling in Jameson Land has been suspended for two years as a result of declining oil prices.

PART THREE

Canadian Arctic Politics

CHAPTER EIGHT

Lessons of the Arctic Pilot Project

JENNIFER LEWINGTON

For many of those who were aware of it, the Arctic Pilot Project (APP) was the epitome of Canadian corporate dynamism. Private- and public-sector entrepreneurs joined together in the late 1970s to propose a futuristic energy transportation venture to bring the first of the high Arctic's natural gas discoveries to market. The project, a demonstration scheme initially estimated to cost $1.5 billion, called for the extraction and pipeline transportation of natural gas from Drake Point to the southern shore of Melville Island, where it was to be liquefied and loaded onto two icebreaking liquefied natural gas tankers, which would sail back and forth to a port in eastern Canada on a year-round basis beginning in 1983. The idea seemed truly promising to begin with. But in the recession-ridden world of the early 1980s, when caution reigned, the APP was able to win few friends in the federal Cabinet or in the boardrooms of the nation.

The project invited extreme reactions. Throughout its brief history, spanning five years of tumultuous energy politics in Canada and abroad from 1977 to 1982, the APP led a roller-coaster life, its fortunes moving up and down with new developments, both promising and forbidding. In retrospect, the APP was remarkable not as a failed attempt to make use of the Northwest Passage but because it took so long to fail. The reasons for such a judgment are complex and offer a commentary on the energy policies pursued by corporations and governments in our time. They also suggest that another APP could emerge, with Ottawa as ill-prepared as before to make difficult choices about Canada's energy future.

For all the APP's complexities, a single feature stands out. From the outset it was a chameleon. Nurtured by strong-minded personalities, it appeared to offer a little of something for everyone. The "something" had a way of changing to suit the needs of the day. At first, adaptability helped the APP to attract support from a diverse community of interests. But in the end, this quality made for defeat. Lacking a clear and compelling purpose, the APP ultimately died as the victim of falling oil prices and recession.

As both prime policy-maker and regulator of northern energy development, the federal government could have forced the sponsors – led by its own federal crown corporation, Petro-Canada – to define the central concept of the APP more clearly from the start. But the government had no coherent view of what it wanted from the Arctic and asked probing questions of the APP only as it neared the end of its life. As well, the APP evaded close scrutiny by governments distracted by a series of politically charged energy dilemmas: the financial and political perils of the proposed intracontinental natural gas pipeline from Alaska, through Canada, to the lower 48 American states; the fate of the Alsands and Cold Lake oil sands projects in Alberta; and the near-demise of Dome Petroleum Ltd and the collapse of its Beaufort Sea oil dream. These issues, which drew far more attention than the APP, were played out in a context of abrasive energy politics between Ottawa and Edmonton, and highly variable oil prices on the international scene.

At different times, the APP seemed to capture the imagination of federal politicians, from Prime Minister Pierre Trudeau on down, who saw the project as part of the cherished dream of opening up the Canadian north.[1] Arctic energy development in federal territory also appealed as a means of offsetting the prominent role of Alberta in national energy politics. By contrast, Energy, Mines and Resources (EMR) bureaucrats were never enthusiastic about the venture. Compared to the major energy issues of the day, the APP was a minor matter for EMR. But since Petro-Canada asked only for incremental sums of money for the project, EMR officials had no interest in a fight with the corporation, whatever their misgivings over the scheme. In the absence of organized opposition from the leading federal agency on energy matters, the corporate sponsors of the APP were free to embellish and adapt the concept as conditions changed.

ORIGINS

The seeds of the APP germinated at Petro-Canada soon after the corporation's creation in 1976. Eager to establish a presence, the fledgling state oil company looked for projects with which to build a diversified national base and, not incidentally, to silence its critics.[2] Wilbert "Billy" Hopper, Petro-Canada's president and later chairman, was suited to the dual public-private sector objectives of the new corporation. Like many Calgary oilmen, he saw the frontier as the key to Canada's future growth as an energy-rich nation. As an influential energy bureaucrat in Ottawa, he saw a role for government to support new ventures with a payoff, in terms of the national interest, some years down the road. An ebullient personality, Hopper was at his convincing best when he had a new project to promote. For Petro-Canada, the APP was a symbol of the new company's boldness: an all-Canadian energy project to pioneer year-round shipping by tankers through the Canadian portion of the Northwest Passage. With characteristic flair, Hopper said that the APP was "akin to opening up the Canadian West by railroads 100 years ago."[3]

Already a company with diverse interests in oil sands, natural gas, and oil properties in the Canadian West, Petro-Canada was also a player on unknown, at the time, prospects off the coast of Nova Scotia and Newfoundland. As well, the company had a 45 per cent stake, later rising to 53 per cent, in Panarctic Oils, a public/private-sector consortium of oil companies active in the high Arctic islands. From the mid-1960s, the Panarctic partners had been successful in finding some oil and a lot of natural gas, but they had no way of delivering the gas to southern markets. Without a transportation system, the partners had to sit on their discoveries. Meanwhile, Petro-Canada's rivals were busy elsewhere in the north. Dome Petroleum Ltd, long the private-sector favourite of federal politicians, had a strong hold on offshore play in the Beaufort Sea. Dome, a pioneer in offshore winter drilling, was also the leading and most persuasive advocate of tankers to deliver oil from the western Arctic. But Petro-Canada saw itself as a new, national oil giant that would take second place to none, including part-Canadians like Dome as well as foreign multinationals active in Canadian frontier areas. The APP, then, was a means to establish Petro-Canada's primacy in the eastern Arctic in the way that Dome had done in the western Arctic.

Donald Wolcott, credited with the original idea for the APP, shared Hopper's vision of the north. An experienced oilman and engineer, Wolcott had spent a decade with Dome Petroleum in natural gas and pipeline operations. As one of the few industry veterans to join Petro-Canada in its early days, Wolcott was a valuable asset, not least because he gave the company credibility with its critics. A former fighter pilot, Wolcott was a domineering personality who forged ahead with the APP and swept others along with him. At Petro-Canada, Wolcott was named senior vice-president with responsibility for special projects, a position that allowed him to develop his Arctic ideas. One was a scheme to use tankers to exploit northern hydrocarbon resources at an early date. He saw that tankers had an advantage in being able to deliver natural gas in volumes smaller than those required by pipelines, which needed to move large quantities to justify their high capital cost. At first, his colleagues were sceptical, questioning both the economics of the proposition and the technological capability of Canadian industry to do the job. But Wolcott pushed ahead with Hopper's support. The combined force of their never-say-no enthusiasm gave the APP its initial momentum.

On paper, Wolcott's scheme had a good deal of appeal. It was a pilot project, using only small quantities of gas to test the feasibility of year-round shipping through the Passage. Small in scale, the then-$1.5 billion APP was less threatening to the environment and to native communities than a rival proposal, the $6.1 billion Polar Gas Project, which envisaged delivery of high Arctic gas reserves by pipeline to markets more than 2,000 miles away in Ontario. The APP had other attractions. It would generate the first revenues from Arctic gas discoveries that dated back a decade. As a pioneering transportation venture, the project was touted as a way to lift Canadian industry to the forefront of Arctic marine technology, making Canada a world leader to rival the Soviet Union and Finland.[4] Not least, the project would strike a blow for Canadian sovereignty over its Arctic waters, the country's third and most neglected sea area.

In sum, the APP set out in a haze of objectives – corporate aggrandizement and profit, Arctic marine transportation leadership, energy supply, and political sovereignty – with no single purpose clearly paramount. Depending on the conditions, one objective would get more emphasis than another. But without a prime purpose, such as energy supply or transporation innovation, the APP rested uneasily on shifting ice.

In the beginning, the APP was portrayed primarily as a small-scale transportation experiment for the Arctic. Early in 1977, Wolcott turned to Michael Bell, a senior Montreal shipping executive, to assemble a consortium to assess the Arctic marine dimension. Bell put together Melville Shipping, a marriage of four Canadian and American shipping firms, some with years of experience in Arctic barge work. Later, the consortium was reduced to three Canadian companies. Bell was a long-time Arctic marine enthusiast. Although he had some doubts about the feasibility of Wolcott's idea, Bell also saw opportunities. "Everything depends on the shipping element. He who controls the transportation system controls the Arctic," he once declared.[5] For the Melville Shipping partners, the APP was a stepping-stone to a potentially lucrative future in Arctic marine transportation. The partners also saw Dome as a shipping competitor in the Arctic, with its ambitious plans for a fleet of oil tankers operating from the Beaufort. If the Melville group established a shipping presence in the eastern Arctic, it could head off a virtual monopoly by Dome in northern tanker traffic.

Transportation considerations also motivated Alberta Gas Trunk Ltd (AGTL) – later renamed Nova – to join the APP partnership. Under its chief executive officer, Robert Blair, AGTL was a major pipeline transmission company in Alberta that was determined to project its corporate presence northward. The company had recently been awarded the right to build the Canadian section of the intracontinental pipeline to bring Alaskan natural gas to the "lower 48" U.S. states. An experienced builder of pipelines in cold-weather conditions, AGTL stood to gain a strong position in frontier work with the APP by building the feeder pipe from Panarctic's Drake Point field to the proposed liquefaction plant on Melville Island. At the time Petro-Canada and AGTL also were partners in an $800 million-plus natural gas project to extend the existing cross-country gas pipeline eastward to Quebec and the Maritimes, which were regarded as potential consumers of Arctic gas. For AGTL, there were risks, too. The APP would open the door to some 13 trillion cubic feet of gas located in the high Arctic, adding these reserves to the official inventory of Canadian gas. Arctic gas was a possible competitor to Alberta gas, AGTL's bread and butter, in the drive for new exports to the U.S. market. Still, the attractions outweighed the possible risks.

For Panarctic Oils, the transportation aspect of the APP was a crucial means to a long-standing end. Though Panarctic had struck gas in the mid-1970s, the rate of new discoveries had slowed by 1977 and partners were beginning to defect. Lacking evidence either of new finds or of a way to market them, the partners had little reason to contribute indefinitely to the consortium. After spending years in exploration and more than $700 million in public- and private-sector money, Panarctic was anxious to obtain natural gas revenues. Panarctic President Charles Hetherington was not, however, an early enthusiast of the APP. He preferred the Polar Gas project because it involved the sale of much larger volumes of Arctic gas. But the expensive Polar Gas plan was stalled, lacking sufficient reserves to make it a viable proposition in the short term. Eventually, Hetherington switched to the APP as an opportunity for Panarctic to generate early income from the Drake Point field, which held about 5 trillion cubic feet of gas.

The diverse corporate interests of the various players thus converged to bring about the birth of the APP. For a time, too, the economic and political conditions were favourable as well. In 1977–8, talk was not of natural gas surpluses, as was the case as early as 1982, but of impending gas shortages in Canada and the United States. Major new gas finds in Alberta and off Nova Scotia and Newfoundland had not yet occurred. Accordingly, corporate promoters were prepared to bet on the high Arctic and Beaufort Sea as two promising, if costly, regions where mega-schemes could succeed. As well, overland energy transportation projects were running into increasing political difficulty. The Alaska natural gas pipeline, which had been the subject of major government investigations into environmental and native rights issues, had become a thorn in the side of the Canadian and U.S. governments because of financial risks. Pipelines were indeed creeping northward, but they were fraught with controversy. By contrast, the APP looked downright modest, given its comparatively low cost and incremental approach to transportation.

A FALSE START

In January 1979, after two years of groundwork by Wolcott and his small team, Petro-Canada and AGTL went public as the two APP partners. Melville Shipping was not a full partner but played an integral role because of its responsibility for the design and construction of the tankers. Panarctic, as the gas supplier, would drill the necessary wells at its Drake Point field. In the partnership, Petro-Canada had 55 per cent as operator, and AGTL the remaining 45 per cent. Together, they announced an application to the National Energy Board, the federal regulatory authority, for the right to export 250 million cubic feet of gas a day starting in 1983. In total, this would represent 1.9 trillion cubic feet of gas exports over the following 20 years, or the equivalent of less than 10 per cent of all Canadian gas exports in 1979.

The $1.5 billion scheme involved four major elements. Eight onshore wells were to be drilled by Panarctic at Drake Point, on the Sabine Peninsula of northeast Melville Island. A $100 million, 22-inch buried pipeline was to be built by AGTL from Drake Point to Bridport Inlet, a natural harbour at the south end of Melville Island. A $450 million barge-mounted liquefaction plant was to be built for Petro-Canada in southern Canada and floated north to Bridport Inlet; on-site storage tanks were to hold 200,000 cubic metres of gas at -160° Celsius. Finally, two tankers, each longer than three football fields, and built stronger than Arctic class 7 icebreakers, would be designed to move continuously through seven feet of new ice. With 32 trips in all per year, the winter voyage would take twice as long as in summer: the tankers would pass through Melville Sound, Barrow Strait, Lancaster Sound, and across Baffin Bay; then they would cut south through Davis Strait near the coast of Greenland and down past Newfoundland to a southern destination in Canada (or, later, in Western Europe). Wolcott predicted that if the pilot project succeeded, 25 to 30 ships would ply the Northwest Passage in the 1990s.[6] Such a forecast was characteristic of the APP. It held out the promise that Canada, which did not have even a Coast Guard icebreaker for year-round operation in the north, would finally make its mark as an Arctic nation.

Initially the project drew applause. For example, the Ottawa *Citizen* commented: "Petro-Canada and Alberta Gas Trunk Ltd. have come up with another dynamic idea to improve Canada's energy position and thrust Canada forward in the development of new technology ... It's just this kind of bold vision ... that Canada needs right now."[7] Even the Canadian Arctic Resources Committee, a public interest group concerned with northern environmental and native issues and later a strong critic of the APP, praised its gradualist approach. Indeed, the project's modest size was one of its strengths, making it look all the more rational when compared with pipeline schemes like the Polar Gas plan.

Still, the APP's billing as a "pilot" project belied the scale of the effort that was envisioned. The AGTL pipeline would be the first built through continuous permafrost, costing between five and seven times as much as required to move Alberta gas. And while not technologically innovative, the barge-mounted liquefaction plant required to chill and liquefy the pipelined gas would be the first to operate in Arctic conditions. The tankers, moreover, did represent a real technological advance. Designed to carry 140,000 cubic metres of gas each, these ships would be among the most powerful and sophisticated merchant vessels ever built.

Canadian shipbuilders and repairers, and the electronics and engineering industries, were both encouraged and troubled by the APP. The shipbuilders, then in financial distress like their counterparts around the world, desperately needed orders to maintain their dwindling labour force. Employment aside, the APP offered Canadian yards the hope of gaining valuable experience in building a new class of ship. For the electronics and related industries, the APP could be a catalyst in securing entry into the global market for high-technology marine components. And yet the shipbuilders feared that they might not reap great benefit from the project. For one thing, the APP partners intended to go abroad for the tanker hulls, technologically the most interesting feature of the project. In 1979, no Canadian yard was big enough to build the massive structures that had to be reinforced for ice conditions. As well, by contracting abroad for a major part of the shipbuilding work, the sponsors could make the most of price-competitive and experienced builders in South Korea and Japan. Even with a 20 per cent Canadian shipbuilding subsidy, and a 25 per cent duty on the importation of foreign-built ships, the APP still expected to pay a premium on tankers built at home.

In a sense, then, the APP was a contradiction. It was supposed to be a "high tech" venture for Canada, a departure from the country's traditional role as resource extractor. The project was to have 73 per cent Canadian content in all, but only 36 per cent of the ships' value would originate in Canada. In other words, the most job- and technology-intensive segment of the project would be in foreign hands. Moreover, since Canada had no experience in the design or construction of storage facilities for liquefied natural gas (LNG), the technology would be imported from France. In these circumstances, an early go-ahead for the APP relied on heavy use of foreign technology which would defeat the interests of Canadian industry. But if the APP delayed its initial start-up date of 1983 to allow domestic industry an edge in supplying the goods and services, the project cost would jump. Never a robust business venture, the APP would become less attractive to the partners.

After the first unveiling of the APP in early 1979 – there would be another one later – one of the few critics of the project was the Inuit Tapirisat of Canada (ITC), which represented 25,000 Inuit in communities across the Canadian north. Tiny settlements at Resolute, Grise Fiord, Arctic Bay, and

Pond Inlet, some less than 100 miles from the proposed tanker route, were home for a sea people who hunted and fished along the coasts. Six months of the year, Inuit hunters used the ice as land. They feared a potentially damaging disruption of their hunting grounds if tankers were to cut through the land-ice. Though the ships would not take long to pass any one point, it was thought that the break-up of ice and the noise would scare off marine life, interfere with mammal mating habits, and thus threaten the renewable-resource way of life of the Inuit. In truth, neither the sponsors nor its Inuit critics were sure what effect the tankers would have on Arctic marine life. But the very uncertainty raised alarm among native groups.

Despite attempts by APP officials to win support for the project during a number of tours of northern communities through 1979, native groups remained suspicious. The ITC made a basic demand that, before any resource project won federal approval, Ottawa first had to settle outstanding land claims in the eastern Arctic. Without that precondition, native groups suspected that the APP would simply open the door to large-scale Arctic development that ignored their interests. Indeed, other possibly more environmentally hazardous projects seemed to be waiting in the wings. Panarctic hoped to use tankers to market small quantities of oil reserves in the high Arctic, using a route similar to that of the APP. Other companies wanted to ship iron ore from the north by tanker. Added to these was Dome Petroleum, with its potential to deliver Beaufort Sea oil eastward by tanker. In short, the Inuit saw the APP not as a low-risk research project, as argued by the sponsors, but as the thin edge of an industrial wedge into the north where native rights had yet to be established.

And then there was the all-important question of markets. From the beginning, the partners were not sure if they would sell to the United States or to Western Europe. The answer depended on what market looked more favourable at the time. Initially, the preferred option was to land LNG either in the Maritimes or on the east coast of the United States, tying into existing delivery systems to serve American consumers. When the APP was first announced in 1979, Hopper predicted that the gas could command a premium price in the United States because Americans were in need of long-term gas supplies. But there were already some disquieting signs. U.S. government regulatory authorities had recently rejected a plan by Tenneco Inc. to import high-priced Algerian LNG through a proposed terminal in New Brunswick. Moreover, the U.S. government now ranked imports of liquefied gas as its least-preferred supply source. That decision eventually forced the APP sponsors to drop the U.S. east coast terminal option.

More important, the sponsors withdrew their application from the National Energy Board in mid-1979, only months after it first had been presented. The withdrawal of the APP application owed something not only to marketing uncertainties but also to Petro-Canada's new political preoccupation – survival. The new Conservative government, elected in May 1979, had promised to sell off the crown oil company and indeed worked actively on a sale plan throughout the remainder of the year. But though there were potential buyers for some of Petro-Canada's activities, no one showed much interest in the corporation's ideas for the high Arctic.

HOPE AND DISMAY

Just as the APP seemed headed for oblivion, a remarkable turn of events reversed its fortunes. The return of Ayatollah Khomeini to his Iranian homeland and the subsequent revolutionary turmoil there in 1979 touched off a new world energy crisis, the second in less than a decade. The fear of oil shortages sent tremors throughout the West. As governments and industry moved to secure scarce supplies, hoarding started a run-up in prices. The spot price for Middle East light oil, a stable $13 U.S. per barrel until late 1978, rose to $18 U.S. in early 1979. Then it hit $27 U.S. a few months later and soared to $38 U.S. by year's end. Transfixed by the oil price explosion, forecasters in government and industry now predicted an inexorable rise in the cost of energy. In an atmosphere of threatened scarcity and price pressure, even high-cost frontier projects began to look more economically realistic. "Initially we did not feel our project was economic," Wolcott commented in 1980, observing how the second oil price shock turned to the advantage of the APP. "Then Khomeini came along and natural gas prices started going up to substantially beyond the inflation rate."[8]

Thanks to fast-rising oil prices, the APP flourished as a credible economic proposition. In reworking the project, the sponsors now assumed a 2 per cent annual increase in oil prices after inflation. In addition, they expected natural gas to be priced equivalent to oil, an understandable premiss given the fear of supply shortages. Under such assumptions, the sponsors could count on earning about $10 U.S. per thousand cubic feet at the 1983 start-up, more than twice the export price in 1979. By 2005, the export price was supposed to rocket to an astounding $85 per thousand cubic feet. The new financial underpinnings for the project allowed the backers to predict a healthy 20 per cent on the capital invested, which was comparable to pipeline projects, instead of only 9 per cent when the APP was first conceived.

By the spring of 1980, the APP was moving ahead vigorously. The Liberals had returned to power, ending the threat to Petro-Canada. The project had a new look too. Dome Petroleum, which had been knocking at the APP's door for months, now joined as a partner. Petro-Canada remained the operator, but reduced its share to 37.5 per cent while Alberta Gas Trunk

Ltd dropped to 25 per cent. Dome came in for 20 per cent and Melville Shipping, until now an associate, became a full partner with 17.5 per cent. But it was an uneasy alliance, since the new partners were each other's rivals for a leadership role in the Arctic. "Dome was trying to develop a virtual monopoly over the Northwest Passage," a Petro-Canada official said later.[9] "They wanted to control the shipping," he added, noting that Dome's acquisition of Davie Shipbuilding had given the company additional means to realize its objectives. More important, in joining the APP, Dome was able to hedge its bets on Arctic transportation. If Ottawa gave financial and political support for only one transportation project in the Arctic, Dome wanted to be in on it, whether it was in the west or east Arctic, in oil or natural gas.

Dome's arrival effectively pushed Melville Shipping to the background. With its own ship design team already working on oil tankers, Dome became the principal architect of the LNG tankers. Melville had reached the final design stage after three years of work, but its partners had worried privately that the shipping consortium lacked critical design expertise.[10] Under Dome's management, the look of the ships changed radically. Dome relied on a Finn, Bengt Johansson, who had designed the company's highly praised Beaufort Sea drill ship, the *Kigoriak*, the first to operate year-round in the Arctic. "When Dome came in, they looked at it in an entirely different way. They saw it as a totally Arctic project," recalled a former APP official, noting that the ships subsequently looked more like Arctic icebreakers than standard LNG carriers.[11]

Dome's participation brought in new design strength, but it troubled the Inuit still more by underlining the APP's potential as a precursor for large-scale transportation of Beaufort Sea oil. Dome President William Richards did little to allay these fears. "It's no secret that Dome is planning to use tankers to get the oil out of the Beaufort and the eastern route is the obvious way of getting to the refineries in Montreal," he commented when Dome became a partner.[12] Still, continuing Inuit opposition was a minor irritant when set against the rising fortunes of the project in 1980. At mid-year, the partners signed a letter of intent, the first step to a real contract, with Panarctic Oil as the gas supplier. A few weeks later, as part of the same process, the sponsors signed another letter of intent with four large American natural gas buyers, led by Tenneco.

These improvements in the overall outlook as of 1980 brought out new colours in the chameleon. Although the APP's "chief benefit" in 1979 was to be gas revenues,[13] the new emphasis in 1980 was on the transportation challenge as the key to wider development of frontier natural resources. Once we get it [the gas] moving," Petro-Canada Chairman Hopper claimed in a newspaper interview, "there will be all kinds of commercial development possible."[14] The fluid nature of the project – sometimes transportation-oriented, sometimes energy-related – masked one of its most troubling aspects. However much the sponsors pointed to a variety of potential plusses, the APP was in truth an export project that added nothing to domestic oil security.

Buoyed by the rise in energy prices, the APP partners submitted a new application to the National Energy Board in October 1980, just weeks before the Liberal government announced its nationalist energy program. Transcanada Pipelines Ltd, the country's biggest gas transmission company, joined the project but not the partnership. Transcanada's job was to build a $217 million terminal somewhere in eastern Canada – the site was left vague – to regassify the liquid from the tankers. The company coyly kept open its options between rival regassification sites in Quebec and Nova Scotia.

The APP also had a new marketing strategy designed to strengthen its appeal to American customers. As before, the plan was to deliver 225 million cubic feet a day of Arctic gas into the Maritimes, with an equivalent amount of Alberta gas sold to the United States. However, the swap arrangement presented some risk of supply interruption to the Americans because they were buyers of the Arctic gas even if they physically received Alberta gas. Therefore, as a sweetener, the APP sponsors now offered an additional direct sale of 225 million cubic feet of Alberta gas, with both the regular and extra sales going at the prevailing export price. Nevertheless, for all the seeming attractions of the APP, the American buyers were prepared to accept few risks. While the purchasers were required to take and pay for all the gas, regardless of need, they did not share in the cost of possible cost over-runs, as is normally the case in such energy deals. Curiously, the APP sponsors optimistically banked on only a 25 per cent over-run, in spite of extreme Arctic conditions and forecasts of high inflation. As one Petro-Canada official remarked later, "The market was not prepared to take any significant risk."[15]

At the official level, the newly revised APP received a cool reception from federal bureaucrats. Given the frontier emphasis of the October 1980 energy program, officials in the federal Department of Energy, Mines and Resources (EMR) should have been enthusiastic. In fact, they were sceptical. The energy policy document released that month gave the high Arctic a low rating as an early supply source. "In the case of natural gas, the need for Arctic gas in Canadian markets may not arise for many years," the authors declared.[16] Their scepticism was prompted in part by a banner exploration year in 1979, led by the discovery of the Hibernia oilfield and the Sable Island gas field. With these major plays, and a run of successful gas finds in western Canada, energy planners were reluctant to race to develop high-cost Arctic gas first.

While they showed little enthusiasm for the project, EMR officials were not ready to kill it, either. For one thing, given the relatively modest sums invested by Petro-Canada at the time, one official said later, "It [the APP] was not something we were prepared to go to the mat on."[17] For another, energy bureaucrats and federal politicians were mired in a more urgent conflict with Alberta over oil prices and taxes. Again, Hopper was able to capitalize on the lack of concentrated official opposition to steer the project through the political shoals of Ottawa in 1980 and early 1981.

The concept did indeed appeal to federal politicians such as Prime Minister Trudeau, Energy Minister Marc Lalonde, and Indian Affairs and Northern Development Minister John Munro. All were attracted by the idea of developing the potential of the north. But there was an extra fillip for Lalonde, who was battling Washington over his energy program. With Europe now becoming a possible market for APP gas, Canada could diversify its exports away from sole reliance on the United States. On a visit to Canada early in 1981, West German Chancellor Helmut Schmidt urged Trudeau to push ahead with the APP to fill Canada's potential as a resource exporter. Excited by the growing interest of the West Germans and the French (who saw the APP primarily as a means of selling technology to Canada), the Department of External Affairs supported the project as a means of building new industrial links with Western Europe. For Indian Affairs and Northern Development, the APP would promote "orderly" economic activity in the Arctic. By contrast, native groups had become increasingly vocal critics, now using networks such as the Inuit Circumpolar Conference, which represented Inuit from Alaska, Canada, and Greenland. Anxious to quell a swelling tide of Greenlandic opposition, Petro-Canada asked John Munro to fly to Denmark in late 1980 to ease concerns over Danish sovereignty, tanker noise, and threats to the livelihood of native Greenlanders.[18] This diplomatic effort was one of several through 1980 and 1981 designed to assuage mounting criticism about the potentially damaging environmental effects of the project.

Under the weight of record-high interest rates – one of the repercussions of the energy shock – megaprojects began to come apart. In mid-1981, Imperial Oil cancelled its $12 billion oil sands plant. Daunted by rising energy prices and the promise of further price hikes in the wake of the Ottawa-Alberta accord of September 1981, consumers started curbing their appetite for oil and gas. The recession deepened the conservation trend. After more than a decade of increasing sales, the demand for LNG tumbled in 1981, along with oil and natural gas consumption world-wide.

Just as a convergence of circumstances gave the APP credibility in 1980, the new series of events through 1981 conspired to highlight the inherent frailty of the project. Though the sponsors anxiously pressed the National Energy Board (NEB) to open hearings as soon as possible, NEB officials persisted in demanding more information to fill in the gaps. Personally frustrated by the delays, Wolcott had stepped down as project leader in mid-1981 in order to set up his own company. Although he remained a consultant to the APP, his diminished involvement was tacit admission that the project was running out of steam. "He was an instigator, not an implementer," an ex-colleague observed, arguing that a promoter's personality – essential to the APP's genesis – was unsuited to the needs of project implementation.[19]

In the summer of 1981 the sponsors once again modified their marketing concept. In this latest revision, they dropped the proposal to sell additional Alberta gas to the United States and returned to the original notion of selling only Arctic gas. The decision was a tactical manoeuvre, designed to avoid an appearance before a major gas export hearing scheduled by the NEB for early 1982. By dropping the "sweetener" volume of Alberta gas, the APP application would not be heard with other applications by western Canadian gas producers for licences to export new gas supplies to the United States. Given the troubling signs of weakening gas markets in the United States, Alberta gas producers were sure to have launched a strong attack on the APP's plan. In effect, the APP sponsors had decided to leave the NEB battlefield before the war opened. That way, the APP could marshal its forces for a separate NEB hearing, now expected in late 1981, to consider the frontier project.

Associated with the tactical withdrawal was a costly blunder. It turned out that the sponsors had met privately with NEB officials and Chairman Geoffrey Edge in the summer of 1981 to discuss procedural changes for the upcoming APP hearing. After the private meeting, the board revised a previously announced agenda for the APP hearing, putting export questions first and leaving environmental and social issues for later.

The Inuit Tapirisat of Canada and the Baffin Regional Inuit Association were enraged. They charged that the new agenda put them at a disadvantage. With the hearings just a few months away, the intervenors argued that they had insufficient time to prepare for a discussion of exports. In opposing the NEB's change of procedure, the native groups formed an unlikely alliance with the Ontario government. The province was a determined opponent of the APP, viewing it as a threat to the Polar Gas project, part of which was owned by the government of Ontario. In what would be the first of many legal skirmishes, the Inuit and Ontario went to the Federal Court of Canada to protest the private meeting of the APP sponsors and the board. Round 1 went to the Inuit and Ontario. Geoffrey Edge was forced to step down as chairman of the hearing, which was delayed three months, until February 1982, to give the intervenors time to prepare.

When the hearing finally began, APP officials counted on a quick review, lasting no more than three months. But rancorous testimony dragged on for seven months without the hearings reaching a conclusion; the books were formally closed on the project by the NEB only in August 1984. Looking back on the proceedings in 1982, APP officials complained that the board was overly solicitous of the Inuit and their time-consuming interventions. In reality, larger forces, some of the project's own making, worked against quick approval. In December 1981, the federal Cabinet had frozen Petro-Canada's APP budget, except for $12.5 million needed for the NEB hearing. Meanwhile, the other partners were reluctant to spend any more than necessary to keep going. Dome was financially strapped after its gluttonous corporate buying bout and privately threatened to pull out of the APP. Alberta Gas Trunk Ltd, now known as Nova, also wanted to pare down its commitment. By this time, Hopper was no longer enthusiastic about the APP's prospects, given the economic climate. "Morale could not have been worse," one participant said later, "we were cutting staff as we went into the hearing."[20]

At the NEB, resistance to the APP gathered force just when the sponsors could least afford it. Hopper and Joel Bell, senior vice-president of Petro-Canada, secretly talked to Ontario in a bid to neutralize its opposition. In one overture in late 1981, the two executives suggested a marriage of the APP and Polar Gas, but Ontario refused to co-operate. At the same time, Alberta gas producers grew increasingly hostile. They viewed the APP as a double threat: not only did it offer competition to Alberta's declining gas sales to the United States, but Alberta producers were not to be allowed a share in the export revenues flowing from the APP – contrary to the terms of the Ottawa-Alberta pricing agreement of September 1981. Instead, the APP sponsors planned to take all the export revenues to give themselves an adequate return.

If this were not enough, the American gas buyers turned on the sponsors. Once supportive of the APP concept, Tenneco had become indifferent by early 1982. Early purchases of high-cost Arctic gas, using an untested delivery system, now held little attraction in view of weak gas markets and stiff regulatory hurdles in the United States. But Tenneco was not ready to give up its right of first refusal to the Melville Island gas. While Petro-Canada told the NEB that the gas buyer's rights had expired, Tenneco asserted that its rights were still valid and that it had no desire to free Petro-Canada to talk to potential French and West German buyers.

Nor were the APP partners in a position to redeem the project by demonstrating that it was vital to the national interest. In view of falling energy prices, it was increasingly evident that the Canadian taxpayer would face a substantial bill if APP markets failed to materialize. Petro-Canada had budgeted about 5 per cent of its capital spending for the project and now planned to borrow $832 million through 1987. But if the APP consortium collapsed or the other partners failed to come up with their full share, Petro-Canada would need the government of Canada to foot the bill. There were other potential financial burdens. Transcanada planned to incorporate the cost of its southern receiving terminal – by now an estimated $300 million – into the company's overall rate base, which was approved annually by the NEB. This meant that domestic gas consumers would pick up the tab for the terminal and any cost over-runs. In short, Canadian consumers stood to pay heavily for what was in essence an export project.

Given the mounting opposition and financial risks, the sponsors might have been expected to pursue a strategy of conciliation at the NEB hearings. Instead, they tied the viability of the project to the board's granting a series of special favours. The need to adopt such a strategy stemmed from the inherent weakness of the APP concept. Common sense suggested that the project was no longer economic. But the sponsors reasoned that the project still had a chance if the board agreed to extend certain costly allowances. For one thing, they argued that the board should give the sponsors, not Alberta producers, the APP gas revenues flowing back to the Alberta border. It should, in addition, excuse the sponsors from the same gas surplus test applied to other exporters of gas from the West (the test ensured that there was enough gas for Canadians before supplies were sold abroad, but the sponsors had no desire to see other frontier projects get the same favourable treatment). Further, it ought to give the sponsors special freedom to replace APP gas with supplies from anywhere in Canada, in case of delivery interruptions; but the sponsors did not want APP gas exports curtailed in case of domestic shortages. Finally, it should give royalty and tax relief for Panarctic, so that it would not have to pay taxes in the early years of the project – in effect, having subsidized Panarctic's exploration work for years, taxpayers would receive no revenue from its gas sales until years later. Thus the APP represented an extraordinarily high price for Canadians to pay for a venture that did little for oil self-sufficiency, orderly resource development, native interests, environmental concerns, or Canadian energy revenues.

Midway through the hearings, in the summer of 1982, the sponsors made a last bid to save the project. Having talked on and off about Europe as an alternative buyer, they now presented that area as the preferred solution, in view of the depressed U.S. market. Accordingly, in July, APP asked Transcanada to withdraw its application for the southern Canadian terminal. At the same time, the sponsors wanted the NEB to press on with the nearly completed hearings on the northern portion. In so doing, they stoutly maintained that the project was still intact, even though it was no longer clear if, and where, markets existed for the gas. Not surprisingly, the intervenors vigorously protested that the APP no longer had a leg to stand on. As one lawyer recalled, "The APP stepped over the line from having the skeleton of a project to having the possibility of nothing."[21] Hearing chairman Livia Thur agreed with the intervenors. In late August 1982 she adjourned the hearings until the APP could put its marketing program together.

Notwithstanding the long odds on deals with French and West German buyers, world gas markets being so weak, APP officials were publicly optimistic for months about contracts in Europe. For their part the Europeans were quite willing to talk, since they had nothing to lose. While there was no immediate need for Arctic gas, the French, West Germans, and British all required imports in the next century, and new supply sources from Canada could become a sensible alternative. In this vein, the sponsors discussed a possible 50 per cent equity interest with the French and West Germans. While not committing themselves, both countries were prepared to invest some time and a little money in the APP for the long term. For the French, keen to maintain their shipping industry as a leader in LNG transportation, the APP was a vehicle for industrial spin-offs rather than a new gas source. But the greater the French participation, the fewer the industrial benefits for Canada, contrary to the original concept of the APP.

The APP discussions with the Europeans continued into 1983. But in reality the project had died months earlier, with the NEB adjournment. In many ways, the APP was a victim of circumstance in that it entered the regulatory stage during one of the worst recessions in 50 years. But in another respect,the APP's downfall was of its own making: a shapeless concept lacking inner substance was revealed as such. Lacking a set of purposes that could withstand unfavourable economic conditions, the APP was unable to justify itself as being either commercially sound or in the public interest. Though they blamed their misfortunes on the NEB hearings, the sponsors should have looked at their own performance more closely. Having failed to assemble a coherent concept, they were ultimately unable to prevent others from concluding that the project was premature or, worse, ill-conceived.

LESSONS

One of the lessons of the 1980s for Canadian energy entrepreneurs is that not all oil and natural gas projects are created equal. As the sponsors of the Alsands tar sands project learned so painfully in 1982, even the offer of major government subsidies could not save a scheme that was dependent on high oil prices, which had evaporated in the midst of economic recession. As had been the case with the Alsands partners, the APP sponsors eventually had to come to terms with the discipline of the market. As a first rule of thumb, an energy megaproject must make economic sense when judged in the harshest and not the most favourable circumstances. If it fails that tough test, then both sponsors and governments must negotiate what, if any, subsidies are required to put the project over the top in the interest of the nation. In the case of both Alsands and Cold Lake, the answer lay in scaling down the size of the effort in order to create a workable approach to oil sands development. Even then, governments had to provide tax relief to get the projects going in 1984 in an environment of stable oil prices.

Unlike the APP, the oil sands developers had a convincing case for an early push to production. Given the alternatives for new oil development in Canada, it made more sense to extract known resources on provincial lands before moving to frontier regions, where costs of production were even higher and where there were fewer spin-offs for the local economy. By contrast, the APP could not offer a winning argument to justify the development of Arctic natural gas reserves before Alberta oil or, for that matter, to exploit high Arctic resources for export in advance of the less costly East Coast alternatives.

For the future, the successful corporate energy sponsor will need a better check-list against which to assess the odds on moving through the economic and regulatory maze to ultimate success. Size alone is not the determinant of success or failure, although the larger the scale, the higher the risk that heavy government subsidies will be needed to launch the enterprise. More important than size are criteria such as market demand, whether export or domestic; viability in the absence of government subsidies; extent of subsidies required; alternative supplies; environmental considerations; and net benefit to the region and the country. In the case of the APP, the project made little economic sense in conditions of soft oil prices. It offered no energy security to Canadians. It posed high financial risks for taxpayers if the project foundered. It ranked behind alternative natural gas sources. And it offered mixed benefits at best to Canadian industry. Little wonder, then, that when oil prices collapsed, the APP had not much left to prop it up.

Governments, too, have their responsibilities. For all its rhetoric about energy development after 1980, to say nothing of the situation in earlier years, the Canadian government had no coherent priorities against which to judge the APP. Before another frontier megaproject takes shape, Ottawa must decide what it wants to achieve on the frontier and at what cost. If transportation is the primary initial objective, government and industry could begin to co-operate in the development of an Arctic icebreaking capability and in gaining essential operating experience in Arctic conditions. If energy self-sufficiency is paramount, then the government must select the most promising lower-cost sources first, before moving to more expensive frontier locations.

The Arctic's hour will come. Its energy resources will be needed. While there is time, Ottawa must collaborate with all those who have a direct stake in the Arctic to ensure that the rewards of a future Arctic Pilot Project outweigh the risks.

CHAPTER NINE

Environmental Politics and Inuit Self-Government

PETER BURNET

Depending on the constitutional structure of the country concerned and on the distribution of planning responsibility and powers of decision over resource use, conservation policies may be required at more than one level of government. Roles and responsibilities should be clearly and effectively related to those levels of government above and below [the one primarily concerned]. – *World Conservation Strategy*[1]

In 1972, Jean Chrétien, then Minister of the Department of Indian Affairs and Northern Development (DIAND), announced a federal policy for northern Canada. Entitled *Northern Canada in the 70's*, the policy listed seven goals. Among them were the following: "To maintain and enhance the northern environment with due consideration to economic and social development," and "To further the evolution of government in the northern territories."[2]

When the policy was announced, the Canadian public was beginning to express a growing concern about the environmental hazards posed by large-scale industrial development in the north. The petroleum industry and the federal government were planning huge hydrocarbon exploration and transportation projects to bring the substantial oil and gas reserves of the north to southern markets. Environmentalists were claiming that these projects were ill-planned, ill-timed, and threatening to the Arctic environment, which was perceived as uniquely sensitive to damage from such ventures owing to the simplicity of its ecosystems, its low regenerative ability, and its reduced capacity to absorb pollutants.[3] When the federal government appointed Mr Justice Thomas Berger to conduct an inquiry into proposals to build pipelines down the Mackenzie Valley and across the North Slope of the Yukon, it provided a forum through which those voices of protest became a popular national cause.

This opposition was complemented by that of many native northerners who expressed similar, but not identical fears. They shared the environmental concerns, especially as they related to threats to northern wildlife, upon which the natives relied for food and their traditional ways of life. Native groups also resisted a rapid industrialization for which their peoples were not prepared and did not want in any event. But whereas environmentalists spoke of a collective, national responsibility to protect Canada's Arctic heritage, the northern natives expressed a deep resentment that their lands and adjacent marine areas were to be used for industrial activity without their consent. As part of the growing national native rights movement, the northern aboriginal peoples began demanding that the government recognize their rights to use northern lands and waters and that they should have a say in how resources would be developed.

APPARENT ALLIANCE

Despite their different emphases, environmentalists and native groups were able to make common cause before the Berger inquiry, where they registered an effective protest against a common adversary. This alliance continued in the face of several subsequent industrial proposals, such as the Arctic Pilot Project and the Norman Wells Pipeline, which both groups sought to halt or modify. As protesters outside the decision-making process for northern development, their reactive efforts harmonized very effectively, and the two groups were seen as pursuing the same goals. Throughout the 1970s, it was commonplace for journalists to depict environmentalists and native groups as holding identical opinions on controversies over northern resource development proposals such as the Mackenzie Valley Pipeline and offshore drilling in Lancaster Sound.[4]

These highly visible controversies succeeded in doing more than stopping development projects. Throughout the late 1960s and the 1970s, the values both groups were espousing gained considerable public support. Both in the north and nationally, the environmental ethic and the cause of native rights became increasingly popular. The federal government responded by announcing policies, such as the 1972 DIAND policy, that committed it to redress native grievances and promote environmental protection in national and northern development strategies. Public monies were made available to those studying and promoting these values, and the federal bureaucracy was expanded to accommodate these new federal responsibilities and goals.

The increasing integration of these values into government planning changed the nature of both groups in two significant ways. First, the number of people who were personally and professionally involved in the causes rose dramatically. The environmental "movement," broadly speaking, expanded from a loose collection of private conservationists to include large numbers of corporate employees, public institutions, scholars, professional consultants, and, especially, civil servants. While by no means a unified, integrated force, environmentalists did acquire both an established presence in bureaucratic decision-making and a measure of political influence. Ottawa's decisions to fund native organizations, negotiate comprehensive land claims agreements, and enter into constitutional negotiations with native groups had a similar effect on the native rights movement, although on a more modest scale. The 1970s saw the evolution of a trained group of lawyers, professional advisers and consultants, scholars, and, again, civil servants who presented, negotiated, studied, and implemented the political development of Canada's native peoples.

Second, both movements went from reactive protest to prescriptive advocacy. The "cause" of conservation developed into a quasi-scientific discipline called environmental management. The native political rights movement evolved into a complex attempt to test the creativity of Canadian federalism through sophisticated legal, political, and constitutional theories. There was much less co-operation and mutual understanding between the two movements in these efforts of policy development, if only because both had become so professional, inwardly focused, and inscrutable to the passing observer.

The increasingly complex and comprehensive solutions advanced by the two groups tended to have a more profound significance for the entire political, economic, and social future of northern Canada than they would have had in the south. By comparison, the north is politically and economically undeveloped. The non-native population is small and unsettled. There is no manufacturing base and relatively little industrial activity aside from mining and oil exploration. Both northern territories are governed, temporarily in theory, by the federal government, which owns and controls the use of all lands in the north. A corollary of this state of affairs was that the range of alternatives for the north appeared much broader than for the south. The political and economic development of the north lay largely in the future, and the direction of that future was not constrained by the vested interests of an established non-native population, the realities of an existing economic base, or the dictates of a permanent constitutional structure. The north was Canada's "last frontier," and our last chance to do things right![5]

What must be appreciated is that issues in the North tend to take on a significance and to produce more hostility and much tougher bargaining than the terms of the issue would seem to justify simply because they are in the North. While an issue in the South will tend more to be decided on its merits, in the North the issue will be argued in terms of its implications for the basic northern issues to which it is seen to be related. This interdependence of key issues defines northern politics. It tends to bring northern political debate regularly back to first principles and invariably those first principles have to do with the basic question of what is the most desirable future for the North.[6]

This perception led to numerous creative, sweeping proposals by environmental and native groups. Environmentalists tended to advocate comprehensive planning and resource management policies that would determine the scope of, and conditions for, various land and water uses throughout the north before specific industrial demands arose. Northern native groups focused on their comprehensive land claims negotiations with Ottawa, proposing that land claims settlements be the primary vehicle for determining the permanent political and administrative structures that would replace direct federal control over northern lands and, in the case of the Inuit, the northern offshore.

The situation in the offshore was complicated further by the fact that Inuit political organizations had yet to overcome the serious conceptual problems involved in articulating just what their claim would entail. The doctrine of aboriginal rights grew out of the common law theory of real property, which is based upon private "interests" or rights to land. No corresponding rights exist for the "offshore," which traditionally was divided between territorial waters and the high seas. Thus, although the historical use and occupancy of the Arctic offshore, which is frozen most of the year, by the Inuit was incontestable, the administrative and legal regimes that govern the offshore appeared to provide little basis for an accommodation of the collective private rights of the Inuit.

Despite some efforts by the Inuit organizations to grapple with this conceptual hurdle, both they and the government elected to concentrate on claims respecting land and to reserve offshore claims for the future. The James Bay Settlement specifically stated that the offshore claim was to be negotiated at a future date, while the COPE (Committee of Original Peoples Entitlement) settlement extinguished the rights of the Inuvialuit to the offshore in the western Arctic. Both of these agreements imply some recognition by the government that Inuit offshore rights do exist, and the issue is certain to be a difficult one in negotiations with the Inuit of the eastern Arctic, who have been the most assertive about their rights to the offshore.

It was not until 1981 that the federal government agreed to a comprehensive land use planning policy,[7] and no final land claims settlement was initialled until 1983.[8] The 1970s came and went with the apparent alliance between environmentalists and native groups still intact. As neither group succeeded in changing the course of federal northern policy in any substantial way, they could and did continue to co-operate in their individual, reactive efforts to stop or modify development proposals.

That a large segment of the public perceived them as Davids challenging the Goliaths of industry and government helped to obscure the fact that the two groups were not arguing for the same thing. Despite the priority both gave to the wise management of land and marine resources, they had quite different answers to the issue of on whose shoulders the management responsibility should best lie.

At the root of this divergence of views between Natives and non-Natives lie both real and conceptual differences in the ownership of land and resources. What frequently, in recent years, united Native people, environmentalists and conservationists around such issues as northern pipelines and hydro-electric development was, among other things, a sense of collective ownership and responsibility for land and resources, a sense that no individual or group in society has the right to appropriate or destroy resources of benefit to all. Behind the rhetoric of stewardship and the environmental ethic, however, lay unclarified just whom this collectivity consisted of.

Pressed on this question, southern environmentalists would probably respond that this collectivity is national or even international in scope. Although Native people may at times have been a more responsible (or less destructive) part of that collectivity, they are only a part. Consequently the entire nation has a management responsibility, to be exercised in keeping with international obligations of stewardship ...

Native people, on the other hand, maintain that they are the collectivity to which the land and resources belong. They were the first inhabitants and the traditional users, and although they are not unwilling to share with others, it is their responsibility and prerogative to determine how that will be done. They, as prime users and beneficiaries of faunal resources, have the greatest vested interest in and capability of sound management.[9]

Nor is the drive towards political development in the north restricted to the land claims of the aboriginal peoples.

SOUTHERN DECISION-MAKING AND NORTHERN DEVOLUTION

The territorial governments of Yukon and the Northwest Territories (NWT) have long stood for the devolution of jurisdiction over lands and resources to them, as a step on the road to provincial status. All northerners are sensitive to the fact that direct rule from Ottawa denies them the regional political representation and authority enjoyed by the majority in the south. The territorial governments have chafed, particularly under their inability to secure more than an advisory role in decisions on major non-renewable resource development: "The North can be studied as a society – actually a set of several societies – but it can only be understood as a colony. Basically, a society is colonial to the extent that major decisions affecting it are made outside it. Colonialism is weakness and dependence ... the North is totally dependent constitutionally on Ottawa. It is also a colony as a matter of practical politics in that the territories lack the political resources to sway Ottawa ... In addition, they may find that they have to take a back seat to southern or foreign-based firms that are well positioned to lobby Ottawa on questions of northern development."[10]

The issue of the devolution of political authority and legislative jurisdiction to northern governments has not been linked as closely to the environmental movement as has that of native claims. The government of the NWT has often expressed its wariness of the social and environmental impact of proposed projects, especially after the election of the ninth assembly in 1979, with its native majority, but rarely has it expressed views as forceful as those of environmentalists and native groups. The Yukon territorial government (YTG) has frequently expressed its resentment at the perceived outside interference of environmentalists and has tended to see the members of this group as a part of the colonial regime Yukoners live under.[11]

There is a consensus in the north that provincehood is the ultimate goal for the territories. The federal government has sometimes acknowledged this,[12] although current policy continues to be expressed in vague words about responsible government and constitutional development.[13] It is difficult to gauge how serious Ottawa is about devolution of jurisdiction over lands and resources, as it has set the settlement of land claims as a precondition for any negotiation on changes to its own authority in this area. Nevertheless, the change of government in Ottawa in 1984, and the signing of land claims agreements with the Council of Yukon Indians and COPE, raise the likelihood that devolution will be given a higher priority in the coming years.

Political development through land claims and devolution to northern governments are the primary public issues in the north in the 1980s.[14] If northern non-renewable resource development and environmental protection were national issues in the 1970s, it was, at least in part, because the federal government has jurisdiction in these areas. But as northerners move from protesting bystanders to duly constituted decision-makers, they will be less inclined to welcome the views of non-northerners aggressively urging them to exercise this new authority in a particular way.

However sympathetic individual environmentalists may be to the aspirations of northerners to "control their own destiny," there is an inherent conflict between the general philosophical basis of environmental thinking and the motivation of northerners working towards political evolution. Environmentalists, lacking any private rights in land and resources, emphasize a collective responsibility for conservation and tend to define that collectivity as widely as possible. This sentiment is well expressed in the introduction to *World Conservation Strategy*, which states it in terms of "the global interrelatedness of actions, with its corollary of global responsibility. This in turn gives rise to the need for global strategies both for development and for conservation of native and natural resources."[15] Such sentiments generally are expressed as moral imperatives rather than detailed proposals for centralized decision-making. Likewise, it would be unfair to suggest that environmentalists would automatically favour a continuation of the Canadian north's current colonial status. Yet, in an era of political change, environmentalists may be concerned about the transfer of jurisdiction to native or non-native northerners if they have doubts about the capabilities of these groups to manage resources, or if they suspect that these groups will not give enough priority to good conservation practices.

Even when they favour local or community decision-making, environmentalists are primarily concerned with "how" resources are managed and can be expected to relate this closely to the question of "who" should have the authority to do it. Northerners, in contrast, see devolution as a first principle, a good in itself. It is not difficult to see how these different emphases could result in arguments about the scope and timing of devolution. If we take the term *environmentalist* to include the large number of federal politicians and civil servants who are charged with the responsibility of ensuring the health of the northern environment, and who often represent the interests of environmental organizations within the federal government, there is a potential for some federal departments to argue that devolution be subject to institutional assurances that northern resources will be well managed in the national interest.

Native and non-native northerners seeking political change are interested not in global responsibility but in local control over decision-making. There are three different aspects to the northerners' perception that the role they should play in northern government is circumscribed by Ottawa's current authority. First, there is the feeling that territorial status confers a kind of second-class citizenship on northerners by denying them the political rights other Canadians enjoy under the country's federal structure. This sentiment was expressed by Chris Pearson, leader of the YTG, at the Canadian Arctic Resources Committee's Third National Workshop in 1983: "Our position with respect to resource management is simply that Yukoners deserve the same rights and responsibilities other Canadians have to develop and protect their resources."[16]

Second, the northern aboriginal peoples perceive Ottawa's jurisdiction over the north as an unlawful usurpation of their own aboriginal rights to use and manage northern lands. Their case is epitomized in the statement that "The term 'land claims' itself, from the governments perspective, means that the native people or the aboriginal people are claiming land. Our position has always been that the Dene are not claiming land. We own the land. The government, the institutions, and the corporations are claiming land."[17]

Finally, it is a characteristic of all northern peoples, with their small populations and limited, fragile renewable resource base, to resent the tendency of populous southern metropolitan centres to place the highest priority on the extraction of non-renewable resources in the name of the national interest:

Whether Europeans like the Icelanders, Faroese, and Shetlanders or aboriginal people like the Inuit of Greenland, Canada and Alaska, the Dene or the Sami (Lapps), the circumpolar people have their land and resources rights disputed by more powerful majorities farther south. These more southerly interests have their own development imperatives which often differ widely from the renewable resource economies on which the small northern societies are built. While powerful interests – be they military, oil and gas, other forms of energy or shipping – bear down on the north with the support of governments motivated by revenue needs or other economic factors, the small societies may feel themselves fighting for survival.[18]

These three sentiments have led to firm, persistent demands for political change in northern Canada. All three bespeak a resentment of overly centralized government and too much influence by non-northerners in northern decision-making. This is in sharp contrast to the notions of global responsibility and collective decision-making that environmentalists generally find so attractive.

Although any major political change for the north remains in the future, there have already been several instances of conflict between those promoting conservation and those giving priority to transfer of political authority to northern governments or native groups. Conservation groups supported by sports hunters, such as the Canadian Wildlife Federation, have long been hostile to the recognition of preferential hunting rights for natives and can be expected to resist any special role for native groups in northern wildlife management. Professional wildlife biologists and resource managers have clashed with native groups over the need for restrictions on native hunting. For more than a decade, the YTG sought to develop the North Slope of Yukon and was openly hostile to environmental groups who called for the preservation of this area and its wildlife. And two federal departments with conservation mandates refused to agree to a signed wildlife agreement between Ottawa and the Inuit on the grounds that it placed conditions on their rights to veto a decision of a proposed joint Inuit-government wildlife management board.

These examples will be discussed in more detail below. They warn of impending controversies that will accompany political change in the north.

However wise comprehensive conservation policies may be from an environmental perspective, they have meant and will continue to mean an increasingly pervasive federal bureaucratic presence in the north. The comprehensive regulation of land and ocean use demands the close involvement of federal officials at all levels of decision-making, with the result that the federal government's role will continue its subtle shift from that of governor to that of manager. The YTG has commented bitterly on this increased federal role acquired in the name of good conservation: "In spite of the fact that in the 1960s DIAND recognized itself as trustee of northern lands, it is now interpreting its mandate as: the federal agency responsible for the control, management and administration of public lands north of 60°."[19] This "hands on" approach to federal northern administration can only escalate the resentment of all northerners toward southern control of northern lands. It also threatens to retard the process of political evolution by promoting established bureaucracies with a stake in the future of the north and firm opinions on how, and at what pace, that future should evolve.

Constitutional change and imaginative land claims settlements in the onshore and offshore arrangements remain, theoretically, as possible as they always were.[20] Yet as individual federal departments and agencies, such as DIAND, Fisheries and Oceans, and Environment Canada, expand to implement and administer increasingly detailed resource management and conservation policies, they become forces in their own right and associate the national interest with the enhancement of their authority:

In a democratic state, bureaucracies are entrusted with the efficient translation into policies and administrative procedures of the goals set by their political masters. If they become policy makers in their own right, which of course they do from time to time, there is a danger that politicians, instead of aggregating the interests of their constituents and responding to the requirements of the public, become the captives of their officials. While this does happen from time to time and has even been known to produce felicitous results, it is more likely that governmental outputs will, under these conditions, increasingly reflect only the interests of the administrative state, thus alienating the people from their government.[21]

Whether promoting conservation or development, federal departments tend to guard their mandates jealously. Northerners seeking increased political authority are as much a threat to DIAND as other federal departments asserting an overlapping mandate. DIAND's draft discussion paper, *A Comprehensive Conservation Policy and Strategy for the Northwest Territories and Yukon*, contains a remarkably assertive warning to anyone proposing to challenge its authority:

DIAND, then, still has the function of "trustee" or "steward" described by Laing over twenty years ago. It can be argued that much has changed over the past twenty years; that northern conditions have changed, are dynamic and demand a changing approach and a need for flexibility. The roles and responsibilities of DIAND elaborated above, however, are not in dispute, have not altered substantially over the years, and are not negotiable. These roles and responsibilities need to be restated constantly to ensure that everyone concerned fully understands the department's position. This should not be interpreted as meaning that DIAND's role is simply one of facilitation and co-ordination; it extends beyond that to include the development of a comprehensive northern policy on conservation and recreation to provide the basis for these two functions.[22]

It should be noted that this statement purposes to define the national interest or the authority not of the federal government in the north *but of one department of that government*. It indicates a bureaucratic perception that desirable conservation policies require a strong central administrative authority. Diffusion or sharing of decision-making undermines the efficiency of these policies.

A second and related problem is the lack of understanding among environmentalists of how the issues surrounding political devolution to northerners relate to current policies on the environmental protection and management of northern resources. This is particularly the case with land claims, which are little understood in government and by the public generally. Although these claims will determine the ownership and administration of all lands in the north, they are largely ignored in government policies designed to develop or conserve the north.

Serious discussion of aboriginal claims is often avoided in northern policy debates. Whenever a spokesman from industry, government, or a conservation group advocates a particular policy initiative for the north, he or she will often conclude a detailed description of content and structure of the proposed policy with a phrase like "But, of course none of this should prejudice the settlement of land claims" or "And, of course, land claims will have to be settled, too." Rarely is any serious thought given to the contradictions inherent in such a statement, and the audience is left with the impression that land claims are off on the side somewhere, out of the mainstream of northern policy.

The federal government's land claims policy is designed to replace the vague, undefined aboriginal title of natives to northern lands and marine areas.[23] Future agreements will recognize native ownership of large tracts of land and provide native peoples with compensation monies to be used to promote economic development. But most of the agreements will provide also for a role for native groups in northern decision-making. Participation in administrative structures will allow natives to regulate wildlife harvesting, review and monitor development projects, participate in non-renewable resource development, and control development on their lands. They may give the Inuit a role in the management of the Arctic offshore. They will provide some measure of political authority for northern natives over future resource development. At the same time as these agreements are being negotiated, DIAND is trying to implement a comprehensive land use planning policy and develop a comprehensive conservation policy, both of which are strongly supported by environmentalists who see those policies as the primary vehicles for determining land use in the north.

In 1983, Environment Canada released a fifty-page document outlining in detail its mandate and policies in the north. Nowhere does the document mention land claims, and, indeed, the opinions of the native peoples, who form the majority in most of the north, are accorded one paragraph in a section entitled "Some Concerns." The above-mentioned draft document, *A Comprehensive Conservation Policy and Strategy for the Northwest Territories and Yukon*, makes only passing reference to land claims and no effort to analyse how these claims relate to DIAND's conservation efforts.[24] Likewise, DIAND's land use planning policy makes no attempt to explain how comprehensive land use planning can be reconciled with a land claims policy that will determine the title and control of large tracts of northern lands and marine areas.

This failure of federal officials not directly involved in negotiations to understand the goals of the land claims policy, and the scope of the matters that will be determined under the land claims process, can have unfortunate practical consequences for native groups. These officials may react with alarm when they learn that the terms of a given agreement affect their jurisdiction. Departments with environmental mandates are no less prone to respond in this manner than are departments with a development mandate, as the Inuit of the eastern Arctic discovered when they signed a wildlife agreement in principle with the federal government on 27 October 1981.

The wildlife agreement in principle is a complex document that recognizes preferential Inuit hunting and fishing rights in the eastern Arctic, referred to as Nunavut. In addition to defining the extent of Inuit hunting and fishing rights, the agreement establishes an administrative framework for the management of wildlife resources. The responsibility for managing wildlife is vested in a joint Nunavut wildlife management board, consisting of Inuit and government nominees. The board would have general authority to set hunting quotas in Nunavut for both natives and non-natives.

The wildlife agreement begins with several principles that it was designed to promote. In addition to acknowledging the legal rights of Inuit to harvest wildlife, the agreement states that these hunting rights shall be subject to principles of conservation, that a long-term, healthy renewable resource economy is both attainable and desirable, that there is a need for an effective system of wildlife management to complement Inuit hunting and fishing rights, and that the federal government retains the ultimate responsibility for wildlife management. One would suppose that these principles would be applauded by the majority of environmentalists and would be consistent with their general goals in protecting and managing northern wildlife.

The decisions of the Nunavut Wildlife Management Board were to be subject to the veto of whatever federal Minister exercised jurisdiction over the wildlife concerned. The Inuit were concerned that ministers would fall into the habit of vetoing board decisions without fully investigating the reasons for them. To meet these concerns, the Inuit and the federal negotiator agreed to a disallowance clause, which was designed to make it more cumbersome for the government to reverse a decision of the board. The clause provided that a ministerial veto could be exercised only in certain circumstances and that the Minister would first have to refer his decision back to the board before ultimately exercising the veto. While this clause did not change the principle that the ultimate responsibility for wildlife management resides with the government, it did somewhat restrict the power of individual ministers and provided the remedy of judicial review to the Inuit if they felt that the veto had been exercised capriciously or for improper purposes.

The board is consistent with the general terms of the federal government's comprehensive land claims policy, under which northern native groups have been negotiating for more than ten years. While the policy is distressingly vague and contradictory on the general question of political devolution to native groups, it clearly foresees the sharing of administrative regulatory powers: "Meaningful and influential Native involvement in land management and planning decisions on Crown lands could be initiated and strengthened by providing membership on those appropriate boards and committees whose decisions affect the lives of their communities."[25]

Despite the fact that the wildlife agreement in principle was consistent with both good conservation management and the federal land claims policy, two federal departments refused to agree to its ratification, and the agreement continues to languish in the depths of the federal bureaucracy, to the considerable bitterness of the Inuit. The two departments were Fisheries and Oceans, and Environment, both exercising an environmental mandate over wildlife management. Their refusal to ratify the agreement was based upon a perception not that the agreement in principle was bad conservation but simply that it reduced the absolute authority they had previously enjoyed over wildlife management. Robert Mitchell, the former federal negotiator who concluded the agreement on behalf of the government, recounts the experience:

That idea gained a measure of acceptance at senior levels of the bureaucracy in Ottawa – a sufficient measure, I think, for me as a negotiator to conclude an agreement on the basis of it. But two [federal] departments were just not going to live with it. The basis for [their] not living with it was simply this: it diminished the power of their minister ...

I think that position is totally inconsistent with the concept that was enunciated by the government ten years ago and restated in the [federal land claims policy] document *In All Fairness*. I think that the concept involves a sharing of control ... and that it is absolutely incumbent upon the bureaucracies involved to understand and accept that sharing is an integral part of the land claims policy. Until they do I believe that the land claims process is going to have difficulties, and, indeed, may not work.[26]

As environmentalists continue to call for more comprehensive policies, they must be aware that these policies will spawn bureaucratic structures that may compete with northerners for the rights to administer and manage northern lands and resources. This phenomenon, combined with appeals to the national interest and global responsibility, will be perceived as a threat to northern native groups trying to establish their right to participate in decision-making over wildlife management and land use generally.

This suspicion has already led one native group to reject DIAND's land use planning policy as a vehicle for determining land use in the area covered by their agreement. In December 1983, COPE signed a draft final agreement with the federal government that provides for a joint Inuvialuit-government environmental screening process for development proposals on the North Slope of Yukon. As environmentalists favour comprehensive land use planning supplemented by open, public reviews, COPE's decision to turn down the agreement may represent a setback for a major conservation initiative in the north. COPE rejected the policy because it perceived it as a federal stratagem to maintain administrative control over northern lands![27]

NORTHERN SELF-GOVERNMENT AND THE CONSERVATION ETHIC

If northern native peoples learn to mistrust the motivations of environmentalists, it will be difficult for the latter group to maintain co-operative relations with the aboriginal peoples once the agreements are signed. These groups will be faced with the formidable challenge of implementing complex agreements, investing large sums of compensation money in economic projects, and participating in the administrative and regulatory structures created under their agreements. It would be unwise for the environmentalists to allow native groups to associate the conservation ethic with a high-handed assertion of priority by a powerful outside establishment. It is incumbent upon those promoting northern conservation policy to understand the land claims policy and to ensure that conservation efforts do not prejudice the ability of native groups to negotiate creative, imaginative settlements.

It is inevitable that native northerners will have a greater say in wildlife management in northern Canada. Aboriginal hunting and fishing rights are now entrenched in the Canadian constitution. Natives hold the majority of the seats in the legislative assembly of the NWT. The federal government is negotiating land claims agreements that will recognize the priority of native hunting rights and accord natives a role in wildlife management. These developments are sufficient to lay to rest the perennial debate on whether natives "should" have special hunting rights. Such a question has now become as abstract and academic as the question of whether Canada should be unilingual. What is now being debated is the degree of control that northern aboriginal groups should have over northern wildlife and what legal and policy structures can best reconcile native rights and the national interest in northern wildlife.

Conflicts between environmental and northern political interests can take the form of conflicts between competing public decision-making processes. Even in cases where there is no substantial disagreement between the two interests, northerners may find that what they see as largely a political issue to be resolved in a bilateral forum, such as land claims negotiations, is being assessed through a public environmental review process in which they are but one of numerous "interests." Relegated to an equal status with southern industrialists and environmental groups, they experience the frustration of trying to defend their unsettled, fundamental long-term political rights to land and resources in a forum designed to review the environmental implications of a specific industrial proposal.

A good example of this type of conflict is the lengthy assessment process that the government conducted of the proposal by Norlands Petroleum (now Consolidated Oakwood Magnorth) to drill an exploratory well in Lancaster Sound at the mouth of Baffin Bay. The sound has long been recognized as perhaps the most biologically productive and sensitive area in the Arctic.[28] It supports a large and varied marine wildlife population that sustains the surrounding Inuit communities and is an important nesting ground for hundreds of species of birds. When DIAND gave Norlands approval-in-principle to drill a well in 1974, both the Inuit and environmental groups mobilized to challenge the project.

Faced with considerable pressure from both sides, DIAND referred the project in 1978 to an Environmental Assessment and Review Panel (EARP), the federal process for reviewing major development proposals publicly. Norlands had still not fulfilled certain conditions of its original approval to the government's satisfaction and had yet to drill. The EARP held hearings throughout the Lancaster Sound region, thus affording the Inuit communities and organizations an opportunity to participate intensively in the review.

The Inuit raised two basic concerns at the hearings. They shared the environmental and technical concerns relating to the proposed drilling operation and the impact that the project might have on the renewable resource base. They joined environmentalists in arguing that any sensible environmental review should not be restricted to the specific potential effects of one well but should assess the capacity of the entire region to sustain industrial activity, an argument that was ultimately accepted by the panel. They expressed fears that their communities were not economically or culturally prepared to cope with the effects of large-scale hydrocarbon development.

However, in addition to their environmental and socioeconomic concerns, the Inuit noted that for several years they had been engaged in direct negotiations with Ottawa over their legal rights to the region's lands and resources, including the rights to use and manage the marine region and their right to share in any development undertaken in the area. The Inuit understood that their land claims negotiations were being undercut or ignored by the very existence of the EARP. How, they asked, could the government commit itself to negotiate their permanent legal rights and then assess the most significant development in the region as if it were totaly unrelated to this process? As Eric Tagoona, then president of Inuit Tapirisat of Canada, told the panel: "Most of you may not realize that these hearings conflict and are contradictory to the process of comprehensive claims and negotiations now in process between the Inuit Tapirisat and the Government of Canada. We would hope that the environmental assessment and review panel recognizes that any decisions affecting drilling in any areas of the Arctic would have serious ramifications on the comprehensive claims negotiations and would predictably stall the negotiations whereby the aspirations and objectives of Inuit in Canada would be seriously affected."[29]

The EARP concluded eventually that the Norlands proposal could not be intelligently assessed in isolation and that a broader review of the capacity of Lancaster Sound to support hydrocarbon development was necessary: "The questions of potentially conflicting resource uses must be identified, and thus the desire of the local residents to participate in the development of resource use strategies must be recognized. The Panel supports their participation and recommends that a comprehensive review be carried out as soon as possible of potential resource uses of the Lancaster Sound area."³⁰ This led DIAND to commission the Lancaster Sound Regional Study, a four-year study of the future of the area, particularly the future of resource development. The study, chaired by Professor Peter Jacobs of l'Université de Montréal, became known as the Green Paper exercise. The study held extensive public hearings and produced a report that outlined six possible strategies for planning the development of Lancaster Sound. These ranged from accelerated industrial development to a total ban on such activity, but the study did not, and could not, recommend a particular course to be followed. Jacobs clearly understood that the outstanding claims of the Inuit would have to be resolved before any definite course could be followed. To do otherwise would be to risk prejudicing settlement, which, after all, was supposed to determine the long-term rights of the inhabitants of the region to their lands and surrounding marine areas.

The EARP hearings and the Green Paper exercise together took seven years to complete. The Inuit communities and their representative organizations invested a great amount of time and financial resources in participating in both and, through them, succeeded in raising the profile of their political, economic, social, and cultural concerns. Yet, as a decision-making process, these exercises failed to resolve the issue of whether drilling should or should not occur. In fact, the Norlands proposal appears to have quietly disappeared without any firm decision ever being made. Among the Inuit and industry, the credibility of the environmental assessment process suffered considerably. In the end, all parties realized that, if the comprehensive land claims policy was to be respected by the government, political settlements with the northern aboriginal peoples would have to be concluded before any major industrial development could be properly and fairly assessed by a process designed solely to consider environmental factors.

A NORTHERN PERSPECTIVE ON THE NATIONAL INTEREST

The future transfer of lands and resources to northern governments, whether abrupt or gradual, poses a different kind of challenge to environmentalists. It may well be argued that it is in the national interest to devolve this authority to northern governments. However much this is so, such a shift would obviously mean that decisions on resource development and management will be taken less from a national perspective and more with regional and local interests in mind. It is difficult to predict what the implication of devolution would be for the northern environment, and, in fact, there is unlikely to be consistency across the north. Few observers would doubt that, had the YTG had jurisdiction over land and resources during the 1970s, there would have been far more development on the environmentally sensitive North Slope of Yukon. However, a future Nunavut government, representing a native majority in the eastern Arctic, might very well exercise more responsibility and caution in its development policy than has the federal government.

Whatever their nature, northern governments will clearly feel limited accountability to a national environmental movement, the majority of which resides in the south. The degree to which northern governments currently feel that there is a national interest in northern resource management varies widely. The YTG is particularly aggressive in asserting that Yukon resources are to be developed for the primary benefit of Yukoners.[31] By contrast, current proposals by the Nunavut Constitutional Forum show a less exclusive view: "It is recognised that a legitimate interdependence on interests between Nunavut and national and international society expressed through the Government of Canada exists in respect of lands and resources, and that co-operative planning and accommodation of each other's interests is necessary."[32]

The almost total absence of universities, private citizens' groups, consulting firms, and large bureaucracies in the north[33] means that the Canadian environmental movement is still very much southern-based, even that part that concerns itself with northern Canada. The future ability of environmentalists to play a role in northern resource development and to have a voice in northern affairs will depend very much on their ability to maintain the respect of northerners and northern governments. This will not be accomplished by loudly insisting upon the preservation of every wildlife species and sensitive or beautiful landscape "in the national interest." There must be much greater sensitivity and understanding of northern economic realities and the understandable wish of northerners to build a secure economic future.

Past failure to do so may account, in part, for the long-standing hostile relations between environmentalists of any stripe and the YTG. In 1983, this hostility exploded into a national controversy over industrial plans to build a port on the North Slope. In March 1983, Gulf Canada Resources applied to DIAND for permission to build a marine support base at Stokes Point on the North Slope. For years the North Slope had been a focus of efforts by conservationists to create a national wilderness park. The area is recognized as having a uniquely rich and sensitive ecology. Mr Justice Berger recommended that the area be closed to development in perpetuity, and the NEB refused permission to Canadian Arctic Gas to build a pipeline across it to Alaska. In 1978, the federal government, by order-in-council, withdrew the lands from disposition pending a final land claims settlement with COPE and the Council for Yukon Indians and the creation of a national park.

The YTG had long been in favour of the development of hydrocarbon exploration support facilities on the North Slope. It opposed the idea of making the whole North Slope into a park, as this would have denied Yukon access to the Beaufort Sea and made it much more difficult for the Yukon economy to benefit from future oil development in the area. Its 1980 resource management model proposed a park in the western half of the North Slope, with the eastern half being left open to controlled development.

The YTG strongly supported Gulf's application for Stokes Point. When John Munro refused permission to Gulf in November 1983, the YTG angrily accused Ottawa of putting the interests of Yukoners behind those of national environmental groups such as the Canadian Arctic Resources Committee.[34] The fact that federal departments with an environmental mandate, such as Environment Canada and the Department of Fisheries and Oceans, also opposed the Gulf application served to heighten the YTG's perception that the Yukon economy was being held hostage to environmentalists.

It is not to deny the validity of environmentalists' opposition to Stokes Point to note that they have traditionally given little consideration to the YTG's economic arguments. To be sure, the YTG showed little inclination to discuss these questions and seemed to favour aggressive rhetoric over mature dialogue. But one cannot dismiss the position of a democratically elected government and, at the same time, claim to have the best interests of Yukoners at heart without appearing very paternalistic.

The point is not that environmentalists should learn to get along better with northern governments which hold different views. The point is that the national environmental movement must learn to view the evolution of the Canadian north from a northern perspective as well as a national and global one. This will mean taking a far keener interest in the northern economies and their potential. If environmentalists fear large-scale, unplanned non-renewable resource development above all, they should take the lead in proposing realistic alternatives. This is the only way they can help northern governments which will face the difficult job of administering new jurisdictions with far fewer resources than the federal government now enjoys.

Political evolution and environmental protection are not two different subjects or sectors competing for priority in the north. However much the environmental movement helps or hinders the course of political evoution in the north, it will be the land claims process and the march towards responsible government that ultimately determine the course of northern decision-making on lands and resources. The future usefulness of environmentalists to northern governments will be determined by their ability to understand the new evolving political structures and to make them work.

The immediate priority for the environmental movement is to understand and support the evolution of the federal government's land claims policy, native participation in wildlife management, and the development of a sound northern economy.

CHAPTER TEN

Defence and Policing in Arctic Canada

W. HARRIET CRITCHLEY

Defence and policing or constabulary functions in Canada's Arctic are performed by several institutions that have nation-wide responsibilities: the Department of National Defence and the Canadian Armed Forces perform the defence function; the Royal Canadian Mounted Police (RCMP) and the Canadian Coast Guard perform the constabulary function in providing order in conformance with Canada's civil and criminal laws. For each of these institutions, their activities in the Northwest Territories (NWT) are only a small fraction of their overall operations, even though in terms of area the NWT adds up to approximately one-third of Canada's territorial expanse. The combination of a sparse, scattered population of some 46,000 and physical factors including adverse terrain, climate, permafrost, and ice has served to create a situation in which there are relatively few activities that might require monitoring and enforcement for defence or constabulary purposes. Moreover, the area surrounding the various waterways through the Arctic archipelago constitutes only a small, but significant, portion of Canada's far north. In considering the defence and constabulary implications of Arctic resource development and increased transportation in the Passage, it is necessary first to appreciate the range of activities that currently require monitoring and the capabilities currently available to perform these functions.

CURRENT DEFENCE ACTIVITIES AND CAPABILITIES

The current roles for the Department of National Defence (DND) and the Canadian Armed Forces (CAF) were originally set out in the 1971 defence White Paper, *Defence in the 70s*. A recent restatement of these roles puts them as follows:

Role 1 – the protection of Canada and Canadian national interests at home and abroad (short title, Sovereignty);

Role 2 – The defence of North America in co-operation with the United States (short title, Defence of North America or Defence of Canada);

Role 3 – the fulfilment of NATO commitments as may be agreed upon (short title, NATO); and

Role 4 – the performance of such international peacekeeping duties as Canada may from time to time assume (short title, Peacekeeping).[1]

Of these four main missions, DND and CAF activities in the north are almost exclusively concerned with the first two – sovereignty and defence of North America.

Defence activities related to sovereignty include Northern Patrol flights by long-range aircraft, occasional naval exercises, periodic army exercises of up to battalion strength, and some search and rescue tasks. Activities related to defence of North America include the manning of Canadian Forces Stations Inuvik and Alert (Ellesmere Island) and providing a small number of CAF personnel at three main Distant Early Warning (DEW) Line stations in Canada. Two other sets of activities – manning Northern Region Headquarters (Yellowknife) and maintaining the Canadian Rangers – support both roles.

A more detailed examination of these defence activities reveals that they are being performed on a modest level. In recent years there has been an annual average of 16 or 17 Northern Patrol flights, each with a duration of three to four days.[2] These flights, using CP-140 *Aurora* aircraft from bases at Comox, BC, or Greenwood, NS, generally cover the whole of Canada's north over the year's series but will monitor the same specific locations for only a fraction of the flights. The *Auroras* are equipped for their main task – anti-submarine surveillance off Canada's Atlantic and Pacific coasts – and land or take off from only two airstrips (Yellowknife, Frobisher Bay) in the NWT. Their Arctic patrols consist essentially of *visual observation* in support of "pollution control, fisheries surveillance, wildlife protection and ice reconnaissance."[3] The limitations on visual observation imposed by adverse weather conditions are increased in high Arctic areas by the three-to-four-month period of 24-hour-a-day darkness from November to February.[4]

The occasional naval exercises referred to above consist of periodic, but not annual, visits by surface ships attached to Maritime Command to ports in southwestern Greenland and annual voyages (Operation NORPLOY) from Halifax along the coast of Labrador and into Hudson Bay. As none of the ships of Maritime Command is ice-strengthened, they cannot operate in ice-covered or even moderately ice-infested waters. This effectively bars these ships from almost all of the waters in Canada's Arctic archipelago at any time of the year.

The army exercises for up to battalion-size units (Sovereign Viking) were instituted in 1981. There are one or two exercises per year, each of approximately four weeks' duration, but their location and range of operations are governed by the limited number of sites that can be used to provide the essential air transport and logistical support.[5] Prior to the Sovereign Viking series, exercises in the north were for much smaller groups and concentrated on providing northern survival training for selected officers and NCOs. Where search and rescue in the north are concerned, the only northern-based aircraft available to DND are the two CC-138 *Twin Otters* based in Yellowknife. Other DND aircraft available for search and rescue are based in Edmonton and Trenton, Ontario.

Activities in the north associated with the defence of North America are at an equally modest level. The DEW Line stations are manned largely by civilian contract employees. The few CAF personnel at three main stations report to the two Regional Operations Control Centres (co-located at North Bay, Ontario), which together control Canadian air space for NORAD purposes. CFS Inuvik and CFS Alert are manned by CAF personnel, but their communications research activities are controlled by the Canadian Forces Supplementary Radio Systems Headquarters in Ottawa.[6]

More generally, Northern Region Headquarters (NRHQ), with a current complement of 77 officers, other ranks, and civilians, was created in 1970 as the regional administrative, liaison, and support unit for the whole of Yukon and the NWT. This headquarters is responsible for the largest military region in the world,[7] but, aside from the *Twin Otter* detachment, the headquarters does not have any operational military units under its direct command. NRHQ does administer the Canadian Rangers, which number some 700 individuals located in 36 communities in the north.[8] In the high Arctic communities, members of the Canadian Rangers are usually Inuit hunters who provide a paramilitary presence and are able – by virtue of their local hunting and fishing expertise – to assist the regular forces of the CAF with their special survival and operational skills during exercises.

The modest level of defence activities in Canada's north is matched by an equally modest level of defence capabilities. If we include CAF units and groups that are on exercise in the north along with regular forces personnel who are stationed there, the total at any given time would amount to well under 1,000 of the approximately 83,000 people in the armed forces. Mobile Command, as a result of the experience gained in the Sovereign Viking exercises, can move up to battalion-sized units into the high Arctic, but only to a severely limited number of specific locations and after detailed advanced planning and preparations. Once units are on location, their mobility and range of operations are restricted by climate, terrain, and the presence of either ice or open water. None of Maritime Command's destroyers and other surface ships can operate in the waters of the high

Arctic. They do exercise in waters along the southeastern fringe of the region, but only for one to three months of the year, depending on ice conditions. Air Command's fighter aircraft cannot routinely land at or take off from any airstrips north of Cold Lake, Alberta. In unusual circumstances, one or perhaps two fighter aircraft can fly into Canada's high Arctic air space, but only after detailed preparations have been made for in-flight refuelling.[9] The unarmed *Aurora* long-range patrol aircraft fly over the Arctic, but again their capabilities are limited to visual observation. In addition, the unarmed CC-130 *Hercules* aircraft of Air Command's Air Transport Group provide transportation for Mobile Command exercises in the Arctic and resupply for CFS Alert. They are also available for search and rescue missions. The two unarmed *Twin Otter* aircraft in Yellowknife function as air transport for NRHQ and are available for search and rescue missions. Finally, Canada has an obsolete trip-wire radar early warning system located along, or close to, 70th parallel north latitude, which is manned largely by civilians, and a civilian paramilitary reserve force in some northern communities.

It should be noted that both the low level of defence activities and the slender defence capabilities outlined above reflect the judgment of successive federal governments that potential threats to Canada's security emanating from the north are also at a low level – consisting exclusively of the potential for attack by Soviet long-range bomber aircraft and land-based intercontinental ballistic missiles.

In summary, current defence activities in Canada's north – regardless of which of the two formal defence roles are attached to them – fall largely into the areas of selective training, logistical support, and the monitoring of compliance with Canadian statutes, laws, and regulations. In fact, the Senate Sub-Committee on Defence has reiterated the latter part of this observation in a critical recommendation: "Because the first item of commitment of the Canadian Armed Forces, the protection of Canadian sovereignty, has been narrowly interpreted to include only police functions, the sub-committee recommends that it be recast so as to include specific reference to the defence of Canada."[10] Canada's defence capabilities in the north are quite modest as well. Nevertheless, given the cutbacks in manpower, resources, equipment, and defence budgets over the past two decades, the provision of even such a modest capability places a noticeable strain on the overall defence capabilities of the CAF and DND.

CURRENT CONSTABULARY
ACTIVITIES AND CAPABILITIES

The delivery of all policing services in the NWT is the responsibility of the RCMP. That is, in addition to its federal responsibilities, "G" Division of the RCMP provides police services for the NWT and all communities in the NWT under contract with the territorial government. The total complement of "G" Division is approximately 250, of which some 190 are regular force personnel and 30 are special constables. Divisional headquarters is in Yellowknife, but the RCMP's activities in the NWT are managed through a system of three subdivisions, with headquarters in Frobisher Bay, Inuvik, and Yellowknife. Each community within the boundaries of a subdivision has a detachment that ranges in size from a total of two (one regular force corporal or constable and one special constable) in the small communities, to 14, 18, or 24 in the larger communities. Of the total complement of 190 regular force personnel, some 35 serve at divisional headquarters. This leaves only 155 regular force personnel to cover the whole territory and 40 communities.[11] Each subdivision has one DHC-6 *Twin Otter* to provide transportation among the communities. As there are very few roads in the NWT, aside from those within each community, air transportation is the main means of moving personnel and supplies between communities and of conducting inspections within a subdivision.

In addition to law enforcement, security, criminal investigations, commercial crime investigations, and police-community relations, RCMP personnel also serve as customs and excise officers throughout the NWT. The presence of the RCMP – particularly in the communities of the high Arctic – has been, and still is, seen as a major ingredient in the assertion of Canada's sovereignty. Most of the high Arctic, as defined in this chapter, is within the Frobisher Bay subdivision, and small portions are within the Inuvik and Yellowknife subdivisions. Therefore the regular force RCMP presence in the high Arctic is less than 50 out of the 13,300 uniformed personnel in the RCMP. Given the modest numbers of regular force personnel in the high Arctic and the three *Twin Otters* at its disposal, the RCMP barely manages to carry out its constabulary and sovereignty functions at current levels of demand for its services.

The Coast Guard also has some constabulary functions in Canada's northern waters. The functions and roles of the Coast Guard are derived from a series of statutes (including revisions), cabinet decisions, and orders of the Governor in Council that date from 1867 to the present. Among others, these include the British North America Act, the Navigable Waters Protection Act, the Canada Shipping Act, and the Arctic Waters Pollution Prevention Act. In general, the Coast Guard's responsibilities can be reduced to the following: to develop and maintain safe and efficient marine transportation.[12] Where northern waters are concerned, there is an additional responsibility to "mitigate dangerous [marine] operating conditions ... [and thereby] reduce the threat of environmental and biological damage to the delicate Arctic ecology."[13] The fulfilment of these responsibilities includes providing and operating navigation aids, ice surveillance, monitoring recovery of wrecks, providing icebreakers for route assistance and escort during the Arctic shipping season, marine search and rescue, and operating a vessel reporting system. The Coast Guard also co-ordinates and supports the eastern Arctic sealift – the annual resupply to communities, private companies, and individuals in the high Arctic – and administers the Canada Shipping Act and Arctic Waters Pollution Prevention Act (AWPPA) in the sense of enforcing the provisions, regulations, and standards set forth in these statutes.

Constabulary functions of the Coast Guard are associated with the following activities: recovery of wrecks, small vessel safety, search and rescue, and administering the AWPPA. With respect to the latter, provision is contained within the AWPPA for the appointment of pollution prevention officers.[14] Some members of the Coast Guard have been so appointed for the purpose of boarding ships in the shipping safety control zones to determine whether they comply with the standards of the AWPPA regulations, that is, whether they have deposited a substantial quantity of waste in Arctic waters or are in danger of doing so, and to order ships to take part in the clean-up or control of such waste.[15]

The duration of the shipping season in Canada's high Arctic varies slightly with ice conditions in these waters but lasts approximately three months, from late July until late October. The Coast Guard has a fleet of 292 vessels, of which 8 are heavy icebreakers and 13 are medium-sized and small icebreakers. In the 1984 season, for example, 9 of these icebreakers saw service in Arctic waters. Thus, although Coast Guard activity in the high Arctic serves a very important function, that activity is a slight portion of total Coast Guard operations in Canada's waters.

As is the case with the RCMP, the Canadian Coast Guard is seen as an instrument of Canadian sovereignty in the north. That is, all Coast Guard activities in the high Arctic during the shipping season contribute to effective occupation of the area by an agency of the federal government.

Senior administrators of the Coast Guard (Northern Branch) have responsibility for developing an organizational structure to administer Coast Guard activities in support of proposed year-long shipping in Arctic waters and, at the appropriate time, implementation of "the full range of Coast Guard support systems with technologies and systems appropriate to the Arctic environment."[16] Bids for the construction of the proposed Polar 8 icebreaker have been submitted, and a decision to build such a vessel has now been made. In addition, more research and development are required to provide improved systems for ice reconnaissance, navigation, communications, and traffic management.

DND, the RCMP, and the Canadian Coast Guard assist each other in the performance of their search and rescue responsibilities, while the RCMP and Coast Guard support one another in meeting some of their constabulary responsibilities. All three institutions perform sovereignty roles in the north, either directly or indirectly. The Coast Guard, however, is an entirely civilian service in Canada, rather than a military or paramilitary force, as is the case in many other countries. None of the Coast Guard vessels is armed or fitted to be armed if such a requirement should occur. Therefore the Coast Guard has no capability – planned or ad hoc – to perform any defence tasks. This situation has been a matter of periodic concern in some quarters in the past. The Senate Sub-Committee on Defence is perhaps the most recent body to express such concern. Whereas the committee foresees that "the Coast Guard will continue to carry out the great bulk of Canadian maritime tasks in the Arctic in the years ahead"[17] and finds "no compelling reason to acquire icebreakers" for Maritime Command,[18] it nevertheless recommends that new Coast Guard heavy icebreakers be constructed to allow military helicopters to land on them and, if necessary, to be able to accommodate containerized weapons systems.[19] The committee also recommends that Maritime Command personnel be seconded on a regular basis to the Coast Guard for practice in Arctic navigation.[20]

FUTURE DEVELOPMENT OF
DEFENCE AND CONSTABULARY
ACTIVITIES

The two major factors in the future political economy of the Northwest Passage are changes in the level of commercial activity and changes in the level of military activity in or near the high Arctic.

Any significant changes in commercial activity are likely to be related to the exploitation of such non-renewable resources as oil, natural gas, lead, zinc, and iron. While most analysts agree that this kind of commercial activity will increase in the high Arctic, there is disagreement and uncertainty over the timing and pace of the non-renewable resource development upon which commercial activity depends. Development of these types of resources is highly dependent on the size and quality of the resource deposit, the cost of development, national and world demand for that resource, and its world price. For example, changes in price and demand for petroleum hydrocarbons over the past two decades have often been sudden and unforeseen. As a result, forecasts for oil and natural gas development in the high Arctic have fluctuated widely. A 1976 Department of Energy, Mines and Resources study forecasted that, at high energy prices, the Mackenzie Delta-Beaufort Sea and Arctic Islands areas would be supplying *half* the natural gas domestic demand by 1990.[21] A recent attempt at forecasting included a series of scenarios in which exploitation of Beaufort Sea oil reserves started either in 1987 (with production rates ranging from 75,000 to 200,000 to 776,000 barrels per day) or did not start before the year 2000, while exploitation of natural gas reserves began either in 1990 or after 2000.[22] The scenarios excluded any change in current levels of exploitation of the lead, zinc, or iron ore deposits in the high Arctic before 2000. The degree of commercial activity and its fiscal impact in the NWT vary across the scenarios from nearly negligible to very substantial. It should be noted that decisions on when and at what pace the resources will actually be developed are largely in the hands of the private companies that own the leases. Those companies will base their decisions on the economic factors mentioned above.

The commercial activity associated with any exploitation of non-renewable resources – regardless of the pace of development – is highest during the initial phases of development. This is when mines or production wells are being constructed, supplies and personnel for such construction are being delivered and stored or housed at the sites, and the transportation system for delivering the resource to its markets is being constructed. Once the production and transportation systems are in place, commercial activity declines rather sharply to level off at production and maintenance operations.

The exploitation of resources in the high Arctic – whether in the construction or production and maintenance phases – will involve marine transportation. Construction and production materials, supplies and fuel in particular, are shipped into the high Arctic from Atlantic or Pacific ports or barged down the Mackenzie River to the Beaufort Sea and then transferred to ships for distribution. In addition, the resource produced *may* be delivered to market by marine transportation, but the choice of transportation system depends on a host of economic factors as well as the geographic location of markets and regulatory (environmental and/or export) decisions.

In the past, the routes for such marine transportation have varied with ice conditions, the size and draft of the ships, and their destination in or through the Arctic.[23] This variation in routing is likely to continue and expand incrementally for surface vessels as exploitation activities at new sites commence. A recent study has argued that rather than there being a single Passage through the Canadian archipelago, there are five main routes that together constitute the Canadian portion of the Northwest Passage.[24] The routes used by marine transportation in association with future commercial activity are all likely to transit many, if not all, of these waters. Therefore, consequent with any increase in commercial activity, more extensive and effective aids to navigation will be required. If increased marine transportation includes a lengthening of the high Arctic shipping season, those aids will also have to be available for a longer annual duration and, perforce, under more difficult navigation conditions.

If changes in commercial activity in the high Arctic are difficult to forecast with any accuracy, and are largely dependent upon economic factors and the decisions of private enterprise, changes in military activity in the region are even more conjectural. Future levels of military activity in this area are largely dependent on the interaction of the two superpowers, the United States and the Soviet Union. The likelihood of any change in military activity is best examined by treating the four environments – land, water, air, and space – separately.

As indicated earlier, the current level of military land activity in the Canadian high Arctic is quite modest. If one recalls that the region is in the zone of continuous permafrost, north of the tree line, that most of the region is a polar desert that experiences nearly twenty-four hours of darkness per day for four months of the year, it is clear that the high Arctic presents an exceedingly forbidding environment for land operations. Any sized unit must either carry all of its requirements for shelter, food, and fuel – not to mention weapons and ammunition – or be able to receive these basic supplies by air. Training exercises by Canadian forces personnel over the past several decades have repeatedly shown that approximately 80 per cent of an individual's energy is devoted to sheer physical survival in this environment. This leaves only some 20 per cent available for such other activities as fighting. In addition, there is little, if anything, of any significant strategic value in that vast expanse that is likely to be attacked – or require defence – by land forces.

It is only prudent – as a hedge against an unpredictable future involving one-third of Canada's territory – that the Canadian Armed Forces acquire and retain the skills and equipment to operate in the high Arctic. However, in this author's estimation, the only future development in the region that might require a defence capability by land forces arises from a significant increase in oil and natural gas activity. If Canada, or the United States, were heavily dependent on Arctic oil and gas and that fuel source were a major factor in a severe crisis between the superpowers, there might be a requirement to defend the wells and pipelines associated with producing oil and gas fields against sabotage by commando-type units. It seems that other possible land operations by hostile forces can be dealt with by preventing their resupply of food and fuel, thereby forcing a surrender. In the high Arctic, prevention of resupply would involve air, not land, forces.

In the maritime environment, the current level of naval surface vessel activity in the high Arctic is also quite slight. It seems highly unlikely that this level of activity will change in the future. The surface vessel elements of both the Soviet and u.s. navies are designed for, and used in, only blue (open) water. This is also true of Canada's navy. While it is possible to design new, or refit older, surface vessels with ice-strengthened hulls, the added expense of doing so and the increased fuel requirements for operating such heavy vessels would have to be balanced by a clear requirement for surface vessels to defend, or attack, or deter an attack on strategic assets of high value. In addition, ice conditions for most of the year and in most of the waters in, or adjacent to, Canada's high Arctic are such that even ice-strengthened vessels would require icebreaker escort, thus adding to the expense and decreasing the response time to incidents for such naval vessels. It is difficult to image any future development in the high Arctic that would satisfy these criteria for an increase in military activity by surface naval vessels.

The situation may be quite different for the subsurface maritime environment in the high Arctic. Nuclear-powered submarines can, and have, operated under the ice in the high Arctic at least since the late 1950s and early 1960s, as published accounts of some of these voyages indicate.[25] Two of the published accounts describe transits of the Northwest Passage by submarines of the u.s. Navy,[26] and it is reasonable to assume that there have been others by u.s. submarines, if only as training exercises. In addition, although there have been occasional rumours of Soviet submarines in these same waters, the only verified public report concerns the Lincoln Sea.[27] Recently, however, some analysts have argued the distinct possibility of the near-future deployment of Soviet nuclear-powered submarines into Arctic waters, including some waters in and near the Canadian archipelago.[28] If or when such deployments are made by Soviet submarines, one can expect the u.s. Navy to respond by increasing the deployment of some of its submarines into Arctic waters, if only for anti-submarine monitoring purposes. Canadian military activity associated with such deployments could range from nothing, to the installation and operation of an underwater detection grid, to the acquisition and operation of a small number of nuclear-powered submarines.

Military activity related to the air environment has been the major feature in nearly all military operations in the high Arctic. Canada, particularly Canada's high Arctic, lies astride the shortest air route between the continental United States and the Soviet Union. This geographical fact led to the formation of NORAD and the construction of the DEW Line. The purpose of the latter was to provide early warning of an attack on North America by bombers from the Soviet Union. When land-based intercontinental ballistic missiles (ICBMs) became the major element in each superpower's strategic nuclear arsenal, the bomber threat and the DEW Line declined in relative importance. Some DEW Line stations were shut down and military activity in the north associated with the DEW Line declined.

However, the recent advent of strategic-range air-launched cruise missiles and their deployment on bomber aircraft by the Soviet Union is leading to an increase in the bomber threat to North America. The

Canadian and U.S. response to this development has been an agreement, announced in March 1985, to modernize continental air defence. As part of the agreement, the DEW Line will be replaced by the North Warning System (NWS) – a series of 13 long-range radars and 39 short-range radars located across northern Alaska, northern Canada, and down the Labrador coast.[29] Only the long-range radar stations will be manned and the eleven of these in Canadian territory will be manned by CAF personnel and civilians under contract. Some five airstrips in Canada's north will be improved to allow CF-18 fighter aircraft to land and take off on a contingency basis, and at least two airstrips will be improved to allow for the landing and take-off of U.S. AWACS aircraft. Therefore the construction and operation (starting in 1989) of NWS in Canada should result in a slight increase in military activity, while the construction phase itself will cause a short-term increase in commercial activity. After 2000, it is likely that air defence warning systems for North America will be based in space. This should result in a decrease in military activity on the ground in the high Arctic.

Military activity in space is likely to increase in the future with the further development of ballistic missiles, satellites for many military and quasi-military purposes, and, possibly, anti-satellite satellites. But only a small proportion of military activity associated with space takes place on the earth's surface *near* Canada's high Arctic: the U.S. Ballistic Missile Early Warning System (BMEWS) has stations in Thule, Greenland, and Clear, Alaska. There is no military activity associated with space *in* Canada's high Arctic, to my knowledge. Given the size and complexity of the systems that launch, monitor, or analyse data collected from satellites, it seems highly unlikely that military activity associated with space will take place in Canada's high Arctic. These systems already exist in southern Canada and the continental United States.

In summary, changes in military activity in the Arctic, and more specifically in the vicinity of the Passage, are largely dependent on the interaction of the two superpowers. The current level of activity is slight, and, while there may be some incremental increases in the future – associated with submarine monitoring and air defence – the analysis presented here indicates that, overall, such activity will continue to be characterized at best as "modest."

Changes in requirements for constabulary capabilities will be associated almost exclusively with an increase in commercial activity. Whether such changes relate to the customs and standard policing activities of the RCMP because of temporary increases in population at construction sites and/or in some communities, or to the enforcement functions of the Coast Guard because of increases in surface marine transportation in Arctic waters, any sudden and significant increase in commercial activity is likely to place a severe strain on – if not outstrip – current RCMP and Coast Guard resources and capabilities.

In most instances, there would be some advance warning of significant increases associated with non-renewable resource development: the environmental regulatory process for approving such development projects takes at least two or three years to complete; if the export of petroleum hydrocarbons is involved, the export regulatory process for approval takes a similar period of time. However, it is likely that this two- or three-year advance warning will not provide sufficient lead time for the increase of some enforcement capabilities. For example, the process of designing, building, and conducting sea trials for a new heavy icebreaker requires some five to seven years, while the process of designing, construction, and launching into orbit of satellites for navigation or ice reconnaissance may take even longer. Therefore, even with the advance warning provided by the regulatory process, the Coast Guard and, perhaps, the RCMP may experience a period of several years' duration when their capabilities to handle increased constabulary requirements are less than the demand for them.

Although most development scenarios for the high Arctic involve overland or surface marine transportation, some include submarine tanker transportation of non-renewable resources from the Arctic to markets in the Far East or Europe. Most tanker submarines are at the "gleam in the engineer's eye" stage of development. Some projects have reached the preliminary design stage, but none has been constructed. The one thing that many of these possible projects have in common is the large size of the submarine – it would have a larger displacement than current ballistic missile–carrying submarines. If such tanker submarines are ever built, their size alone will dictate what waters they can, and cannot, use. Many of the channels between the islands in Canada's high Arctic will be too shallow – when ice-covered – for the operation of such submarines. Submarine navigation of the deeper channels – including the Parry Channel route through the Passage – could be involved, but avoidance of these waters entirely may be even more likely. Depending on the site of the resource in the high Arctic and the location of the market for it, tanker submarines may find easier and more economical routes: from the Beaufort Sea, through the Arctic Basin either to the west, through the Bering Strait and Bering Sea to the Pacific, or to the east, through the Norwegian or Greenland seas to the Atlantic. If such routes are used, the constabulary, navigation aid, and ice reconnaissance requirements for Canada will be minimal, in part because the voyage would be under the surface of the ice-covered and ice-infested waters, and in part because most of the voyage would be in the high seas, well away from territorial waters, the 100-mile pollution prevention zone, and the 200-mile economic zone.

The situation is quite different for surface marine transportation of non-renewable resources to markets in the Far East, Europe, southern Canada, or the continental United States. Because of severe ice conditions in the Arctic Basin, it seems most unlikely that surface vessels would take the high seas routes mentioned above for submarine tankers. Rather, on voyages to the west, they would use routes in the Beaufort Sea close off the Canadian and Alaskan coasts to the Bering Strait, while voyages to the east would use routes through Canada's archipelago to the Labrador Sea. Increased navigation of these routes *will* require improved navigation aids, ice reconnaissance, and icebreaker escort. It will also require the presence of experienced ice pilots on board the commercial vessels and an increased capability for marine search and rescue. Finally, in the interests of safe navigation and pollution prevention, this list of requirements clearly indicates a further need to develop and enforce a series of standards for the vessels themselves – to use navigational aids and ice reconnaissance information effectively, to have the appropriate ice-strengthening, and to report to a marine traffic authority on progress, conditions, and problems.

Canada had made a thorough beginning on such standards in the annexes (and their subsequent revisions) to the Arctic Waters Pollution Prevention Act.[30] In addition, the treaty that was the result of the Third United Nations Conference on the Law of the Sea assigns rights regarding pollution prevention to coastal states "where particularly severe climatic conditions and the presence of ice covering such areas for most of the year create obstructions or exceptional hazards to navigation, and pollution of the marine environment could cause major harm to or irreversible disturbance of the ecological balance."[31] Thus it seems reasonable to conclude that according to Canadian statutes and international law, Canada has the authority to act in these matters. The United States, however, disagrees with Canada's position on the status of the Passage and may not recognize these recent additions to the international law of the sea, since it has not signed the new treaty.

In such circumstances, lack of sufficient Canadian capability to enforce the pertinent national and international laws – a constabulary function – undermines Canadian authority, jurisdiction, and, ultimately, sovereignty. For example, while vessels of Canadian registry will abide by Canadian standards and regulations by virtue of their registry, there is no certainty that foreign flag vessels will do so unless Canadian authorities can effectively enforce standards and regulations on all vessels in Arctic waters, regardless of the time of year and route they use.[32]

In summary, changes in constabulary activity in the high Arctic – especially in the vicinity of the Passage – are dependent on changes in the level of commercial activity in that region. The current level of constabulary activity is modest, reflecting a modest level of commercial activity. If commercial activity continues at its present pace or declines, a modest constabulary capability may be sufficient for the future. If, however, commercial activity associated with non-renewable resource development in the Arctic rose suddenly or substantially, there would be a requirement for increases in constabulary capabilities that Canadian authorities may be able to provide only after a time lag of several years. In that interim, the enforcement of Canadian laws, regulations, and standards – however slight the tasks may be at present – will decline. Such a decline would undermine Canadian sovereignty over Arctic waters that are in and adjacent to the Canadian archipelago.

CONCLUSION

Canada's defence and constabulary capabilities barely meet current requirements in the Arctic. Any future increase in such requirements will necessitate at least a commensurate increase in capabilities. There are two features of high Arctic activity that present major difficulties for the analyst and policy-maker. First, the sources of any increase in activity, and therefore an increase in defence or constabulary requirements, in the Arctic are largely external to Canadian public administration and the federal government: the interaction of the superpowers dominates Canadian defence activities, and world economic factors and decisions by private enterprises drive commercial, and therefore constabulary, activities. Second, it is extremely difficult to predict with accuracy and confidence events and trends and their impact on the high Arctic for the next 15 years. These two sets of difficulties would seem to place us in the unenviable position of trying to promote Canada's national interests by reacting post hoc to events and decisions taken by others whose interests may not coincide at all with those of Canada.

The degree to which that unenviable situation already exists or will arise depends on three factors: the clarity of Canadian jurisdiction and interests as they are understood in domestic and international forums; the co-ordination of public policies and of the activities of federal agencies; and the capability to monitor events and trends closely. Each of these factors presents a range of policy options.

Canada's interests in the high Arctic are not sufficiently well appreciated within the federal government or by the Canadian public, to say nothing of others abroad. Pollution prevention has been articulated in law and policy as a major interest over the past 15 years, but how does this interest link with, or compare to, others, such as energy self-sufficiency, national defence, and the rights of the aboriginal peoples who live in the Arctic? Many southern Canadians have a rather mythical image of the Arctic. Nevertheless they feel strongly that the region is a major part of their heritage, identity, and future. At the same time, observers in other states witness the modest defence and constabulary capabilities of federal agencies in the Arctic and understandably conclude that Canada's interests in the region are minimal. How can this contrast in perspectives and values be resolved?

Canadian sovereignty over the land in the high Arctic is undisputed, but such is not the case for the waters in the region. If Canada's views with regard to the status of the waters are to prevail, these views must be clarified in such international forums as the United Nations and its agencies, the North Atlantic Treaty Organization, and, if necessary, the International Court of Justice. Of equal importance, however, is the demonstration of adequate capability to exercise and enforce the jurisdiction that Canada claims. It is doubtful that an adequate capability exists now or that it will exist in the near future.[33]

Many analysts of Arctic development have highlighted the need for co-ordination of the various existing public policies that have a bearing on the region and for creation of a general "Arctic policy." In the past, public policies concerning the Arctic have been created largely in a piecemeal, ad hoc fashion in reaction to discrete events. Greater co-ordination of these policies would, in my estimation, be a key ingredient to initiating Canadian priorities and activity in the Arctic, rather than simply reacting to the initiatives of others.

A second type of co-ordination must be considered as well: binational and multinational co-ordination with our immediate Arctic neighbours and other allies, for the purposes of both national defence and managing constabulary activity in the high Arctic. The basis for such co-ordination already exists in two international treaties and a binational agreement – the recent UN Convention on the Law of the Sea, the North Atlantic Treaty, and the NORAD agreement. A common multinational or binational set of tasks, regulations, standards, and management systems for the high Arctic may not be in Canada's sovereign interest, particularly where the waters of the region are concerned. However, the co-ordination of complementary national sets of tasks, regulations, standards, and management systems could serve our sovereign interest, our defence interests, and the efficient performance of constabulary activities.

Finally, a third type of co-ordination should be carefully examined. The analysis presented above indicates that there is very little overlap between DND and the CAF in the performance of their defence functions, and between the RCMP and the Coast Guard in the performance of their constabulary functions. Given the modest levels of activity in the high Arctic by all four institutions and the scanty resources at their disposal, some future requirements for increased capability and/or activity may be co-ordinated or shared on a contingency basis for greater effect and efficiency. In fact, careful moves to build in this type of complementarity across defence and constabulary activities may be highly desirable for sovereignty, as well as budgetary, reasons. Examples of such co-ordination already exist: at sea in the Atlantic and Pacific, where Maritime Command vessels assist in pollution prevention and fisheries monitoring, as well as marine search and rescue, and in the Arctic, where *Aurora* aircraft perform similar monitoring functions. For the future, the Senate recommendations cited earlier indicate one possible facet of co-ordination on a contingency basis. Others may include shared use of surveillance and communications satellites, or of control radar in the high Arctic, if such a capability is required.

The capability to monitor closely events and trends that may affect defence and constabulary activities in the high Arctic is essential to proactive, rather than reactive, decision-making and policy creation. If the results of careful monitoring promptly reach people at senior decision-making levels, the length of the advance warning for potential new demands or activities could be considerably increased over that currently provided by the regulatory process. This would also allow for the creation of more realistic contingency plans and, where appropriate, incremental increases in defence or constabulary capabilities. In some cases, an incremental increase in capability may consist of simply an increase in the pace of research and development on the monitoring systems themselves. Examples of the latter type of incrementalism include more research on underwater detection techniques for ice-covered and ice-infested waters, or more research on systems for ice reconnaissance satellites. A recent example of a more familiar incremental increase in capability is the plan to upgrade some northern airstrips to allow fighter aircraft to land for refuelling if required.

The linkage between the three factors – clarity, co-ordination, and monitoring – is obvious to even the most casual observer of policy formation. Each of the four federal agencies that are the subject of this chapter do follow these basic precepts. However, as their Arctic activities are only a small fraction of each agency's overall operations and as the region apparently enjoys a rather low priority on the national agenda, the necessary linkages among high Arctic activities are not always made in sufficiently effective fashion. If the defence and constabulary implications of Arctic resource development and transportation are to be recognized and dealt with in a timely manner, each of the agencies and their political masters must attach a higher priority to Arctic issues.

CHAPTER ELEVEN

Polar Icebreakers:
The Politics of Inertia

KIM RICHARD NOSSAL

The ice that covers Canada's navigable inland, coastal, and archipelagic waterways for some, most, or all of the year has posed a political and economic problem of some significance for the state in Canada. The relatively thin "annual" ice that forms on the East Coast, in the St Lawrence River, on the Great Lakes, and in the approaches to Hudson Bay offers a perennial obstacle to marine transportation. Year-round navigation in Canadian waters south of the Arctic Circle has required the acquisition of an icebreaking capacity of considerable size, technological sophistication, and cost. However, a capability to navigate Arctic waters, particularly Canada's portion of the Northwest Passage, on a year-round basis raises a special challenge. It requires a "polar" icebreaker, a vessel of sufficient power (measured in either horsepower or kilowatts of shaft power),[1] mass, and endurance to break the thick ice-fields – a combination of multi-year, annual, and "glacial" ice – that clog the narrow channels of the Arctic archipelago for most of the year.

In the century after 1876, the Canadian government slowly acquired an icebreaking capacity for waters south of the Arctic Circle – a comparatively large fleet of heavy, medium, and light icebreakers.[2] However, the polar capability of this fleet is exceedingly limited, and as of early summer 1985 it seemed likely to remain that way. Although funds had been approved for the design of a Canadian polar icebreaker, the government evidently preferred not to move to the acquisition of such a vessel. It seemed prepared to have no more capacity to navigate Arctic waters on a year-round basis than it did when it acquired its first icebreaker nearly a century before.

Then, on 10 September 1985, in the aftermath of the voyage of the u.s. icebreaker *Polar Sea* through the waters of the Canadian archipelago, Ottawa announced a decision to build a polar-class vessel, the Polar 8, the designing of which had been prompted by the voyages of the s/t *Manhattan* 15 years earlier. Some government officials claim that the time from go-ahead to deployment will be 60 months; others say that, more realistically, it will not be until 1992 that the Polar 8 will be in service in the far north. Further, those considerations that made for Canada's long-standing reluctance to invest in year-round Arctic icebreaking capabilities seem likely to persist in some form or another and to influence the politics of polar icebreaker acquisition in the years ahead.

The purpose of this chapter is to explore the government's policies towards acquisition of a polar icebreaker in the period up to mid-1985 and to examine why Canada was so slow to acquire such a capability. It argues that the leisurely pace of polar icebreaker acquisition in the 1970s and 1980s can be attributed to what might be thought of as policy inertia – the propensity of the state to act as it always has on a policy issue. For, as I will show, distinct and consistent patterns in icebreaker acquisition have emerged over the last century. These had an inertial impact on the state's consideration of the acquisition of a polar icebreaker in the 1970s and early 1980s, directly shaping policy outcomes. The origins and development of the government's icebreaking capacity are thus discussed in some detail, for they help explain the constrained character of the polar icebreaker acquisition process that began with the transit of the Passage by the *Manhattan* in 1969. And they may also alert us to difficulties that lie ahead as the decision to build the Polar 8 is implemented by a state apparatus that is set in its ways.

CANADA'S ICEBREAKING CAPABILITY: THE HISTORICAL DIMENSION

The government's capacity to break the ice that annually appears in Canada's coastal and inland waters evolved in three distinct eras: from Confederation to the end of the Second World War; from 1945 to 1970; and from the voyages of the *Manhattan* to mid-1985.

1876–1945

The government first acquired icebreakers for two southern tasks. First, there was a need for icebreakers to aid in the spring break-up of ice in the upper reaches of the St Lawrence River, particularly between Montreal and Trois Rivières, to prevent flooding. Second, an icebreaker was required to maintain a link between Prince Edward Island and the mainland during the winter months. When that province joined Confederation in 1873, the islanders had secured a commitment from the federal government to maintain a year-round link across Northumberland Strait.[3] In 1876 the Cabinet approved the expenditure of $50,000 for "a steamboat specially adapted for the Winter service and running through the ice."[4] The *Northern Light*, a wooden vessel displacing 357 tonnes and developing less

TABLE 1
Canadian Government Icebreaker Acquisition, 1876–1984

Name	Completed	Class	Shipyard[a]
1876–1945			
Northern Light	1876	—	E.W. Sewell
Stanley	1888	—	UK
Minto	1899	—	UK
Montcalm	1904	—	UK
Champlain	1904	—	UK
Lady Grey	1906	—	UK
Earl Grey	1909	—	UK
Mikula (ex J.D. Hazen)	1916	—	Vickers
Saurel	1929	—	Vickers
N.B. McLean	1930	Medium	Halifax
Ernest Lapointe	1941	b	Davie
1945–1970			
Edward Cornwallis	1949	Light[c]	Vickers
d'Iberville	1953	Heavy	Davie
Labrador[d]	1954	Heavy	Marine
Walter E. Foster	1954	Light	Vickers
Montcalm	1957	Med/NA[e]	Davie
Sir Humphrey Gilbert	1959	Med/NA	Davie
Sir William Alexander	1959	Med/NA	Halifax
Alexander Henry	1959	Med/NA	Port Arthur
Camsell	1959	Med/NA	Burrard
Wolfe	1959	Med/NA	Vickers
Tupper	1959	Light	Marine
Simon Fraser	1960	Light	Burrard
Thomas Carleton	1960	Light	Saint John
John A. Macdonald	1960	Heavy	Davie
John Cabot	1965	f	Vickers
J.E. Bernier	1967	Med/NA	Davie
Norman McLeod Rogers	1969	g	Vickers
Louis S. St. Laurent	1969	Heavy	Vickers
Griffon	1970	Med/NA	Davie
1970–1984			
Pierre Radisson	1978	1200[h]	Burrard
Sir John Franklin[i]	1979	1200	Burrard
Des Groseilliers	1982	1200	Port Weller

TABLE 1 (*Concluded*)

Unnamed #1[j]	1985	1100[k]	Burrard
#2	1985	1100	Burrard
#3	1985	1100	Marine
#4	1985	1100	Marine
#5	1986	1100	Collingwood
#6	1986	1100	Halifax

a Current Canadian shipbuilders: Burrard Yarrows Corporation, Vancouver & Victoria, BC; Collingwood Shipyards, Collingwood, Ont.; Davie Shipbuilding Limited, Lauzon, Que.; Halifax Industries Limited, Halifax, NS; Marine Industrie Limitée, Sorel, Que.; Port Arthur Shipbuilding, Thunder Bay, Ont.; Port Weller Dry Docks, St Catharines, Ont.; Saint John Shipbuilding and Dry Dock, Saint John, NB; Versatile Vickers Inc., Montreal, Que. Since 1969, Versatile Vickers has been primarily a ship repair facility; Port Arthur Shipbuilding has also specialized in ship repairing.
b Official classification is "St.Lawrence Ship Channel Icebreaking Survey and Sounding Vessel."
c Light = light icebreaking aid-to-navigation vessel.
d HMCS *Labrador* was originally commissioned for the Royal Canadian Navy. It was transferred to the Ministry of Transport in February 1958.
e Med/NA = medium icebreaking aid-to-navigation vessel.
f Combination cable repair ship and icebreaker.
g Although rated as a "heavy" icebreaker, used primarily in the Gulf of St Lawrence and on the East Coast.
h Ships in the 1200 class (or "R" class, as they were known in the 1970s) are medium gulf/river icebreakers; they are lighter and develop less power than heavy icebreakers like the *Louis S. St. Laurent* and the *John A. Macdonald*.
i Named the *Sir John Franklin* in 1979.
j In September 1983, the government ordered six new icebreakers; these as yet unnamed vessels were under construction in mid-1985.
k Ships in the 1100 class are light icebreaking aid-to-navigation vessels.

than 90 kw in shaft power, was built by E.W. Sewell of Lévis, PQ. But, according to T.C. Pullen, it was "totally unequal to the task"[5] and was frequently out of service because of ice damage.

The first generation of Canadian icebreakers came after Prince Edward Island's legislature petitioned Queen Victoria in 1885 over the link with the mainland. In 1888, Ottawa responded by withdrawing the *Northern Light* from service and purchasing a larger and more powerful steel ship from Scotland. This was followed by a substantial expansion of the fleet in the next 20 years (see Table 1). Because Canadian shipyards did not possess the necessary technology during this early period, Canadian icebreakers were all purchased offshore – from shipyards in the United Kingdom.[6] It was not until 1914 that the government felt confident enough about indigenous capabilities to place an order with Canadian Vickers of Montreal for the *J.D. Hazen*.[7]

Part of this initial fleet was disbanded in the course of the First World War, when three ships were sold to the Russian navy. The remainder of the fleet, however, proved exceedingly durable. One was given as a present to the Soviet Union in 1942; and another lasted until 1955, when it sank after a collision on active duty in the St Lawrence.

The inter-war fleet remained small. The major acquisition was a medium-sized icebreaker to aid navigation in Hudson Bay. The opening of the port of Churchill, Manitoba, on Hudson Bay, and the movement of grain through Hudson Strait during the summer months, necessitated an expanded icebreaking capacity. The *N.B. McLean*, built by Halifax Shipyards in 1930, displacing 4,869 tonnes and developing 4800 kw in shaft power, was purchased in 1931; it remained in service into the early 1980s. The *Saurel* was acquired in 1929, and the *Ernest Lapointe* in 1941. These were, however, light vessels, used primarily for southern tasks.

Until the end of the Second World War, the Canadian government's icebreaking capability remained largely limited to southern waters. To be sure, navigation in the Arctic was not impossible, even through the Northwest Passage – the RCMP schooner *St. Roch* transited the Passage in one season in 1944, for example. Similarly, the government began to engage in regular voyages to the eastern Arctic in the 1920s. But movement by ship through Arctic waters was always limited to the short melt season.

The reason for the limited development of Arctic icebreaking during this period was simple. Over the 70 years after Prince Edward Island's admission to Confederation, successive governments defined icebreaker acquisition in terms of responding to demonstrated and palpable needs. These interests were political (the commitment to Prince Edward Island), commercial (the needs generated by the opening of Churchill, or the needs of merchant shipping in the Gulf of St Lawrence), and environmental (flooding in the upper reaches of the St Lawrence River). Until the late 1940s, little thought was given to the acquisition of an icebreaker large and powerful enough to navigate the waters of the Arctic archipelago, for little need was seen for such a vessel.

1945–70

In the two decades following the war, the government embarked on a major program of icebreaker acquisition that was to result in considerable expansion of the fleet. By 1970, 19 new vessels would be added to the modest fleet of four icebreakers in service in 1945. Most of these were icebreakers best suited to southern tasks. Eight medium-sized icebreaking aid-to-navigation vessels were acquired, five of them ordered for delivery in 1959 and 1960; between 1949 and 1960, five light navaids vessels were purchased; in addition, the *John Cabot*, a combination icebreaker/cable repair ship, was acquired in 1965 (see Table 1).

Additions to Canada's Arctic icebreaking capability were, however, made during this expansion: five heavy icebreakers were acquired between 1945 and 1970. HMCS *Labrador* was commissioned by the Royal Canadian Navy in 1954. It was the heaviest icebreaker in the Canadian fleet: with a displacement of 7,100 tonnes, it developed 7,500 kw of shaft power; its diesel/electric propulsion system gave it an effective cruising range of between 25,000 and 35,000 nautical miles. When it was decided in the late 1950s that the Department of National Defence would no longer engage in icebreaking activities, the *Labrador* was transferred to the Department of Transport (DOT) in February 1958.

DOT also acquired the *d'Iberville*, completed in 1953, and the *John A. Macdonald*, completed in 1960. Both had a greater displacement and more power than the *Labrador*, but less range. The *John A. Macdonald*, also powered by a diesel/electric system, had a cruising range of 20,000 nautical miles. The *d'Iberville* had a steam propulsion system that reduced its ability to cruise for lengthy periods in the Arctic: its Skinner uniflow engines and its eight boilers consumed massive quantities of oil while breaking fast ice, limiting the effective range to 11,000 nautical miles.[8]

These three vessels were the "capital" ships of the icebreaking fleet until the end of this period, when the *Norman McLeod Rogers* and the *Louis S. St. Laurent* were both completed in 1969. The former, while rated as a heavy icebreaker, was designed primarily for use on the East Coast and in the St Lawrence. The *Louis S. St. Laurent*, by contrast, was the first Canadian icebreaker intended primarily for Arctic work. It remains the government's largest and most powerful icebreaker: it displaces 14,500 tonnes, and its steam turbo/electric propulsion system develops 17,900 kw shaft power. However, like the *d'Iberville*, it also burns black oil, and it thus has a cruising range of only 16,000 nautical miles.

The considerable expansion of icebreaking capabilities in the post-war period was necessary for four reasons. First, the icebreaking needs of the St Lawrence River and Gulf steadily increased. The existing fleet in 1945 – one medium and three light icebreakers – was proving inadequate for the task of winter and spring icebreaking in the St Lawrence. One of the key reasons for the acquisition of the *d'Iberville* was for service in this area.

Second, the entry into Confederation in 1949 of Newfoundland, with its long coastline, placed an added burden on the capabilities of DOT, which was responsible for erecting and maintaining such aids to navigation as lighthouses and buoys. (Transporting staff to and from lighthouses, it might be noted, accounts for 10 to 15 per cent of the work of the Coast Guard fleet.) Third, the opening of the St Lawrence Seaway in 1959 heralded the expansion of inland water traffic – and a concomitant requirement for higher levels of aid to navigation on the Great Lakes. Indeed, it was not coincidental that 8 of the 13 smaller vessels added to the fleet between 1945 and 1970 were completed between June 1959 and July 1960 – the first full season of Seaway traffic. The tasks associated with both Newfoundland and the Seaway required smaller ships – medium or light icebreaking aid-to-navigation vessels – and thus the bulk of the expansion was in the acquisition of light or medium navaids (13 of the 19 icebreakers acquired between 1949 and 1970).

Fourth and finally, the increased strategic importance to the United States of the Arctic forefield or "glacis"[9] had an impact on icebreaker acquisition. Strategic considerations impelled the Canadian government to acquire greater capacity to navigate the waters of the far north. The construction of Distant Early Warning (DEW) Line facilities from 1954 to 1957 created a need for summer supply operations: in these three years, over 300 ships carried 1.25 million tons of cargo to the high Arctic. Likewise, American interest in the Arctic led to the establishment after 1948 of five weather stations north of 60°N operated jointly with Canada; these, too, required summer resupply.

Until 1953, resupply operations for the weather stations were conducted exclusively by U.S. vessels – for the simple reason that until then Canada did not have the capacity to travel by sea to the far north.[10] After the acquisition of the *Labrador* and the *d'Iberville*, this capacity was expanded, but not greatly: much of the supply for DEW Line construction was undertaken with the assistance of U.S. icebreakers. But in 1958 the Diefenbaker government decided to assume responsibility for the entire Arctic summer resupply operation; this was a prelude to its decision in 1959 to take over operational control of the DEW Line installations. The decisions to acquire the *John A. Macdonald* in the late 1950s and the *John Cabot* and the *Louis S. St. Laurent* in the early 1960s were all underwritten by the need to ensure that the Canadian government had an expanded capability to assist the United States in Arctic aspects of continental defence.

While the substantial expansion of the Canadian icebreaking fleet during this period did give Ottawa greater ability to navigate the Arctic archipelago than before, the heavy icebreakers acquired during this period did not give Canada significant polar capability. Even the most powerful ships – the *John A. Macdonald* and the *Louis S. St. Laurent* – were limited to the summer months and to less harsh ice conditions of eastern and southern Arctic waters.

1970–85

In 1969, the year that the *Louis S. St. Laurent* was completed, the supertanker *Manhattan* made its historic transit of the Northwest Passage. Paradoxically, the pace of icebreaker acquisition slowed after this, despite the political and environmental concerns raised by the prospect of more commercial traffic moving through the Passage. After the completion of the *Griffon* in 1970, the only other icebreakers acquired during the Trudeau era were light navaids and medium vessels. In August 1981, the design contract for type-1100 light navaids icebreakers was announced.

These vessels – displacing 3,800 tonnes, and developing 6,000 kw shaft power – were intended to "become the workhorse of the fleet."[11] In September 1983, it was announced that orders for six 1100s had been placed with five shipyards across the country, to be delivered in 1985 and 1986.[12]

In the late 1970s and early 1980s three medium icebreakers were also completed – the *Pierre Radisson* (1978), the *Sir John Franklin* (1979), and the *Des Groseilliers* (1982). These ships, which had been designed in the early 1970s, were intended to replace the *N.B. McLean* and the *d'Iberville*, which were retired in the early 1980s. They belong to the Coast Guard 1200-class (also known as "R" class). The 1200s displace 6,600 tonnes and develop 10,100 kw shaft power and thus fall between the medium and heavy classes.

However, 1200-class icebreakers did not add significantly to Canada's Arctic capabilities. While they are capable of limited Arctic navigation, and incorporates the latest icebreaker technology, they are designed primarily for southern tasks. For example, their shallow draught (they draw only 6.2 m, compared with 9.5 m for the *Louis S. St. Laurent*, 8.6 m for the *John A. Macdonald* and 9.3 m for the *Labrador*) allows them to work the Seaway and the Great Lakes.[13] But it also makes Arctic operations more difficult: the deeper an icebreaker's propellers are, the less likely they will suffer damage by ice. Certainly, the 1200-class icebreakers do not represent a substantial improvement in the Canadian government's Arctic icebreaking capabilities.

Icebreaker acquisition in the latter years of the Trudeau period was not impelled only by provision of icebreaking services per se. The process of acquisition was also accelerated by the needs of the Canadian shipbuilding industry itself. As early as 1978, Cabinet recognized that declining capital acquisitions by government were having a severe impact on the shipyards. On 21 December 1978, it approved a Government Programme for the Economic Stimulation of the Canadian Shipbuilding Industry. The *Des Groseilliers*, approved by the government of Joe Clark in December 1979, was acquired under this program.[14]

But by the end of 1982, the industry was in more serious difficulty than it had been in the late 1970s. Now both Canadian and export commercial orders placed in Canadian yards had "virtually dried up," according to the Canadian Shipbuilding and Ship Repairing Association.[15] This was largely because of the downturn in world shipping construction during the recession of 1982 and the growing dominance of Japan and South Korea in commercial shipbuilding, but also because of Canadian customs legislation which encouraged firms to purchase their shipping offshore and import the completed vessels into Canada duty-free.[16]

The 1982 crisis in the shipbuilding industry – particularly the rapid decline in shipyard employment from 14,000 in March to 8,500 in

December – prompted the government to introduce a Special Recovery Capital Projects (SRCP) program in its April 1983 budget. By October, the government had placed orders for nine vessels with shipyards, including $306 million in orders for 1100-type light navaids icebreakers. In addition, the acquisition of a fourth 1200-type medium icebreaker was also speeded up. These orders targeted those shipyards that had not received government contracts for ferries or for the Canadian Patrol Frigate.[17] Government work thus represented 81 per cent of the gross tonnage under construction in Canadian yards by the end of 1983. (These accelerated acquisitions would be criticized by the auditor-general in his report for 1982–3: he argued that rapid acquisition encouraged waste because a major asset like an icebreaker tends to be used "just because it is there, and substantial operating costs will be incurred unnecessarily.")[18]

Acquisitions 1876–1985: An Overview

Three inertial tendencies can be identified in the first century of government icebreaker acquisition. First, the pattern of icebreaker acquisition was consistently reactive over the period examined. Historically, governments in Ottawa moved to acquire a particular icebreaking capability only *after* Ministers were convinced that there was an obvious, demonstrated, and easily justifiable need for the expenditure of funds on large capital acquisitions that are also expensive to operate once built and in service. This was evident in the case of Northumberland Strait in the 1880s, the opening of Churchill in the 1930s, the accession of Newfoundland in 1949, the construction of the DEW Line in the 1950s, the opening of the Seaway in 1959, and in the periodic decisions to replace vessels nearing the end of their useful lives. Icebreaker acquisition has thus traditionally followed from electoral, strategic, or, more frequently, commercial demands.

From this stems a second, related historical tendency to seek clearly identifiable "clients" or beneficiaries for icebreaker acquisition. The acquisition of icebreaker capability has never been seen by the government as a pure public good. Put another way, governments in Canada have not historically been prone to justify the ability to break ice in Canadian waters for such intangible beneficiaries as "all Canadians." Rather, icebreaking has tended to be justified as providing benefits to specific groups in Canadian society with concrete interests either in the provision of icebreaking services or in the actual building of icebreakers themselves. In the 1870s, the government was impelled to gain a rudimentary icebreaking capacity; from the late 1920s, it was the needs of prairie farmers and merchant shipping; from the 1950s, both Seaway icebreaking and Arctic summer resupply and hydrography have been justified in terms of service to clients with concrete and tangible interests in icebreaker capability. And in the late 1970s and early 1980s, the identifiable clients with concrete interests were not so much the "consumers" of icebreaking services as the "consumers" of state expenditures on icebreaker acquisition: the shipyards who benefited by the placing of orders.

The third tendency that emerges from this overview is the overriding importance of domestic construction and the requirements of regional distribution of government contracts. Since 1914 the Canadian government's icebreakers have been acquired exclusively from Canadian shipyards. The failure of the Canadian-built *Northern Light* forced the government to purchase the first generation of icebreakers from British yards. But from 1914, when sufficient technological capacity had been transferred from the United Kingdom, the government in Ottawa looked exclusively to Canadian yards to supply its icebreaking capability.

Similarly, particularly in the post-Second World War period, the federal government's capital acquisitions in water transportation, of which icebreakers have been a substantial part, have been made with an eye to regional distribution of contracts. Thus while the industry's principal yards – Davie in Quebec and Burrard Yarrows in British Columbia – have received the lion's share of icebreaker contracts over the seventy years since the *J.D. Hazen* was ordered in 1914, an effort has been made to diversify construction contracts. Acquisition has thus also been targeted to Atlantic yards (Halifax Industries, Saint John Shipbuilding) and the Great Lakes yards (Collingwood, Port Arthur, and Port Weller Dry Docks).

These three inertial tendencies – the reactive nature of icebreaker acquisition, the need for specific "clients," and the reliance on regionally diversified domestic suppliers – all had a critical impact on the process of gaining a polar icebreaking capability.

CANADA'S POLAR ICEBREAKER
CAPABILITY

At the end of Pierre Elliott Trudeau's tenure as Prime Minister in 1984, the Canadian government had no more polar icebreaking capacity than it had in 1969, when the voyages of the *Manhattan* so exercised the new leader and his Cabinet. Canada's fleet of icebreakers in service in 1984 still lacked the capability for extended navigation in Arctic waters.

The more severe ice-covered waters of the Arctic archipelago pose formidable obstacles to any icebreaker, even the most powerful.[19] It should be noted that the ice in the channels, straits, bays, and basins of the Arctic archipelago differs considerably from the polar ice pack that drifts in the currents of the Arctic Ocean. The pack can be navigated by following "leads" or openings in the ice: in July 1977, for example, the Soviet nuclear icebreaker *Arktika* (now the *Brezhnev*) broke through to reach the North Pole.

By contrast, archipelagic ice tends to be extremely difficult to navigate. Leads tend to be few, particularly during the winter months, when ice is packed tightly between the Arctic islands ("landfast" ice); it tends to be a combination of "new" (first-year) and harder "old" (multi-year) ice. The pressure of confinement in narrow channels causes "hummocking" – heavy ice ridges above sea level, often to heights of 8 m. Pressure ridging also works below sea level: ice "keels," often to depths of 50 m, are created. In some months of the year – May is usually the worst – such fast ice is simply impenetrable; even at other times, the most powerful icebreaker can break a channel through a consolidated ice pack only by repeated charging.

The severity of ice conditions differs according to the region of the Arctic. Generally, ice conditions deteriorate in the western and northern portions of the archipelago. The norm in an eastern location like Baffin Bay, for example, is for first-year ice 1.25 m thick, with pack ice to 1.75 m, and ridging and hummocking to 6–8 m. By contrast, around Axel Heiberg in the Sverdrup Basin, the ice is a combination of first-year ice over 2 m thick, and 60 per cent multi-year ice packed to over 3 m, with exceedingly heavy pressure ridging.[20] In the Parry Channel, the severest ice conditions are to be found in M'Clure Strait, which has only been crossed by submarine. On the more common route (through Prince of Wales Strait), the ice conditions are severest in Viscount Melville Sound at the northeastern opening of Prince of Wales Strait.

The Coast Guard's icebreakers are, as T.C. Pullen puts it, "summer visitors only."[21] The current generation of Canadian icebreakers does not have the power, the mass, or the endurance to navigate widely in the Arctic archipelago on a year-round basis. Nor, under Canadian law, are they allowed to.

The Arctic Shipping Pollution Prevention Regulations (ASPPR) made under the Arctic Waters Pollution Prevention Act of 1970 are designed to provide a comprehensive regime to regulate access of marine transportation to Arctic waters. The ASPPR divide Canada's Arctic archipelago into 16 shipping control zones. Boundaries reflect the relative severity of ice conditions in each zone on a year-round basis (zone 1 being the severest, zone 16 the least severe). Schedules VI and VII outline mechanical and hull specifications for nine "Arctic classes" of ascending strength and power – 1, 1A, 2, 3, 4, 6, 7, 8, and 10. Schedule VIII indicates what class of ship may enter the 16 zones at what times of the year. For example, an Arctic class 10 vessel may enter all 16 zones at any time of year; an Arctic class 1 vessel may not enter zones 1 to 5 at any time and is restricted to zones 6 to 16 for varying periods between June and November.[22]

"Arctic class" is frequently used as a shorthand method of describing the

TABLE 2

Arctic Capabilities of Canada's Icebreaker Fleet, mid-1985

Name	Arctic Class or Equivalent[a]	Displacement (Tonnes)	Shaft Power (kw)
Existing Fleet			
Labrador	2–3	7,100	7,500
John A. Macdonald	3	9,300	11,200
Norman McLeod Rogers	2	6,500	8,900
Louis S. St. Laurent	3–4	14,500	17,900
Pierre Radisson	2–3	6,600	10,100
Sir John Franklin	2–3	6,600	10,100
Des Groseilliers	2–3	6,600	10,100
Contemplated			
"R" Class #4	2–3	6,600	10,100
Polar 8	8	33,600	74,600

a The Arctic Shipping Pollution Prevention Regulations (chaps 353–6, *Consolidated Regulations of Canada*, 1978) established nine Arctic classes and outline the design specifications for each class. Technically, there is no such class as "2–3" or "3–4; however, for the purposes of the ASPPR, the Coast Guard regards some of its icebreakers as falling between two classes. The upper and lower classes are given in these cases.

polar icebreaking *capabilities* of a vessel. For example, "Arctic class 10" is usually defined as the capability to maintain continuous headway of approximately 3 knots through fast ice ten feet thick without having to stop, back up, and ram the ice. However, the ASPPR outline not a vessel's icebreaking capabilities, but the structural prerequisites of ships wishing to navigate the archipelago; whether an Arctic class vessel can actually navigate those zones that it is entitled to is another matter altogether. Too often, the shorthand creates the expectation that a class 10 vessel, which has the *right* to travel anywhere in the archipelago at any time, has the *ability* to do so.[23]

As of 2 August 1972, when the Arctic Waters Pollution Prevention Act of 1970 was proclaimed,[24] the Arctic mobility of Canada's icebreaker fleet was restricted by law as well as by nature. The most powerful icebreaker in the fleet in 1985 was the *Louis S. St. Laurent*. Drawing 9.5 m, displacing 14,500 tonnes, and developing 17,900 kw in shaft power, this vessel is rated as "between 3 and 4," according to the Coast Guard. Such a rating restricts the *Louis S. St. Laurent* to south of 60°N from the end of March to the beginning of June. It may enter less severe zones (6–16) for six to ten months of the year. For the severe zones (1–5) an Arctic class 4 vessel is restricted to a short "open" season. In zone 2, for example, which includes the portion of the Prince of Wales Strait route through the Passage, entry is limited to 60 days (15 August to 15 October). The Arctic class ratings for the other large vessels in the icebreaking fleet range from 2 to 3 (see Table 2), and so their movements in Arctic waters are even further restricted. Indeed, the *Norman McLeod Rogers*, rated as a "heavy" icebreaker, but with an Arctic class 2, is denied entry to large portions of the archipelago at any time of the year.

POLAR ICEBREAKER DECISIONS,
1974–85: 7, 8, OR 10?

The idea of acquiring an icebreaker with greater mass and power than the *Louis S. St Laurent* and the *John A. Macdonald* surfaced in the wake of the trials of the *Manhattan* in 1969. In June 1971, for example, the House of Commons Standing Committee on Indian Affairs and Northern Development, after a study of Arctic icebreaking services, urged the construction of an icebreaker with the capability of navigating Arctic waters for 10 to 12 months of the year.[25] Such a sentiment was echoed in an editorial in the *Vancouver Sun* in November of that year. The *Sun* asserted that to control pollution and assert sovereignty in the Arctic, "Canada needs muscle. One way to get it is to build ships, especially icebreakers, of sufficient power and range."[26] In other words, there was a perceived need for a "polar" icebreaker (generally defined as a class 6 or above).

In the following decade, Cabinet did not acquire such a capability: throughout the 1970s, a succession of ministers of transport would have to respond to the perennial written question put by J.M. Forrestal (PC: Dartmouth-Halifax East), the lone voice in the House of Commons plumping for a Canadian polar icebreaking capability – by the late 1970s (or, as it eventually became, the early 1980s), how many icebreakers would the government have to break polar ice seven feet thick? – with the same one-word answer: none. However, the issue *was* under consideration. During the 1970s and early 1980s, Cabinet considered three different plans for acquiring a polar icebreaker. The following section provides a brief overview of those plans.

The Coast Guard's response to demands for a "polar" icebreaker in the early 1970s was to propose a two-track acquisition strategy: an Arctic class 7 for the medium term (the 1980s), and a class 10 for the long term (the 1990s). Because nuclear power was the most efficient propulsion system for a year-round icebreaker (not only would it develop massive power, but it would also afford great cruising range, since refuelling would be needed only once every several years), it was proposed that a class 10 icebreaker be nuclear-powered.

In the mid-1970s, Cabinet approved this proposition – but only in a limited way. Funding was approved for the design phase for a conventionally powered class 7 icebreaker. The Polar 7, which would at that time be the largest icebreaker in the world, would displace 18,200 tonnes, develop 60,000 kw shaft power, and be capable of Arctic operations for eight to ten months of the year. German and Milne Ltd of Montreal, Canada's leading firm of naval architects, was given the contract for the design stage.[27]   In 1975, German and Milne was also authorized to conduct a feasibility study of a larger, class 10 icebreaker. By 1976, Cabinet was persuaded that Canada's polar icebreaker should be nuclear-powered. More properly, the propulsion system would not be entirely nuclear, but rather a "hybrid" or a combination of systems: gas turbine engines would be powered by nuclear reactors. Since the Polar 7 was too small to accommodate the nuclear power plant, Cabinet decided that it would fund a preliminary design of a hybrid class 10 icebreaker, modifying the existing Polar 7 design. The hybrid class 10 would be larger and develop almost twice as much shaft power as the Polar 7 – 112,000 kw.[28]

In March 1978, a $6 million design project for the hybrid was announced; in January 1979, Treasury Board approved the program; and in July 1979, a Request for Proposal was issued by the Department of Supply and Services inviting potential contractors with expertise in nuclear maritime propulsion systems to submit proposals.[29] All potential suppliers of the nuclear propulsion system were located offshore – in the United States, France, Germany, and Britain. However, in the following year, all but one of the potential nuclear suppliers pulled out – for a variety of reasons. By the time the Department of Transport (DOT) was ready to go to Cabinet in the autumn of 1980, only the French remained.

At this juncture, DOT had to secure Cabinet approval for the next step. Its presentation to Cabinet in October 1980 outlined four alternatives suggested by the withdrawal of all but the French nuclear suppliers. First, Cabinet could agree to continue the design phase of the hybrid 10 with an eye to the long term and construct a conventionally powered class 8 for the near term. The impetus for this suggestion rested on a definition of need over the long term (late 1990s and into the new century): a vessel of the power and range of the hybrid 10 would eventually be required, but in the shorter run Canada would still need polar capability. A conventionally powered class 10 icebreaker would be hugely expensive because of its appetite for oil and therefore was dismissed by DOT as not cost-effective. Thus the alternative was a conventionally powered icebreaker of the next class – a Polar 8. The second and third alternatives presented to Cabinet suggested that Canada could abandon the nuclear hybrid altogether and construct either one conventional Polar 8 or, in collaboration with the private sector, build two or more of these vessels for Arctic work. The final alternative was to abandon the acquisition of a polar icebreaker altogether.[30]

TABLE 3
Comparative Arctic Icebreaking Capabilities
(Ships displacing over 6,000 tonnes)

Country	Name	Displacement (Tonnes)	Shaft Power (kw)
Soviet Union	Brezhnev[a,b]	23,800	55,900
	Sibir[b]	23,800	55,900
	Jermak	20,500	26,800
	Adm Makarov	20,500	26,800
	Krasin	20,500	26,800
	Lenin[b]	19,500	32,800
	Moskva	15,600	16,400
	Murmansk	15,600	16,400
	Leningrad	15,600	16,400
	Kiev	15,600	16,400
	Vladivostok	15,600	16,400
United States	Polar Star	13,300	58,100
	Polar Sea	13,300	58,100
	Glacier	8,600	15,700
	Westwind	6,600	7,500
	Northwind	6,600	7,500
Canada	Louis S. St. Laurent	14,500	17,900
	John A. Macdonald	9,300	11,200
	Labrador	7,100	7,500
	Pierre Radisson	6,600	10,100
	Franklin	6,600	10,100
	Des Groseilliers	6,600	10,100
	Norman McLeod Rogers	6,500	8,900
Sweden	Atle	9,700	16,400
	Frej	9,700	16,400
	Ymer	9,700	16,400
Finland	Urho	9,700	16,400
	Siso	9,700	16,400

a Formerly Arktika.
b Powered by nuclear/steam turbine machinery.

In April 1981, Cabinet endorsed none of these alternatives clearly: it decided to abandon all further work on a hybrid 10, but it did not approve anything more than a design phase for one Polar 8 for use by the Coast

Guard.[31] As envisaged by DOT, this vessel would be the flagship of the icebreaking fleet, more powerful than any other icebreaker afloat, including the latest powerful acquisitions by the Soviet Union and the United States (see Table 3). It would displace 33,600 tonnes and develop 74,600 kw in shaft power; drawing 13 m, it would have a cruising range of 30,000 nautical miles and would have sufficient fuel to operate for three weeks at full power.

By 1983, a "funded bid" phase for the Polar 8 had been approved. A funded bid program – under which the costs to the yards of formulating bids are offset by the government – was made necessary because Cabinet had not approved a construction phase, and thus there was no guarantee that after an expensive bid had been formulated Cabinet would approve construction. A total of $1.3 million was allocated for payment to three shipyards with the necessary capacity to build the Polar 8.[32] The funded bid was to be valid for eighteen months; officials worked on the assumption that Cabinet would consider the construction phase of the Polar 8 acquisition by August 1985 at the earliest.

EXPLAINING POLAR ICEBREAKER DECISION-MAKING

At first blush, Cabinet's decisions on polar icebreaker acquisition in the 1970s and early 1980s suggest a marked lack of rational policy direction. In the space of a decade, Cabinet tentatively embraced three very different conceptions of polar icebreaking capability, each having very different implications – for Arctic navigation, for sovereignty, for Arctic ecology, for expenditures, and for the Canadian shipbuilding industry. But the Ministers never grasped the nettle firmly enough to permit the actual acquisition of a polar capability: as Langford concluded from his study, Cabinet was not convinced of the need to expend substantial funds on a polar icebreaker,[33] a conclusion that remained as valid in 1984 as when it was written in 1975. Why that was so is the focus of this section.

For, in fact, the Cabinet's decisions on polar icebreaker acquisition were quite consistent with the three inertial patterns outlined above. Indeed, these factors account for Cabinet's persistent lack of conviction.

Reaction

The evolution of Cabinet's decisions on a polar icebreaker for Canada was in keeping with the traditional pattern of predicating icebreaker acquisition on the basis of reaction to events and pressures both domestic and external. Each phase of polar icebreaker decision-making parallels almost exactly shifts in the policy-making environment during this period.

The Polar 7 emerged largely as a reaction to the symbolism of the voyage of the *Manhattan* and the domestic and foreign policy implications of u.s. flagships cruising Canadian waters. The successful transit of this vessel through the Northwest Passage fuelled nationalistic fears of threats to Canada's sovereignty in the Arctic and heightened environmental concerns about potential damage to Arctic ecosystems. The focus in the early 1970s was thus on the symbolic level: what was needed was a vessel of sufficient power that would by its very presence in the Arctic assert and protect Canadian sovereignty. Little thought was given to what size of icebreaker would be needed for the assertion of sovereignty, though it was recognized that one more powerful than the *Louis S. St. Laurent* would be desirable. In a very real sense, the class eventually chosen emerged arbitrarily.

The oil crisis of 1973–4 accelerated what had been a slow process of consideration at the bureaucratic level and shifted the focus from sovereignty/environmental concerns of the post-*Manhattan* period to the more concrete needs of icebreaker support for the transport of hydrocarbons from the Beaufort Sea and other areas. The embargo of the Organization of Arab Petroleum Exporting Countries – and the surge in crude oil prices – created firm expectations that by the end of the decade there would be pressures placed on Canada to open the waters of the Arctic archipelago to the commercial transport of Arctic resources. A demand for the services of professional polar icebreakers would, it was thought, inexorably follow.

The focus of the government's attention shifted from a Polar 7 to a larger icebreaker in step with this change. A class 7 vessel might have been appropriate for showing the flag, but it would have been inadequate for icebreaking support for commercial carriers through the Northwest Passage. For one thing, its cruising range would have been restricted by the ASPPR, which would have kept it out of the strategic northeastern opening of Prince of Wales Strait (zone 2) from 1 December to 31 July. To navigate the Northwest Passage effectively, a class 8 or a class 10 was required. For this reason, it was decided to abandon the Polar 7.

The decision to upgrade the polar capability directly to class 10 was likewise predicated on the expectation of Arctic resource development. At some juncture, it was argued, the exploitation of resources in the northwestern Arctic (zone 1) would require a class 10 icebreaker. Therefore it made more sense to departmental planners to secure a 10 at the outset rather than acquire a class 8 and then have to engage in another bout of upgraded polar icebreaker construction shortly thereafter.

And a decision to acquire a class 10 demanded a nuclear propulsion system. A diesel propulsion system on such a large icebreaker operating in severe ice at full power would burn so much oil that the Coast Guard would have to establish and operate northern fuel depots outfitted with heated fuel storage and transfer systems. The expense of a conventionally powered class 10 icebreaker was simply cost-ineffective. A nuclear hybrid, by contrast, would require refuelling only once every three or four years at a southern installation. The initial increased capital cost of a hybrid 10 would be more than offset by long-term operating savings.

However, for all its attractiveness, the nuclear option posed formidable problems. First, the government had to go offshore for the propulsion system, for Canada's nuclear technology – the CANDU system – was inappropriate for marine applications. This did not sit well with Canadian manufacturers and evoked critical questions in the House of Commons in November 1976. Second, placing a nuclear power plant on a Canadian icebreaker involved a great deal of uncertainty. The marine use of nuclear power in Western countries was confined exclusively to military applications; ironically, the only country with knowledge of nuclear power applied in the jarring environment of icebreaker operations was the Soviet Union. Eventually, only one state – France – was willing to negotiate the transfer of marine applications of nuclear power to Canada. Third, because there was no regime in place in Canada for the regulation of nuclear power in marine applications, one had to be created while negotiations with the French were under way. The lack of any Canadian standards and delays in formulating a Canadian regulatory regime for a nuclear icebreaker caused both delays and conflicts in negotiations with the French. And, finally, the acquisition of nuclear technology for a class 10 icebreaker would be a singular investment, for no other ship built or registered in Canada would be nuclear-powered.

For these four reasons, the government's enthusiasm for the hybrid 10 option was never unbounded. However, it was not these obstacles that led to abandonment of the nuclear hybrid option in the spring of 1981. It was the revision of the estimates of Arctic resource exploitation. By 1981, much of the initial optimism about northern exploitation had evaporated. While in 1975, Ministers had fixed on the early 1980s as the time when commercial shipments of Arctic resources would begin,[34] by 1981 these had been revised as a result of the shifting needs of industry.

Clients

The client-oriented perspective of earlier periods of icebreaker acquisition continued well into the 1970s and 1980s. And there was little doubt that the major clients were the commercial concerns exploring for, exploiting, and shipping Arctic resources. "The Canadian Coast Guard," noted the former polar icebreaker project manager, "has carried out its planning based ... on the assumption that it is the government's view that Arctic hydrocarbon development should proceed at or near the pace proposed by industry."[35]

The pace proposed by industry became more and more unclear as a result of the recession, the natural gas glut, and the shifting fortunes of Arctic exploration. As we have seen, industry's optimism of the mid-1970s prompted the government to embark on acquiring a Polar 10 nuclear capability; it was the slackening of that pace in the early 1980s that prompted Cabinet to view with increasing scepticism arguments that industry needs in the near term would require a polar icebreaker. While there continues to be an expectation that at some juncture commercial shipments of Arctic resources will be made, there is constant uncertainty about when that will occur. There is agreement on the short-term prospect: commercial shipping of resources through the Northwest Passage will not occur before the 1990s. But beyond that, forecasts of commercial uses of the Passage evince little agreement on the medium term. By 1984, some officials were claiming that they expected year-round commercial shipping through the Northwest Passage to begin in the early 1990s. Others were predicting that given the costs involved, commercial transport of resources through the Passage would not occur until well into the twenty-first century. Still others noted that industry might eschew year-round navigation altogether in favour of using large convoys during the short melt season.

The importance of identifiable clients to the polar icebreaker project is best demonstrated by Cabinet's 1981 decision to terminate work on the nuclear option and authorize a Polar 8 design. In that decision, the Ministers explicitly tied the construction of the Polar 8 to energy industry requirements, directing that when the issue was brought back to Cabinet, DOT and Energy, Mines and Resources (EMR) were jointly to make the submission. The implication was that EMR should sign a recommendation to Cabinet only when it judged that industry demand was great enough to warrant acquisition of a polar icebreaker.

Cabinet's definition of resource extraction firms as the principal "beneficiaries" of a polar icebreaker was reflected in the considerable bureaucratic conflict that ensued from the decision of 1981. First, the reluctance of Cabinet to specify other beneficiaries did nothing to dampen the opposition of central agencies that had been ranged against the polar icebreaker program since the mid-1970s. Lacking a broader definition of "clientele," officials from Treasury Board Secretariat (TBS) and the Department of Finance were free to continue to express their distinct lack of enthusiasm for such a huge expenditure ($451 million in constant 1982 dollars) on a capital project in a period of restraint unless there were immediate and identifiable economic benefits. Certainly, neither TBS nor Finance was disposed to embrace the wider conception of "beneficiaries" implicit in the argument that a polar icebreaker was needed to assert Canadian sovereignty in Arctic waters.[36]

Second, Cabinet's 1981 decision led to conflict among the program departments. While there was general agreement among them on the desirability of a polar icebreaker for Canada, there was no agreement on which "envelope" the project should be funded from.[37] For its part, the Coast Guard initially assumed that since Cabinet had linked acquisition of a polar icebreaker to transport of hydrocarbons, the Polar 8 would be funded out of the energy envelope rather than the economic development envelope; indeed, EMR agreed to help fund part of the design phase of the Polar 8. But EMR's position was consistently that a polar icebreaker could not be justified on energy grounds alone, even if there were commercial hydrocarbon traffic in the Northwest Passage. In EMR's view, therefore, funding for the construction phase of the polar icebreaker project should not come out of the energy envelope.

Because Cabinet had not endorsed a wider conception of "beneficiaries," there was little concrete support from other departments for the Polar 8. While it was recognized that a polar icebreaker in service north of 60°N would provide some benefits, neither Environment nor Indian and Northern Affairs wanted this expenditure to come out of the social affairs envelope. While expenditures on a polar icebreaker would bring benefits to the shipbuilding industry, the Polar 8 was not a priority for Industry, Trade and Commerce (after 1982, Regional Industrial Expansion), for reasons that will be discussed below. Most program departments agreed that a polar icebreaker would be useful to assert Canada's sovereignty, but those departments with the primary policy interest in sovereignty – External Affairs and National Defence – were both unwilling to commit funds from their envelopes for this program. In short, Cabinet's specification of the polar icebreaker's clientele meant that each department, while agreeing in principle to the idea of the Polar 8, had no interest in contributing to its actual acquisition. Further, the opposition of the central agencies to the project meant that they would be disinclined to play the role of a compromising mediator in the funding dispute.

The dispute over funding was an important factor in delaying the process of acquisition. Unlike the new fighter aircraft program, for which Cabinet had narrowly structured the decision-making process to dampen the budget-maximizing tendencies of the different bureaucratic players,[38] in this case, Cabinet's decision actually encouraged the many departments involved to pursue and protect parochial interests. This parochialism spawned reluctance at the bureaucratic level to endorse the Polar 8, tightly constraining the lead player, the Coast Guard. In particular, the position of EMR, upon which the Coast Guard was dependent for endorsement, was critical. EMR's position was in essence that the Coast Guard did not have the clientele specified by the Ministers, and without those clients justification for the Polar 8 largely evaporated.

Nor did the Coast Guard itself have the bureaucratic political resources to transcend the constraints of this inertial tendency. The Coast Guard, like its earlier bureaucratic incarnations in Transport and (before 1936) the Department of Marine, has by tradition been a "service" agency, rendering assistance to identifiable clients who demand it. Indeed, its planning for a polar icebreaker reflected this service role. As early as 1974, the Coast Guard was working on the assumption that its polar icebreaker would operate on a cost-recovery, or "dedicated" basis.[39] By 1980, DOT's submission to Cabinet claimed that 40 per cent of the polar icebreaker's operational ship days would be devoted to "dedicated" icebreaking.[40] However, it would appear that such a "service" orientation is difficult to alter, even when Ministers themselves decide to change it. Thus, for example, Cabinet had confirmed in 1977 that the Coast Guard, and not Maritime Command of the Canadian Armed Forces, would be responsible for asserting Canadian sovereignty in ice-covered Arctic waters. But there was no concomitant decision to allocate sufficient political or budgetary resources to fulfil this role.

In sum, the client-oriented perspective of both the ministerial and bureaucratic levels is critical to an explanation of the process of polar icebreaker acquisition in the late 1970s and early 1980s. The inability of the Coast Guard – the lead agency – to convince other players to embrace a wider conception of "clientele" for polar icebreaker services, the unwillingness of Cabinet to abandon a tradition of authorizing expenditures only when a need for icebreaking is clear and obvious, and the uncertainty of the hydrocarbon industry's own plans for cargo shipments through the Passage all contributed to the lack of progress in acquiring a polar icebreaker during the Trudeau era.

Canadian shipbuilders

One of the traditional clients in icebreaker policy has been the Canadian shipbuilding industry: not since 1909 has the government in Ottawa acquired its icebreaking capability offshore, and in the seven decades after the first contract was let to Canadian Vickers in 1914, the pattern has been to diversify Coast Guard (and naval) construction contracts. This inertial tendency also had a minor, but not insignificant, effect on polar icebreaker decision-making after 1970. Certainly the preferences of the shipbuilding industry played a part in determining Cabinet's icebreaker decisions.

At first glance, it might be assumed that the shipbuilding industry would favour an acquisition program that would have meant an initial capital expenditure of more than $450 million in Canadian yards (to which must be added later expenditures on repairs and refits). Certainly the industry's association, the Canadian Shipbuilding and Ship Repairing Association, had preferences on the issue of polar icebreaker acquisition. For example, of the three options considered by Cabinet from the early 1970s to the early 1980s, the least-favoured option was the nuclear/hybrid 10 option, the propulsion system of which would have to be procured offshore. Canadian shipyards, lacking a nuclear capacity in marine applications, naturally favoured options that would maximize indigenous expenditures: icebreakers with conventional propulsion systems.

However, even for the conventionally powered Polar 7 and 8, the enthusiasm of the shipbuilding industry has been distinctly restrained. There were two compelling reasons for this. The first was that a ship is a relatively indivisible acquisition. The outcomes are basically zero-sum, since there are only two major components: the propulsion system and the hull. The allocation of $450 million for one Polar 8 would therefore be of great benefit to one or at most two of the industry's members. The industry's preference was for divisible programs: it thus enthusiastically embraced the Canadian frigate program, and the 1100- and 1200-class icebreaker acquisiton programs, mainly because the benefits of such expenditures could more easily be distributed by the state across the industry.

In this, the preferences of the shipbuilding industry and the state coincided. For its part, the government was seeking to aid an industry forced into a severe slump by a dry order book. Its priorities were thus to place government orders in such a way as to diversify its purchases regionally and to maximize employment. The choice between a polar icebreaker and the icebreakers slated for construction under the capital replacement program highlighted these priorities. Accelerating the ice-breaker replacement program in the early 1980s allowed the state to target more than $300 million on a regional basis at a number of yards. A second reason for the lack of enthusiasm on the part of the shipbuilding industry was the unique nature of the acquisition. One of the industry's assumptions was that even if the Canadian government approved the Polar 8, it would not be acquiring a fleet of polar icebreakers, regardless of the level of commercial cargo traffic in the Passage.

Nor was there assumed to be a significant commercial market for world-class polar icebreakers. The Canadian hydrocarbon extraction industry has acquired its own icebreakers and icebreaking cargo vessels, but these ships have been class 4 or lower. And while Dome Petroleum kept alive its stated intention to purchase a class 10 vessel icebreaker, there has been little concrete activity on this private-sector acquisition over the last several years.[41] There was likewise assumed to be a highly limited export market for a polar icebreaker of the power and strength of the Polar 8, given the indigenous technological capabilities of other states with an interest in polar icebreaking.

Indeed, it might be concluded that, paradoxically, the shipbuilding industry itself was a not unimportant impediment to the acquisition of a polar icebreaking capability. As the industry's members and their employees felt the effects of many years of low government levels of procurement, an adverse customs regime, and a world-wide slump in commercial orders, the demands of industry upon the state increased in the late 1970s and early 1980s. The rapid economic decline in the shipbuilding industry in 1982 prompted the Government to respond to regional needs by using icebreaker procurement as an explicit tool of social and economic policy. Construction of a polar icebreaker, with its massive concentration of funds at one shipyard, was less advantageous to this end than a large number of smaller acquisitions.

CONCLUSIONS

When Cabinet approved the construction phase of the Polar 8 in September 1985, it was expected that it would not be until 1990 that the Canadian government would have the capacity to navigate the Northwest Passage beyond the short summer season. And even by mid-1985, before the passage of the *Polar Sea* prompted the Mulroney government to accelerate the Polar 8 acquisition program, the uncertainty that hung over the program was quite in keeping with the politics of inertia that had long been part of icebreaker acquisition in Canada.

I have argued that the process of polar icebreaker acquisition as it emerged in the 1970s and 1980s is best understood in the context of consistent inertial patterns of icebreaker policy over the last century. Acquiring icebreaking capability has been marked by a tendency for both Ministers and bureaucrats to wait until the state is presented with clear and unambiguous demands for icebreaking services by readily identifiable clients before contracting with indigenous shipyards for icebreaker construction. Indeed, the polar icebreaker program followed those patterns precisely from its inception in the early 1970s to mid-1985. These inertial factors explain why the Canadian government was not much closer to acquiring polar capability a decade and a half after the voyage of the *Manhattan*. They also suggest that the September 1985 decision to proceed with the construction phase of the Polar 8 was a singularly out-of-character step for the Canadian state. For there was little palpable demand for icebreaking services in the Arctic; there were few readily identifiable clients; and a minimum number of shipyards stood to benefit from the acquisition decision.

PART FOUR

Conclusions

CHAPTER TWELVE

Beyond the Arctic Sublime

FRANKLYN GRIFFITHS

It is an irony that the challenge to Canada's control over its Arctic waters comes from the government and the people with whom Canadians have the most in common. The dilemma is compounded by the fact that whereas the United States is only secondarily an Arctic country and approaches the region from the standpoint of a maritime power with global interests, the Arctic figures prominently in Canadians' conceptions of themselves as a people and is viewed primarily from the perspective of a coastal and regional state. Add to this the gross disparity of national power and Canada's economic dependence on the United States, and it becomes clear that Canada is engaged in a potentially very damaging dispute that will be difficult to resolve with success. Recent events in the Passage have served to heighten Canada's dilemma and to bring nearer the time of decision.

The intrusive voyage of the u.s. icebreaker *Polar Sea* through Canada's Arctic waters in August 1985, and the decisions of the Canadian government announced on 10 September have altered political calculations about the future of the North American portion of the Northwest Passage and about Canada's portion in particular. Acting in accordance with its view of the Northwest Passage as an international strait,[1] the United States prompted Canada to enclose the channels of the Arctic archipelago as Canadian waters effective 1 January 1986 and to declare its readiness to have both an adjudication by the International Court of Justice (ICJ) and bilateral talks with Washington.[2] Ottawa thus accepted the possibility of a binding decision one way or the other on its sovereignty claim. It also indicated an interest in what might be called an out-of-court settlement with the United States. As well, by reaffirming its preparedness to support and regulate commercial shipping and by undertaking to acquire a polar icebreaker, the government of Canada brought closer the day when it will be able to provide for safe and efficient Arctic shipping. Risks and costs for Canada have risen in the Passage. So also has the need for Canadian preparedness.

In putting its Arctic waters claim on the line, the Canadian government has reduced uncertainty about what lies ahead for the political development of the Passage. It is now somewhat easier to envisage alternative futures for the Passage and to consider their implications for Canadian policy. Talks that began between Canada and the United States late in 1985 will condition what is required of Canada in dealing with the many issues that bear on the future status and use of the Passage. If the two sides are able to agree on a framework for relations on the Passage, existing uncertainties will be substantially reduced, if not eliminated. Otherwise, the political evolution of the Passage will continue to be shaped by trends in the international political environment, by developments in Arctic marine transportation, and by U.S.-Soviet strategic military interaction. Established Canadian propensities in dealing with Arctic marine issues will also have an effect. So will the capacity of Canadians to evoke and act upon a vision of their northern spaces that transcends the notion of the Arctic sublime, that is suited to the needs of a leading regional state in the twenty-first century. Such are the themes of this concluding essay.

ALTERNATIVE FUTURES FOR THE PASSAGE

To help order the consideration of Canada's choices, an idea of how things might turn out in the waters of the archipelago is essential. Looking for likely end results in terms of jurisdiction and use by the end of the century, we may identify several more or less plausible futures for the Passage. Each of these has different implications for Canadian and American policy. Some are obviously to be preferred by Canada over others.

The Passage as an international strait

The many channels that make up the Passage could acquire recognized status as an international strait by decision of the ICJ, by unilateral American action, or through the evolution of international practice. In the first instance, the U.S. government would one way or another bring about an adjudication of Canada's act of enclosure. Or conceivably it could override Canadian objections by making use of the Passage as it saw fit and refusing to accept the ICJ's jurisdiction in the matter. As to an evolutionary transition, it would see the Passage acquire de facto status as an international strait to the degree that increasingly frequent subsurface and surface navigation were accompanied by continued objections to Canada's claim and a failure on Canada's part to gain the capabilities needed to exercise effective control over foreign operations. Given enough time, a de facto international strait could become one in law. Indeed, in such forbidding and exceptional waters as these, infrequent international navigation could suffice to establish international strait status in relatively short order – a consideration that figured in Canadian thinking about the need for a firm response to the voyage of the *Polar Sea*.

However it came about, a fully internationalized archipelagic waterway that afforded transit passage rights or virtually unlimited access for aircraft, surface vessels, and submarines from one part of the high seas to another would constitute an extraordinary setback for Canada. Land, water, and superjacent airspace are, after all, the essential resources with which a people builds a country. To lose control over a significant body of water and its related airspace is to suffer reduced opportunity in the present and a diminished outlook for the future. The sense of loss would be made all the more profound in this case by damage wrought on the intangible but vital links between the Arctic and the self-image of Canadians as a people.

In practical terms, international strait status for the Passage would deny Canada the capacity to regulate foreign commercial shipping for purposes of pollution prevention and environmental conservation. Nor would Canada be in a position to prevent deprivations that might be visited upon its Inuit population and their renewable-resources way of life. Further, the channels of the archipelago would be opened to legitimate military-strategic competition by u.s., Soviet, and other armed forces entitled to operate in the air, on the surface, and under the ice if they chose to do so. These eventualities could as well be expected to have a bearing on Canadian-u.s. relations. If the transition to international strait status were evolutionary, the effect on bilateral relations could well be minimal: Canada might gradually acquire a North American view of things Arctic. But it would be quite a different story if a singular defeat were administered to Canada by the icj, or for that matter by the United States acting unilaterally, in the midst of sharp Canadian-u.s. disagreement. The vehemence of public protest that was brought forth merely by the transits of the *Manhattan* and *Polar Sea* suggests that outright loss of the Passage would produce lasting bitterness and resentment toward the United States. Subsequent effects in Canadian domestic politics and on Canada's alliance relations could be substantial.

Whereas international strait status poses the prospect of a great setback for Canada,[3] u.s. interests are likely to be heavily but not entirely favoured. A naval requirement for submarine and related access to and through the archipelago would be fully met,[4] as would the perceived need to hold the line against erosion of the global straits regime by archipelagic states which might otherwise find encouragement and precedent value in Canada's act of enclosure. As well, by maintaining and eventually prevailing in its dispute with Canada, Washington could expect to preserve the option of surface shipping of Alaskan oil or natural gas eastward in time of need. However, as is the case with Canada and Denmark/Greenland, the U.S. government has interests in the prevention of Arctic marine pollution and the avoidance of undue threats to its Inuit population. These interests require national and ultimately international management of marine operations throughout the North American portion of the Northwest Passage. Regulatory arrangements could not, however, be instituted without compromising transit passage rights and hence the global straits regime to the extent that the Northwest Passage were part of it. Further, to seek international strait status for the waters of the Canadian archipelago would be to authorize the presence of Soviet nuclear submarines, surface vessels, and aircraft, thereby complicating the strategic defence of North America if one day Moscow chose to take up its option in earnest.[5] If to the foregoing we add the American interest in stable relations with Canada, the pursuit of straits status may not be wholly advantageous for the United States.

The Passage as a shared-access zone

As Oran Young suggests in chapter 6, Canada and the United States could set aside their conflict over the status of the Passage and proceed to co-operate without prejudice to the legal claims of either party. If they applied the principles contained in Article IV of the Antarctica Treaty of 1959, the two sides would agree (1) to shelve the whole question of jurisdiction, (2) to affirm that the act of setting claims aside did not affect their status in law or the status of pre-existing rights, and (3) to assert that activities subsequently occurring in the Passage would not be used to support or deny differing jurisdictional claims in the event that the agreement were terminated. Young argues that an undertaking of this kind would serve to suspend distributive or "win-lose" conflict and allow the parties to pursue the joint benefits of an integrative approach to problem-solving in the Passage. In particular, non-prejudicial arrangements modelled on the Antarctica Treaty could create preconditions for the development of an integrated transit management regime to regulate surface shipping in the Arctic waters of North America. For maximal effectiveness, participation in a framework agreement on the Passage and in a subsequent regulatory regime could be widened to include Denmark/Greenland and conceivably other interested parties.

The proposal is imaginative. Indeed, elements of the Antarctic solution would seem already to have surfaced in U.S. Arctic waters policy: the voyage of the *Polar Sea* was presented by Washington and accepted by Canada as a venture that did not prejudice the status in law of existing claims and rights over the Passage.[6] But what are the larger implications for Canada?

Employed as a basis for agreement, Young's presentation of the Antarctic solution would see the waters of the Canadian archipelago converted into a complex shared-access zone. Engaging in conflict avoidance over the Passage, participating states would join to promote sound commercial uses of the surface waters of Arctic North America from Bering Strait to Davis Strait. Surface waters would, however, be managed separately from whatever might go on under the surface or over it. The Antarctica Treaty, it should be noted, dealt with the problem of military operations by demilitarizing the continent. Subsurface and overflight military activities are not, however, discussed by Young. If these operations were not subject to regulatory arrangements negotiated by the participating states, the latter, having set aside their jurisdictional claims, would presumably be free to do as they wished. The U.S. Navy, in particular, would gain unrestricted freedom of movement in the Canadian archipelago. Alternatively, subsurface and overflight activities could in principle be regulated by the parties involved. This, however, would entail U.S. negotiation on major matters of national security with Greenland as well as Denmark and Canada, and possibly other parties associated with a framework agreement. For this and other reasons we may assume that subsurface and overflight operations in the Passage would not be susceptible to the regime-building process that applied to surface waters. The effect of Young's proposal would thus be to make the Passage into a multinational management zone for purposes of surface navigation and a de facto international strait for purposes of subsurface and overflight activities. Everyone's claims would remain intact. But in practice the waters of the Canadian archipelago would be internationalized.

Canada may well be obliged to accept some internationalization of the Passage. After all, sovereignty is in the eye of the beholder, whether it be the international community or the ICJ. International recognition of Canada's Arctic waters claim will not soon be established if a bilateral agreement on the matter eludes Ottawa and Washington. Nor is Canada in a position to move ahead rapidly in establishing operational control over the waters of the archipelago. Advances will have to be made step by step. In these circumstances it makes sense for Canada not to close but to open the Passage in a way that affirms its position there. To begin by isolating and dealing with issues of jurisdiction and management associated with the *surface* waters of the archipelago is appropriate, as is the effort to construct an international regime for commercial navigation, as Young suggests. But is it appropriate to make use of the Antarctic precedent in an attempt to decouple not only surface from subsurface and air uses, but also questions of jurisdiction from questions of use and management?

Despite any undertaking made in a framework agreement that subsequent practice would not affect the status of competing jurisdictional claims, it is hard to believe that the conversion of the Passage into a shared-access zone would not colour the judgment of others if after some years a participating state were to abrogate the agreement and seek adjudication of its case. Also, for Canada to enter a framework agreement patterned on the Antarctica Treaty would in effect be for it to recognize that the United States had a claim in the first instance. Although the u.s. government might well reason in equivalent fashion, Canadians believe that the waters of the archipelago are theirs and theirs alone, that Washington has no claim to set aside. To risk lending strength to the American claim and to others' view of the Passage as an international waterway might nevertheless be acceptable if the overall approach offered reasonable benefit to Canada as a permanent solution to its Arctic waters dilemma.

Certainly there would be gains for Canada in the avoidance of mutually damaging conflict with the United States and in the creation of preconditions for efficient management of commercial navigation in the Arctic waters of North America. These would, however, be offset by the disintegration of Canada's future as an intact Arctic country, by a surrender of the right to control military operations in the archipelago, and by the transition of the Passage a good part of the way to de facto international strait status. Aside from these debits, it is debatable whether questions of jurisdiction can effectively be set aside in the creation and operation of a surface waters regulatory regime that would follow upon a framework agreement.

As D.M. McRae argues in chapter 5, the functioning of co-operative arrangements for the management of the waters of the Canadian archipelago would sooner or later raise issues of jurisdiction. To this it could be added that management without authority is likely to be no management at all. Who, for example, would determine and collect damages in the event of an oil spill from a u.s. vessel in Parry Channel? Or from a Canadian vessel off the Alaskan coast? Either the authority would be national, or it would be transferred to a central agency without supranational powers. In the latter case, delegation of authority would necessitate the accommodation of pre-existing national regulations and preferences in the application of civil and criminal legislation to the offshore. Unless the framework agreement and a surface waters regulatory regime were negotiated simultaneously – an impractical task in view of the time required to find a mutually agreeable way through the political labyrinth of the modern Northwest Passage – the process of regime-building would almost certainly necessitate the resolution of national claims, which could not be held in abeyance by a framework agreement on questions of jurisdiction. All in all, to make the Passage into a shared-access zone permanently or for a time would seem to present Canada with more problems than advantages.

Whether or not the separability proposition that worked in Antarctica is applicable in the offshore waters of a region where national rights and obligations are thick upon the ground, an effort to convert the Passage into a shared-access zone would broadly conform to u.s. interests. Military uses of the archipelago would be unconstrained. An international management regime for surface shipping could be established when necessary. But to the extent that a framework agreement itself included a commitment in principle to regulate large-scale marine transportation ventures, it would of course serve to restrict freedom of international navigation. To deal with this problem, the u.s. government could decouple the Northwest Passage from the international straits regime and treat it as a special body of water. This it could do by joining with Canada and possibly Denmark/Greenland in affirming Article 234 of the Convention on the Law of the Sea as a basis for non-discriminatory coastal-state co-operation in managing surface navigation under the special circumstances presented by ice-covered waters. As McRae notes, the United States was intimately involved in the negotiation of Article 234. If a framework agreement on the Passage as a shared-access zone met major u.s. requirements for military mobility and conflict-avoidance with Canada, it might not be excessively difficult for Washington to sever the Northwest Passage from the international straits regime and to make use of Article 234 to facilitate the management of surface navigation in the Arctic waters of North America.

The Passage essentially as is

Although the trend of recent decades toward greater use of Arctic waters is bound to continue, it could produce further political development of the Passage only very slowly. This might well be the outcome if the u.s. and Canadian governments, on examining the alternatives from time to time, persistently chose to leave the basic issues the way they were in the mid-1980s. In so doing they woul continue to disagree or perhaps agree to disagree. The United States would protest Canada's act of enclosure but would not seek a decision by the icj. It would continue to sail nuclear submarines through the archipelago[7] but would refrain from surface and air activity. As to Canada, it would hold to its internal waters claim and proceed with the construction of the Polar 8 and other measures – for example, the installation of sensors to monitor submarine operations – intended to improve political control and strengthen its claim to exclusive jurisdiction. Ottawa would acquiesce in u.s. nuclear submarine traffic and would join the United States in a wait-and-see approach to Arctic marine transportation. Both governments would in effect decide to leave well enough alone. The Passage would be managed so as to remain a minor issue in bilateral relations.

The "as is" alternative for the Passage in the next decade and more does have the virtue of simplicity. It could, however, work against the Canadian interest. And it would maintain the vulnerability of both sides to surprise.

When the *Polar Sea* went through without Washington having requested a by-your-leave, Canadians became concerned despite the American undertaking not to use the voyage to further its case in law. They were concerned because they could *see* the vessel in question and as well Ottawa's need to save face by granting permission that had not been sought. But from the standpoint of international legal opinion, or of a panel of arbitrators in The Hague, one visible voyage through the archipelago, even if conducted with disregard for Canadian law and without a Canadian protest, would hardly contribute more to the evolution of an international practice consistent with international strait status than would one unseen submarine transit for which permission had not been sought. If one day it came to a court test, the United States could be in a position to present excerpts from the logbooks of a good many submarine voyages in the archipelago as evidence for an international straits claim. Disclosures of this kind might well be effective in demonstrating that the varied channels that made up the Passage had frequently been employed as waterways connecting two high-seas areas – this without Canada having been aware of what was going on. For Canada to leave things "as is" might thus be to risk further erosion of its position that the Passage comprises historic internal waters that have not been used to any significant degree for international navigation. By the same token, the strength of the u.s. claim could be affected by a growing number of surface transits made or abstained from in conformity with Canadian law. This consideration could gain force if it were thought undesirable to release information on submarine activity in the waters of the archipelago. If not, submarine voyages, being no doubt more frequent than surface navigation by non-Canadian vessels operating under Canadian regulations, would probably favour the u.s. position.

It is also an unfortunate feature of Canada's present approach to its Arctic waters that in the absence of a clear and pressing need to act, little is accomplished despite the uncertainty that surrounds its title to the Passage. As of early 1986, it was clearly the intention of the Canadian government not to leave things be. But were Washington to disagree quietly with Ottawa on the basic legal question and to refrain from visible moves that could be construed as provocative, the September 1985 commitment to make good on the Canadian claim could gradually be emptied of political support. The Polar 8, for example, could run into greater difficulty as debate deepened on its mission, cost, design, and financing. Nor would Ottawa be as ready to act on related requirements, such as support for Arctic science, or a resolution of Inuit constitutional and land claims issues, as a means of strengthening Canada's case for historic title to the Passage.

"As is" could thus work against Canada's ability to avoid being caught short by the advent of commercial shipping in the Passage or by the need to defend the Canadian position in court.

Finally, if the politics of the Passage were to remain essentially unaltered, both Canada and the United States would continue to accept the risk of real surprise. Suppose, for example, that France announced a plan to send an oceanographic research vessel through the Canadian archipelago in the summer of 1988, without requesting permission. If France persisted, the fundamental issue could go to court or explode in confrontation, despite Canadian and u.s. preferences to avoid such an outcome. Canadian-u.s. relations would suffer, since France would almost certainly be perceived in Canada as a surrogate for the United States. Similarly, at some point in the not-too-distant future the United States could be faced with an authentic emergency that necessitated another icebreaker voyage through or into the Passage, or it might determine that Soviet nuclear submarine activity required the deployment of airborne ASW in the archipelago. The point here is that either as an unintended stalemate or as the result of a co-ordinated effort by the two countries, the "as is" alternative for the Passage would not address the potential for gradual or abrupt change that favoured the interests of one side. Nor would it eliminate the risk of a debilitating confrontation in Canadian-u.s. relations. Far wiser for the two governments to resolve their differences and to gain a measure of control over the political development of North America's Arctic waters.

The Passage as an open Canadian waterway

Either by decision of the ICJ or through bilateral agreement between Canada and the United States, the waters of the Canadian archipelago could acquire recognized status as Canadian internal waters open to navigation by friendly states. In the former case, the United States or another maritime power would either challenge Canada's act of enclosure or oblige Canada to defend it in court. Given an affirmation of its claim, Ottawa could then negotiate access rights for others as appropriate. Alternatively, Ottawa and Washington could move to an agreement that one way or another recognized the Canadian claim and granted the United States reasonable conditions of access for its naval and commercial vessels and aircraft. With American support, Canada's claim could be expected to gain general international recognition.

Let us assume that both sides would prefer to settle the matter themselves without the winner-take-all risks and costs of resolution by the ICJ. A settlement could take various forms. Most obvious and possibly most difficult to obtain would be an outright resolution in which u.s. recognition of Canadian sovereignty were traded for guaranteed u.s. access to the archipelago. An arrangement that, for example, allowed the United States unrestricted mobility for 99 years would reduce Canada to the status of an Arctic Panama. However, an accord that severely constrained u.s. access, and left Canada in a position to deny it altogether once sovereignty had acquired sufficient recognition, could very well be unacceptable to Washington, either on its own merits or in view of its perceived implications for the global straits regime. If the two sides were unable to split their differences in a comprehensive resolution of the problem, another settlement might be considered. The two sides would confine themselves to a reference to Article 234 of the Convention on the Law of the Sea in issuing a joint statement of intent to prepare for the eventuality of surface shipping in the Arctic waters of North America.

By citing Article 234 as a basis in international law for the development of a regulatory regime in ice-covered waters, Canada and the United States would in effect agree that the Canadian portion of the Northwest Passage was subject to some degree of coastal-state jurisdiction and was not part of the global straits regime. There would be no mention of Canadian sovereignty over the Passage, and the United States would refrain from doing more than publicly reserving its position on Canada's legal claim. But in practice the exclusive jurisdiction of Canada in all the waters of the archipelago would be recognized for the specific purpose of surface navigation management and set aside where the under-ice and air environments were concerned. There would be no mention of subsurface operations in the archipelago, and the United States would not seek to conduct overflights. For its part, Canada would turn a blind eye to the operation of u.s. attack submarines; or it would join with the United States in establishing positive control over the subsurface waters of the archipelago; or, better yet, it would mount anti-submarine defences at key choke-points in the archipelago – a glance at the map (pp.28–9) suggests that emplacements in Barrow Strait and Jones Sound would suffice – so as to deny transit to Soviet and to regulate access of allied nuclear submarines.

By distinguishing between surface, subsurface, and overflight uses, an arrangement of this kind would represent progress toward recognition of Canadian sovereignty over its Arctic waters. The United States would avoid adverse effects on the global straits regime by treating the Northwest Passage as a special case, as allowed by the "Arctic exception" in the Law of the Sea Convention. It would also be assured of subsurface mobility in the archipelago. Both sides would act on their common interest in resolving commercial, environmental, and socioeconomic issues associated with large-scale Arctic marine transportation and would begin to do so well before the need for consensual knowledge, uniform standards, and regulatory arrangements became urgent. When appropriate, Denmark/Greenland could be associated with the regime-building effort of the two countries. Meanwhile, Canada would gain time to acquire and deploy the means needed to assert increasingly effective control over the subsurface waters and related airspace. This task, essentially military in nature, could be accomplished in co-operation with the United States and might require deployment of Canadian anti-submarine barriers or acquisition of nuclear or advanced diesel-electric submarines. Given continued good working relations between the two sides, it should eventually be possible to evoke u.s. decisions affirming exclusive Canadian jurisdiction in all three environments of a Passage open to friendly states.

Whatever the modalities of a settlement that led to recognition of the Passage as an open Canadian waterway, some portion of the Canadian population may be expected to condemn the authorization of u.s. nuclear submarine activity in the archipelago. Strongly preferring a demilitarized north and indeed a nuclear-free Canada, they would object to a bilateral settlement along the lines proposed here. The dilemma they would face is the same as would be confronted by the government of Canada if bilateral negotiations failed and the United States both persisted in making submarine transits and refused to accept the jurisdiction of the ICJ in the matter. A war of words would begin, if it hadn't already. Deeds would follow. Canada might be obliged to consider coercive means in its defence of the Passage, for example by attempting to deny the United States all access to the waters of the archipelago. Needless to say, any action of this kind would come very close to a Canadian declaration of armed neutrality. Depending on the value finally attached by Canadians to Arctic sovereignty, the result would be an unprecedented confrontation with the United States or a return to bilateral negotiations in profoundly unsettled circumstances. Surely it would be better to settle before things got out of hand.

A closed Canadian waterway

A fifth and final alternative for the political development of the Passage may be identified. As of the mid-1980s there is little prospect of Canada gaining international support for its sovereignty claim if it renounced its willingness to accept international navigation and declared that all foreign vessels were to be excluded from the waters of the archipelago. This, however, could become an option if the Canadian claim came before the ICJ and the United States accepted the Court's jurisdiction.

Granted a favourable ICJ decision, Canada could be freed to determine that requirements of environmental conservation and protection of the Inuit way of life necessitated conversion of the Passage into an ecological preserve. Shipping would accordingly be confined to Canadian hulls engaged in summer-months resupply of local communities, with a possible exception being made for tourist vessels. Foreign bulk transportation vessels would be excluded, as would Canadian shipping of oil and natural gas, which would be moved south by pipeline. Whether or not it would also be prudent to pay much attention to defence against foreign intrusions under the ice (consider merely the adverse ecological potential of a Canadian attack on a nuclear submarine), the perceived advantages of closing the Passage could be quite substantial.

First, the claim on federal revenues would be minimal in comparison with all but the international strait alternative for the archipelago: since very little would now be happening, little in the way of regulatory and enforcement capabilities would be required. Second, the formidable foreign policy task of fitting a surface shipping regulatory regime into the political labyrinth of the Northwest Passage would be obviated. Third, for southern Canadians to treat the waters of the archipelago as an ecological preserve would require no re-evaluation of their prevailing attitudes toward the Arctic. On the contrary, persistence in a nineteenth-century vision of the Arctic sublime would be quite in keeping with a policy of leaving the Passage alone as a splendid but ultimately unapproachable place. Finally, the closed Canadian waterway solution would be simple, easily communicated, and readily understood by all.

This much said about alternatives for the political development of Canada's Arctic waters, it is the announced intention of the government to secure the Passage as an open Canadian waterway. As of the mid-1980s, the government of Canada is unwilling to leave the Passage "as is." It is instead committed to gaining the means to ensure sovereignty and to encourage commercial navigation in the waters of the archipelago. It shows no sign of interest in converting the Passage into a closed reserve. Nor is it willing to countenance the transition of its Arctic waters into a shared-access zone by the application of non-prejudicial arrangements such as were made for the voyage of the *Polar Sea*. As to a future that would see the Passage become an international strait, it is wholly excluded. All five futures for the Passage considered here could be ranked in hypothetical order of preference for Canada and indeed the United States. But there is now only one preference for the government of Canada, and in my view it is surely the right one for Canadians: an open Canadian waterway.

Provided that the basic legal issues are not quickly brought before the ICJ, the construction of an international regime for the management of commercial shipping will be of critical importance in an effort to open the Passage as a Canadian waterway. As a means of strengthening Canada's legal position, beginning to establish effective political control, and seeing to it that large-scale marine transportation is properly adapted to the special needs of the Arctic physical and social environment, Canadian leadership in the development of international arrangements for surface navigation will be essential. In the new situation created by Canada's act of enclosure, regime-building will be no less important than legal strategy aimed at affirming exclusive jurisdiction over the Passage. Leadership in the construction of a transit management regime will also demand far more of Canada than an Arctic waters policy that continued to draw primarily on the skill and imagination of the legal officers of the Department of External Affairs. These new demands give cause for concern.

As we have noted, a visible American threat to the Passage has thus far been necessary to drive Canada's Arctic waters policies forward. A manifest threat has also been required to bring Ottawa to procure the costly capabilities required to assert political control over waters where not much has thus far been happening aside from probable operations by nuclear submarines. However, collaboration with the United States is an essential precondition for the development of an Arctic waters shipping regime, to say nothing of an out-of-court settlement of the underlying legal and political-military issues. Meanwhile, Canada takes part in joint defence arrangements in the Arctic with an ally that contests Canada's jurisdiction over a significant portion of the space to be defended. Caught in the cleft between conflict and collaboration with the United States, Canadian policies could all too readily revert to "as is" in the period ahead. Something will have to change if Ottawa is to succeed in its aim to secure the Passage as an open Canadian waterway.

THE PASSAGE IN FOREIGN POLICY CONTEXT

One thing that needs to change is the inclination of Canadians to view the Passage as an isolated foreign affairs issue. While the problem originates in Canadian-u.s. relations, its solution requires not only bilateral co-operation but also multilateral arrangements and a better understanding of how the Passage might fit into the broader evolution of Canada's external policies. Let us begin with the need to improve Canada's relations with Greenland and Denmark as a first step in securing the future of the Passage.

As Lars Rasmussen notes in chapter 7, the attitudes of Greenlanders toward shipping in the Arctic waters of North America are beginning to change. Recently united in militant opposition to Petro-Canada's ill-conceived Arctic Pilot Project, Greenland's position has become increasingly ambiguous as oil exploration on its east coast raises the possibility that Greenland itself could one day be engaged in the marine transportation of hydrocarbons. It is worth adding, as further evidence of shifting Greenlandic interests, that only little opposition was offered to Panarctic's Bent Horn Project, which saw initial small amounts of oil move from Cameron Island in the Canadian archipelago to Montreal in the summer of 1985. We should also be aware that in 1983, and with Greenlandic participation, Denmark negotiated with Canada a marine environment co-operation agreement that could in future provide a ready basis for consultations on the management of large-scale commercial shipping in Baffin Bay and Davis Strait.[8] This agreement has added significance in that it cites Article 234 of the Convention on the Law of the Sea in proposing bilateral co-operation to prevent harmful socioeconomic as well as environmental effects of Arctic marine transportation. As such, it offers a point of departure for the elaboration of regulatory arrangements that further distinguish the Passage and its eastern approaches from the global straits regime.

It is nevertheless unwise to assume that as matters stand Greenland and Denmark would respond positively to a Canadian (or for that matter a Canadian-U.S.) initiative to develop a management regime for surface shipping in the Arctic waters of North America. Memories of the Arctic Pilot Project are still too strong. Greater trust must first be built between Greenland and Canada, without Canada intervening in what Copenhagen clearly regards as Danish internal affairs. In close consultation with the Danish government, Canada should seek to develop relations with Greenland on a broad front. Since Greenlanders and the Canadian as well as Alaskan Inuit co-ordinate policy positions through the Inuit Circumpolar Conference (ICC), progress in resolving constitutional and land claims issues of concern to the Canadian Inuit may well be a precondition for effective Canadian-Greenlandic co-operation. Aside from a variety of technical assistance and trade projects, Ottawa could as well consider enlarging its financial support for the ICC itself. Nor should the underlying aims of Canadian policy toward Denmark/Greenland be confined to the promotion of properly regulated commercial navigation. In view of the automatic backing that Greenland can expect from Copenhagen on questions of external affairs, Greenlandic preferences will be significant in determining what happens on the surface waters of Arctic North America. To the extent that Canada and Denmark/Greenland speak with one voice, Canada's leverage on American policy will be improved. Further, as Rasmussen points out, Greenland possesses a "secret weapon" in its strategic value to the Western Alliance. Were Greenland to move further toward autonomy from Denmark and to find itself only remotely connected to any other Western country, Canada's security would suffer. The point here is that where Greenland alone is concerned, the aim of securing the Passage as an open Canadian waterway obliges Ottawa to act on a range of interests that go well beyond today's concern with sovereignty and commercial navigation in the archipelago. The same applies to the promotion of commercial navigation as such.

As was pointed out in the introduction to this volume, the outlook for large-scale marine transportation in the Arctic waters of North America remains uncertain as of the mid-1980s. It was suggested that Ottawa might attempt to reduce uncertainty by prompting others to ship oil or natural gas from the Canadian Arctic in conformance with Canadian regulations. Thereby it would strengthen control over the Passage and provide reason for the development of an international regime to govern surface navigation in the Arctic waters of North America. In addition to inviting Japan to test polar transportation technology by moving limited amounts of oil westward from Hibernia or the Beaufort Sea in the 1990s, Canada could explore West German interest in the development of equivalent technology by moving Beaufort Sea oil to Western Europe. Either way, others' interests in making use of the Passage are likely to be insufficient as long as oil prices are expected to remain low. Informed analysts argue that if new conventional energy sources are not developed, the Western world will once again find itself heavily dependent upon the Persian Gulf in the 1990s. However, the mounting disinclination of oil multinationals and Western governments to develop frontier reserves suggests that a more complacent assessment may prevail for some time to come. To overcome these economic inhibitions, Canada could provide political incentives for others to make use of the Passage.

These new incentives could be generated in the course of an adaptation of Canada's foreign economic and defence policies to important developments in the external environment. But now, rather than beginning with the Passage and seeking measures to assure its use as an open Canadian waterway, Canada would advance its Arctic waters aims by doing other things that ought to be accomplished on their own merit.

To start with, continuing interaction between American and Soviet nuclear forces is serving to heighten the strategic significance of the Canadian Arctic. As Harriet Critchley makes clear in chapter 10, Canada's capacity to defend its Arctic spaces is absolutely minimal, this because of the view of successive governments that the threat of attack from the north consisted solely of the potential for strategic missile and bomber strikes against targets to the south. But the strategic value of the Canadian Arctic is appreciating for the United States. Evidence of this is to be had in a pattern of increased u.s. use of Canada's northern airspace, land, and waters for purposes of testing, basing, transit, deterrence, and defence in depth.[9] Regarded by many Canadians as a problem, this development provides Ottawa with an opportunity to influence u.s. policies. Influence could be gained not by threatening to deny access but by moving to commit more resources to continental defence and less to the defence of Western Europe as such.

As things stand, Canada has a greater number of defence commitments than it is able to meet without substantial increases in spending and the national deficit. Although Ottawa decided in 1985 to add to the strength of its ground forces on NATO's central front, the need to contemplate a reduction of its commitments to the defence of Western Europe remains and will persist in coming years. Indeed, the need will increase to the extent that Canada is drawn into unilateral as well as joint continental defence activity, the purpose of which is not only to counter Soviet capabilities but also to maintain control over the Canadian Arctic.

Were Canada to modify its NATO contribution, it could argue that the Alliance is not an arrangement for North American defence of Western Europe but an agreement of all to defend the area covered by the Atlantic Treaty; that North America, including its Pacific shores, is as much a part of the treaty area as is Western Europe; and that in view of the greater need to take part in the defence of North America, Canada was redeploying its effort within the treaty area. It is in the making of a sequence of decisions on the nature and extent of a redeployment to North Ameria, and indeed eventually to the Pacific, that opportunities would arise not only to influence U.S. policies but also to evoke West German interest in the Canadian Arctic. Quite apart from discussions of possible West German participation in Arctic defence, Ottawa's position would be that in strengthening Canadian sovereignty by embarking on a joint project to test the potential to ship Beaufort Sea oil to Europe, the Federal Republic would reduce Canada's political need to allocate resources to the defence of North America. For this proposition to be credible, it would have to be presented in the context of a considerably larger reassessment of Canada's external relations.

Born of the experience of the Second World War and the darkest years of the Cold War, Eurocentrism in Canada's international security policies is less and less consistent with the needs of a country whose future as a trading nation is ever more closely linked to the United States and to the countries of the Pacific Basin. Whether or not Ottawa and Washington ultimately succeed in marked enhancement of bilateral trade, Canada will continue to experience a need to offset its economic and military dependence on the United States with policies that affirm its political sovereignty and its independence as a contributor to the defence of North America. It will also find it invaluable to build increasingly diverse relationships with the Asian countries, most notably with Japan, whose energy and security needs will grow with what many expect to be continued strong economic performance. Canadian moves in this direction could well include energy exports and co-operation in the development of Arctic marine transportation technology. And sooner or later Canada will be required to add naval forces to the interplay in the Pacific Basin. To remain as heavily committed as it now is to the defence of Western Europe, with which trade cannot apparently grow, is for Canada to use the rear-view mirror as it drives into the future.

The time is approaching when Canada will have to come up with an autonomous strategic perspective that links trade, defence, and diplomacy in a new orientation to external affairs that is adapted more to the needs of 2000 than to the late 1940s. Again, the evolution of a new outlook will be gradual. By no means should it deny the continued value of membership in the North Atlantic Alliance and active relations with Western Europe. But the more dynamic and promising elements of an adapted Canadian approach to world affairs will be found as the country looks south to the United States and possibly Latin America, west to the Pacific Basin, north to the Arctic, and beyond the Arctic to an increasingly limited adversarial relationship with the Soviet Union. Is this too fanciful? John Kirton and Don Munton observe in chapter 4 that the *Manhattan* episode prompted Canada to adopt a qualitatively new approach to external affairs which included, inter alia, heightened concern for the Arctic, a partial withdrawal of Canadian armed forces from Europe, and the first Prime Ministerial visit to the Soviet Union, in 1971. If defence of the Passage figured once in a major reorientation of Canadian foreign relations, it might do so once again.

Were an autonomous strategic perspective to supplant today's preoccupation with foreign affairs "roles" played by Canada for others, the Canadian Arctic could be integrated into the country's external relations in a way that it is not at present. Greater emphasis on Arctic sovereignty would both permit and offset closer economic and defence ties with the United States by affirming Canada's political and cultural autonomy. A greater effort to make use of Canada's Arctic waters and energy reserves would contribute to the energy security of Japan and Western Europe and to Canadian sovereignty. Similarly, a larger commitment to continental defence and ultimately to security in the North Pacific should elicit greater u.s. and Western European readiness to support Canada's aim of securing the Passage as an open waterway. Further, where the Arctic in particular is concerned, an autonomous strategic perspective could extend well beyond the Northwest Passage.

As a region, the Arctic is gradually coming alive under the effects of military-strategic rivalry, resource scarcity, technological innovation, and the growing capacity of governments and peoples to affect one another's internal as well as foreign affairs. Whereas Graham Rowley in chapter 2 discusses the history of the Canadian Arctic to 1968 in terms of southerners "bringing the outside inside," the last decades of the twentieth century are witnessing the intrusion of regional and extra-regional influences into the Canadian domain. Whether it be the ICC, the interaction of superpower strategic nuclear submarines, the cohesion of OPEC, the aspirations of Greenlanders, or even the greenhouse effect, proper management of the Canadian Arctic increasingly requires a multidimensional regional perspective. No longer can Canadians afford to regard the circumpolar north

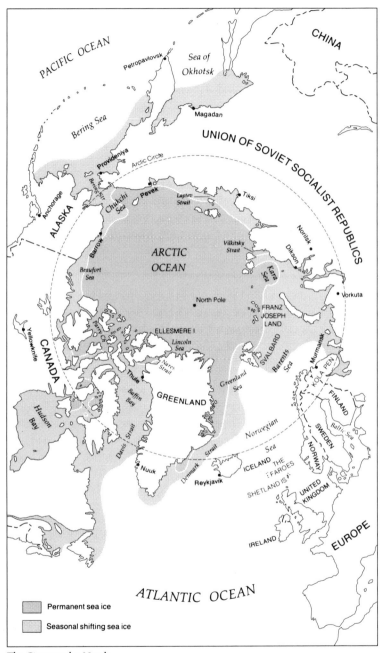

PACIFIC OCEAN

CHINA

Petropavlovsk

Sea of Okhotsk

Bering Sea

Magadan

UNION OF SOVIET SOCIALIST REPUBLICS

Providenlya

Arctic Circle

Anchorage

ALASKA

Barrow

Chukchi Sea

Pevek

Laptev Strait

Tiksi

Norilsk

Beaufort Sea

ARCTIC OCEAN

Vilkitsky Strait

Dikson

Kara Sea

Vorkuta

North Pole

FRANZ JOSEPH LAND

Yellowknife

CANADA

Parry Ch.

ELLESMERE I.

Lincoln Sea

SVALBARD

Barents Sea

Murmansk

KOLA PEN

FINLAND

Nares Strait

Thule

Baffin Bay

GREENLAND

Greenland Sea

SWEDEN

Baltic Sea

Hudson Bay

Davis Strait

NORWAY

Norwegian Sea

UNITED KINGDOM

Nuuk

Denmark Strait

ICELAND

THE FAROES

SHETLAND IS.

Reykjavik

IRELAND

EUROPE

ATLANTIC OCEAN

Permanent sea ice

Seasonal shifting sea ice

The Circumpolar North

with indifference. On the contrary, there is much that Canada could and should do to shape the development of the Arctic as a region in which military and resource-related conflict is minimized, environmental integrity and the needs of aboriginal inhabitants are protected, and southern-based economic development is allowed to proceed. The potential opportunities and benefits of participation in Arctic regional development are substantial. They present Canada with a need to come forward as a leading regional country with much to offer and to protect.

All of this is to underline the proposition that it will not do to view the Passage essentially as an issue in Canadian-u.s. relations, where the tension between competing and common interest is all too likely to immobilize Canadian policy. The Arctic region and Canada's larger foreign environment are changing in ways that at once require and enable a forward-looking and comprehensive approach to the Arctic waters of North America. These changes are evolutionary. They should enable Canada to perform as a country whose Arctic domestic and regional policies add strength to, and derive energy from, its wider involvements in world affairs. They also offer Canada an opportunity to prevail in the Passage by leading the way to commercial navigation and an international regime that ensures the adaptation of shipping to the physical and social environment of the region. Quite apart from any legal strategies that may be pursued, the international setting does offer Canada a fair chance of success in realizing its goals for the Passage and its potential as an Arctic country. But what might it take for Canadians to summon the will to succeed?

THE PASSAGE IN DOMESTIC POLICY CONTEXT

Certain exceptions notwithstanding, the approach of Canadians to Arctic marine issues has been reactive, fragmented, and lacking in the ability to follow through in non-urgent conditions. To improve the prospects of success in gaining international recognition of the Passage as an open Canadian waterway, Canadians need self-knowledge of the strengths and weaknesses they bring to the situation, as well as knowledge of what the international situation may allow. Self-knowledge is to be had from an understanding of Canadian failures, standard responses, and successes as well. Fortunately there is only one outright failure on the record.

Although a less critical assessment could no doubt be offered, Jennifer Lewington's appraisal of the Arctic Pilot Project (APP) in chapter 8 is instructive. Misconceived as a natural gas export venture that offered a wide range of benefits to southern Canada, the APP was as much a menace to the Greenlanders and therefore the Danes, to say nothing of Canadian Inuit, as the *Manhattan* had been to southern Canadians some years earlier. Aborted by falling oil prices and a downturn in the business cycle, the project provides valuable lessons on how not to proceed in making use of the Passage.

Where the APP consortium came on strong, lacked staying power, and was headed for international opposition that promised significant damage to the security interests of Canada and the Atlantic Alliance, Canada's efforts to secure its Arctic waters will have to build slowly and stay the course until conditions to move forward vigorously have matured. Whether it be foreign or Canadian vessels that are proposed for use in the Passage, the proposition can become a firm intention only after a way has been negotiated through the political labyrinth. The APP experience makes it all too clear that it's not the export or shipping venture but the enabling conditions that must be the central concern of federal government departments and industry.

From the APP episode we learn also that the magnitude of the effort required to bring about safe and efficient commercial navigation in the Passage is such as to invite failure if support is confined to the higher reaches of the federal and corporate bureaucracy. To master the Passage is to make a major claim on available economic and political resources. To secure the necessary resources and to demonstrate to others that Canada is determined to make the Passage into an open waterway, a national commitment is required. And yet the fact that the APP consortium promoted and was to some extent guided by a vision of soon-to-be-achieved leadership and excellence provides a caution for any who would seek public support for defence of the Passage by evoking a vision of national self-discovery and greatness in the Arctic. This is not to deny visionary thinking about the Passage. But it is to insist that a challenge to the people of Canada be framed with a proper regard for the long-term requirements of success.

The contrast between the attempt of Petro-Canada and its associates to set icebreaking liquefied natural gas (LNG) tankers moving through the Passage and the federal government's approach to polar icebreaker acquisition is also instructive. Where the APP went overboard with dynamism and the promise of innovation in the development of Canada's Arctic marine capabilities, inertia and an inclination to do what had been done before dominated in Ottawa's icebreaker procurement policies between 1876 and 1985. In chapter 11, Kim Nossal reports that in the 1970s and early 1980s, Ministers had to be convinced of three things before authorizing new acquisitions: a clear and pressing need for the icebreaking services in question; the presence of specific beneficiaries in Canadian society, as distinct from the public good; and the potential to aid a variety of shipyards with new orders. Official reactiveness did prompt consideration of a polar-class icebreaker after the voyages of the *Manhattan* in 1969–70.

Nevertheless, the demand for three-fold proof continued to hold as the prospects of Arctic marine transportation rose and then fell by 1981; as the Coast Guard as lead agency failed to secure from Cabinet and central departments a wider definition of the "beneficiaries" to be served; and as the departments of External Affairs and National Defence, which had major responsibilities for the defence of sovereignty, remained free to resist application of the procurement cost to their budgetary envelopes. The outcome as of mid-1985 was completion of the design phase for a Polar 8 icebreaker and little or no assurance that the vessel would be acquired. Only the appearance of the *Polar Sea* finally produced a procurement decision, and this only just before the government's statement of 10 September 1985.

Inertia and reactiveness in the acquisition of icebreakers would seem to be typical of the approach of the Canadian federal government to the country's Arctic waters dilemma more generally. Lacking an overall policy design that integrates separate requirements (icebreaking, bathymetry, Arctic science, northern constitutional development, promotion of international consensual knowledge on Arctic marine transportation, and so on), Ottawa has tended to judge each item with exceedingly conservative decision rules that slight the public good or national interest in securing the Passage as an open Canadian waterway. This surely is not good enough. Further, in view of the uncertainty inherent in the political and economic development of the Passage, it will be self-defeating to continue to demand near-absolute certainty in establishing the need to move ahead with programs that necessarily have long lead times to completion. Ceasing to react to events, Ministers and officials will have to make greater allowance for anticipatory action. Indeed, uncertainty itself should be reduced by promoting commercial use of Canada's Arctic waters. Whether or not a national vision is appropriate, Canada is in need of an integrated framework for persistent national action on the Passage. Otherwise the Passage will be treated "as is" or worse, despite the best of declared intentions to see it become an open Canadian waterway.

As of mid-decade, Inuit and environmentalists are unlikely to show much enthusiasm for the prospect of large-scale foreign or Canadian transportation of oil and natural gas in the archipelago, much less for a Canadian attempt to encourage commercial navigation by foreign flags. There are major problems to be worked out here.

Arctic waters issues in relations between southern Canada and the Canadian Inuit are in some ways similar to coresponding issues in Canadian-u.s. relations. As noted above, the APP posed a threat to the Inuit that was analogous to that offered by the *Manhattan* to Canada. In both relationships, the more powerful side has been reluctant to surrender control to the weaker. And just as Canada is convinced it has historic rights to the Passage that invalidate the American claim, Canadian Inuit believe that they too have historic rights that are not being acknowledged by Ottawa. The principal difference lies in the fact that the Inuit are not claiming exclusive jurisdiction. Considerations of fairness oblige Ottawa not to do to Canadian Inuit what the United States would do to Canada. Considerations of pragmatism require Ottawa to make use of the opportunity that exists to work out collaborative arrangements with the Inuit for the management of Arctic waters.

As Peter Jull makes clear in chapter 3, cultural survival and self-government within Confederation are the essential demands of Canada's Inuit. Modernization and industrialism having wrought an upheaval in the traditional way of life based on the sea, and the Inuit seek to regain a degree of control over their land and marine environment and over the ability of southern interests to make use of the same. Until the Inuit achieve a decent measure of success in the resolution of long-deferred constitutional and land claims issues, large-scale resource extraction and marine transportation ventures in the North American Arctic will be mired in controversy over environmental and social consequences and the lack of benefit to local communities. And yet, as Jull reminds us, Inuit are not opposed to modernization and development as such. Granted effective self-governing institutions with rights that extend to marine management and development, they could take an active part in maintaining a proper balance between environmental protection and wealth-generating marine activities. Quite simply, it would be in their interest to do so once basic rights and an effective say in decisions had been secured.

Though the modalities of a division of authority over offshore activities between Ottawa and a Nunavut government will no doubt be difficult to agree upon, southern Canada has it within its power to move promptly to constitutional and land claims settlements that would improve the prospect for safe and efficient commercial shipping in the Passage, to say nothing of the Canadian claim in international law. Southern Canada should so move in an effort to join with the Inuit as partners in Arctic marine development, in environmental protection, and in creation of national and international regulatory arrangements to govern navigation in the Arctic waters of North America. But where might this leave the northern environmental concerns of southern Canadians?

"Bringing the outside inside" in the period up to 1968 may be viewed as a process of colonialization of the north by southern Canada.[10] Since then, and with the assistance of the federal government, the "inside" has begun a struggle for limited self-determination and decolonization, which has been paralleled by the remarkable growth of southern concern over the fate of the northern physical environment. Peter Burnet argues in chapter 9 that progress towards settlement of land claims and constitutional issues is creating a new situation that requires a change in the perspective of southern environmentalists. As decisions on Arctic resource development and management are taken less from a "national interest" or global ecological standpoint, and more with regional and local interests in mind, the ability of environmentalists to contribute to the resolution of conservation issues in the Arctic will depend increasingly on their capacity to maintain the good will of northern governments and communities. Attitudinal change in the south may be difficult in view of northern residents' interests in self-determination and resource use, and of the threat posed by political devolution to the prerogative of federal government departments in which southern environmental concerns are institutionalized. Nevertheless, as Burnet suggests, it will be increasingly counterproductive for southern environmentalists to be perceived in the north as agents of an order in which decisions bearing directly on local life are dictated from afar.

However, a national interest approach to Arctic marine conservation surely has a future, if only because the federal government will retain a major say in the use of Canada's Arctic waters. Should Ottawa commit the country to the elaboration of an international regime to regulate commercial navigation in the Passage, southern environmentalists would be in a position to join with Inuit, and with governments and fellow conservationists in the three North American Arctic states, in an effort to develop sound regulatory procedures. The more reliable the ensuing regime and the environmental assessment capabilities of Canada in particular, the more southern conservationists would have contributed to the national and global interest in a proper adaptation of resource development to the natural setting. In brief, northern political development in Canada requires a modification of national interest assumptions that restrict the role of the Inuit in marine conservation decisions and an extension of the national interest perspective to the regional level, which has thus far been slighted.

The foregoing of course assumes that in the Canadian archipelago it is possible to reconcile large-scale commercial shipping with the maintenance of the Inuit way of life and environmental conservation. This is an assumption that underlies long-standing government policy on the Passage, to say nothing of the present chapter and the introduction to this volume. Were it to be proved false, for example by trial voyages of the Polar 8 on an extended-season basis in the biologically rich Lancaster Sound area, Canada could be confronted with a dilemma even graver than it now faces. Ottawa could persist in the aim of securing the archipelago as an open Canadian waterway and accept real risks of social and environmental damage so as better to avoid an international straits future and near-complete loss of the ability to regulate navigation. Or Ottawa could announce that it was closing the archipelago to all but limited summer-months navigation by Canadian vessels, thereby possibly jeopardizing its international legal position and risking an end to its capacity to prevent environmental harm. The decision would be heavily dependent on the quality of the social and environmental assessment and on the political context at the time. For the time being it seems wiser to maintain the assumption that commercial shipping and environmental preservation can be reconciled in practice.

Mention of the international legal implications of Canada's internal environmental politics brings us to a final aspect of the Canadian experience in dealing with the Passage: internal preconditions of success in the international legal arena. Kirton and Munton's account (chapter 4) of the decision-making process of 1968–70 might be considered in this context, but the actions that led to the Arctic Waters Pollution Prevention Act and associated measures were sustained by a visible challenge from the United States. What we are concerned with here are requirements of success when the perceived need to act is not bolstered by an immediate threat. McRae's discussion (chapter 5) of Canada's part in the negotiation of Article 234 is highly apposite.

In six years, as McRae shows, Canada succeeded in making a transition from protests by major states to substantial international recognition of the Arctic Waters Pollution Prevention Act. While Canadians' interest in their Arctic waters dissipated after 1970, a small group of legal officers in the Department of External Affairs stayed the course and produced results. They dealt with many states along the way, but it was finally the United States, the Soviet Union, and Canada that negotiated Article 234.

McRae identifies several elements in the chemistry of success. The timing was right: the environmental movement was on the rise globally, jurisdiction over Arctic waters was only one of a great many issues in an omnibus agreement being negotiated at the Third United Nations Conference on the Law of the Sea (UNCLOS), and, it might be added, détente helped bring the two other main players together. UNCLOS also provided an appropriate forum for the furtherance of Canadian aims. Timing and a proper forum were matters of good fortune, but the secret of success was to do better with good luck. In the Legal Bureau of the Department of External Affairs, Canada had a highly skilled, cohesive, and persistent group of negotiators who gradually built support for what had been a unilateral act made in advance of international consensus. This they were able to do because they operated with a clear mandate, had effective control over inter-agency politics in Ottawa, and displayed persistence and flexibility until the moment came to close. Nor should we forget that the position of the Soviet Union was pivotal in providing direct support for Canada and in making the Canadian stand seem less unreasonable to the United States.[11] Although the pick-and-choose approach of the United States to individual provisions of the 1982 Convention has subsequently deprived Article 234 of the full force hoped for by Canada's negotiators, their effort shows something of what might be accomplished if the country as a whole decided to apply itself to the task of securing the Passage as an open Canadian waterway.

But is it realistic to expect of southern Canadians the cohesiveness, perseverance, and pragmatism required to open the Passage as a Canadian waterway? As of mid-decade we must doubt that the people of Canada are prepared to make the transition from an Arctic waters policy that relies on small and dedicated groups of civil servants to one that requires a substantial outlay of resources over an extended period in which the need to act will remain vulnerable to scepticism and dissension. What's ultimately needed to move the country forward is political leadership.

BEYOND THE ARCTIC SUBLIME

Experience shows that the latent attachments of southern Canadians to the Arctic are loaded with political energy. To set things right with the Passage, Canadian leaders must summon this energy on behalf of a sustained national effort that otherwise risks foundering in the midst of inertia and uncertainty. Needed to begin with is an understanding of why Canadians care deeply about the Passage but act as though they cared hardly at all when there is no immediate challenge in sight.

Louis-Edmond Hamelin provides an insight when he refers to a "double illusion" in which over-idealization joins with excessive pessimism to form a series of dualities in southern Canadian thinking about the north – hopes of great wealth and accounts of fortunes lost, exploratory feats and disasters, euphoria and indifference, enthusiasm and repulsion, and so on.[12] Other polarities could be cited if not only attitudes but actions are considered – conservation and development, corporate vision and official inertia, Canada's interests as an Arctic coastal state and its potential to become a shipping state as seen in the APP episode, a southern perspective on the region and a local view of the same, military co-operation with the United States and the need to "defend against help" from the United States in the defence of North America, powerful public concern over Arctic sovereignty in August 1985 and absent-mindedness by December, and so on again. The result is perplexing. Myth mixes with reality to produce frequently exaggerated attachments and aversions in the domestic and international outlook of a people that has yet to come to grips with the north. Most troubling is the propensity to indulge in overdrawn attitudes and inconstant action.

Many explanations could be offered for antinomies in the way Canadians handle individual domestic and foreign issues that bear on the future of their Arctic waters. But if we are primarily interested in an adaptation of the overall approach of the country so as to improve the likelihood of success in securing the Passage as an open Canadian waterway, we need to probe deeper and question why the Canadian mind seems to be so divided against itself where the Arctic is concerned.

The elucidating power of a single notion is necessarily limited, but it does seem to me that the prime source of Canadian difficulties is more cultural than political, geophysical, or organizational. In the myth of the Arctic sublime we have a fragment of nineteenth-century culture that is lodged deep in the Canadian consciousness. By its very nature sublimity is an internally contradictory construct. It gives rise to exaggeration and oscillation in the country's approach to northern issues.

To the Victorian imagination, sublimity represented astoundingly vast and beautiful natural greatness, the contemplation of which could release and uplift the soul, thereby somehow making the observer greater than ordinary. But it also connoted extraordinary harshness, terrible danger, pitiless inhumanity in the working of blind natural forces.[13] Evoking "exultation and terror" and "a mixed sense of triumph and defeat," the thought of the Arctic sublime gave rise to excessive and conflicting predispositions. These would seem to have taken root in the mentality of a people joined together only a few years after the fate of the Franklin expedition had been revealed. Although time, urbanization, and the increasingly multicultural character of Canadian society have no doubt taken some of the edge off these romantic impulses, it is my impression that the Arctic remains at once appealing and appalling to many southern Canadians. They are both daunted and greatened by the knowledge that the Arctic is there and theirs. On the whole they are more daunted by what they take to be the empty grimness of the region.

If this reading is correct, we might expect to see half-heartedness and self-deterrence predominate in a larger pattern of political behaviour marked by alternating short bouts of activism and long periods of apparent indifference. Vacillation is evident in the "Northern Vision" of 1958 ("roads to riches" that went nowhere), in the vigorous protective reaction to the voyages of the *Manhattan* and the subsequent descent into inaction, and in what could yet be a similar pattern associated with the *Polar Sea* episode. As to half-heartedness and the reluctance to venture much in defence of the Passage, it has been all too evident in the absence of a palpable need to act. The people of Canada do feel deeply about their Arctic spaces, but the lingering myth of the sublime deters them from a persistent effort to set things right. It will continue to subvert public policy until southern Canadians come to new realizations about the Arctic as a region in which the need to act is on the rise.

New realizations might well start with the old. The myth of the Arctic sublime has two sides – the "double illusion," in Hamelin's phrase – and is the product of tension between them. Alter the positive or the negative side substantially, and the myth becomes transparent. Positive feelings – exultation, national distinctiveness and greatness by association, the desire to maintain possession and to protect an unspoiled natural environment – surely deserve to remain and grow. They are wholly in keeping with today's ecological perspective. They will continue to drive the Canadian effort to maintain political control and assure sound uses of the Arctic. But there are problems. For one thing, Nature sublime is necessarily depopulat-ed. Inuit and other northern residents are not really there in a received myth that centres on the physical environment. If southern Canadians are not only to contemplate the Arctic from afar but to make their presence known to others in a way that avoids violence to the local setting, fellow citizens who live in the Arctic will have to be valued. Further, the notion of sublimity is incompatible with economic development and on this count has no doubt lost ground in the Canadian consciousness. Nevertheless, the lingering thought of the Arctic sublime prompts resistance rather than imaginative adaptation in dealing with the intrusion of industrialism from the south. As such, it holds Canadians back from a sustained and effective response to the reality that no part of the world is any longer exempt from change.

As to the negative aspects of sublimity as a guiding vision – fear and the feeling that the Arctic is alien and unapproachable – these are highly destructive to the national purpose in the north and in the Passage in particular. Southern Canadians still think of themselves as interlopers in the largest part of their own country. Until they learn that the Arctic can be approached and approached successfully when the effort is adapted to the physical, social, and political setting, they will continue to feel threatened with defeat, dwarfed by the immensity of what they face, lacking in confidence.

The key to well-founded confidence is reliable knowledge. It is to be gained from research, reflection, and public education. But it is also to be had from the experience of doing things right in the midst of challenging circumstances. This is where political leadership enters the picture directly. If Canada's leaders, ideally from all three political parties, were to communicate to the public what is at stake in securing the waters of the archipelago – something that has yet to be done by any one political party – and then to proceed step by step with practical measures to make the Passage a safe and open waterway, they might just begin to reduce the Arctic aversions of southern Canadians and to build a new sense of pride and confidence in the ability to act.

The Arctic sublime *is* a myth. Canadians must recognize this. It is suited to an era in which little or nothing is thought to be happening in the region, in which the main activity is admiration from afar. To part with the notion of the sublime is to part with the exaggerated view that the Arctic is terrific in the two senses of the word. The region becomes less captivating and more ordinary. But it also loses some of its ability to inspire fear and passivity. Indeed, the contours of an alternative appreciation begin to take shape as we see through the myth of the sublime. Though it retains the power to seize the imagination of southern Canadians, the underlying idea of the Arctic ceases to be a literary conception that is disconnected from the real world. On the contrary, the Arctic is seen to be connected in countless ways, some of which have been discussed in this book, to the national and international setting. At the same time, the viewpoint of southern Canadians begins to change. The Arctic ceases to be something "other" and is increasingly perceived from within. The centre of gravity of the Canadian self-image moves some degrees northward without detriment to the many other things Canada is and might be. Hesitancy in the face of the awesome yields to a more willing exploration and management of the interconnections between the Arctic and its surrounding environments. Canadians learn new things about themselves as they seek to control these interconnections with some idea of the good in mind. What lies beyond the Arctic sublime is a vision of national self-discovery, a vision whose details are best revealed as Canada begins to affirm its potentialities as a leading Arctic country.

The place to start is the Northwest Passage and Canada's portion of it. Vitally important things need to be done there. If they are done right, the large reservoir of political energy that is associated with Canadians' positive feelings about the Arctic may be released to support an increasingly ambitious long-term effort to make the Passage an open Canadian waterway. To the extent that Canada succeeds in its goals for the Passage, it will have gone a good part of the way to becoming a great northern nation.

Appendix

On 10 September 1985, Secretary of State for External Affairs the Rt. Hon. Joe Clark made the following statement in the House of Commons concerning Canadian sovereignty in the Arctic:

Mr. Speaker, sovereignty can be a very emotional issue in this country, and that is quite understandable, since sovereignty involves the identity and the very character of a people. We Canadians want to be ourselves. We want to manage our own affairs and control our own destiny, but we also want to go beyond this to play a constructive role in a world that is become increasingly inter-dependent. We have something to offer and at the same time we have something to gain.

Since it came to power, this Government has shown a keen interest in the sovereignty issue. We have consolidated national unity, because a house divided cannot stand. We have reinforced the national economy, because sovereignty means nothing without solvency. Unity and strength: these are the hallmark of sovereignty and of the policies and achievements of this Government.

We have declared a Canadian ownership policy in respect of foreign investment in the publishing industry. We have made our own Canadian decisions on controversial issues of foreign policy, whether in Nicaragua or South Africa. We have passed the Foreign Extraterritorial Measures Act to block unacceptable claims of jurisdiction by foreign Governments or foreign courts seeking to extend their writ to Canada. We have arrested foreign trawlers poaching in our fishing zones. We have taken important steps to bolster and improve Canada's defences, notably in increasing Canadian forces in Europe and in putting into place a new North Warning System to protect Canadian sovereignty over our northern airspace.

As well, Sir, we have reconstructed relations with traditional friends and allies who have welcomed our renewed unity and strength and the confidence they generate.

Sir, my colleague, the Minister of Communications (Mr. Masse), and other Ministers of this Government on other occasions, will be making announcements through the life of this Parliament on other steps this Government intends to take to assert and guarantee the sovereignty and independence of Canada. In domestic policy, foreign policy, and defence policy the Government has given Canadian sovereignty a new impetus within a new maturity. However, Sir, much remains to be done. The voyage of the *Polar Sea* demonstrated that Canada, in the past, had not developed the means to ensure our sovereignty over time. During that voyage, Canada's legal position was fully protected, but when we looked for ways to exercise our sovereignty we found that the Canadian cupboard was nearly bare. We obtained from the United States a formal and explicit assurance that the voyage of the *Polar Sea* was without prejudice to Canada's legal position. That, Sir, is an assurance which the Government of the day in 1969 did not receive for the voyage of the *Manhattan* and of the two United States Coast Guard ice breakers. Sir, whatever was done this summer, and however it may contrast with what was done before, nonprejudicial arrangements will not be enough in the future.

The voyage of the *Polar Sea* has left no trace on Canada's Arctic waters and no mark on Canada's Arctic sovereignty. It is behind us and our concern must be for what lies ahead. Many countries, including the United States and the Federal Republic of Germany, are actively preparing now for commercial navigation in Arctic waters. Developments are accelerating in ice science, ice technology, and in tanker design. Several major Japanese firms are moving to capture the market for ice breaking tankers once polar oil and gas come on stream. Soviet submarines are being deployed under the Arctic ice pack and the United States Navy has, in turn, identified a need to gain Arctic operational experience to counter new Soviet deployments.

The implications for Canada are clear. As the western country with by far the greatest frontage on the Arctic, we must come up to speed in a range of marine operations that bear on our capacity to exercise effective control over the Northwest Passage and our other Arctic waters. To this end, Sir, I wish to declare to the House the policy of the Government in respect of Canadian sovereignty in Arctic waters, and to make a number of announcements as to how we propose to give expression to that policy.

Canada is an Arctic nation. The international community has long recognized that the Arctic mainland and islands are a part of Canada like any other, but the Arctic is not only a part of Canada, it is a part of Canadian greatness. The policy of the Government is to preserve that Canadian greatness undiminished. Canada's sovereignty in the Arctic is indivisible. It embraces land, sea and ice. It extends without interruption to the seaward-facing coasts of the Arctic islands. These islands are joined, and not divided, by the waters between them. They are bridged for most of the year by ice. From time immemorial Canada's Inuit people have used and occupied the ice as they have used and occupied the land. The policy of the Government is to maintain the natural unity of the Canadian Arctic archipelago and to preserve Canada's sovereignty over land, sea and ice undiminished and undivided.

That Canadian sovereignty has long been upheld by Governments of this country. However, no previous Government has defined its precise limits or delineated Canada's internal waters and territorial sea in the Arctic. This Government proposes to do so. An Order in Council establishing straight baselines around the outer perimeter of the Canadian Arctic archipelago has been signed today and will come into effect on January 1, 1986.

These baselines define the outer limit of Canada's historical internal waters. Canada's territorial waters extend 12 miles seaward off the baselines. While the Territorial Sea and Fishing Zones Act requires 60 days notice only for the establishment of fishery limits, we consider prior notice should also be given for this important step of establishing straight baselines.

Canada's jurisdiction over its continental margin and 200-mile fishing zone is unchallenged in the Arctic as elsewhere. Canada also exercises jurisdiction over a 100-mile pollution prevention control zone in arctic water, in order to protect the unique ecological balance in the area. That too has been recognized by the international community, in a special provision in the United National Convention on the Law of the Sea.

However, no previous Government had ever extended the application of Canadian civil and criminal laws to offshore zones in the Arctic and elsewhere. The present Government will take this action. To this end, one of our priorities will be the speedy passage of legislation covering the offshore application of Canada laws.

The exercise of functional jurisdiction in arctic waters is essential to Canadian interests. However, it is no substitute for Canada's full sovereignty over the waters of the arctic archipelago. Only with full sovereignty can we protect the entire range of Canadian interests. Full sovereignty is vital to Canada's security. It is vital to the Inuit people. And it is vital to Canada's national identity.

The policy of this Government is to exercise full sovereignty in and on the waters of the arctic archipelago and this applies to the airspace above as well. We will accept no substitute.

The policy of the Government is also to encourage the development of navigation in Canadian Arctic waters. Our goal is to make the Northwest Passage a reality for Canadian and foreign shipping as a Canadian waterway.

Navigation, however, will be subject to the controls and other measures required for Canada's security, for the preservation of the environment, and for the welfare of the Inuit and other inhabitants of the Canadian Arctic. In due course the Government will announce the further steps it is taking to implement these policies, and especially to provide more extensive marine support services, to strengthen regulatory structures, and to reinforce the necessary means of control. I am announcing today that the Government has decided to construct a Polar Class-8 ice breaker.

My colleagues, the Minister of National Defence (Mr. Nielsen) and the Minister of Transport (Mr. Mazankowski) will shortly bring to Cabinet recommendations with regard to the design and construction plans. The costs are very high, in the order of $.5 billion, but the Government is not about to conclude that Canada cannot afford the Arctic.

Meanwhile, we are taking immediate steps to increase surveillance overflights over Arctic waters by Canadian Forces aircraft. In addition, we are now making plans for naval activity in Eastern Arctic waters in 1986. Canada is a strong and responsible member of the international community. Our strength and our responsibility make us all the more aware of the need for co-operation with other countries, and especially with our friends and allies. Co-operation is necessary, not only in defence of our own interests, but in defence of the common interests of the international community. Co-operation adds to our strength and in no way diminishes our sovereignty. The policy of the Government is to offer its co-operation to its friends and allies and to seek their co-operation in return.

We are prepared to explore with the United States all means of co-operation that might promote the respective interests of both countries as Arctic friends, neighbours and allies in the Arctic waters of Canada and Alaska. The United States has been made aware that Canada wishes to open talks on this matter in the near future. Any co-operation with the United States or with other Arctic nations shall only be on the basis of full respect for Canada's sovereignty. That too has been made clear.

In 1970, the Government of the day barred the International Court of Justice from hearing disputes that might arise concerning the jurisdiction exercised by Canada for the prevention of pollution in Arctic waters. The Government of that day said to that court, "Your jurisdiction shall not affect Canada. We will not put our case before that court". This Government will remove that bar. Indeed, we have today notified the Secretary General of the United Nations that Canada is withdrawing the 1970 reservation to its acceptance of the compulsory jurisdiction of the World Court.

The Arctic is a heritage for the people of the Canada. They are determined to keep their heritage entire and to keep their heritage intact. The policy of this Government is to give full expression to that determination.

We challenge no established rights, for none have been established except by Canada. We set no precedents for other areas, for no other area compares with the Canadian Arctic archipelago. We are confident in our position. We believe in the rule of law in international relations. We shall act in accordance with our confidence and belief, as we are doing today in withdrawing the 1970 reservation to Canada's acceptance of the compulsory jurisdiction of the World Court. We are prepared to uphold our position in that Court, if necessary, and to have it fully and freely judged there.

In summary, Mr. Speaker, these are the measures we are announcing today: first, immediate adoption of an Order in Council, establishing straight baselines around the Arctic archipelago, to be effective January 1, 1986; second, immediate adoption of a Canadian Laws Offshore Application Act; third, immediate talks with the United States on co-operation in Arctic waters on the basis of full respect for Canadian sovereignty; fourth, an immediate increase of surveillance overflights of our Arctic waters by aircraft of the Canadian Forces, and immediate planning for Canadian naval activity in the Eastern Arctic in 1986; fifth, the immediate withdrawal of the 1970 reservation to Canada's acceptance of the compulsory jurisdiction of the International Court of Justice; and sixth, construction of a polar, class 8 ice breaker and urgent consideration of other means of exercising more effective control over our Arctic waters.

These are the measures which we can take immediately. We know, however, that a long-term commitment is required. We are making that commitment today.

Source: Canada, Parliament, House of Commons, *Debates*, 33rd Parl., 1st Sess., Vol. 128, 6462-4 (10 September 1985).

Notes

1 On this and other aspects of nineteenth-century British thinking about the Arctic see the brilliant essay by Chauncey C. Loomis, "The Arctic Sublime," in U.C. Knoepflmacher and G.B. Tennyson, eds., *Nature and the Victorian Imagination* (Berkeley: University of California Press, 1977), 95–112. I am grateful to Professor Carl Berger, Department of History, University of Toronto, for drawing my attention to this source.

2 Donat Pharand provides a list of known transits in a volume written with Leonard H. Legault, *Northwest Passage: Arctic Straits* (Dordrecht: Martinus Nijhoff, 1984), 50–2.

3 Consider the range of assumptions as to the likelihood of Arctic resource development and marine transportation that pervade the following studies: Senate of Canada, *Marching to the Beat of the Same Drum: Transportation of Petroleum and Natural Gas North of 60°* (Ottawa: Queen's Printer, 1983); National Energy Board, *Canadian Energy: Supply and Demand 1983–2005: Technical Report* (Ottawa: Ministry of Supply and Services, 1984); William E. Westermeyer and Kurt M. Shusterich, eds., *United States Arctic Interests: The 1980s and 1990s* (New York: Springer-Verlag, 1984), especially chap. 3; and U.S. Congress, Office of Technology Assessment, *Oil and Gas Technologies for the Arctic and Deepwater* (Washington, DC: U.S. Government Printing Office, 1985).

4 See, for example, G. Leonard Johnson et al., "United States Security Interests in the Arctic," in Westermeyer and Shusterich, *Arctic Interests*, 268–94; and W. Harriet Critchley, "Polar Development of Soviet Submarines," *International Journal* 39, no. 4 (Autumn 1984), 828–65.

5 See Appendix.

6 Article 38 of the 1982 Convention on the Law of the Sea defines transit passage as "freedom of navigation and overflight solely for purposes of transiting a strait

between one part of the high seas or an exclusive economic zone and another part of the high seas or an exclusive economic zone." Additional wording provides that "all ships and aircraft enjoy the right of transit passage, which shall not be impeded" in situations where it applies. The text of the Convention is to be found in U.N. Doc. A/CONF 62/122, 7 October 1982.

7 Nuclear submarine interaction between the United States and the Soviet Union increases the strategic value of Canada's Arctic waters. Since there is a very heavy concentration of nuclear attack (SSN) and ballistic missile-firing (SSBN) submarines in the Soviet Northern Fleet, which is based on the Kola Peninsula to the east of northern Norway, the use of Soviet strategic naval assets in peacetime, crisis, and war will be marked by patterns of deployment north into the Barents Sea and Arctic waters beyond, and south into the Norwegian Sea and the Atlantic Ocean. In a crisis, and therefore in peacetime preparedness operations, the U.S. Navy will strive for rapid forward movement of its SSNs in order to force the Soviets to maintain a defensive protection of their SSBNs and in order to deter a land battle in Europe by being in a position to fire long-range sea-launched cruise missiles from the Norwegian and Barents seas. Since Soviet SSNs will provide opposition in the Norwegian Sea, American SSNs may be expected to make their way into the Arctic Ocean and Barents Sea by way of the waters of the Canadian archipelago as well as the Norwegian Sea. By the same token, Soviet attack submarines will probably be deployed so as to permit the mining of the Canadian archipelago and otherwise to address the capacity of U.S. SSNs to make use of Canadian waters in reaching the Arctic Ocean and redeploying between the Atlantic and Pacific oceans. What this all means is intensified American and, no doubt in lesser measure, Soviet use of the waters of the Canadian Arctic archipelago in peacetime, which means today. For a general statement of U.S. naval strategy, see Admiral James D. Watkins, "The Maritime Strategy," U.S. Naval Institute Proceedings, January 1986, Supplement, 2–17. On the Soviet perception of U.S. interest in making use of the Passage for submarine redeployment between the Atlantic and Pacific oceans, see G. Morozov and B. Krivitsky, "Rol prolivov v vooruzhennoi borbe na more" [The Role of Straits in Naval Warfare], Morskoi sbornik, no. 8, 1982, 22. I am indebted to Michael MccGwire of the Brookings Institution, Washington, DC, for this latter source.

8 In conversations with Canadians, U.S. international lawyers continue to assert that Soviet access to the Passage and surrounding waters is a price Washington is prepared to pay in order to prevent Canada's "closure" of the Passage from being employed as a precedent by straits states that might restrict U.S. navigation elsewhere around the globe. Aside from the dubious precedent value of Canadian action to affirm exclusive jurisdiction over a body of water that has not been used for commercial navigation and is exceptional in being heavily ice-covered for most of the year, an effort to assimilate the Passage to a global regime for international straits seems unlikely to withstand full recognition of the continental defence implications for the United States.

9 See, for example, the statements by Mitchell Sharp, then Secretary of State for External Affairs, in the *Globe and Mail*, 18 September 1969; and by the current Secretary, Joe Clark, in Appendix.

10 Ernst B. Haas, "Why Collaborate? Issue-linkage and International Regimes," *World Politics*, 32, no. 3 (April 1980), 367–8.

11 Resolution of constitutional and land claims issues in the Canadian Arctic will also be required. If Canada's Inuit are to have an effective say in Arctic marine transportation decisions and if the government of Canada is to present a persuasive case before the ICJ, Canadian lawyers will surely be required to develop the argument of historic Inuit occupancy in major portions of the Passage – a point that cannot readily be made as long as questions of aboriginal title to lands and offshore areas remain undecided within Canada.

12 By the same token, Canadians should recognize that the U.S. government has not been engaged in an attempt to deny Canadian jurisdiction over waters that it secretly acknowledges to be Canadian. All indications suggest that U.S. officials and legal scholars are in earnest in regarding the waters of the Canadian Arctic archipelago as an international strait.

13 Loomis, "The Arctic Sublime."

14 These comments on the possible Japanese interest are based in part on interviews with Arctic marine consultants and Canadian Coast Guard officials, 2 May and 2 August 1985.

15 Not having established an overall policy framework for Canada's Arctic waters, the government had in effect intended its sovereignty statement of 10 September 1985 to drive the necessary implementing actions. The Polar 8, to say nothing of the many related requirements to ensure sound uses of Canada's Arctic waters, was thus projected into something of a policy vacuum. See Jeff Sallot, "Wrangles in Cabinet over Money Delay Report on Defence Policy," *Globe and Mail*, 11 January 1986; and Robert Martin, "Estimates on Icebreaker Are Too High, Firms Say," *ibid.*, 25 January 1986.

CHAPTER TWO

1 Eigil Knuth, *Reports from the Musk-ox Way* (Copenhagen: Eigil Knuth, 1984).

2 Helge M. Ingstad, *Land under the Pole Star* (London: Cape, 1966).

3 Peter Schledermann, "Eskimo and Viking Finds in the High Arctic," *National Geographic Magazine*, 159, no. 5 (May 1981).

4 L.H. Neatby, *In Quest of the North West Passage* (Toronto: Longmans Green, 1958).

5 L.H. Neatby, *The Search for Franklin* (New York: Walker, 1970).

6 For a more detailed description of the various possible routes see Donat Pharand, *Northwest Passage: Arctic Straits* (Dordrecht: Martinus Nijhoff, 1984).

7 The east-west concept, however, dies hard. In November 1974 the federal Cabinet decided that the Northwest Territories should be split into two constituencies. In subsequent discussions the first proposal was to divide the

existing constituency along east-west lines, with the boundary between the two constituencies running from south to north. The boundary was changed to run approximately along the tree line as a result of the firm opinions expressed by the Inuit to the Electoral Boundaries Commission. A tentative agreement reached early in 1985 on the boundary between the two parts into which the Northwest Territories is to be split indicated that the east-west division had prevailed over the treeline concept, but the agreement was subsequently rejected by the Inuit.

CHAPTER THREE

1 Thomas Berger, *Village Journey* (New York: Hill and Wang, 1985).
2 See, for example, Frederik Harhoff, "Greenland's Withdrawal from the European Communities," *Common Market Law Review* (The Hague) 20 (1983), 19–20.
3 An interesting discussion of modern Greenland and its relationship to Canadian Arctic issues is Nils Orvik, *Northern Development: Northern Security* (Centre for International Relations, Queen's University, Kingston, Ontario, 1983). A brief background outline and discussion of Greenland Home Rule is available in Peter Jull, "Greenland: Lessons of Self-government and Development," *Northern Perspectives* 7, no. 8 (1979), published by the Canadian Arctic Resources Committee, Ottawa.
4 The author was made aware of this when working for the Quebec Inuit in Makivik Corporation.
5 Communiqué, Office of the Prime Minister, 3 October 1979.
6 The work to create Nunavut is being carried on by the Nunavut Constitutional Forum (NCF), with offices in Yellowknife and Ottawa. The forum is made up of members of the NWT legislative assembly elected in Nunavut, including the NCF chairman, Dennis Patterson; the national president of the Inuit and the head of the Nunavut land claims negotiating body; and the president and a second representative of COPE, the Mackenzie Delta/Beaufort Sea Inuit organization. NCF is funded by federal and territorial governments and by Inuit organizations. It carries on its work through public meetings, liaison, research, and publications. Its major publications include *Nunavut* (a political history of the Arctic), *Building Nunavut* (a discussion of the nature of a Nunavut government and constitution, now being revised and expanded for a second edition), and two studies by S.M. Malone, *Nunavut: The Division of Powers* and *Nunavut: Financial Perspectives*. A similar body, the Western Constitutional Forum, represents the people of the Mackenzie Valley. Together the two forums make up the Constitutional Alliance, which presents a common front on issues such as greater self-government for the north and a territorial share in resources decisions and revenues.

7 The Liberal government announced support in principle for Nunavut on 26 November 1982; thereafter it added a series of limiting conditions. On 28 September 1984, Prime Minister Mulroney told a press conference in Ottawa that his Conservative government had not yet defined its policy ("Constitution to Be Avoided at Meeting," *Globe and Mail*, 29 September 1984). Party spokesmen had earlier offered assurances of Nunavut's creation as part of a larger furtherance of self-government in Canada's northern territories. Experience shows that much waffling is to be expected before a Nunavut territorial government assumes responsibility in an Arctic capital with a range of powers equivalent to those of a Canadian province minus non-living resources ownership and the constitutional status of a province.

8 Report of the Advisory Commission on the Development of Government in the Northwest Territories, Department of Indian Affairs and Northern Development, Ottawa, 1966.

9 As researchers like McDonald have demonstrated (see "Inuit Nationalism," MA thesis by Allysson McDonald, Institute of Canadian Studies, Carleton University, Ottawa, 1984), the Inuit politicians who have shaped the Inuit political movement were launched *before* these Potemkin village governments began to function.

10 See Minutes of the Nunavut Regional Workshop, Cambridge Bay, 9 September 1984, available from the Nunavut Constitutional Forum (NCF), Ottawa.

11 For comment on the NCF, see note 6. On the offshore issue, the attitude of the Conservative government in Ottawa is not fully known but is thought to be more open than that of the previous government. The latter had repeatedly refused to yield to coastal jurisdictions seeking more power offshore. The offshore position of NCF is presented in *Building Nunavut*, first issued in May 1983.

12 An example is Bill C-52, introduced in the House of Commons by John Munro in the dying hours of the Trudeau government's last session of Parliament, in 1984.

13 See, for example, the exchanges of chairman Patterson and COPE delegates Haogak and McDiarmid in Minutes of the Nunavut Regional Workshop.

14 *The Western Arctic Claim: The Inuvialuit Final Agreement*, Department of Indian and Northern Affairs, Ottawa, 1984.

15 "Further Brief to the Royal Commission on the Economic Union and Development Prospects (The Macdonald Commission), a Commission on Canada's Future, from the Canadian Section of the Inuit Circumpolar Conference," presented by Mark R. Gordon, vice-president (Canada) and Rhoda Innuksuk, Canadian executive council member, ICC, Ottawa, July 1984. Ocean section, 11–15; quotations in text here, 14–15.

16 A recent book, *Sikumiut: "The People Who Use the Sea Ice"* (Ottawa: Canadian Arctic Resources Committee, 1984), brings together a number of excellent

papers on this subject. See also David VanderZwaag and Donat Pharand, "Inuit and the Ice: Implications for Canadian Arctic Waters," *Canadian Yearbook of International Law*, 21 (1983), 75–8.

17 Eben Hopson Sr, "Welcoming Address, First Inuit Circumpolar Conference, Barrow, Alaska, 12–19 June 1977," *Arctic Policy Review* (North Slope Borough, June–July 1983), 2.

18 The founding and subsequent history of the ICC are discussed in Philip Lauritzen, *Oil and Amulets* (St John's: Breakwater Press, 1983). This book surveys changes and issues in the circumpolar Arctic today.

19 A Canadian perspective on the 1980 Nuuk assembly is the author's "Diplomats of a New North," *Policy Options* (Institute for Research on Public Policy, Ottawa) 2, no. 2, (May–June 1981), 21–6.

20 This office was opened in late November 1983, in the suite of offices where Canada's national Inuit organizations are located.

21 See, for example, Samuel E. Fry, *Native Arctic Peoples: A Growing Political and Economic Identity*, 26th Session, Executive Seminar in National and International Affairs, Foreign Service Institute, u.s. State Department, 1983–4, 34, and note 6, 35.

22 In Greenland, where functional organizations already exist, this makes good sense.

23 See Jull, "Diplomats," 24.

24 See Fry, *Native Arctic Peoples*.

25 The Soviet Inuit homeland is excepted, although one may assume that there, too, change is dramatic and perhaps traumatic. A disturbing article indicates that removal and dispersal may be the lot of these Inuit: B. Chichlo, "Les Nevukaghmiit ou la fin d'une ethnie," *Etudes Inuit Studies* (Laval University, Quebec) 5, no. 2 (1981), 32–46.

26 *Beaufort Sea Hydrocarbon Production and Transportation*, Final Report of the Environmental Assessment Panel, Federal Environment Assessment Review Office, Ottawa, July 1984. The report is diverse and has many interesting and useful aspects. Although disappointing on the needs of the living, it is remarkably bold and progressive about dead Inuit, as per the archaeology proposals on 99. Some of the best recommendations, for example on resources revenue sharing (97), do not appear in the formal list of recommendations.

27 Peter Jacobs and Jonathan Pulluq, *Public Review: Public Prospect* (The Lancaster Sound Regional Study), Department of Indian and Northern Affairs, Ottawa, November 1983. Known widely as "the Peter Jacobs report," this paper is as concise and clear as most others are inaccessible; pp. 9–16 are particularly useful.

28 For example, during the NCF workshop on regional government, held in Cambridge Bay on 9 September 1984, Peter Katorka addressed the need for greater powers offshore for a Nunavut government. Citing the activity of an exploration vessel in Hudson Bay and the lack of information provided by

government or industry to Inuit, he stated simply, "Hudson Bay is ours." See Minutes of the Nunavut regional workshop, NCF, Ottawa, 15.

29 CBC Northern Service Radio news, Yellowknife, 2 October 1984.

30 "After Opposing Arctic Plan, Greenland Eyes Oil Royalties," *Globe and Mail* Report on Business, 21 September 1984.

31 CBC news, 2 October 1984.

32 Katherin Graham et al., *A Climate for Change: Alternatives for the Central and Eastern Arctic*, Final Report of the Eastern Arctic Study, Centre for Resource Studies, Queen's University, Kingston, Ontario. This is perhaps the most detailed, and certainly the most neutral, study of northern political development in Canada.

CHAPTER FOUR

1 Notably Edgar Dosman, *The National Interest* (Toronto: McClelland and Stewart, 1975); Edgar Dosman, ed., *The Arctic in Question* (Toronto: Oxford University Press, 1976); and Richard Rohmer, *The Arctic Imperative* (Toronto: McClelland and Stewart, 1973). On the basics of the case see Maxwell Cohen, "The Arctic and the National Interest," *International Journal* 26, no. 4 (Winter 1970–1), 52–81, and Thomas Tynan, "The Role of the Arctic in Canadian-American Relations," PHD dissertation, Catholic University of America, 1976.

2 The precepts of traditional liberal-internationalism are specified in David Dewitt and John Kirton, *Canada as a Principal Power* (Toronto: John Wiley, 1983). The new tendency conforms in its major elements to the perspective of "complex neorealism" outlined in that work. On the concept of a tendency see Franklyn Griffiths, "A Tendency Analysis of Soviet Policy-Making," in H.G. Skilling and Franklyn Griffiths, eds., *Interest Groups in Soviet Politics* (Princeton: Princeton University Press, 1971), 335–87.

3 In addition to published sources and press accounts, this article is based largely on confidential interviews and colloquia on Canadian-U.S. relations, involving both authors, extending over the past decade, supplemented more recently by selective documentary and interview evidence dealing with the *Manhattan* case. Standards of reliability meet those specified and employed in John Kirton, "The Conduct and Co-ordination of Canadian Government Decisionmaking toward the United States, 1970–1975," PHD dissertation, Johns Hopkins University, 1977.

4 On the legal status of the Passage see Donat Pharand, *The Law of the Sea of the Arctic* (Ottawa: University of Ottawa Press, 1973), and Donat Pharand, "The Legal Regime of the Arctic: Some Outstanding Issues," *International Journal* 39, no. 4 (Autumn 1984), 742–99.

5 In legal and geographical terms, the more precise distinction is that between "territorial" and "internal" waters, both of which give the coastal state exclusive jurisdiction, but only the latter of which allows it to control rights of passage.

6 "A New Defence Policy for Canada," Statement to the Press by the Prime Minister, Mr. Pierre Elliot Trudeau, 3 April 1969. The Prime Minister also chose a group of party faithful and oil industry officials before which to outline his defence policy a week later. See "The Relation of Defence Policy to Foreign Policy," Statement by the Prime Minister, Mr. Pierre Elliott Trudeau, to the Alberta Liberal Association, Calgary, 12 April 1969. The location of the speech, and its identification of Canada's "three-ocean," Arctic interests, strongly suggest that the new defence priorities were conditioned by the impending *Manhattan* voyage. And while the Prime Minister provided another, rather weak explanation for the rushed timing of the 3 April defence policy announcement, it may be significant that the *Manhattan*'s voyage was originally thought to begin in April 1969.

7 John Dafoe, *Globe and Mail*, 16 May 1969.

8 Dosman, *The Arctic in Question*, 42.

9 *Ibid.*, 46.

10 Mitchell Sharp, "A Ship and Sovereignty in the North," *Globe*, 18 September 1969.

11 *Ibid.*

12 "MPs Urge Full Claim to Waters of Arctic," *Toronto Star*, 8 September 1969.

13 Sharp, "A Ship and Sovereignty."

14 Peter Thomson, "MP Won't Allow Arctic Challenge," *Telegram*, 25 October 1969.

15 "Trudeau Will Meet U Thant to Discuss Arctic Pollution," *Globe and Mail*, 25 October 1969.

16 For a full account of the Brussels process see R. Michael M'Gonigle and Mark Zacher, *Pollution, Politics, and International Law: Tankers at Sea* (Berkeley, Calif.: University of California Press, 1979).

17 "Claim Waters of Arctic Now, MPs of All Parties Urge," *Globe and Mail*, 17 December 1969.

18 The group comprised Ivan Head, Allan Gotlieb, and Messrs Robertson, Uffen, and Dewhirst of the Privy Council Office, Messrs Legault and Lee of External Affairs, Mr Thorson of Justice, Messrs McDonald and Hunt of DIAND, Messrs Needler and Omere of Forestry and Fisheries, Mr Isbister of EMR, and Mr MacGillway of Transport.

19 John Doig, "Arctic Pollution," *Toronto Star*, 20 February 1970.

20 By this phrase was meant both the Alaskan and Canadian portions.

21 John Aitken, "U.S. Prepares for Arctic Legal Fight?" *Telegram*, 18 February 1970.

22 The possibility of a 12-mile territorial sea limit, without an ICJ reservation, rested in between.

23 Allan Gotlieb had served formerly as the legal adviser in External Affairs and was, in 1969 and 1970, deputy minister of the Department of Communications.

24 Paul Martin had studied international law and international affairs at Cambridge University, where he had been taught by Arnold McNair, who, in 1970,

was serving as president of the ICJ. Moreover, as a product of the inter-war generation, Martin believed that the wars against the Kaiser and Hitler had been fought in order to construct an international system centred in the United Nations and the ICJ. And as an international lawyer his commitment to the Court was as intense as that of his contemporary, Lester Pearson, to the United Nations. Indeed, so strong was Martin's commitment, nurtured by his two years of post-graduate education in international law, that in 1946 he attempted to get Canada to support the bid of a prominent American for another term on the ICJ, even when the U.S. government had repudiated the candidacy of its national. Martin's desire to have the Court grow, and his consequent opposition to a reservation, were thus ideological, catholic, and almost religious in nature. Indeed he felt as strongly about this issue as about any in his twenty years in Cabinet. See Paul Martin, *A Very Public Life* (Ottawa: Deneau, 1983).

25 As another lawyer with exposure to international law, Trudeau fully understood the argument and felt the obligation to resist a small transitory national advantage in favour of the larger task of building the international system. Indeed, as he sat next to Martin at Cabinet he could be overheard whispering his private support for the internationalist position. Also evident was Trudeau's fear that Martin might resign over the issue. Yet Trudeau's Jesuitical approach, and his position as head of the government, affected his views when he saw that the majority of the Ministers favoured a reservation. In addition he felt the Arctic waters were Canada's, recognized the pollution problem, saw the Act as a practical step, and felt that Canada could reduce the damage to the international system by withdrawing its ICJ reservation at a later stage. Finally, he wanted to settle the issue and found it difficult to repudiate a policy that he had introduced and which had been developed by his close associate Ivan Head.

26 Most other Ministers were primarily concerned that Canada not lose any ICJ case. And as none of the major Ministers was a lawyer who understood international law, they did not feel keenly about building up the international system. Their approach was more pragmatic. And as a second generation (i.e. post-war) internationalist, Mitchell Sharp's commitment was less ideological than that of Martin.

27 Clyde Sanger, "Challenge to Arctic Sovereignty May Go to Court, Sharp Says," *Globe and Mail*, 13 March 1970.

28 "Documents Concerning Canadian Legislation of Arctic Pollution and Territorial Sea and Fishing Zones," *International Legal Materials* 9 (May 1970), 598–9.

29 The other three reservations concerned disputes dealt with in other forums, disputes with Commonwealth members, and disputes exclusively within the jurisdiction of Canada.

30 For a scholarly statement of these concepts, directed at the American legal community, see Allan Gotlieb and Charles Dalfen, "National Jurisdiction and International Responsibility," *American Journal of International Law* 67, no. 2 (April 1973), 229–58.

31 Dewitt and Kirton, *Canada as a Principal Power*, 295.
32 For example, editorial support in the United States was evenly balanced between the Canadian and u.s. position.
33 Ivan Head, "The Foreign Policy of the New Canada," *Foreign Affairs* 50, no. 2 (January 1972), 237–52. See also Harald von Riekhoff, "The Impact of Prime Minister Trudeau on Foreign Policy," *International Journal* 33, no. 2 (Spring 1978), 267–86.

CHAPTER FIVE

1 Canada, Senate, *Debates*, 1906–7, 266.
2 For Canada's historical claim to the waters, see Ivan Head, "Canadian Claims to Territorial Sovereignty in Arctic Regions," *McGill Law Journal* 9 (1962–3), 219.
3 See R.Y. Jennings, *The Acquisition of Territory in International Law* (Manchester: Manchester University Press, 1962).
4 D.P. O'Connell, *The International Law of the Sea*, I (Oxford: Clarendon Press, 1982), chap. 1.
5 *Ibid.*, chap. 11.
6 Earlier this century, however, the status of the waters of Hudson Bay was debated. See, e.g., T.W. Balch, "Is Hudson Bay a Closed or an Open Sea?" *American Journal of International Law* 6 (1912), 409–59; V.K. Johnston, "Canada's Title to Hudson Bay and Hudson Strait," *British Yearbook of International Law* 15 (1934), 1–20.
7 See Head, "Canadian Claims," 220–4.
8 [1951] ICJ Rep. 116.
9 A/CONF.13/L.52. The Convention has never been ratified by Canada.
10 Article 4(4). The Convention added a qualification, not found in the *Fisheries Case*, to the effect that there would still be a right of innocent passage where the waters so enclosed were previously territorial.
11 The first such legislation was adopted in 1964; Territorial Sea and Fishing Zones Act, 13 Eliz. 2 c. 22 (1964).
12 Fisheries Council of Canada, "A Brief Concerning 'Canada's National and Teritorial Waters'," 28 January 1963.
13 A.E. Gotlieb, "The Canadian Contribution to the Concept of a Fishing Zone in International Law," *Canadian Yearbook of International Law* 2 (1964), 55–76.
14 Letter of Department of State to the Department of Justice (Territorial Waters) 13 November 1951; A.L. Shalowitz, *Shore and Sea Boundaries*, I (Washington: u.s. Department of Commerce, Coast Guard and Geodetic Survey, 1962), App. D.
15 Order-in-Council PC 1967-2025, 26 October 1967.
16 Order-in-Council PC 1969-1109, 29 May 1969.
17 See generally R.S. Reid, "The Canadian Claim to Sovereignty over the Waters of the Arctic," *Canadian Yearbook of International Law* 12 (1974) 111–36.

18 The voyage of the *Manhattan* was not, however, the first occasion on which the status of Arctic waters had been brought into question. In 1958 the passage of the USS *Nautilus* under the polar ice-cap raised the issue of Canadian jurisdiction over the waters.

19 J.A. Beesley, "Rights and Responsibilities of Arctic Coastal States: The Canadian View," *Journal of Maritime Law and Commerce* 3 (1971–2), 7.

20 *Ibid.*

21 The statement is reproduced in *International Legal Materials* 9 (1972), 600.

22 A.E. Gotlieb and C.M. Dalfen, "National Jurisdiction and International Responsibility: New Canadian Approaches to International Law," *American Journal of International Law* 67 (1973), 229–58.

23 R.M. M'Gonigle and M.W. Zacher, "Canadian Foreign Policy and the Control of Marine Pollution," in B. Johnson and M.W. Zacher, eds., *Canadian Foreign Policy and the Law of the Sea* (Vancouver: University of British Columbia Press, 1977), 124.

24 Originally set up in 1958 to deal with the technical regulation of international shipping, following the *Torrey Canyon* disaster in 1967, IMCO developed a major role in the international regulation of marine pollution from ships. In 1982 the organization's name was changed to the International Maritime Organization (IMO). For a full analysis of IMCO's role in marine pollution, see R.M. M'Gonigle and M.W. Zacher, *Pollution Politics and International Law* (Berkeley: California University Press, 1979).

25 M'Gonigle and Zacher, "Canadian Foreign Policy," 125.

26 Report of the Intergovernmental Working Group on Marine Pollution; A/CONF.48/1WGMP.II/5, 22 November 1971.

27 Decisions of the UN Conference on the Human Environment relating to the preservation of the marine environment and marine pollution, A/AC/138/S.C. III/L.17, 24 July 1972.

28 For an account of the treatment of the Canadian initiative at the IMCO conference, see Donat Pharand, "La contribution du Canada au développement du droit international pour la protection du milieu marin: le cas spécial de l'Arctique" *Etudes internationales* 11 (1980), 458. Similar Canadian initiatives were also made at the London Dumping Conference in 1972, *ibid* 456.

29 IMCO Doc. MP/CONF/C.1/W.P.36. The co-sponsoring states were Greece, the Netherlands, Norway, Sweden, and the United Kingdom.

30 The right of "innocent passage" that exists in the territorial sea can be suspended for limited periods of time by the adjacent coastal state for such purposes as environmental protection. Passage cannot be suspended in territorial waters that constitute an international strait. The transit passage regime involved an absolute right of passage, innocent or not.

31 For the definition of an archipelagic state, see Convention on the Law of the Sea, 1982, Article 46.

32 Acceptance of a special regime applicable to ice-covered waters nevertheless

posed problems for the Soviet Union. It could be seen as a retreat by that nation from its position that it had full sovereignty over Soviet Arctic waters.

33 Article 234 refers to severe climatic conditions, the presence of ice covering such areas for most of the year creating obstructions or exceptional hazards to navigation and where pollution of the marine environment could cause major harm to or irreversible disturbance of the ecological balance. Moreover, laws established by the coastal state are to have "due regard to navigation."

34 M'Gonigle and Zacher, "Canadian Foreign Policy," 142–3; see also D.M. McRae and D.J. Goundrey, "Environmental Jurisdiction in Arctic Waters: The Extent of Article 234," *University of British Columbia Law Review* 16 (1982), 197-228.

35 Donat Pharand, *The Northwest Passage: Arctic Straits* (The Hague: Sijthoff, 1984), 119–20.

36 The wording of Article 234 does not preclude a sovereignty claim to ice-covered waters.

37 B.G. Buzan, "Negotiating by Consensus: Developments in Technique at the United Nations Conference on the Law of the Sea," *American Journal of International Law* 75 (1981), 324–48.

38 Canada was, of course, concerned that the straits regime should not apply to southern waters, such as the Strait of Juan de Fuca or Head Harbour Passage, which are claimed as internal waters of Canada. This issue was predominantly a bilateral matter with the United States.

39 In particular, the United Kingdom and the Federal Republic of Germany.

40 Pharand, "La contribution du Canada," 465–6.

41 D.A. Colson, "Political and Boundary Issues Affecting Arctic Energy Resources," paper presented to the 18th Annual Law of the Sea Institute Conference, San Francisco, 26 September 1984, 22.

42 W.E. Westermeyer, "Jurisdiction and Management of Arctic Marine Transportation," paper presented to Canada–United States Arctic Policy Forum, Banff, October 1984, 25.

43 Presidential Proclamation of 10 March 1983.

44 Chapter 6 in this volume.

45 Pharand, *The Northwest Passage*, 108.

CHAPTER SIX

1 On the distinction between distributive and integrative bargaining, see Howard Raiffa, *The Art and Science of Negotiation* (Cambridge: Harvard University Press, 1982), parts II and III.

2 T.C. Pullen, "Arctic Outlet," an address to the Canada-Japan Trade Council of Ottawa, Ottawa, 1981, and "Great Arctic Energy Rush," *Business Week* 24 (January 1983), 52–7.

3 John C. McCaslin, ed., *International Petroleum Encyclopedia* (Tulsa: Penwell Publications, 1984); Bob Williams et al., "North American Arctic Report," *Oil and Gas Journal*, 25 June 1984, 55–77; David B. Brooks, "Black Gold Redrilled: Are the Economics of Beaufort Sea Oil Getting Better or Worse?" *Northern Perspectives* 11, no. 3 (1984), 1–4; and M.B. Todd, "Development of Beaufort Sea Hydrocarbons," *The Musk-Ox* 32 (1984), 22–43.

4 For relevant background, consult J.W. Devanney III, *The OCS Petroleum Pie*, Report No. MITSG 75-10 (Cambridge: MIT, 1975).

5 John Dyson, *The Hot Arctic* (Boston: Little Brown, 1979).

6 McCaslin, *Encyclopedia*, 316–22.

7 John F. Helliwell, Mary E. MacGregor, and Andre Plourde, "Changes in Canadian Energy Demand, Supply, and Policies, 1974–1986," *Natural Resources Journal* 24 (1984), 297–324.

8 Consult, inter alia, O.S.C. Robertson, "The Canadian Arctic Water Basin," in Maja van Steensel, ed., *People of Light and Dark* (Ottawa: Queen's Printer, 1966); O.S.C. Robertson, "The Russian Arctic Water Basin," *ibid.*; T.C. Pullen, "The Development of Arctic Ships," in Morris Zaslow, ed., *A Century of Canada's Arctic Islands* (Ottawa: Royal Society of Canada, 1981); and A.S. McLaren, "Transporting Arctic Petroleum: A Role for Commercial Submarines," *Polar Record* 22 (1984), 7–23.

9 François Bregha, "CARC's Memorandum to Cabinet," *Northern Perspectives* 10, no. 3 (1982), 1–12.

10 Williams et al., "Report.".

11 See E.J. Dosman, ed., *The Arctic in Question* (Toronto: Oxford University Press, 1976); Lisle A. Rose, "Recent Trends in U.S. Arctic Policy," *Arctic* 35 (1982), 241–2; and R. Tucker Scully, "Arctic Policy: Opportunities and Perspectives," in *Proceedings of a Conference on Arctic Technology and Policy* (New York: Hemisphere Publishing Corp., 1983).

12 See the essays in Dosman, ed., *The Arctic in Question*.

13 R. St J. Macdonald, ed., *The Arctic Frontier* (Toronto: University of Toronto Press, 1960).

14 Dosman, ed., *The Arctic in Question*; Brian D. Smith, "United States Arctic Policy," Ocean Policy Study 1, no. 1 (Charlottesville: The Mitchie Company, 1978); and Hal Mills et al., *Ocean Policy and Management in the Arctic* (Ottawa: Canadian Arctic Resources Committee, 1984).

15 The disadvantages to Canada of having the entire Arctic carved up into an elaborate network of national zones might well outweigh any advantages Canada might obtain from extending its own jurisdiction in the Arctic. On the realism of this scenario see also W. Joseph Dehner, "Creeping Jurisdiction in the Arctic: Has the Soviet Union Joined Canada?" *Harvard International Law Journal* 13 (1972), 271–88.

16 National Security Council, "National Security Decision Memorandum 144," (Washington 1971), and William E. Westermeyer and Kurt M. Shusterich,

eds., *United States Arctic Interests: The 1980s and 1990s* (New York: Springer-Verlag, 1984).

17 For a broader discussion of Arctic security issues, consult Nils Orvik, *Northern Development: Northern Security* (Kingston: Queen's University, 1983).

18 See Gurston Dacks, *A Choice of Futures: Politics in the Canadian North* (Toronto: Methuen, 1981), especially chap. 4.

19 For a brief but accurate account see Central Intelligence Agency, *Polar Regions Atlas* (Washington: Central Intelligence Agency, 1978).

20 See the essays in E.F. Roots, ed., *Lancaster Sound: Issues and Responsibilities* (Ottawa: Canadian Arctic Resources Committee, 1980).

21 David Boeri, *People of the Ice Whale: Eskimos, White Men, and the Whale* (New York: Dutton, 1984).

22 Peter Burnet, "Stokes Point, Yukon," *Northern Perspectives* 11, no. 2 (1983), 1–12.

23 "State Lifts Beaufort Broken-Ice Restrictions," *Arctic Policy Review* 2, no. 6 (1984), 9–13.

24 Gerald MacBeath, *North Slope Borough Government and Policymaking*, MAP Monograph no. 3 (Anchorage: Institute of Social and Economic Research, 1981), and Philip Lauritzen, *Oil and Amulets* (St John's: Breakwater Press, 1983).

25 Richard Nelson, *Hunters of the Northern Ice* (Chicago: University of Chicago Press, 1969), and Alan Cooke and Edie Van Alstine, eds., *Sikumiut: "The People Who Use the Sea Ice"* (Ottawa: Canadian Arctic Resources Committee, 1984).

26 David M. Hickok et al., *United States Arctic Science Policy*, monograph of the Alaska Division of the American Association for the Advancement of Science (Anchorage: AAAS, 1981).

27 Ken MacQueen, "Canada Probes Arctic Ice to Back Claim to Ownership," reprinted in *Polar Times* 96 (June 1983), 11.

28 William E. Butler, *Northeast Arctic Passage* (Alphen aan den Rijn: Sijthoff and Noordhoff, 1978).

29 See also Lincoln P. Bloomfield, "The Arctic: Last Unmanaged Frontier," *Foreign Affairs* 60 (1981), 87–105.

30 For a standard treatment consult J.L. Brierly, *The Law of Nations*, 6th ed. (New York: Oxford University Press, 1963).

31 For a discussion of these concepts see Raiffa, *The Art and Science of Negotiation*, part II.

32 Thomas C. Schelling, *The Strategy of Conflict* (Cambridge: Harvard University Press, 1960).

33 McLaren, "Transporting Arctic Petroleum."

34 See also Donat Pharand, *The Law of the Sea of the Arctic* (Ottawa: University of Ottawa Press, 1973).

35 Douglas Pimlott, Dougald Brown, and Kenneth Sam, *Oil under Ice* (Ottawa: Canadian Arctic Resources Committee, 1976), especially chap. 8.

36 For a more extensive analysis see Oran R. Young, *Resource Management at the International Level: The Case of the North Pacific* (London and New York: Pinter, 1977).

37 Pharand, *The Law of the Sea,* and Bloomfield, "The Arctic."

38 Cooke and Van Alstine, eds., *Sikumiut.*

39 For a discussion that raises doubts about the authoritativeness of the Law of the Sea Convention see James L. Malone, "Who Needs the Sea Treaty?" *Foreign Policy* 54 (1984), 44–63.

40 For the full text see United Nations, "United Nations Convention on the Law of the Sea," A/Conf.62/122 (1982).

41 For a thoughtful Canadian discussion of this issue see D.M. McRae and D.J. Goundry, "Environmental Jurisdiction in Arctic Waters: The Extent of Article 234," *University of British Columbia Law Review* 16 (1982), 197–228.

42 Dosman, ed., *The Arctic in Question,* and Richard B. Bilder, "The Canadian Arctic Waters Pollution Prevention Act: New Stresses on the Law of the Sea," *Michigan Law Review* 69 (1970), 1–54.

43 F.M. Auburn, *Antarctic Law and Politics* (Bloomington: Indiana University Press, 1982).

44 Oran R. Young, *Resource Regimes: Natural Resources and Social Institutions* (Berkeley: University of California Press, 1982).

45 Oran R. Young, "International Regimes: Problems of Concept Formation," *World Politics,* 32 (1980), 331–56, and Oran R. Young, "Regime Dynamics: The Rise and Fall of International Regimes," *International Organization* 36 (1982), 277–97.

46 See also Stephen D. Krasner, ed., *International Regimes* (Ithaca: Cornell University Press, 1983).

47 For relevant background, consult Christopher B. Joyner, "Oceanic Pollution and the Southern Ocean: Rethinking the International Legal Implications for Antarctica," *Natural Resources Journal* 24 (1984), 1–40.

48 For some imaginative suggestions regarding new types of international regimes, see Finn Sollie et al., *The Challenge of New Territories* (Oslo: Universitet Forlaget, 1974).

49 Anatol Rapoport, "Strategic and Non-Strategic Approaches to Problems of Security and Peace," in Kathleen Archibald, ed., *Strategic Interaction and Conflict* (Berkeley: Institute of International Relations, 1966), 28–41.

50 For a parallel discussion of the international seabed regime see Oran R. Young, "International Resource Regimes," in Clifford S. Russell, ed., *Collective Decision Making: Applications from Public Choice Theory* (Baltimore: Johns Hopkins University Press, 1979), 120–38.

51 See also Young, *Resource Regimes,* especially chap. 3.

52 See also William B. Kemp and Lorraine Brooks, "A New Approach to Northern Science," *The Northern Raven* 2, no. 1 (1983).

53 For an extensive case study consult Willy Ostreng, *Politics in High Latitudes: The Svalbard Archipelago* (London: C. Hurst and Co., 1977).

54 For details see the essays in Dosman, ed., *The Arctic in Question*.

55 See Young, "International Resource Regimes.".

CHAPTER SEVEN

1 *Meddelelser om Grønland*, no. 1 (1980), 15.

2 Ministry for Greenland, *Annual Report 1982*.

3 *Ibid.*.

4 *Information*, 2 December 1984.

5 Conversation with u.s. embassy official, Copenhagen, 15 March 1983.

6 *Ibid.*, 10–11 September 1983.

7 Joint Council Document, dated 6 June 1983.

CHAPTER EIGHT

1 Interviews with federal government officials, January–March 1984. Also see *Globe and Mail*, 23 September 1980. The author reported on the APP story for the *Globe and Mail* from 1981 to 1984.

2 Interviews with Petro-Canada and government officials, January-March 1984.

3 *Wall Street Journal*, 2 February 1982.

4 *Calgary Herald*, 18 January 1979 and 26 June 1980.

5 *Ibid.*, 14 February 1981.

6 *Ibid.*, 16 April 1981.

7 *Ottawa Citizen*, 24 January 1979.

8 *Calgary Herald*, 14 October 1980.

9 Interview with former Petro-Canada official, March 1984.

10 Interviews with Petro-Canada, APP, and government officials, January–March 1984.

11 Interview with former APP official, March 1984.

12 *Calgary Herald*, 16 October 1984.

13 Petro-Canada press release, 17 January 1979.

14 *Globe and Mail*, 10 June 1980.

15 Interview with Petro-Canada official, January 1984.

16 National Energy Program, October 1980.

17 Interview with federal official, March 1984.

18 Interview with federal official, February 1984.

19 Interview with former APP official, March 1984.

20 Interview with former APP official, March 1984.

21 Interview with lawyer-intervenor at National Energy Board hearing, March 1984.

CHAPTER NINE

1 *World Conservation Strategy: Living Resource Conservation for Sustainable Development*, published in 1980 by the International Union for Conservation of Nature and Natural Resources (IUCN) in conjunction with the United Nations Environment Programme (UNEP), the World Wildlife Fund (WWF), and others.

2 *Canada's North 1970–1980* (Ottawa: Indian and Northern Affairs, 1972), 10. The other five goals were to provide for a higher standard of living, quality of life, and equality of opportunity for northern residents by methods compatible with their own preferences and aspirations; to encourage viable economic development within regions of the northern territories so as to realize their potential contribution to the national economy and the material well-being of Canadians; to realize the potential contribution of the northern territories to the social and cultural development of Canada; to maintain Canadian sovereignty and security in the north; and to develop fully leisure and recreational opportunities in northern territories.

3 Gurston Dacks, *A Choice of Futures* (Toronto: Methuen, 1981), 9.

4 "Ottawa Reverses Stand on Native Land Claims," *Globe and Mail*, 9 August 1973, and "Moral Lobby Outguns Industry at Pipeline Hearings," *ibid.*, 7 June 1976.

5 Letter dated 23 June 1982 from D.J. Gamble, Director Policy Studies, Canadian Arctic Resources Committee, to Pierre E. Trudeau.

6 Dacks, *A Choice*, 2.

7 *Northern Land Use Planning: Discussion Paper* (Ottawa: Indian and Northern Affairs Canada, 1981).

8 Agreement in principle between COPE and the federal government, signed December 1983.

9 Peter J. Usher, *Environmental Conservation, Wildlife Management and Native Rights in Northern Canada*, 16.

10 Dacks, *A Choice*, 208.

11 Yukon *Hansard*, 26 October 1983, 492–3.

12 Douglas H. Pimlott, Kitson M. Vincent, and Christine McKnight, eds., *Arctic Alternatives* (Ottawa: Canadian Arctic Resources Committee, 1973), 40.

13 Indian and Northern Affairs Canada, *Annual Report (1982–1983)* (Ottawa: DIAND, 1983), 8 and 17.

14 *Northern Perspectives*, July–August 1983 (published by the Canadian Arctic Resources Committee, Ottawa), 2.

15 *World Conservation Strategy.*

16 Hon. Chris Pearson, *Northern Perspectives*, July–August 1983, 3.

17 Herb Norwegian, *ibid.*, 6.

18 Brief to the Macdonald Commission on Canada's Future, presented by the Canadian Section of the Inuit Circumpolar Conference (ICC), 16 December 1983, 6.

19 *Yukon Indian Land Claim: A Fair Deal for Yukoners?* (Whitehorse: Government of Yukon, March 1983), 45.

20 *In All Fairness: A Native Claims Policy* (Ottawa: Indian and Northern Affairs Canada, 1981), 19.

21 John Meisel, "The Reformer and the Bureaucrat: A Remediable Dissonance?" Alan B. Plaunt Memorial Lecture, Carleton University, Ottawa, 8 April 1983, 3.

22 *A Comprehensive Conservation Policy and Strategy for the Northwest Territories and Yukon. Draft Discussion Paper* (Ottawa: Northern Environment Directorate, DIAND, October 1982), 17–18.

23 *Ibid.*

24 *Ibid.*, 5–6.

25 *In All Fairness*, 23.

26 Bob Mitchell, *Northern Perspectives*, July–August 1983, 5.

27 Private conversation with Robert Delury, chief negotiator for COPE, October 1983.

28 E.F. Roots, ed., *Lancaster Sound: Issues and Responsibilities. Report of an Environmental Science Workshop Held in November 1979* (Ottawa: Canadian Arctic Resources Committee, 1980).

29 Inuit Tapirisat of Canada, "Presentation to E.A.R.P.," Pond Inlet, NWT, October 1978, 4.

30 Letter to the Minister of Environment from D.W.I. Marshall, in *Report of the Environmental Assessment Panel: Lancaster Sound Drilling* (Ottawa: Federal Environmental Assessment Review Office, 1979), 2.

31 *Northern Perspectives*, July–August 1983, 3.

32 *Building Nunavut: A Discussion Paper Containing Proposals for an Arctic Constitution* (Ottawa: Nunavut Constitutional Forum, May 1983), 25.

33 The Yukon Conservation Society being the notable exception.

34 *Whitehorse Star*, 7 November 1983.

CHAPTER TEN

1 Canada, Senate, *Canada's Maritime Defence* (Ottawa: Supply and Services Canada, 1983), Appendix A, 101.

2 Department of National Defence, *Defence 83* (Ottawa: Supply and Services, 1984), 76.

3 *Ibid.*, 50.

4 For the purposes of this article, "high Arctic" is defined as those areas of Canada's north that lie north of the mainland.

5 For a recent listing of these exercises, see *Defence 83*, 55 and 76.

6 On 17 April 1985 it was announced that CFS Inuvik was to be closed.

7 *Defence 83*, 75.

8 Department of National Defence, *Defence 84* (Ottawa: Supply and Services, 1985), 79.

9 One of these rare instances occurred in September 1976, when one flew north to observe the Soviet-occupied ice island NP-22. More recently, a few fighter aircraft have landed and taken off at Yellowknife on a feasibility-testing basis.

10 *Canada's Maritime Defence*, 28.

11 Oral briefing by "G" Division to author.

12 "Canadian Coast Guard Proposed Operational Plan Framework" (unpublished, Ministry of Transport document, 1983 revised edition), 1.

13 *Ibid.*, 9.

14 Statutes of Canada, Arctic Waters Pollution Prevention Act, vol. 1, Eliz. 2 18–19, c. 47 s. 14.

15 *Ibid.*, s. 15, 3.

16 "Canadian Coast Guard," 11.

17 *Canada's Maritime Defence*, 92.

18 *Ibid.*, 51.

19 *Ibid.*, 92.

20 *Ibid.*, 52.

21 Canada, Department of Energy, Mines and Resources, *An Energy Strategy for Canada* (Ottawa 1976), 67.

22 W.H. Critchley and J.C. Stabler, *Fiscal Viability and Constitutional Evolution in the Yukon and Northwest Territories* (forthcoming).

23 Donat Pharand with Leonard H. Legault, *Northwest Passage: Arctic Straits* (Dordrecht: Martinus Nijhoff, 1984), 6–21.

24 *Ibid.* Also see figure 2 in the maps attached to the inside back cover of the book.

25 *Ibid.*, 148–9.

26 J.P. Steele, *Seadragon Northwest under the Ice* (New York: E.P. Dutton, 1962), and J. Calvert, "Skate's Breakthrough at the Pole," *Life* 46, no. 18 (4 May 1959).

27 Mark Arnold-Forster, "Russian Missile Subs Edge Nearer U.S.," *Manchester Guardian Weekly*, 6 March 1977.

28 See, for example, W.H. Critchley, "Polar Deployment of Soviet Submarines," *International Journal* 39 (Autumn 1984), 828–65.

29 Canada, "Memorandum of Understanding and Exchange of Notes on the Modernization of the North American Air Defence System" (March 1985).

30 See the original in Canada, *Gazette*, part II, 106, no. 16, *Arctic Waters Pollution Prevention Act, Shipping Safety Control Zones Order*, SOR/72-303, 2 August 1972, and Canada, *Gazette*, part II, 106, no. 20, *Arctic Waters Pollution Prevention Act, Arctic Shipping Pollution Prevention Regulations*, SOR/72-426, 10 October 1972, as well as subsequent revisions.

31 United Nations Convention on the Law of the Sea, section 8, Article 234.

32 An additional source of enforcement is the requirements set out by marine insurance underwriters before they will insure vessels going into high Arctic waters. However, the most influential underwiters – Lloyd's, for example – are not obliged to use Canadian standards.

33 The news, in June 1985, that a U.S. Coast Guard icebreaker planned to transit

294 Notes to pages 216–19

the Passage in August without asking the permission and assistance of Canadian authorities, and the fact that Canadian authorities could do little if anything in response, were a recent example of this problem. Although the government announced a series of counter-measures on 10 September 1986, aside from the establishment of straight baselines around the Arctic archipelago little of the announced response has so far been implemented.

CHAPTER ELEVEN

I am most grateful to the officials in the following departments who so readily gave of their time and expertise: Department of Transport (Canadian Coast Guard, Coast Guard Northern, Coast Guard Fleet Operations, and Polar Icebreaker Project Office), Department of Indian and Northern Affairs, Department of External Affairs, Department of National Defence, and Department of Energy, Mines and Resources. In addition, my appreciation to Capt. T.C. Pullen, RCN (ret), for his kind assistance.

1 There are three methods of rating a ship's power in horsepower. The power at the output shaft of an engine may be measured in brake horsepower (BHP) or shaft horsepower (SHP), depending on whether an absorption dynamometer such as a brake or a transmission dynamometer such as a torsion meter is used. In larger reciprocating engines, power is often measured in indicated horsepower (IHP), determined by the pressure in the cylinders. The metric measurement is expressed in kilowatts of shaft power (1 h.p. = 746 w).

2 Canada's icebreaker classifications include: "heavy icebreaker," "medium icebreaker," "medium icebreaking aid to navigation (navaid) vessel," and "light icebreaking navaid vessel." These classifications are based on the displacement of the icebreaker, the power-displacement ratio, and the capacity to maintain continuous movement through an icefield of varying depths. Thus, for example, the *John A. Macdonald*, displacing 9,307 tonnes, developing 11,185 kw shaft power, and capable of continuous headway through a metre of fast ice, is classed as a heavy icebreaker; the *N.B. McLean*, displacing 4,869 tonnes and developing 4,800 kw shaft power, is a medium icebreaker; the *J.E. Bernier*, at 3,150 tonnes and 3,169 kw, is a "medium navaids" icebreaker; the *Simon Fraser* is a "light icebreaking aid to navigation vessel" – it displaces 1,374 tonnes and develops 2,162 kw shaft power.

3 Donald Creighton, *Canada's First Century, 1867–1967* (Toronto: Macmillan of Canada, 1970), 21.

4 PC 244, 4 April 1876. See Canada, Transport Canada, Canadian Marine Transportation Administration, Marine Policy and Planning, "Canadian Government Icebreaking Policy: An Administrative and Historical Review," by Thomas E. Appleton, mimeo., Ottawa, February 1978, appendix.

5 T.C. Pullen, "The Development of Arctic Ships," in Morris Zaslow, ed., *A*

Century of Canada's Arctic Islands, 1880–1980, 23rd symposium (Ottawa: Royal Society of Canada, 1981), 157.

6 For a discussion of the technological – and therefore the commercial – dominance of the yards in Paisley, Dundee, and Barrow-in-Furness in this early period, see Canada, Department of Transport, *Usque ad Mare: A History of the Canadian Coast Guard and Marine Services*, by Thomas E. Appleton (Ottawa: 1968), 178–9.

7 PC 748, 14 March 1914, authorized the expenditure of $998,000 to Canadian Vickers. The *J.D. Hazen* was completed in 1916 but immediately sold to Russia.

8 Pullen notes that when "labouring in fast ice three to six feet thick, she consumes oil at the rate of 180 tons a day. Diesel/electric icebreakers would burn one-third of that or less"; "Development of Arctic Ships," 158.

9 James Eayrs, "The Foreign Policy of Canada," in Joseph E. Black and Kenneth W. Thompson, eds., *Foreign Policies in a World of Change* (New York: Harper & Row, 1963), 676; also J. Gellner, "The Military Task: Sovereignty and Security, Surveillance and Control in the Far North," in E.J. Dosman, ed., *The Arctic in Question* (Toronto: Oxford University Press, 1976), 85.

10 See A.H.G. Storrs, "East Arctic Marine Resupply," in Canada, Department of Transport, *Arctic Transport* (Ottawa) 2 (February 1971), 88–9; also T.A. Hockin and P.A. Brennan, "Canada's Arctic and Its Strategic Importance," in Dosman, ed., *The Arctic in Question*, 109.

11 Canada, Department of Transport, Press Release 140/81, 5 August 1981.

12 *Globe and Mail*, 30 September 1983; also Canadian Shipbuilding and Ship Repairing Association, "Production Summary for the First Three Quarters of 1983," Ottawa, 7 November 1983.

13 For example, the *Pierre Radisson* was dispatched to Lake Superior in April 1979 to cut a path for five lakers and an ocean-going vessel carrying wheat for export; Department of Transport, Press Release 79/79, 3 April 1979.

14 In 1960, government procurement comprised 27 per cent of the construction in Canadian yards; by 1970, that figure had dropped to 2 per cent. For an examination of some of the problems faced by the shipbuilding industry, see Canada, Sector Task Force on the Canadian Shipbuilding and Repair Industry, *Final Report*, 1978; also Transport Canada, Coast Guard, *Tri-Annual Status Report*, 1 April 1982.

15 Canadian Shipbuilding and Ship Repairing Association, "Canadian Shipbuilding, Ship Repairing and Allied Industries: The Challenge, Problems and Solutions," submission to the Royal Commission on the Economic Union and Development Prospects for Canada (Macdonald Commission), 12 December 1983, 8.

16 Canada, Department of Industry, Trade and Commerce/Department of Regional Economic Expansion, "Canada's Shipbuilding Industry: Performance, Prospects and Policy Options," *Background Paper* (Ottawa 1982).

17 *Globe and Mail*, 30 September 1983, B1.

18 *Ibid.*, 13 December 1983, 10.

19 The following is based on my discussions with officials and T.C. Pullen, an Arctic navigator and former commander of HMCS *Labrador*. For the uninitiated southerner, a useful complete introduction to the severities of Arctic (and Antarctic) ice conditions is Edwin A. MacDonald, *Polar Operations* (Annapolis, MD: United States Naval Institute, 1969). Illustrations and a glossary are included.

20 See the description in G.J. German, "Bulk Shipping and Icebreaker Support in the Arctic," *Arctic Transportation* 3, 178–9.

21 Pullen, "Development of Arctic Ships," 159.

22 Arctic Shipping Pollution Prevention Regulations, chaps 353–6, *Consolidated Regulations of Canada, 1978*.

23 Pullen, "Development of Arctic Ships," 160, table II, note b. A comparable assumption is made by the Report of the Subcommittee on National Defence of the Senate's Standing Committee on Foreign Affairs, *Canada's Maritime Defence* (Ottawa, May 1983), 50, and J.W. Langford, "Marine Science, Technology, and the Arctic: Some Questions and Guidelines for the Federal Government," in Dosman, ed., *The Arctic in Question*, fn. 9.

24 The Arctic Waters Pollution Prevention Act, passed in April 1970, was not proclaimed immediately because it was discovered that the regulations made under the act would have made liability provisions so costly that no shipping company would sail to Churchill, Manitoba. By 1972, new insurance provisions had been rewritten after consultations with London-based insurance groups.

25 Canada, Parliament, House of Commons, Standing Committee on Indian Affairs and Northern Development, *Minutes of Evidence and Proceedings*, 28th Parl., 3rd Sess., issues 1–4, 10, 11, 13, and especially 25.

26 See T.C. Pullen, "Arctic Marine Transportation: A View from the Bridge," *Northern Perspectives* 11 (December 1983), 6.

27 Langford, "Marine Science and the Arctic," 166.

28 The details are outlined by the former project manager: I.K. Leslie, "The Polar Icebreaker Project and Its Impact on the Canadian Shipbuilding and Allied Industries," in Canadian Shipbuilding and Ship Repairing Association, *Prelude to a New Canadian Shipbuilding Era: Opportunities and Plans*, papers presented to the 34th annual technical conference (Ottawa, March 1982).

29 Department of Transport, Press Release 39/78, 6 March 1978; also the Department of Transport's cabinet discussion paper, "Polar Icebreaker Program," TC 31-80, 27 October 1980.

30 Department of Transport, Cabinet discussion paper, TC 31-80, 27 October 1980.

31 Department of Transport, Press Release 64/81, 22 April 1981.

32 Because contract negotiations were continuing at the time of writing, neither government nor industry officials were prepared to disclose which yards would be funded. However, given the size of the Polar 8, it may be assumed that Burrard Yarrows, Davie Shipbuilding, and Saint John Shipbuilding would be chosen.

33 Langford, "Marine Science and the Arctic," 166.
34 "The government," declared Cliff McIsaac, the parliamentary secretary to the Minister of Transport, in January 1975, "does not foresee a firm requirement for polar icebreakers before the early 1980s"; Canada, Parliament, House of Commons, *Debates*, 30th Parl., 1st Sess., vol. 3, 2489.
35 Leslie, "Polar Icebreaker Project."
36 A good indication of this negative attitude towards the "public good" argument was the comment of a Department of Finance official to Langford in 1975: he "asked me what would be wrong with a situation where U.S. and German icebreaking cargo vessels were the exclusive users of high Arctic waterways." See Langford, "Marine Science and the Arctic," 186. Plus ça change: by 1984, program department officials were complaining that the central agents were "underselling" the sovereignty argument.
37 The envelope system, introduced by the Conservative government in 1979, was supposed to reduce interdepartmental quarrelling over the allocation of resources. The polar icebreaker case suggests that unless Ministers in Cabinet specify clearly and unambiguously their preferences, interdepartmental feuding over budgets will not abate.
38 For an examination of the new fighter aircraft program, and the importance of ministerial decisions in narrowing the "rules of the game" for the different bureaux, see Michael M. Atkinson and Kim Richard Nossal, "Bureaucratic Politics and the New Fighter Aircraft Decisions," *Canadian Public Administration* 24 (Winter 1981), 531–62.
39 R.G.A. Lawrence, "Canadian and International Icebreaker Needs and Technology," paper presented to the Marine Technology Society, Newfoundland and Labrador Section, St John's, undated [1979], 8, outlines the roles planned by the Coast Guard in the mid-1970s: escort and assistance of liquefied natural gas (LNG) and oil carriers, support of Arctic supply ships, support to drilling, ice surveillance, research and development projects for industry and government, pollution monitoring and clean-up, support to transport of minerals, support to pipelaying, and search and rescue operations and marine aid.
40 Department of Transport, "Polar Icebreaker Program," TC-31, October 1980.
41 For a discussion of commercial icebreaking developments in the late 1970s, see Pullen, "Development of Arctic Ships." It should be noted that the recession and reverses in the fortunes of Dome in the early 1980s have to a certain extent overtaken Pullen's description.

CHAPTER TWELVE

1 In the U.S. view, the waters of the Canadian archipelago consist of high seas except for a 12-mile band of territorial waters around each island and off the mainland shores. As a State Department official summarized it in July 1985,

"The American legal position has always held that the Northwest Passage is an international waterway"; *Maclean's*, 22 July 1985, 10. The voyage of the *Polar Sea* was made for reasons of operational efficiency, to allow the vessel to complete scheduled tasks including support for u.s. Navy underwater acoustic research in the western Arctic, as well as the unforeseen need first to assist the resupply of the u.s. military base in Thule, Greenland. Evidently the u.s. government, and no doubt the Navy in particular, concluded that work to be done in the western Arctic took precedence over the maintenance of good relations with Canada. Washington did, however, make an effort to reduce the potential for confrontation inherent in the voyage of the *Polar Sea*. The u.s. Coast Guard co-operated with its Canadian counterpart in providing information on the voyage and in taking Canadian observers aboard. As well, the State Department asserted that the voyage was not a challenge to Canada's claim of jurisdiction and was being conducted without prejudice to the legal position of either country. This last point was made clear in a State Department press guidance issued on 14 June 1985, the day after the Canadian public first learned of the impending transit from a page seven piece in the *Globe and Mail*. The u.s. government thus did everything but ask for permission to make the transit. In so doing, it put Canada in the position of having to grant permission that had not been sought.

2 See Appendix.

3 A great but not necessarily a complete setback for all Canadians. The Arctic Pilot Project episode indicates that Canada may also be in process of acquiring a maritime as well as a coastal state perspective on Arctic marine transportation issues. For the Passage to be treated as an international strait could well mesh with the corporate interests of Dome Canada, Petro-Canada, and the oil multinationals in less stringent and time-consuming regulation of the environmental and social effects of commercial shipping. The same could also apply to the government of Canada insofar as it might wish to export Beaufort Sea oil or high Arctic natural gas to Western Europe or Japan. Chapter 5 in this volume indicates that in the early 1970s the Department of Transport in particular had an inclination to endorse the American view of the Passage as an international strait.

4 The emergence of an active American interest in the Passage as an international strait coincided *inter alia* with the deployment of its nuclear submarine force. During the 1950s, the United States had requested authorization to enter Canadian waters for its vessels engaged in supply operations to various sites, including DEW Line stations. Access arrangements were made at annual meetings between representatives of the u.s. and Canadian Coast Guards, which as today had an easy working relationship and were on the whole left to work things out for themselves. Then, in 1958–9, the Diefenbaker government took over the operation and resupply of DEW Line stations, and in 1960 the USS *Seadragon* made a publicized transit of the Passage. By the early 1960s, and in

the wake of the Second United Nations Conference on the Law of the Sea, the Department of External Affairs and the Department of State had begun to occupy themselves with questions of access and jurisdiction, and differences over the status of the Passage became increasingly clear. In 1963–4, the Pearson government indicated to Washington an interest in enclosing the waters of the Arctic archipelago as internal waters but desisted in the face of strong U.S. reaction. Information for this note is culled from a variety of sources, including J.L. Granatstein, "A Fit of Absence of Mind: Canada's National Interest in the North to 1968," in E.J. Dosman, ed., *The Arctic in Question* (Toronto: Oxford University Press, 1976), 28–9, and an interview with Gordon W. Smith, retired but active historian, Ottawa, 19 April 1985.

5 However, it might be concluded in Washington that in view of Canada's inability to control and defend its Arctic waters, the Soviets would enjoy more or less free access for their nuclear attack submarines whether or not Canada's exclusive jurisdiction were recognized by the United States. For Washington to acknowledge Canadian sovereignty could thus be thought to work against the U.S. interest: Canada would gain a say in American submarine operations in the archipelago and could in principle order their cessation, whereas the Soviets would remain unencumbered in their subsurface activities. Indeed, Moscow might be thought to have the option of deploying ballistic missile-firing and long-range sea-launched cruise missile (SLCM) submarines into the Canadian archipelago, which could become something of a sanctuary for Soviet strategic nuclear forces in the absence of a countering American effect. International strait status for the Passage might accordingly be seen to leave the Soviet navy where it is and to advance the strategic ASW interests of the American naval establishment. However, from a U.S. Air Force point of view, international strait status could well complicate the strategic defence of North America if transit passage rights gave Soviet bombers with air-launched cruise missiles a free ride over the more southern Arctic waters of North America. Indeed, if Fury and Hecla Strait is to be regarded as one of the passages of the Northwest Passage, Hudson Bay, which Canada regards as its internal waters, could conceivably be internationalized. If Hudson Bay is a high seas area, why not James Bay as well? Quite apart from SLCM-carrying submarine deployments into these southerly waters, the Soviet Union could be entitled in peacetime and crisis to fly ALCM-equipped strategic bombers right down to Moose Factory if it wished. The implications of straits status for continental air defence are troubling.

6 Department of State, press guidance, 14 June 1985, and see Appendix.

7 Canada does not have an effective capability to monitor transits by U.S., Soviet, or other nuclear submarines, and strictly speaking it is not known for a fact that American nuclear attack submarines are currently making use of Canadian Arctic waters. The Deputy Chief of Naval Operations for Submarine Warfare has, however, noted: "Today's SSNs thread narrow passages in hostile Arctic

waters scarcely 30 or 40 feet under the ice pack and with a similar distance between the keel and the ocean floor"; Vice-Admiral N.R. Thunman, "Diesel Submarines for the u.s. Navy?" *Proceedings*, u.s. Naval Institute, August 1985, 137. Thunman asserts that the Arctic operations of American SSNs are confined to international waters, but such is the status of the Passage in the u.s. view. In a list of "announced" Arctic submarine operations, mention is made of the voyage of the uss *Archerfish* into Baffin Bay and Nares Strait between Ellesmere Island and Greenland in 1979; Norman Polmar, "Sailing under the Ice," *ibid.*, June 1984, p. 122. For further comment on the u.s. strategic naval interest in the waters of the Canadian archipelago, see note 7, chap. 1.

8 Agreement between the Government of Canada and the Government of the Kingdom of Denmark for Cooperation Relating to the Marine Environment, Copenhagen, August 26, 1983 (in force on the same date). As yet unpublished, the text of this agreement is available from the Department of External Affairs, Ottawa. Canada and the United States have also been conducting annual reviews, at the official level, of hydrocarbon and related developments in the Beaufort Sea and environs for some years now. These meetings could provide a point of departure for a bilateral effort to develop consensual knowledge necessary to the creation of a surface shipping regulatory regime in the western Arctic waters of North America and then for the region as a whole.

9 The pattern of recent years is evident in the following: the 1983 agreement to permit testing in the Canadian north of u.s. air-launched cruise missiles (ALCMs), the most recent tests being widened (January 1986) to develop the capacity to track and defend against Soviet ALCMs flying south over Canada; the 1985 agreement on modernization of the DEW Line, now called the North Warning System, for purposes of improved defence and deterrence against Soviet strategic bomber and long-range ALCM attack; the construction of five Arctic bases for Canada's CF-18 interceptor aircraft and presumably u.s. interceptors in event of need; lengthening of runways at two locations to support the operation of u.s. airborne early warning command and control (AWACS) aircraft, also performing an anti-bomber and anti-ALCM role; a request for an additional low-level flight training area for B-52 bombers north of Cold Lake, Alberta; the unfolding of the u.s. Strategic Defence Initiative and its potential to draw Canada into integrated continental defence arrangements, including possible forward-based ground defences against Soviet ballistic missile attack, plus a concomitant need for more active air defences to counter Soviet strategic bomber and cruise-missile capabilities in the event that Moscow assigned priority to coming in under an anti-ballistic missile dome of protection; and a probable increase in the use of Canada's Arctic waters by u.s. attack submarines for purposes of transit to the Arctic Ocean and Barents Sea in performance of deterrence and defence missions, and in order to deny the use of these waters to Soviet nuclear submarines.

10 See, for example, Gurston Dacks, *A Choice of Futures: Politics in the Canadian North* (Toronto: Methuen, 1981), 208-11.

11 Several months before the government of Canada's announcement of 10 September 1985, which formally enclosed the Canadian Arctic archipelago as of 1 January 1986, the Soviet government would seem to have enclosed two Arctic archipelagos surrounding Vilkitsky Strait and Laptev Strait on the Northern Sea Route of the Soviet Union. The Soviet announcement, as yet not readily available, is contained in what appears to be USSR Notice to Mariners 4450, which refers to a Council of Ministers decree of 15 January 1985.

12 Louis-Edmond Hamelin, *Canadian Nordicity: It's Your North, Too*, translated by William Barr (Montreal: Harvest House, 1979), 4–6.

13 I am relying here on Chauncey C. Loomis, "The Arctic Sublime," in U.C. Knoepflmacher and G.B. Tennyson, eds., *Nature and the Victorian Imagination* (Berkeley: University of California Press, 1977), 95–112, and on 98 for the two phrases quoted.

Contributors

PETER BURNET is senior policy adviser in the Circumpolar Affairs Directorate of the Department of Indian and Northern Affairs. A lawyer by training, and previously executive director of the Canadian Arctic Resources Committee, he has served as legal and political adviser to national Indian and Inuit organizations in Canada.

W. HARRIET CRITCHLEY is associate professor of political science and director of the Strategic Studies Programme at the University of Calgary. Her research interests include Canadian defence and Arctic security issues.

FRANKLYN GRIFFITHS is professor of political science at the University of Toronto. The author of *A Northern Foreign Policy* (1979), he writes on Arctic and international security and Soviet affairs.

PETER JULL is a consultant and adviser on Arctic native and constitutional issues. He has worked in the Privy Council Office on northern and native affairs and since 1979 has provided staff support for various Canadian Inuit organizations and the Inuit Circumpolar Conference.

JOHN KIRTON is associate professor of political science at the University of Toronto. Co-author of *Canada as a Principal Power* (1983), he has written extensively on Canadian-American relations and Canadian foreign policy decision-making.

JENNIFER LEWINGTON is a member of the Washington bureau of the *Globe and Mail*. From 1981 to 1984 she reported from Ottawa on national energy affairs for the same newspaper.

D.M. MCRAE is professor of international law at the University of British Columbia. From 1983 to 1986 he was academic in residence at the Department of External Affairs, Ottawa.

D O N   M U N T O N is visiting professor of political science at the University of British Columbia. His research interests centre on environmental protection and Canadian-American relations.

K I M   R I C H A R D   N O S S A L is associate professor of political science at McMaster University. The author of *The Politics of Canadian Foreign Policy* (1985), he has also studied the Canadian weapons acquisition process.

L A R S   T O F T   R A S M U S S E N is diplomatic correspondent with the Danish national news agency, Ritazu. From 1981 to 1984 he lived and worked in Nuuk, Greenland, first as a reporter with Grønlandsposten and then as press secretary for the Inuit Circumpolar Conference.

G R A H A M   R O W L E Y is research professor at the Institute of Canadian Studies, Carleton University. Among his accomplishments, he carried out the original exploration of part of the western coast of Baffin Island from 1936 to 1939, was scientific adviser to the Department of Indian Affairs and Northern Development in later years, and served as consultant aboard the *Lindblad Explorer* and *World Discoverer* in their transits of the Northwest Passage in 1984 and 1985.

O R A N   R .   Y O U N G , a political scientist, is director of the Center for Northern Studies in Wolcott, Vermont. In addition to his work on the Arctic, he studies social choice, conflict resolution, and property rights.

Index

Aboriginal peoples: and Arctic exploration, 35–6; and environmentalism, 181–5; and hydrocarbons, 117–18; Independence I culture of, 135; land claims of, 187–90; rights of, 187–8, 193–4; Small Tool Tradition of, 25, 35; Thule people, 25, 135–7. *See also* Inuit

Advisory Committee on Northern Development (ACND), 71

Aklavik, 38

Alaska, 9, 25, 41, 44, 45, 77, 122, 126, 164, 197; Arctic National Wildlife Refuge of, 118; Highway, 39, 40, 43; Inuit in, 46–8; land claims settlement, 47; Native Review Commission, 47; North Slope of, 34, 46, 47

Alaska Boundary Commission, 37

Alberta, 74, 164, 167, 174, 175, 177

Alberta Gas Trunk Ltd (AGTL/Nova), 166–7

Alert, 201

Alpha Ridge, 122

Alsands oil project, 164, 178–9

Amundsen, Roald, 4, 37, 39; first crossing of Passage by, 27, 30

Antarctic Treaty, 128, 244–6; and demilitarization, 245; as model for dispute settlement, 128, 132, 244–7; non-prejudicial provisions of, 128

Anti-submarine warfare (ASW), Arctic, 5, 9n7, 244n5; airborne, 10, 249; as Canadian option, 250–1, 252; U.S. interest in, 119

APP. *See* Arctic Pilot Project

Arctic, 17–18, 46, 257–9; climate change in, 34; increased strategic significance of, 119, 255; legal concepts for, 127; regional perspective on, 257–9, 263. *See also* Arctic sublime

Arctic animals: Bowhead whale, 121; caribou, 46, 144; cod, 142–3; harp seal, 26; musk-ox, 25; narwhal, 26; polar bear, 144, 146; salmon, 104; seals, 143–4, 151, 156; walrus, 25; whales, 25, 32, 144, 151, 155, 156

Arctic Bay, 169

Arctic birds, 32, 194

"Arctic exception." *See* Article 234

Arctic Institute of North America, 74

Arctic Pilot Project (APP), 5, 49, 50, 120, 134, 156, 182, 254; analogy with *Manhattan*, 259–60; consortium, 166–8, 171–2, 176; Danish opposition to, 152–5; economics of, 170–1, 173, 176–7; and environmental risk, 152, 155; and foreign technology, 169; Greenlandic opposition to, 49, 148–55; and ICC, 154; and Inuit way of life, 170; lessons of, 178–80; market strategy of, 170–1, 173, 175–8; National Energy Board hearings on, 150–1, 154, 168, 170, 175–8; objectives of, 163–6, 168; Ontario opposition to, 60, 175–6; origins of, 164–7; proposed route of, 168; and ship building industry, 169; technological challenge of, 168–9; as threat to Greenland, 134–5; working group, 152–3

Arctic shipping control zones, 88, 226–8

Arctic Shipping Pollution Prevention Regulations (ASPPR), 226–7, 232

Arctic sublime, 17–18, 242, 252, 265–8; alternative vision to, 266–8; myth of, 267–8; political consequences of, 265–7

Arctic Waters Pollution Prevention Act, 67, 70, 87, 88, 90, 101, 115, 127, 204, 205, 212, 226–7; and Coast Guard, 205; as embodied in Article 234, 110, 114; and exercise of sovereignty, 86, 93; gaining international acceptance of, 94, 102–3; initial U.S. response to, 94–6; and ICJ, 89–90, 127–8; novelty of, 101–2; regulations of, 106; U.S. view of, 112–13, 115

Arktika (Brezhnev), 226

Arrow, 85

Article 234, 115, 127, 264–5; and APP, 153–4; assessed, 112–14; and Canada-Denmark marine environment agreement, 254; negotiation of, 104–12; and Passage, 212, 247, 250

Atlantic Ritchfield Company (ARCO), 77, 157

Audubon Society of America, 9

Aurora aircraft, 201, 203, 205

Australia, 105

AWACS (airborne warning and control aircraft), 210

Axel Heiberg Island, 37, 226

Baffin, William, 26

Baffin Bay, 30, 32, 130, 134, 135, 168, 194, 254

Baffin Island, 26, 36, 38, 52, 153

Baffin Regional Inuit Association (BRIA), 175

Ball, George, 85

Ballistic Missile Early Warning System (BMEWS), 210

Barrow, 34, 47, 48, 56, 57

Barrow Strait, 30, 31, 67; as anti-submarine barrier site, 250; Canadian territorial water in, 82, 92; Inuit hunting on, 33

Beaufort Sea, 9, 19, 34, 37, 54, 121, 167, 212; drilling in, 121; environmental assessment, 50, 60; hydrocarbon reserves of, 11, 116, 165, 172, 206–7; movement of ice pack in, 32

Beesley, J. Alan, 91, 111

Bell, Joel, 176

Bell, Michael, 166

Berger, Thomas, 47, 181, 197

Bering Sea, 9, 27, 46, 55, 211

Bering Strait, 27, 31, 211, 212

Bernier, J.E., 37

Black Angel Mine, 144

Blair, Robert, 166

Bowie, Douglas, 150

Bretton Woods, 132

British Petroleum, 77

Button, Thomas, 26

Bylot, Robert, 26

Cabot, John, 8, 12, 26

Cadieux, Léo, 76, 78, 91

Cambridge Bay, 33

Cameron Island, 5, 253

Canada: acceptance of foreign shipping in Passage, 13–14, 76, 241, 271; Arctic dilemmas of, 16, 20, 241, 248, 253, 263; Arctic Expedition of 1913–18, 37–8; Arctic Islands Preserve, 38; and development of international law, 70, 81, 90, 92; Fisheries Act, 83; and Greenland, 158, 253–4; icebreaker decision-making of, 218–19, 224–5, 228–38, 260–1; icebreaking capabilities of, 85, 91, 92–3, 168, 204–5, 216–24, 226; and ICJ jurisdiction,

15–16, 88–9, 92; land-use policy of, 184–5; liberal internationalist traditions of, 70, 79, 96, 97; northern development of, 39–44; northern politics of, 183–4; Shipping Act, 84, 205; Standing Committee on External Affairs and National Defence (SCEAND), 74; Standing Committee on Indian Affairs and Northern Development (SCIAND), 78, 228. *See also* Passage; Sovereignty, Canadian Arctic

Canadian Arctic archipelago. *See* Passage

Canadian Arctic Resources Committee (CARC), 9, 150, 168, 198

Canadian Rangers, 75, 201, 202

Canadian Wildlife Federation, 86, 188

Carrothers Report, 53

C.D. Howe, 43

CF-18 fighter aircraft, 210

Chesterfield Inlet, 36

China Sea, 116

Chrétien, Jean, 73, 76, 91, 97, 180, 181

Christensen, Mads, 154

Chukchi Sea, 9, 47, 55

Churchill, Man., 36, 220, 224

Clark, Joe, viii, 50, 223, 269

Clear, Alaska, 210

Clerke, Charles, 27

Coast Guard, Canadian, 168, 200, 204–5, 206, 211; Arctic responsibilities of, 204–5; and polar icebreaker acquisition, 228–36

Coast Guard, U.S., 71, 72, 241n1

Cold Lake oil sands project, 164, 179

Committee of Original Peoples Entitlement (COPE), 54–5, 184, 193, 197

Consensual knowledge, 15, 250, 261

Conservation. *See* Pollution prevention

Continental margin, 17, 104

Continental shelf, 73, 74, 87–8, 91

Convention for the Protection of the Mediterranean Sea against Pollution, 129

Convention on the Protection of the Marine Environment of the Baltic Sea, 129

Convention on the Territorial Sea and Contiguous Zone, 99, 105

Cook, James, 27

Council for Yukon Indians, 197

Cruise missiles, 119, 255n9; air-launched (ALCMS), 10, 209, 244n5, 255n9; sea-launched (SLCMS), 10, 244n5, 276n5

Davie Shipbuilding, 172

Davis, John, 26

Davis Strait, 9, 33, 130, 135, 157, 158, 245, 254

Denmark, 9, 10, 11, 95, 119, 125, 131; Danish National Oil and Gas Company, 151; and Greenland, 48–9, 135–40; Joint Council on Mineral Resources, 144; responsiveness to Greenlandic interests, 11, 135, 146–8, 157, 254; and transit management regime, 11, 244–5, 247, 254

Defence, Canadian Arctic, 40–2, 73, 76, 78, 80, 82, 200–3, 208–10; and armed neutrality, 251; and Eurocentrism, 256; strategic perspective on, 255–7; and voyages of *Manhattan*, 73n6

Defence, Department of National (DND), 200–1; Arctic capabilities of, 202–3; and icebreaker acquisition, 235; and *Manhattan*

voyages, 75, 76, 78, 82, 91; Northern Patrol flights of, 201; and sovereignty, 236

Devolution, northern political, 185–8

d'Iberville, 221, 222, 223

Diefenbaker, John G., 179; "northern vision" of, 21, 43

Distant Early Warning (DEW) radar line, 10, 42, 81, 119, 201–2, 209–10, 222, 224. *See also* North Warning System

Distributive bargaining, 115, 129

Dome Petroleum, 4, 5, 120, 164, 165, 171, 172, 237

Drake Point, 81, 163, 167

East Greenland Current, 32

Eastern Arctic Patrol, 38, 39, 43

Ecosystems, Arctic, 97, 121, 232

Edge, Geoffrey, 175

Edge, Hans, 137

Energy, Mines and Resources (EMR), Department of, 72, 75; and APP, 164, 173–4; and icebreaker acquisition, 234–5; and *Manhattan* voyages, 72, 78, 82–3, 87–8; and pipelines, 82

Environment, Arctic marine, 32–4, 121–2, 126, 170; and anti-submarine warfare, 252; Canadian-Danish agreement on, 254; custodianship of, 70, 81, 92, 97; and Inuit way of life, 33–4, 122, 134–5, 170; proposed conference on, 70, 94–5; shipping risk to, 14, 32–3, 121, 126, 170, 263

Environment Canada, 191, 192

Environmentalism, 110, 121, 181, 182–3, 264; and aboriginal rights, 181–5,

193–4, 261–2; and bureaucracy, 189–93; northern perspective on, 198–9, 262–3; and political devolution, 186–7, 196–7; and resource management, 185. *See also* Transit management regime

Erebus, 27, 31

Ernest Lapointe, 220

Ertl, Joseph, 143

Eskimo. *See* Inuit

Evensen Group, 108–9

Exclusive economic zone, 17, 107–8, 109, 113, 211

Exercise Muskox, 40–1

External Affairs, Department of (DEA), 72, 75, 78, 107, 253; and APP, 174; and icebreaker acquisition, 235; Legal Bureau of, 111, 253; and *Manhattan* voyages, 72, 78, 83

EXXON, 70

Faroe Islands, 139

Finland, 95, 166

Fisheries and Oceans, Department of, 189, 191, 192

Fishing zones, 67, 73, 77, 87, 100, 143

Foighel, Isi, 139

Forrestal, J.M., 228

France, 4, 249; and APP, 174, 176, 178; LNG technology of, 169; nuclear propulsion technology of, 229, 233

Franklin, Sir John, 3, 27, 34, 266

Frigate, Canadian Patrol, 224

Frobisher, Martin, 26

Frobisher Bay (Iqaluit), 150, 201, 204

Fury and Hecla Strait, 31, 33; biological richness of, 32; as shipping route, 32, 153

Gallagher, Jack, 12

Gauss, 37

German and Milne Ltd, 229

Germany, East, 148

Germany, West, 4, 19, 229, 255, 256; and APP, 174, 176, 178; and Greenland, 142–3
Gibraltar, 76
Gilbert, Sir Humfrey, 12
Gjoa, 4, 27, 30, 37
Gjoa Haven, 33
Gotlieb, Allan, 89
Greene, Joe, 87
Greenland, 5, 9, 10, 11, 14, 25, 30, 32, 131, 174, 253–4; Atassut Party of, 140, 155; cod dispute with West Germany, 134–5, 142–3; and EC, 134–5, 146–7; economy of, 141–5; foreign relations of, 145–9; history of, 48–9, 135–8; home rule in, 33, 48–9, 135, 138, 139–40; Inuit Ataqatigiit Party of, 140–1, 145, 157; and ICC, 49, 149; Jameson Land, oil exploration in, 135, 145, 155–7, 158; and NATO, 148; opposition to APP, 49, 134–5, 149–55, 174; renewable-resources way of life in, 134, 142–4, 151, 156; Siumut Party of, 140; strategic significance of, 147–8, 158
Greenland Sea, 211
Griffon, 222
Grise Fiord, 150, 169
Gromyko, A.A., 80
Group of 77, 107
Gulf Canada, 197–8
Gulf of Mexico, 116
Gulf Stream, 32

Hamelin, Louis-Edmond, 265, 267
Haze, Arctic, 126
Head, Ivan, 83, 88, 91, 95
Hearne, Samuel, 27
Hedtoft, Hans, 137
Herschel Island, 32, 77
Hetherington, Charles, 167
Hibernia oilfield, 19, 118, 173

Holman Island, 33–4, 52
Hopper, Wilbert, 164–5, 170, 172, 174, 176
Hopson, Eben, 47, 56, 60
Hudson, Henry, 26
Hudson Strait, 31, 32
Hudson's Bay Company, 27, 35, 39, 41, 53
Humble Oil, 70–1, 77
Hydrocarbons, Arctic, 11–12, 19, 116, 206–7, 233; discoveries of, 11, 44, 70, 116, 118, 165; economics of, 5, 11, 77, 116–17, 170–1, 173, 175–7; and energy independence, 117, 118, 119–20; exploration for, 135, 145, 157; transportation of, 4, 5, 11–12, 19–20, 70–1, 83, 116, 165–6, 207, 232
Hydrographic charting, 34

Ice reconnaissance, 35
Icebergs, 30
Icebreakers, Canadian Arctic, 42, 44, 78, 155, 205; classification of, 226–7; and DND, 206, 221; and *Manhattan* voyages, 71–2, 92; nuclear option for, 228–9, 232–3; and shipbuilding industry, 223–5, 236–7; "summer visitors only," 44, 226
Icebreaking, 78, 220–3, 225–7; Canadian tendencies in, 224–5; Greenlandic restrictions on, 134; history of, in Canada, 216–24
Icebreaking tankers, 116, 156, 165, 167. *See also* Arctic Pilot Project; *Manhattan*
Icy Cape, 27, 32
Igloolik, 33
IHI (Ishikawajima-Harima Heavy Industries), 19
Imperial Oil, 174
Independent Petroleum Association, 74
Indian Affairs and Northern

Development, Department of (DIAND), 181, 194; and Lancaster Sound studies, 194–6; land-use policy of, 191, 193; mandate of, 189–90; and *Manhattan* voyages, 72, 75, 82, 84, 88
Indonesia, 76, 106
Innocent passage, 76, 78, 79, 82, 100, 105n30; defined, 72n5
Integrative bargaining, 115, 129
International Court of Justice (ICJ), 15, 21, 214, 245; Canada and jurisdiction of, 67, 88–90, 92, 101–2, 127–8, 241; *Fisheries Case*, 99; and future of Passage, 242, 247, 251; reason to avoid, 249
International Maritime Consultative Organization (IMCO), 76, 80, 82, 102, 103, 104, 108, 109
International Monetary Fund, 132
International Polar Year: first, 36; second, 39
International Seabed Authority, 132
Inuit, 9, 15, 46, 55; in Alaska, 46–8; and Arctic shipping, 49, 148–55, 169–70, 174, 175, 261–2, 263–4; and Canadian Arctic waters sovereignty, 56, 243, 248; claims of, 170, 184, 262; concentrated into villages, 48, 52, 137; dependence on sea, 33–4, 50, 83, 122; desire for political change, 60–1; in Greenland, 48–9, 135–8; and industrialization, 62, 121–2, 262; in Labrador, 49–50; and Lancaster Sound, 195–6; and marine management, 33, 47–8, 50, 53–4, 55, 56, 61, 191; in NWT,

52–4; sense of powerless-
ness among, 14, 61; Soviet,
57; in Western Arctic,
54–5
Inuit Circumpolar Con-
ference (ICC), 9, 47, 49, 122,
254; and Alaskan funding,
57, 58; and APP, 60, 62,
149, 154, 174; charter of,
57–8; environmental
concerns of, 56–7; and local
self-government, 56–7,
60; Soviet absence from, 57
Inuit Tapirisat of Canada
(ITC), 169–70, 175
Inupiat, 47
Inuvik, 201, 204
Itteqqortoormiit (Scores-
bysund), 156, 157

Jacobs, Peter, 196
James Bay Agreement, 51,
184
Jameson Land. See
Greenland
Jamieson, Don, 76, 80, 85,
87, 91
Japan, 4, 11, 12, 107, 131,
169, 223, 256; as poten-
tial surrogate for the U.S.,
90; as potential user of
Passage, 19–20, 255
J.D. Hazen, 219, 225
Johansen, Lars Emil, 142,
145, 150, 157
Johansson, Bengt, 172
John A. Macdonald, 72, 77,
221, 222, 223, 228
John Cabot, 220, 222
Johnson, Alexis, 76, 91
Jones Sound: as anti-
submarine barrier site,
250
Jorgensen, Anker, 143, 146,
147
Jurisdiction: definition of,
124

Keewatin, 52
Kennedy, William, 36
Khomeini, Ayatollah, 171
Kigoriak, 172

King, W.F., 37
Kingigtorsuak, 26
Kitikmeot, 52
Knuth, Eigil, 25
Kotzebue, 59
Kruse, Lukas, 134
Kuujjuaq (Chimo), 52

Labrador, 49–50
Labrador, 44, 220, 221, 222,
223
Labrador Inuit Association,
50
Labrador Sea, 212
Laing, Arthur, 87, 88, 91
Lalonde, Marc, 174, 180
Lancaster Sound, 30, 31,
121, 156; biological
richness of, 32; environ-
mental assessment of,
60, 195–6; as international
strait, 76; and oil dril-
ling, 182, 194–6; and Polar
8, 263
Land claims. See Aboriginal
peoples; Inuit
L'anse aux Meadows, 26
Larsen, Henry, 39
Law of the sea, 101. See also
Arctic Waters Pollution
Prevention Act; Article
234; Innocent passage;
International straits;
Sovereignty, Canadian
Arctic; Transit passage
Lincoln Sea, 209
Lindblad Explorer, 4, 31
Liquefied natural gas (LNG),
151, 163, 169, 170, 260.
See also Arctic Pilot Pro-
ject; Hydrocarbons
Louis S. St. Laurent, 222,
223, 227, 228, 232
Low, A.P., 37
Lynge, Arqaluk, 145, 157
Lynge, Finn, 146, 147, 149,
150–1, 154

M'Clure Strait, 30, 77, 92,
226
Macdonald, Donald, 90
Mackenzie, Alexander, 27

Makivik Corporation, 51, 58,
61
Mammals, marine, 25–6, 32,
126. See also Arctic
animals
Manhattan, analogy with
Arctic Pilot Project,
158; and Canadian foreign
policy, 96, 102, 257;
and Canadian polar ice-
breaking, 216–17, 222,
232; and Canadian public
opinion, 16, 74, 77–8,
81, 86, 115, 266; Canadian
support and regulation
of, 72, 92–3; icebreaker assistance to, 75, 77, 84–
5; as shipping demonstra-
tion, 5, 77; voyages of,
4–5, 34, 38, 42, 67, 71, 73,
90–1
Martin, Paul, 89, 90n24, 97
Melville Bay, 32
Melville Island, 27, 163
Melville Shipping, 166, 172
Michener, Roland, 73
Middle East, 5, 76
Minerals, hard, 5, 40, 144–5,
206
Mitchell, Robert, 193
Mobil Oil, 19, 145
Motzfeldt, Jonathan, 57,
138, 144, 147, 152, 153,
156, 157
Munro, John, 150, 153, 174

Nascopie, 38, 39, 43
National Energy Board
(NEB), 150, 154, 168,
170, 173, 174–6, 197
Natural gas. See Hydrocar-
bons; Liquefied natural gas
Navigation aids, 207
N.B. McLean, 220, 223
Neptune, 37
Newfoundland, 19, 49, 168,
221, 224
Niaqornat, 134
Nielsen, Jonas, 156
Nilsson, Poul, 151
Nixon, Richard, 73, 81,
85–6, 93

Non-prejudicial arrangements, 241n1, 244; in Antarctic Treaty, 128–9, 131

Nordic Council, 149

Norlands Petroleum (Consolidated Oakwood Magnorth), 194

Norman McLeod Rogers, 221, 228

North American Aerospace Defence (NORAD) agreement, 209, 214

North Atlantic Treaty Organization (NATO), 106, 148, 214, 257

North Passage, 12

North Slope Borough, 47, 56, 122

North Warning System (NWS), 119, 210. *See also* Distant Early Warning

North Water, 32

Northern Light, 217, 219, 225

Northern Sea route, 123

"Northern Vision," 21, 43

Northumberland Strait, 217, 224

Northwest Passage, 3, 25, 60, 158, 209, 222, 232, 234; definition of, 3; distinction between Passage and, 3–4; exploration for, 3, 26–7, 36, 99; illusions and visions of, 3, 12, 18, 20–1; as metaphor, 3; and North Passage, 12; realization of, 5–8; and straits regime, 105–6, 110. *See also* Passage

Northwest Territories (NWT), 52–5, 185

Northwind, 77

Norway, 35, 95, 108

Norwegian Sea, 211

Nunavut, 52–4, 61, 191–3, 197

Nunavut Constitutional Forum, 53, 55, 197

Nuuk, 49, 57, 59, 140, 141–2

Oil. *See* Hydrocarbons

Ontario, 166, 175

Operation Norploy, 201

Operation Polarquest, 81

Organization of Petroleum Exporting Countries (OPEC), 117, 232, 257

Panama Canal, 19

Panarctic Oils, 120, 177; and APP, 165, 167; Bent Horn project of, 5, 253; Drake Point gas field of, 81

Parry, William, 27

Parry Channel, 30, 42, 226, 246

Passage, 4, 8, 12, 16, 25–32, 35–9, 71, 100, 124, 130, 165, 216, 222; antisubmarine barriers for, 250–1; "as is," 247–9, 253, 261; Canadian acceptance of foreign shipping in, 13–14, 76, 241, 271; and Canadian defence, 244, 245, 247, 250, 251, 252; Canadian domestic practice and, 259–65; and Canadian foreign policy, 96, 102, 253–9; and Canadian identity, 16–20, 119, 265–8; Canadian interest in, 16, 20–1, 243, 246, 248–9 263–4; Canadian legal view of, 8, 82, 98–102, 105, 110, 124, 241; and Canadian policing capabilities, 203–6, 210–13; Canadian-U.S. conflict over, 8, 76, 93, 94, 115, 118–23, 132–3, 241, 249, 251; Canadian-U.S. talks over, 241, 242, 249–50; as commercial seaway, 12, 20, 77; crossings of, 4, 209, 220; definition of, 3–4; enclosure of, by Canada, 8, 119, 241, 251–2; future of, 4, 242–52; ice conditions in, 30–2, 225–6; as internal Canadian waters, vii, 8,

73n5, 78, 82, 99, 100, 112; as international strait, 71, 100, 126, 242–6, 248, 252; maritime approaches to, 4, 9, 26, 27; and Mercator projection, 26–7; nuclear-free, 78, 251; as open Canadian waterway, 249–51, 252, 253, 259, 260, 261, 265, 267; political labyrinth of, 8–11, 18, 246, 252, 260; prevailing winds in, 30; risk of inaction in, 12–16, 249; as shared-access zone, 113–14, 244–7; shipping in, 5, 8, 12, 206–7, 210–12, 232–4; Soviet access to, 9; U.S. legal view of, 8–9, 15, 71, 76, 93, 119–20, 241; and U.S. nuclear-powered submarines, 5, 9n7, 94, 209, 243n4, 247, 248, 250, 251. *See also* Northwest Passage; Sovereignty, Canadian Arctic; Transit management regime

Pearson, Chris, 187

Pearson, Lester B., 43, 78, 243n4

Peary, Robert E., 37

Pelly Bay, 52

Pepin, Jean-Luc, 89

Permafrost, 127

Persian Gulf, 5, 19, 255

Petro-Canada: and APP, 150, 152, 164–5, 168, 171, 175, 260

Philippines, 76

Pierre Radisson, 223

Pingos, 34

Pipelines, 11, 72, 82–3, 117–18, 158, 167, 252; Alaska Natural Gas Transport System (ANGTS), 120; Canol, 39; Mackenzie Valley pipeline project, 77, 87, 183; Norman Wells, 182; Polar Gas project, 166, 167; Trans-Alaskan Pipeline System (TAPS),

77, 87; TransCanada Pipe-
lines, 173
Poirier, Pascal, 98
Polar 8, 13, 14, 205, 236–8,
263–4; as bargaining chip,
13; difficulties of, 13,
20n15, 248; origins of,
228–31
Polar Sea, vii, viii, 4, 13, 16,
93, 241, 243; and Polar
8, 216, 238, 261; U.S. approach to voyage of,
241n1, 244
Pollution, 14, 71, 76, 80, 84,
113–14, 126, 156, 158,
228, 232; control zones, 67,
83, 87, 88, 89, 91, 211;
noise, 32, 153, 156, 158,
170; prevention, 15, 79,
80, 84, 96, 97, 103, 243,
244. *See also* Arctic
Waters Pollution Preven-
tion Act; Article 234
Pond Inlet, 33, 170
Polynias, 32
Prince Edward Island, 217,
219, 220
Prince of Wales Strait, 30,
67, 76, 77, 82, 92, 226–
7, 232
Prudhoe Bay, 44, 70, 72,
116, 118
Pullen, Thomas, 87, 219, 226

Quebec, 50–2, 72
Queen Elizabeth Islands, 33,
42
Queen Maud Gulf, 31

Rasmussen, Knud, 41
Regimes, international, 80,
84, 85, 97, 104, 113,
124, 128, 132; defined,
128–9; for ice-covered
waters, 104–7, 108; and international straits, 104,
105–6, 110. *See also* Transit management regime
Resolute Bay, 33, 42, 169
Richards, William, 172
Rosing, Hans-Pavia, 62
Royal Canadian Mounted

Police (RCMP), 38, 39,
200, 211, 220; Arctic capabilities of, 203–4; Arctic
responsibilities of, 203–4,
205–6
Rupert's Land, 35

Sable Island, 118, 173
St. Roch, 34, 42, 220
Saurel, 220
Scoresby Sound, 156, 157
Schluter, Poul, 147
Schmidt, Helmut, 143, 174
Seadragon, 5
Search and rescue, 201, 203
Sector principle, 17, 73, 91,
97, 119, 126
Sharp, Mitchell, 73, 76, 79,
84, 88, 90, 91
Shipping, North American
Arctic, 4, 34, 115, 157–8,
165, 168; Canadian interest
in, 4, 18–20, 100, 120, 121,
122; Canadian readiness to
accept, 13, 20, 76, 241; environmental implications
of, 32–3, 121, 170, 263–4;
Greenlandic plans for, 135,
145, 155–7, 253; infrastructure for, 12–15, 21, 34–5,
123, 131–2, 211; and Inuit,
32–4, 56, 61, 122, 170,
263–4; likelihood of, 5–8,
12, 20, 44; Mackenzie River
route for, 38; management
of, 8–9, 14, 113–14, 125–6,
210–11, 212–13, 213–15,
245–7; and regime-
formation, 128–9; uncer-
tainty of, 11–12, 18–19,
116–18, 206–7, 234,
254–5; U.S. interest in,
120, 121, 122, 243–4
Sigyn, 134
Simon, Mary, 59
Sir John Franklin, 223
Skraeling Island, 26
Smith Sound, 32
South Korea, 169, 223
Sovereign Viking, 202
Sovereignty: defined, 124
Sovereignty, Canadian Arc-

tic, 10, 13, 36–8, 39–40,
67, 94, 118–19, 122–3, 166,
213; Cabinet considera-
tion of, 75, 87–90, 97;
claim to, 8, 15, 91, 92,
98–100, 101, 241; and
Coast Guard, 205, 236;
constraints on assertion of,
vii–viii, 98–100, 234,
245; functional approach
to, 100–1, 103; and ICJ,
76, 88, 101–2, 127–8, 241,
242, 243, 245, 247, 249,
251; and Inuit, 16n11, 56,
96–7, 262; and national
defence, 73, 76, 80, 83,
210–13; official action
to strengthen, 13, 37–8,
39–40, 67, 72–3, 75, 79,
84, 86, 100–1, 232, 264;
official statements on,
8, 17, 74, 75–6, 84, 91, 100,
269–73; and Polar 8,
13; public pressure to assert, 74, 77–8, 81, 86,
93; and RCMP, 204; unquestioned over islands, 119,
214
Soviet Union, 4, 9, 19, 119,
129, 166, 208, 231, 257;
and Arctic environment,
82; and Greenland,
148; Inuit of, and ICC, 57;
legal positions of, 105,
107n32, 109, 110, 264n11;
and negotiation of Article
234, 105, 107n32, 108, 109,
110, 111, 264; supporting
Canadian positions, 77, 80,
95, 105, 111, 253, 264
Spence Bay, 33
"Star Wars," 10
Steenholdt, Otto, 155
Stefansson, Vilhjahlmur, 37
Stockholm Conference on
the Human Environment,
102–3
Stokes Point Controversy,
121, 197–8
Straight baselines: and archipelagic states, 106;
Canadian consideration of,

73, 82, 85; Canadian use of, 8, 100, 127; definition of, 99; U.S. view of, 100

Strait of Hormuz, 76

Straits, international: Canadian positions on, 105–6, 108, 110, 111; regime for, 104–6, 110, 250; Soviet view of, 105; U.S. views on, 100, 105, 108, 111, 243, 244. *See also* Transit passage

Sublime, the. *See* Arctic sublime

Submarine tankers, 11–12, 44, 77, 116, 125–6, 155, 158, 211

Submarines, nuclear-powered attack (SSNS), 5, 11, 105, 253, 257; as Canadian defence option, 209, 251; and marine environment, 252; monitoring of, 209, 247; and Passage, 5, 9n7, 10, 94, 209, 243n4, 244n5, 247, 248, 249, 250, 251, 252, 253; Soviet, 5, 8–9, 9n7, 10n8, 244n5, 247n7, 249, 250, 255n9; Soviet, sighted off Greenland, 148, 209; U.S., 5, 8, 9n7, 42, 94, 209, 243n4, 247n7, 248, 250, 251, 255n9

Submarines, nuclear-powered ballistic missile-firing (SSBNS), 9n7, 10, 119

Surveillance, under-ice, 215

Sverdrup, Otto, 37

Sverdrup Basin, 226

Sweden, 95

Tagoona, Eric, 195

Task Force on Northern Oil Development (TFNOD), 72, 73, 75

Tenneco, 170, 172, 176

Terror, 27, 31

Territorial sea, 77, 82, 87, 88, 91–2; Canadian 12-mile, 67, 77, 89, 91–2, 100,

101; and internal waters, 73n5, 124; U.S. position on, 74, 92

Territorial Sea and Fishing Zones Act, 67, 73, 83, 87, 89, 91, 100

Thule, 210

Thur, Livia, 178

Transit management regime, 12, 15, 87, 115, 128–32, 244–7, 252; and Arctic environment, 244, 263; and Article 234, 247, 250; Canadian interest in, 11–12, 12–15, 21, 113–14, 125, 214, 252–3, 259; and consensual knowledge, 15; features of, 130–2; and Greenland, 131, 245, 250–1, 254; and Inuit, 131, 244, 262; lead times for, 12–13, 14–15, 20; and nuclear-powered submarines, 9–11; and transit passage, 244; U.S. interest in, 13, 244, 250. *See also* Regimes, international

Transit passage, 9, 244; and archipelagic states, 106; and Canada, 105–6, 107, 109, 110, 243; defined, 9n6; and Soviet Union, 10, 105, 244; and transit management regime, 244; U.S. interest in, 105, 106, 115, 120, 124, 243. *See also* International straits

Transport, Department of (DOT), 71, 78, 107, 229, 231, 234; and *Manhattan* voyages, 71–2, 78, 82, 84, 87, 91

Transportation, air, 41, 43–4

Trudeau, Pierre Elliott, 73, 74, 90n25, 91, 225; and APP, 164, 174; and Canadian foreign policy, 96–7; and Inuit, 96–7; and pollution prevention, 79, 80, 81, 83, 85, 88, 96–7; and

sovereignty, 73, 75, 79

Tuktoyaktuk, 34

Twin Otter aircraft, 203, 204

U Thant, 80

United Kingdom, 3, 4, 35, 95, 107, 229

United Nations: Convention on the Law of the Sea (1958), 78, 83, 98, 127, 153, 214; Convention on the Law of the Sea (1982), 110, 112; Environment Programme (UNEP), 129; First Conference on the Law of the Sea (1958), 99–100; Second Conference on the Law of the Sea (1960), 89, 100; Third Conference on the Law of the Sea (UNCLOS III), 104, 109, 115, 153, 212

United States, 4, 8, 9–10, 37, 100, 105, 108, 113, 229, 231; Arctic Policy and Research Act of 1984, 122; Arctic political interests of, 119–20; and Arctic Waters Pollution Prevention Act, 84, 115; and Canada's Arctic waters claim, 76, 120, 124; Coast Guard and *Manhattan* voyages, 71; commercial interest in Passage, 44–5, 119–20, 243–4, 247; Continental Energy Plan of, 85, 93; and Convention on Law of the Sea (1982), 112, 115; and Greenland, 148; and ICJ, 76, 128; legal view of Passage, 85, 93, 110, 241n1; naval interest in Passage, 72, 76, 105, 119–20, 255n9; Strategic Petroleum Reserve of, 117, 120; Task Force on Oil Policy, 74; and transit management regime, 9–10; and transit passage, 10. *See also* Alaska

Upernavik, 143

Uummannaq, 134, 143

Vesterbik, Lars, 147
Vikings, 26, 35, 137
Visions, 3, 4, 19, 21, 261;
and APP, 260; of Arctic
sublime, 17–18, 265–7;
and political leadership,
265, 267–8; "northern vi-
sion," 21, 43, 266

Wakeham, William, 36
Wartsila, 19
Watson, Ian, 78
West Greenland Current, 32
Western Arctic Regional
Municipality (WARM),
55
Whaling, 32, 37, 47
Wolcott, Donald, 151, 171,
175

World Bank, 132
World Council of Indigenous
Peoples, 59
World Discoverer, 4

Yakovlev, A.N., 57
Yellowknife, 80, 201, 204
Yukon territorial govern-
ment (YTG), 185–6,
197–8

FC
192
.P64
1987 / 54,791

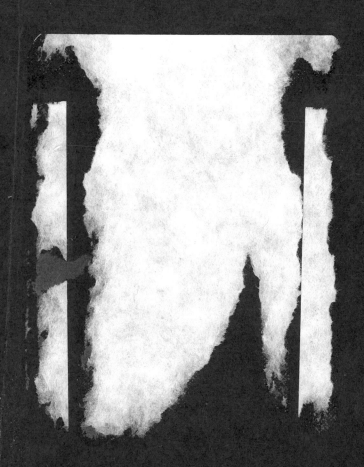

CAMROSE LUTHERAN COLLEGE
LIBRARY